Y0-BSN-591

THE CHARLOTTETOWN ACCORD, THE REFERENDUM, AND THE FUTURE OF CANADA

In the Fall of 1992, public events in Canada reached a climax that had far-reaching effects for the future of the country. For the first time in their history, Canadians were asked to give their approval to a sweeping set of constitutional proposals in a national referendum. The first serious and informed analysis of these proposals took place at a conference at York University that September. Sponsored by the Centre for Public Law and Public Policy, and the Robarts Centre for Canadian Studies at York University, the conference drew major speakers including Peter Lougheed, former premier of Alberta; Peter Hogg of Osgoode Hall Law School; Judy Rebick, president of the National Action Committee on the Status of Women; Senator Gérald-A. Beaudoin; Professor Ronald Watts of Queen's University; Michael Adams of Environics Research Group; Jeffrey Simpson of the *Globe and Mail*; Reg Whitaker of York University; Maude Barlow, National Chairperson, Council of Canadians; David Elton, president of Canada West Foundation; and Raymond Giroux of *Le Soleil*, among others.

The papers of the conference, most of which were later revised in light of the 26 October referendum results, present a record of Canadian thought during a period of profound national change. They are grouped here under such topics as 'The Reform of Central Institutions,' 'The Division of Powers,' 'Distinct Society, Aboriginal Rights, and Fundamental Canadian Values,' 'The Referendum,' and 'The Future of Canada.'

In this book, leading scholars, government decision-makers, interest groups, and journalists come together to debate the country's future. Their papers provide an independent and informed analysis of the choices confronting Canadians at a decisive moment in their collective history.

KENNETH McROBERTS is professor of Political Science, York University, and Director of the Robarts Centre for Canadian Studies.
PATRICK MONAHAN is professor, Centre for Public Law and Public Policy, Osgoode Hall Law School, York University.

The Charlottetown Accord, the Referendum, and the Future of Canada

Edited by
KENNETH McROBERTS and
PATRICK J. MONAHAN

UNIVERSITY OF TORONTO PRESS
Toronto Buffalo London

© University of Toronto Press Incorporated 1993
Toronto Buffalo London
Printed in Canada

ISBN 0-8020-2989-2 (cloth)
ISBN 0-8020-7442-1 (paper)

Printed on acid-free paper

Canadian Cataloguing in Publication Data

Main entry under title:

The Charlottetown Accord, the referendum, and the
future of Canada

Proceedings of a conference held Sept. 23–24, 1992,
at York University, Toronto.

ISBN 0-8020-2989-2 (bound)   ISBN 0-8020-7442-1 (pbk.)

1. Consensus Report on the Constitution (1992).
2. Canada – Constitutional law – Amendments.
3. Federal government – Canada. 4. Canada – Politics
and goverment – 1984–   . * I. McRoberts, Kenneth,
1942–   . II. Monahan, Patrick.

JL65 1993.C53 1993   342.71'03   C93-094681-2

Contents

Preface

September 23 and 24, 1992, was the occasion for a public conference at York University, entitled 'The Constitution: Year of Decision.' Jointly organized by our two centres, the Centre for Public Law and Public Policy and the Robarts Centre for Canadian Studies of York University, the conference was also sponsored by the Osgoode Hall Law School.

As it happened, September of last year was an especially opportune time for a public conference on the constitutional question: the pre-referendum debate over the Charlottetown Accord was just getting into full swing. Moreover, we had succeeded in bringing together academics, journalists, and public activists from across the country who were playing leading roles in that debate. A highlight of the conference was the inaugural Pierre Genest Memorial Lecture, delivered by the Honourable Peter Lougheed, former premier of Alberta. In short, the conference was the occasion for a thorough and stimulating discussion of the accord, and of the process through which it had been produced.

In light of both the importance of the conference's theme and the general quality of the discussions, we invited the participants to prepare formal versions of their remarks for publication. We also gave them the opportunity to take into account the results of the 26 October referendum. Happily, almost all the participants responded to our invitation. Given the extent to which most contributors revised and updated their original conference presentations, the present volume stands as more than the normal conference proceedings.

We wish to thank the following sources of financial support for the conference: the Pierre Genest Lecture Fund, Osgoode Hall Law School; York University; the Social Sciences and Humanities Research Council; the Secretary of State, the Federal-Provincial Relations Office, and the Department of Justice, Government of Canada; and the Ministry of Intergovernmental Affairs, Government of Ontario.

At the same time, we are deeply appreciative of the crucial roles that the staffs of our two centres played in organizing the conference. In particular, we would like to thank Denise Boissoneau and Krys Tarkowski, administrative assistants of the Centre for Public Law and Public Policy and the Robarts Centre for Canadian Studies, respectively, for the professional and committed manner in which they went about their many tasks. The coordinator for the conference was Jonathan Batty, a member of the 1993 graduating class at Osgoode Hall Law School. And we appreciate the support that Virgil Duff and the University of Toronto Press provided for the preparation of this volume.

Finally, we thank our contributors both for making the conference an outstanding success and for preparing their texts for publication. We believe that this volume offers important insights into not only the dynamics of this most recent attempt at constitutional renewal but also the options facing Canada in the potentially difficult years to come.

KENNETH McROBERTS
PATRICK J. MONAHAN

THE CHARLOTTETOWN ACCORD, THE REFERENDUM,
AND THE FUTURE OF CANADA

KENNETH McROBERTS and
PATRICK J. MONAHAN

Introduction

With the defeat of the Charlottetown Accord in the referendum of 26 October 1992, all is now quiet on the constitutional front. Canadians and their political leaders are clearly exhausted by over five years of intense but ultimately futile discussions designed to reshape the fundamental law of the country. Canada may be a country that is divided on many questions, but it is difficult to find any dissenters from the view that the constitutional issue should be put on the back burner for the time being.

Given the widespread constitutional fatigue across the country, some might regard this as an odd time to publish yet another book on the Constitution. But, in our view, the breathing space that we are currently enjoying on constitutional issues presents an ideal opportunity for the appearance of this volume. We can learn and profit from our history only by scrutinizing it closely. The current constitutional calm that we are experiencing provides us with the perfect opening for reasoned and critical reflection on our most recent attempt to rewrite the Constitution. Better that we begin this reflection now, when the issue has faded from public view – and well before the next constitutional storm clouds have appeared over the horizon.

The simple reality, in our view, is that the result on 26 October may have ended the debate on the Charlottetown Accord, but it has not resolved any of the larger issues which gave rise to the accord in the first place. The question of Quebec's place within Canada – the catalyst for most of the constitutional discussions over the past thirty years – remains uncertain. It may be that Quebeckers will be asked in the next provincial election, which must be held before the fall of 1994, to choose between federalism or some form of sovereignty. As for the West, its demands for better representation for 'outer Canada' in the country's central institutions remain frustrated. The appointment of several senators by Prime Minister Mulroney at the end of his time in office, echoing a similar rash of patronage appointments by a prime minister in the fifth year of his mandate nearly a decade ago, will ensure that Senate reform remains high on the Western agenda. And Aboriginal Canadians, who seemed so close to achieving recognition of their inherent right to self-government, have once again been politically marginalized. But having had their constitutional expectations raised in this way, Aboriginal peoples will surely find the failure of the Canada Round negotiations a particularly bitter pill to swallow.

Given the fact that these issues are certain to reassert themselves on the national agenda at some point in the future, it is both necessary and inevitable that they be the subject of informed scholarly attention and analysis. What is remarkable, in our view, is the almost complete absence of this kind of serious analysis in the months immediately following the demise of the Charlottetown Accord. This volume, then, represents an attempt to initiate the kind of debate and reflection that we regard as essential.

As the title to the volume suggests, there are three overarching themes that the papers in this collection seek to explore. The first is the question of the meaning and significance of the Charlottetown Accord itself. The questions that arise in relation to this theme include: What were the forces and interests that shaped the accord during the consitutional discussions of 1991–2? Did the accord represent a fair compromise between the various constituencies and interests in the country as a whole? Finally, had the accord been ratified, in what way would it have shaped Canadian politics in the decades ahead?

The second overarching theme focuses on the meaning and significance of the referendum campaign. For the first time in our 125-year history, Canadians across the country were given the opportunity to pronounce themselves on the desirability of proposed constitutional amendments. What does the referendum experience tell us about constitutional reform in Canada, both now and in the future? Is it possible to account, even in a tentative way, for the rejection of the accord by Canadians on 26 October? Has the referendum itself created a new rule of constitutional amendment, namely, that any future constitutional change must be submitted directly to the people?

The third and final theme of the book relates to the larger implications of the Canada Round exercise for the political future of Canada. At the moment, relatively few Canadians are openly questioning the future unity of the country. But it would appear certain that 'unity questions' will arise in the near future, either during the upcoming federal election in 1993 or the Quebec election scheduled for 1994. What does the Canada Round experience tell us about how Canadians are likely to respond to these issues? Will the country be able to resolve satisfactorily the matters that have been left in doubt by the failure of the Charlottetown Accord?

These are the themes and questions that the essays in this volume seek to answer. As might be expected, there is little or no consensus amongst our contributors on most of these issues. But this is hardly surprising, given the experience of the referendum campaign itself. The same sorts of divisions that dominated the referendum debate are reflected in the contributions here. A number of the contributors were clear supporters of the accord and attempt to explain the basis for that support; others are sharply critical, both of the accord itself and of the process that was employed in the negotiations preceding it. Yet, if there is one point on which all the essays agree, it is on the difficulty of achieving comprehensive constitutional change in a deeply segmented country such as Canada. The failure of both the Meech Lake and Charlottetown accords has been a sobering experience, such that virtually all the contributors in this volume advise great caution before returning to the constitutional file in the future.

The essays in part I of the volume analyse the provisions in the accord that would have reformed the institutions of the central government. The opening essay by Professor Ronald Watts argues that the accord was not a 'grab-bag' of sixty items but rather represented an attempt to arrive at a coherent framework. Professor Watts, who participated throughout the process as a key adviser to the Government of Canada, explains and defends the trade-offs that led to the proposed reforms to the Senate, the House of Commons, and the Supreme Court. Professor Watts argues that the reformed Senate would have been an influential body, primarily because the senators would have been elected and would have represented larger constituencies than members of the House of Commons. He also suggests that the proposed 'joint sitting' process that would have been employed to resolve deadlocks between the Senate and House would have left a meaningful role for senators. While the larger size of the House of Commons would have given the Commons predominance in joint sittings, the Senate could have been able to wield significant influence and power where the government had only a small majority or was in a minority situation. Professor Watts also suggests that the proposed reforms to the House of Commons would have brought the Commons closer to the principle of representation by population, even taking account of the guarantee of 25 per cent of the seats for the province of Quebec.

The essay by Professor David Elton focuses more fully on the question of whether the Senate proposed in the Charlottetown Accord would have been 'effective or emasculated.' Professor Elton attempts to answer this question by comparing the proposed Senate with various models put forward for a 'Triple E' Senate by the government of Alberta and by the Canada West Foundation. He concludes that the Charlottetown Senate was not intended to be a powerful legislative chamber in the traditional sense. Compared to the United States or Australian Senates, the Charlottetown Senate would have had far fewer absolute levers of power to pull when it disagreed with proposed government legislation and programs. Professor Elton concludes that the departures of the Charlottetown model from the proposals put forward by Triple-E advocates were too substantial. He argues that the Charlottetown Senate was a creative way to perpetuate the status quo rather than a fundamental restructuring of Canada's national institutions.

Shelagh Day's essay explains why many women and minority groups were opposed to the proposals for Senate reform contained in the Charlottetown Accord. Ms Day points out that, for the Triple-E Senate proponents, the first 'E' meant equality of the provinces; for women and others, however, that 'E' meant equality for those who are currently marginalized. She criticizes the failure of the accord to guarantee the principle of equality for women and minorities in any reformed Senate. In her view, this outcome is a product of the fact that representative government in Canada is not representative. Instead, it is government by a privileged minority, namely, white professional men. The parameters of the accord – which focused on competitive regional interests rather than on equality and other non-region-based interests – were determined by the fact that the negotiations were dominated by governments and first ministers. She calls for a major debate regarding the reform of the country's democratic system, suggesting the need for more participatory and representative institutions.

The final essay in this first section, by Senator Gérald Beaudoin, suggests that the proposed Senate would have had relatively few decisive powers. But its members would have considerable influence, given the fact that they would be elected and would represent, in some cases, more than a million constituents. He contends that it is impossible to predict with any certainty the precise degree of influence of the proposed Senate, arguing that this would depend on the development of informal conventions and political understandings that would not be part of the formal constitution. But he concludes that the Senate would not have rendered the country ungovernable, suggesting that decisive power on major national questions would probably have remained in the hands of the Cabinet and the House of Commons. Turning to the consequences of the 'no' vote on 26 October, Senator Beaudoin suggests that this outcome means that the constitutional status quo will remain in place for the foreseeable future. But he notes that this may not necessarily be a bad thing, since many issues can and ought to be resolved at the political level without resort to formal constitutional amendment.

The four essays in part 2 examine the proposals in the Charlottetown Accord for changes in the division of powers. The first essay, by Professor Peter Hogg, suggests that the key changes to the division of powers involved limitations on the federal spending power along with constitutional protection for federal-provincial agreements. After detailing and reviewing these changes, Professor Hogg concludes that the division-of-powers provisions in the Charlottetown Accord were the least satisfactory part of the agreement. In Hogg's view, the accord would have effected very little significant change to the division of powers, since most of what the accord contemplated could proceed under the present constitution through federal restraint in the exercise of the spending power and through federal-provincial agreements. But he finds that these changes, while relatively minor, would have contributed to a host of complexities in the Constitution of Canada, making the Constitution resemble the Income Tax Act. While a supporter of the accord as a whole, he expresses no unhappiness at the demise of the division-of-powers provisions that it proposed.

The next essay in part 2, by Professor Jacques Frémont, examines the proposed changes in the division of powers from a Quebec perspective. Professor Frémont begins by reviewing the 'traditional demands' of Quebec for substantial increases in the powers of the provincial government. Frémont argues that the Charlottetown Accord fell short of what has been seen over the years as minimally necessary for Quebec's survival and development as a francophone society. Frémont concludes that the division-of-powers proposals were inadequate since they largely confirmed the status quo. In fact, Professor Frémont claims that the accord may actually have contributed to an increase in federal authority, since it recognized the legitimacy of federal interventions into areas of exclusive provincial jurisdiction through the use of the spending power. In this sense, the Charlottetown Accord contradicted the principle of the exclusiveness of provincial powers. He concludes that the failure of Quebec to obtain a more satisfactory package on division-of-powers issues may well have been a result of a mistaken strategy on the part of the provincial government: Frémont suggests that Quebec mistakenly attempted to obtain recognition of new formal heads of exclusive jurisdiction, when it ought to have focused on the ability to exercise fully the jurisdictions already recognized under the Constitution Act, 1867.

Judy Rebick's essay criticizes the division-of-powers proposals on the basis that they proceed from a faulty premise – the concept of the equality of the provinces. According to this principle, all provinces should be accorded the identical constitutional treatment. But Ms Rebick argues that this approach results in a situation where everyone's demands are frustrated. Quebec's claims for more autonomy are stymied by the fact that anything Quebec gets must also be given to all the other provinces. At the same time, the desire in the rest of the country for a strong central government is undermined by the attempt to respond to Quebec's agenda, even in a limited way, through a general decentralization of powers. Ms Rebick proposes an alternate approach, based on a 'three nations' vision of the country. Under this approach, which emerged during the public constitutional conferences in early 1992, Quebec could be granted additional powers that would not necessarily be available to the remaining provinces. In this way, the constitutional aspirations of all parts of the country might be better satisfied.

The final essay, by Reg Whitaker, pursues and develops this theme. According to Professor Whitaker, some form of 'asymmetrical' federalism (in which Quebec alone would have received greater powers) represented the best hope of resolving the conflicting constitutional demands relating to the division of powers. But this model, despite enjoying some support in the early stages of the negotiations, essentially disappeared from the agenda in the final stages of the process. In attempting to explain the unhappy fate of asymmetrical federalism, Whitaker zeroes in on the fact that the threat of Quebec sovereignty lost credibility in English Canada. Because the rest of the country came to the view that the threat of Quebec separation was not serious, the premiers saw little reason to treat Quebec as anything but a province *comme les autres*. Whitaker argues that certain strategic errors on the part of the Quebec government contributed to this outcome. In his view, asymmetry could have represented a settlement between peoples and societies, in much the same way that the provisions on aboriginal self-government represented a historic agreement. Unfortunately, in his view, the idea of asymmetry now appears a dead letter – which may, in the long term, lead to an even greater 'unity crisis' for Canadian federalism.

The third section of the book contains five essays which address the interrelated issues of Quebec's distinct society, the recognition of Aboriginal rights, and fundamental Canadian values. The first essay, by Professor Mary Ellen Turpel, examines the Charlottetown Accord from the perspective of Aboriginal peoples. Professor Turpel, who headed the legal team for the Assembly of First Nations during the Canada Round negotiations, attempts to situate the accord within the context of the struggle by Aboriginal peoples for fundamental political change. Noting that the status quo is utterly unacceptable for Aboriginal peoples, Turpel argues that the Charlottetown Accord would have gone part way towards addressing the concerns and proposals advanced by Aboriginal groups over the past twenty-five years. Through a detailed review of the various components of the Aboriginal package, Professor Turpel demonstrates that the Aboriginal leadership was able to achieve many of its objectives, but that it was forced to compromise on a number of issues in order to secure the agreement of the federal and provincial governments. These concessions meant that the accord ran into political difficulties in the Aboriginal communities during the referendum campaign. Turpel also reviews the objections to the Aboriginal package that were voiced in the national debate on the accord, arguing that many of these objections were unfounded or misleading. She concludes with an analysis of the implications of the 'no' vote in terms of the position of Aboriginal peoples within Canada.

In his essay, Raymond Giroux examines the Charlottetown Accord from a Quebec perspective. Giroux argues that the Charlottetown Accord negated the national identity of Quebec, since it attempted to reduce Quebec's distinct society to the bare bones of language, culture, and civil law. As for Quebec's agenda – the redesign of the division of powers between Ottawa and the provinces – Giroux concludes that it was completely absent from the accord. Instead, Quebec is treated as just one of ten provinces and two territories, placed in the position of asking for 'undue privileges.' Giroux suggests that the accord was rejected in Quebec because it failed to recognize the emergence of a new national identity in Quebec over the past two decades. This new national identity, according to Giroux, is one that is sensitive to the concerns of minorities as well as to the special position of Aboriginal peoples. He calls for a constituent assembly in Quebec sometime in the future to attempt to define a 'made in Quebec' solution to the questions left unanswered by the failure of the Charlottetown Accord.

Maude Barlow's essay argues that much of the constitutional debate of the last few years has come down to a fundamental disagreement over the nature of Canada. Some see Canada as a federation of equal provinces. But a contrasting view, favoured by Ms Barlow, sees Canada as an association of three equal nations – French, English, and Aboriginal. The problem with the Charlottetown Accord, according to Ms Barlow, was that it was the result of a process driven by itself, rather than by a vision of the nature of the country. The constitutional proposal was the result of horse-trading, and was rejected for as many reasons as there were differing agendas in its creation. She believes that a different model for constitutional reform will be needed whenever the constitutional issue returns to the agenda. This new model should reflect a commitment to participatory democracy whereby individuals are granted direct influence in the decisions that affect their lives. The commitment to direct democracy as the basis of any future constitutional reform is an important shared value that Ms Barlow sees as having emerged from the Canada Round experience.

The fourth essay, by Professor Errol Mendes, focuses on the continued reliance on an élitist, executive-driven process for negotiating constitutional

change in Canada. Professor Mendes notes that, in the aftermath of the failure
of the Meech Lake Accord, the federal and provincial governments made great
efforts to include public and interest-group participation in the constitutional
process. However, the latter stages of the negotiations saw a return to the
traditional forms of élite accommodation, in which public and group opinion
was 'harvested' by governments. Despite his reservations over this return to an
élite-driven model, Professor Mendes indicates that he supported the accord on
the basis that some of its flaws were capable of being remedied. He also
believes that the Aboriginal package was an essential beginning to the restoration of group dignity to Aboriginal peoples, and that the accord would have
secured Quebec's place within Canada. With the failure of the accord, he
suggests that Canada may once again be plunged back into the 'quagmire' of
constitutional reform.

The final essay in this section, by former Alberta Premier Peter Lougheed,
attempts to place the Charlottetown Accord in historical context. Mr Lougheed
argues that the imperative driving the Charlottetown process was the lack of
legitimacy of the existing constitution, owing to the failure of the Quebec
government to agree to patriation in 1981. Looking back on the 1981 period,
Lougheed offers the observation that Quebec Premier René Lévesque may well
have been trapped by party politics and thus been precluded from agreeing to
any form of renewed federalism. But, Lougheed suggests, this failure of Quebec to agree to the 1981 constitutional revision illustrates the fact that the early
1980s may not have been the right time to proceed with the patriation project.
Turning to the Charlottetown Accord, Mr Lougheed argues that the accord
represents a fair and balanced attempt to accommodate the diverse interests
that constitute Canada. He argues that a failure to ratify the accord will inevitably lead the country back to the constitutional issue at some point in the future.
This preoccupation, he argues, will divert Canadian attention away from the far
more important issue of Canada's competitive position in a globalized world.

The essays in part 4 focus on the referendum campaign. The first essay, by
Michael Adams, provides a helpful context, by examining changes in Canadians' attitudes towards government and politics in recent decades. Based on
extensive polling data, Adams argues that the current mood amongst Canadians is one of anxiety and disillusionment. Canadians are increasingly questioning the ability of leaders and institutions to solve the problems we see around
us. He concludes that the growing crisis of confidence in today's politicians is
indicative of an erosion of confidence in the basic elements of the country's
political institutions and in the system of party politics. In the absence of major
democratic reforms, he argues, the Canadian political system is in danger of
losing its legitimacy in the public mind. But it is unclear whether Canadians

will be able to agree on a new set of political ground rules that will allow them to have confidence in the system. He also suggests that the constitutional issue is almost certain to re-emerge on the public agenda, whether Canadian voters and politicians want it or not. Quebec's desire for a different status in Canada is most likely to drive this issue back onto the agenda, and Adams concludes that no one can predict the outcome of this debate. At this stage, Canadian leaders appear to lack both a vision and a process for keeping the country together, which will make the successful resolution of these issues very difficult.

In the next essay, Jeffrey Simpson argues that those who negotiated and supported the Charlottetown Accord faced an insuperable obstacle: securing support in every province. The Charlottetown consensus lulled its negotiators into believing that their unanimity would be contagious. But this belief failed to account for the deep cleavages in Canadian society, which made the search for unanimity a futile one. Charlottetown's opponents attacked the accord 'like a swarm of bees from every angle and with great ferocity,' demonstrating that in a referendum campaign it is sufficient to oppose. Simpson argues that the main lesson of the referendum is that social and economic pressures are manifestly ill suited for relief by formal constitutional amendments. The task for concerned citizens, he argues, is to recast the entire debate towards the alleviating of these pressures and grievances by means other than formal constitutional amendments. If this is the lesson taken from the Charlottetown debate, then the country will save itself future grief and direct its energies into solutions that lie in the territory of the possible rather than the search for constitutional castles in the sky. But, he notes, this will likely produce a polarization of debate in Quebec, a polarization that many Quebeckers do not want. Thus the rest of Canada will try to get Quebec to choose between the status quo and secession, while Quebeckers, with their innate preference for keeping options open, will try to avoid making that choice.

The third essay in this section, by André Blais, focuses on the referendum campaign in the province of Quebec. Professor Blais analyses the twenty-nine polls that were published in Quebec between 22 August and 26 October, suggesting that public opinion evolved through five distinct periods or phases during the campaign. Noting that the polls tended to underestimate systematically the size of the 'yes' vote, he nevertheless finds that there was a steady erosion of support for the accord from early September onward. In his view, it is unclear whether the infamous 'Wilhelmy affair' had any discernible impact on public attitudes. He also argues that opposition to the deal among non-sovereignists in Quebec stemmed from a belief that Quebec had lost in the negotiations; this was coupled with the confidence that the victory of the 'no' side would not lead to Quebec separation. The dissatisfaction with the accord appeared to stem from the view that not enough powers had been devolved to the provincial level, precisely the main complaint about the accord voiced by Liberal dissidents such as Jean Allaire and Mario Dumont.

The book's final section examines the larger political implications of the failure of the Charlottetown Accord for the future of Canada. Peter Russell's essay examines the practice of 'mega constitutional politics' – which he defines as politics concerned with reaching agreement on the identity and fundamental principles of the community. Russell argues that, while the practice is not unique to Canada, this country must surely win the 'booby prize' for the duration and intensity of its involvement in mega constitutional politics. Russell argues that it is essential that Canadians eschew this type of constitutional debate for the foreseeable future. He suggests that more attention should be paid to the resolution of political problems through non-constitutional means. For example, a federal prime minister bold enough to depart from the tradition of strict party discipline in the House of Commons and of political patronage in the selection of judges and senators could do much to enhance the credibility of the federation's central institutions. Russell concludes with the observation that Canadians may lack a popular consensus on a new set of constitutional arrangements, but may nevertheless acquiesce in the constitutional status quo, in the absence of any practical alternatives.

The essay by Patrick Monahan argues that the Canada Round ought to be regarded as at least partly successful, since it featured a unanimous agreement amongst seventeen governments and Aboriginal organizations. Monahan argues that this unanimous agreement was the result of three factors: the role played by the federal government, the absence of Quebec from the early stages of the negotiations, and the recognition of the serious consequences of failure. But while the parties to the negotiations were able to agree, their proposals were soundly rejected by the people themselves. Monahan argues that the conventional explanation of this result – that Canadians were simply voting against their political leaders – is inadequate and misleading. He argues that the referendum result needs to be examined in a comparative perspective. The international experience with constitutional change over the past thirty years suggests that fundamental constitutional reform is the exception rather than the rule. The only instances of genuine 'reconstitutions' have been in cases where established interests have been shattered by war, revolution, external threat, or similar disruption. None of these conditions was present in Canada in late 1992. Turning to the future, he suggests that attempts to secure formal constitutional amendments are a practical non-starter. The future of constitutional politics in Canada depends on events in the province of Quebec and, in particular, on the outcome of the looming showdown between the status quo and sovereignty.

In his chapter, Kenneth McRoberts traces the failure of this most recent constitutional exercise to fundamental differences in the conceptions of political community that are held by English Canadians and Québécois. The 7 July agreement fell squarely within the English-Canadian vision. In attempting to render the agreement more acceptable to Québécois, the framers of the Charlottetown Accord diluted the major component sought by English Canadians, Senate reform, rather than responding directly to Quebec's concerns by assigning greater powers to Quebec through asymmetry. Apparently, the predominant English-Canadian conception of the Canadian political community precluded any serious exploration of asymmetry. As a result, there was little incentive for either English Canadians (at least outside Ontario) or Québécois to support the accord. Rather than incorporating the primary projects of constitutional change, the accord frustrated them. Professor McRoberts concludes by showing how the contradition between English-Canadian and Québécois conceptions of the Canadian political community arose from the efforts of the federal government, under Pierre Trudeau, to counter Quebec nationalism through a pan-Canadian identity.

Roger Gibbins's essay explores the possible consequences of Quebec's departure for the 'residual Canadian state,' consisting of the nine remaining provinces and the northern territories. He suggests that the issue of Quebec secession continues to be relevant in light of the outcome of the referendum, since the threat and possibility of Quebec's departure remain with us. His analysis concentrates on the longer-term implications of Quebec sovereignty, rather than on the short-term transitional situation. He suggests that, if Quebec were to leave, Canadians would face much more fundamental institutional reform than was proposed in the Charlottetown Accord. He believes that any new federal system that would emerge would probably be more centralized than the current one. But the emergence of new institutions would depend upon shifting the terms of political debate away from territorial questions and towards non-territorial issues such as feminism, environmentalism, and globalization. Gibbins also argues that Quebec's departure would not only lead to changes in the institutional status quo: it could also set in motion quite significant changes to the Canadian political culture. Canada would be a very different entity, one in which virtually all citizens shared a single language, and in which there would be greater emphasis on the equality of individuals. Gibbins concludes that there might be many long-term benefits for the rest of Canada if Quebec were to leave. Canada would have the chance to get out from under the dead weight of old ideas and old issues and to move to a political agenda that is not dominated by the linguistic and territorial issues that preoccupy the country today.

We believe that these essays, considered as a whole, provide a comprehensive, diverse, and timely analysis of Canada's recent experience with constitutional reform. As our summary has indicated, the areas of disagreement amongst our contributors far outweigh the areas of agreement. Nevertheless, there are at least three conclusions that are common to all the essays in this volume. The first is that revising Canada's constitution has become an exceedingly difficult task; some, but not all, would say that it has become impossible. The second is that any return to constitutional politics in Canada will likely be in a much more polarized context in which the choices will essentially be the status quo versus some radical restructuring of the country. The third is that Canadians appear to lack an acceptable process for resolving any future constitutional questions that might arise. The overall conclusion that emerges is that continued uncertainty will likely be the predominant feature of Canadian politics in the months and years ahead.

PART ONE

The Reform of Central Institutions in the Charlottetown Accord

I

The Reform of Federal Institutions

RONALD L. WATTS

INTRODUCTION: THE CONTEXT

The specific proposals for reform of federal institutions that were set out in the Charlottetown Consensus Report of 28 August 1992 need first to be placed in the broader context of the nature of that agreement itself. That agreement was not, as some have described it, a grab-bag of sixty items, but rather represented an attempt to arrive at a coherent framework. As Donald Lenihan has perceptively noted, it represented an attempt to provide an overarching framework integrating the Charter of Rights and Freedoms and federalism.[1]

In the effort to formulate such a coherent framework, the initial federal proposals of September 1991, the Beaudoin-Dobbie report in February 1992, and finally the Charlottetown Consensus Report in August 1992 each combined in their proposals three major elements that, as the comparative study of federations indicates, are essential elements in any federation that is to be stable and effective over the long term.

The *first element* is the constitutional articulation of shared values. In most other federations this element has been embodied in one or more of the following forms: a preamble, interpretive clauses, a statement of objectives, or a bill of rights. Normally, these include the recognition and acceptance of diversity and the identification of common values that could serve as the cement to bind the members of the federation together. The Canada Clause in the Charlottetown agreement would have recognized the diversity that contributes to the richness of Canadian society including the distinctiveness of Quebec, the place of the official language minorities, and the aspirations of the Aboriginal peoples within Canada. At the same time, the Canada Clause would have recognized the values that Canadians hold in common: parliamentary democracy, federalism, and the rule of law; racial and ethnic equality; respect for individual and collective human rights and freedoms; equality of women and men; and equality of the provinces. Since the Canada Clause would have provided the courts with a basis from which to interpret the Constitution, it represented an interpretive framework for the Constitution as a whole embodying a vision integrating the values of the Charter and of federalism. In addition, the Charlottetown agreement would have also inserted in the Constitution a statement of the basic objectives of the social and economic union. The contribution the Charlottetown agreement might have made to the constitutional articulation of shared objectives is discussed elsewhere in this book in the papers in the section on distinct society, Aboriginal rights, and fundamental values.

The *second element* required in any effective federation is a *distribution of powers* that can take account of changing social and economic conditions. The distribution of powers must give the federal government the capacity to operate effectively while leaving the provinces scope to deal with the different particular concerns of their own populations. Part III of the Charlottetown agreement made modest adjustments rebalancing the roles of federal and provincial governments and added provisions for effective cooperation and collaboration through intergovernmental agreements and arrangements for the exercise of the federal spending power within areas of exclusive provincial jurisdiction. Those provisions are discussed elsewhere in this volume in the papers in the section on the division of powers.

The *third crucial element* in any federation is the establishment of *effective federal institutions*, to ensure not only their responsiveness and public legitimacy, but also the balanced representation of both majority and minority views in the formulation of policies for the federation as a whole. An important feature in every bilingual or multilingual federation, therefore, has been balancing representation by population, the interests of the smaller provinces and the concerns of major official language minorities. The Charlottetown agreement therefore aimed at improving our federal institutions by (1) reforming the Senate into an elected, provincially equal, and effective body that, while being consistent with the principles of parliamentary institutions, would have given the smaller provinces a stronger voice; (2) improving representation by population within the House of Commons, while at the same time giving Quebec guaranteed representation to offset the substantial reduction by three-quarters in its Senate representation; (3) entrenching the Supreme Court as an independent interpreter of the Constitution; and (4) providing for annual first ministers' conferences, including a role for that body in establishing bodies to monitor the social and economic union. It is this third broad element of the Charlottetown agreement, the establishment of effective federal institutions, upon which this chapter is focused.

There is a considerable literature on Canadian federalism that considers what Donald Smiley defined as interstate and intrastate federalism. Interstate federalism refers to the powers that are distributed between federal and provincial governments (the second element identified above) and intrastate federalism to the means for providing a regional voice within federal institutions (the third element above). Often in the Canadian literature on these concepts adjustments to one or the other of these are seen as alternative strategies. In my view, they are not alternatives. Every federation that has been stable over the long term has found both interstate and intrastate federalism to be essential and complementary elements. Indeed, I would go further and say that in addition to these two elements the constitutional articulation of shared values is also an essential element.

It is worth noting, furthermore, that in the original negotiations for the founding of the Canadian federation and also at the origin of the United States, Swiss, Australian, and German federations, in each case it was not the constitutional distribution of powers that proved to be the most intractable issue but rather conflicts among the constituent units about the appropriate composition, powers, and structure of the federal institutions and particularly of the federal second chamber. This is not surprising because the organization of these common institutions determines the control over federal decision making. It was the Connecticut Compromise proposing a bicameral federal legislature that broke the deadlock at the Philadelphia Convention in 1787, and similarly it was the adoption of a bicameral federal legislature that helped the Swiss to reach agreement on the federal constitution replacing the previous confederal one in 1848. In the Confederation debates in Canada more time was spent debating the proposed Senate than any other item, in part because of the difficulties that had been experienced in the preceding attempt to move towards an elected second chamber in the United Province of Canada. Just as the organization of the common federal institutions has always been a particularly contentious issue during the creation or recreation of every federal union, so the recent constitutional deliberations have been true to this pattern.

Two points have particularly accentuated the importance of the issues relating to the reorganization of our federal institutions in the recent constitutional round. One of the lessons drawn by the federal government, and indeed by most of the participants in the deliberations, from the failure of the Meech Lake Accord was that partial constitutional reform that would leave the concerns and interests of a major portion of the country unaddressed was unlikely to achieve the degree of support necessary for adoption. That is why this round of constitutional deliberations was consciously described as 'a Canada Round' to emphasize that it was intended to take account of the concerns not only of

Quebec but also of other Canadians as well. This explains why Senate reform became a central issue in this round. It was thought necessary to address the long-standing concern of the Western and Atlantic provinces that, owing to the ineffectiveness of the current Senate in representing their interests, Ontario and Quebec (who together elect over 60 per cent of the members of the House of Commons) have dominated policy making within Parliament. This concern has led during the past decade to increasing pressures for Senate reform, and contributed to the strong opposition to the Meech Lake Accord because the proposed changes to the amendment formula would have made such reform in the future much more difficult. Indeed, the tentative but ill-fated agreement reached in the effort to rescue the Meech Lake agreement in Ottawa on 9 June 1990 included as a major component a commitment to a subsequent process for significant Senate reform.

A problem complicating the redesign of federal institutions, and particularly the Senate and the House of Commons in the Canadian case, has been the need to find a balance between adequate representation by population, the interests of the smaller provinces, and safeguards for the major linguistic community concentrated in Quebec. In most multilingual or multicultural federations, weighted representation favouring the smaller constituent units within the federal second chamber has provided at the same time a way of reinforcing the voice of the major linguistic minorities within the federal institutions. The need to take both these considerations into account did not of course arise in the two other federations, the United States and Australia, where strictly equal representation for each constituent unit was adopted, since both were unilingual federations to begin with. In the Canadian case, however, the concentration of our major linguistic community in one of the larger provinces has meant that any increase in the proportionate representation of the smaller provinces, for instance by equal representation of the provinces in the Senate, means a commensurate reduction in that body of representatives from the official language minority. This has created a clash between the two objectives for Senate composition – (a) equality of the provinces and (b) adequate representation of major minority communities – that need to be balanced against representation by population within our federal institutions. This clash was expressed during the Ministerial Meetings on the Constitution by the struggle between the advocates of an 'equal' Senate and of an 'equitable' Senate.

Given the importance and contentiousness of these issues it is understandable why the federal proposals of 1991, the Beaudoin-Dobbie Joint Parliamentary Committee, the Ministerial Meetings on the Constitution (MMC) between March and June 1992, the premiers' meetings on 3 and 7 July, and finally the first ministers' meetings and conferences in July and August found it necessary to devote so much time to the issue of the reform of our federal institutions and particularly of the Senate. The balance of this paper will turn to an examination of the proposals relating to the Senate, House of Commons, Supreme Court, and first ministers' conferences.

THE SENATE

The public discussion and subsequent negotiations on Senate reform turned around four interrelated but distinct sets of issues.

1. The Functions of the Reformed Senate

The issue was whether the primary function of a reformed Senate should be to represent provincial electorates in the central legislative process or to serve an intergovernmental function by providing provincial-government input into the central legislative process. Both in Joe Clark's Cabinet committee during the summer of 1991 and again early in the MMC process in the spring of 1992 serious consideration was given to the latter approach through some form of a House of the Provinces, although in the end in both instances the consensus came down in general favour of the former. Nevertheless, when it was subsequently agreed in response to Premier Bourassa's preference to include in the Charlottetown agreement a provincial option to enable indirect election by a provincial legislature for those provinces so choosing, the result was in fact something of a hybrid.

2. Method of Selection

Here there were four sub-issues. The first was whether senators should be directly elected (as in Australia, the only parliamentary federation with a directly elected second chamber), indirectly elected by provincial legislatures (as in the parliamentary federations of India and Malaysia), or appointed by provincial governments (as in Germany). As noted above, there was a general preference for the first of these options, but in the final stages of the first ministers' negotiations a provincial option allowing the second was agreed upon. The notion of a provincial option for the method of selecting federal second-chamber members is not unique: the Swiss Constitution of 1848 left the method of selection entirely to the discretion of the cantons and only recently have all the cantons come to exercise that option in favour of direct election.

The second sub-issue was the form of election to be specified if senators were to be directly elected. The alternatives considered were first-past-the-post, some form of proportional representation based on a party list, and proportional representation with the single transferable vote. Both at the Calgary conference and during the MMC process prior to August there was a leaning in favour of proportional representation with the single transferable vote as the means most likely to express the social diversity of Canadians, including multiculturalism and gender equality. In the MMC deliberations, Nova Scotia and Alberta accepted this tentative agreement only reluctantly, and in the final stages, Premier Bourassa's concerns that proportional representation would fragment the voice of each province led to the decision not to specify any reference to proportional representation in the Charlottetown agreement. The method of election was instead left to be determined by Parliament, with the opportunity for provinces to provide for indirect elections or special arrangements to ensure gender equality.

A third question was whether Senate elections should be timed simultaneously with House of Commons elections, timed simultaneously with provincial elections, or be stand-alone elections with senators having fixed terms. The least favoured was having them coincide with provincial elections, because with an average of three provincial elections a year that would produce a constantly shifting Senate membership, complicating the legislative process. Both at the Calgary conference and in the early MMC deliberations stand-alone elections were favoured as increasing the independence of the Senate. Some worried, however, about the impact that mid-term separate elections would have on the Senate composition and the likelihood that the protest vote normally experienced in by-elections would accentuate sharply different party compositions in the two houses, encouraging clashes and deadlocks between them. In the end it was the additional cost of separate stand-alone elections, estimated to be over $100 million for each one, and the likely negative public reaction to such additional expenditure on more elected politicians that led to agreement within the MMC upon elections simultaneous with those of the House of Commons.

A fourth question was whether jurisdiction over the method and details of Senate election should be federal or provincial. Although there was considerable pressure within the MMC for the latter, it was in the end agreed that jurisdiction over regulations governing elections to a federal body should lie with Parliament, except in relation to some specified matters where the provinces would be able to exercise options, for example, specifying whether senators should be directly or indirectly elected and providing for gender equality.

3. The Powers of the Senate in Relation to the House of Commons

This proved to be a vexed issue because there is no simple absolute measure of effectiveness, and also because of the need to reconcile the powers of the Senate with a parliamentary system in such a way that the Senate would have real influence without frustrating the will of the House of Commons as the 'confidence house.' All the participants in the intergovernmental negotiations agreed from the outset that the Senate should not be a confidence chamber, that is, that votes of confidence in the government should be the prerogative solely of the House of Commons. The problem then was how to create an effective Senate that would not undermine the principle of cabinet responsibility to the House of Commons. Absolute veto powers for the second chamber, which may be more suitable to central institutions based on the principle of the separation of powers, raise difficulties in a parliamentary system by denying a government supported by a majority in the House of Commons the ability to carry out its program. What was sought, therefore, was a deadlock-breaking mechanism enabling the Senate to influence but not frustrate decisions of the House of Commons. The resulting agreement arrived at was to provide for a suspensive veto for routine revenue and expenditure bills and to provide for a joint-sitting process to break deadlocks on most ordinary legislation. In the case of most ordinary legislation, differences between the two houses would have been dealt with first by a reconciliation-committee process and, if that failed, by a simple majority of the combined membership of the two houses. In two special areas, an absolute veto was in fact provided for: (1) bills involving fundamental tax-policy changes directly related to natural resources (the so-called anti-National-Energy-Program power), and (2) legislation materially affecting French language and culture supported by a majority of senators, including a majority of French-speaking senators.

4. Composition of the Senate

The basic issue here, common to all multilingual and multicultural federations, is how within a bicameral federal legislature to provide at the same time for (1) representation by population, (2) reinforced representation for the smaller provinces, and (3) protection for the interests of the major official language minority, mostly but not totally concentrated within Quebec and which represents a quarter of the federal population. In most multilingual federations the composition of the federal second chamber has attempted to take account of both the second and third factors. Thus, with the exception of the United States and

Australia, both of them monolingual, the composition of the second chamber in most federations has been based on a varied or weighted rather than strictly equal representation of the constituent units.

The federal proposals of September 1991, therefore, came down in favour of an 'equitable' Senate without specifying a precise composition, and the Calgary conference, despite a representation at that conference weighted towards 'outer Canada,' also concluded in favour of an equitable Senate rather than one with provincially equal representation.[2] Subsequently, the Beaudoin-Dobbie Committee proposed several alternatives for a distribution of seats in an equitable Senate, the proposed allocations apparently being arrived at on the basis of judgment rather than any formula.[3]

In the intergovernmental negotiations that followed, while all agreed on the need for Senate reform, it was the composition and related powers of the Senate that proved to be the most intractable issues. In all, between March and 28 August, some thirty distinct proposals for the composition and powers of the Senate were considered during the Ministerial Meetings on the Constitution and the first ministers' meetings before agreement was eventually reached.

Early in the MMC process four basic models for a reformed Senate were identified, together with a number of variants of each:

1. *A Triple-E Senate with provincially equal representation.* Initially Alberta, Newfoundland, Manitoba, Saskatchewan, and Nova Scotia advanced different variants of this approach, differing mainly in terms of the powers of such a Senate. By early June these had coalesced into a single common position in support of eight senators per province and two per territory, with limited powers over supply bills, an absolute veto over a restricted range of subjects, and a joint-sitting process for resolving deadlocks over most ordinary legislation.[4]

2. *An Equitable Senate* with provincial representation based on a sliding scale weighted in favour of smaller provinces. This approach was supported by the federal government, Ontario, New Brunswick, Prince Edward Island, and later Nova Scotia. In the basic model considered by the MMC, provinces and territories were divided into five categories: those with a population above 5 million (Ontario and Quebec) receiving 24 seats each; those between 2 and 5 million (British Columbia and Alberta) 12 seats each; those between 500,000 and 2 million (Manitoba, Saskatchewan, Nova Scotia, New Brunswick, and Newfoundland) 8 seats each; those between 100,000 and 500,000 (Prince Edward Island) 4 seats; and those below 100,000 (Yukon and Northwest Territories) 1 seat each. This approach would have produced a Senate with 118 seats in which the

population per seat progressively increased up the scale from 27,000 for the smallest unit, Yukon, to 417,454 for Ontario.[5] A number of variants of this approach were proposed early in the process by British Columbia. Later, Nova Scotia, after it had abandoned the Equal Senate camp in June, proposed an equitable variant of its own.

3. *A Regionally Equal Senate.* This was British Columbia's preferred position, based on a five-region model in which British Columbia together with the two territories would constitute a fifth region. Two variants were advanced, one for a Senate of 80 seats and one for a Senate of 120 seats.[6] Except for some interest shown in this approach by Quebec, it attracted little support from the other provinces.

4. *Equal Provincial Representation with Special Majorities Required.* This proposal would have allocated Senate seats equally among the provinces, but would have required a super-majority of 75 per cent for the Senate to reject a House of Commons bill. This was intended to ensure some protection to larger provinces by limiting the ability of a simple majority of smaller provinces to block House of Commons legislation. Originally advocated by Peter Nicholson, a vice-president of the Bank of Nova Scotia, in letters to a number of participants in the MMC process and enthusiastically supported by *Globe and Mail* editorials, the proposal initially invoked little enthusiasm within the MMC because it satisfied neither the supporters of a provincially equal Senate nor those of an equitable Senate. Subsequently, however, in the efforts to resolve deadlock between the two groups, the Nicholson approach became a major feature of the premiers' agreement for Senate reform, on 7 July. Nevertheless, in the end the elements requiring special majorities were eliminated in the final resolution agreed to at Charlottetown.

By early June, when it was apparent that the proponents of an equal Senate and of an equitable Senate were deadlocked, a number of efforts to devise hybrids combining elements of both approaches were advanced as compromise proposals. The Beauchamp and Saskatchewan proposals advocated a provincially equal Senate, but with individual senators having different weights for voting. There was also a federal proposal for an equitable composition, but with provincially equal voting for some purposes. The notion of 'inflated' or 'deflated' voting was too easily open to public ridicule, however. Consequently, while there was reluctance among members of the MMC to reject outright such efforts at compromise, these particular proposals aroused insufficient enthusiasm for adoption.

The next effort at compromise emerged out of the meetings of the premiers on 3 and 7 July, and involved a Senate with a provincially equal membership but with the requirement of special super-majorities along the lines embodied in the Nicholson proposal. The agreement of the proponents of an equitable Senate to this proposal was based on two factors. First, the requirement of special majorities would avoid a situation where a simple majority composed of the six smallest provinces representing only a small minority (17 per cent) of the federal population would be able to block the majority in the House of Commons. Second, all premiers including Premiers Wells and Getty agreed that a condition of this Senate reform would be their acceptance of a veto for Quebec on all future constitutional amendments relating to central institutions. This agreement, they thought, would make it possible for Premier Bourassa to accept the proposal in spite of the reduced voice of Quebec and of francophones in an equal Senate. In the event, such an assurance was ridiculed in Quebec as providing meaningless protection once an equal Senate was already in place.

Consequently, further possible compromises were raised for consideration at the Harrington Lake meetings. A final resolution was reached at the first ministers' meeting at the Pearson Building from 18–22 August and this was embodied in the Charlottetown agreement. This resolution derived mainly from initiatives taken first by New Brunswick and then by Saskatchewan. The essence of the solution was a creative compromise making possible equal provincial representation in the Senate by placing the guarantee for the representation of the linguistic community in Quebec in the House of Commons rather than in the Senate. This solution involved transferring seats lost in the Senate by Ontario and Quebec as additional seats in the House of Commons and guaranteeing that the 25 per cent representation in the Commons to which population currently entitles Quebec would continue even if its percentage of the population were to decline. A further important feature of the compromise involved adapting the proposal of the proponents of an equal Senate that deadlocks between the two houses over ordinary legislation be resolved by a joint sitting process, but specifying a smaller Senate with six rather than eight senators per province in order to ensure that Quebec's voice in joint sittings would remain significant.

Assessment of the Proposed Senate

The Senate proposed in the Charlottetown Consensus Report would have been composed of six senators from each province and one from each territory, with provision for the subsequent addition of an unspecified number of seats for representation of the Aboriginal peoples. Elections would have taken place under federal jurisdiction and at the same time as elections to the House of

Commons. Elections would normally have been directly by the people although there would have been provision for a province to specify indirect election by its legislature and to provide for gender equality. For most ordinary legislation, defeat or amendment in the Senate would have been ultimately resolved by a joint sitting process with the House of Commons. Senate powers over ordinary revenue and expenditure bills would have been more limited, with power only to act within thirty days to force the House of Commons to repass such bills. By contrast, the Senate would have had absolute veto powers in two specified areas: (1) fundamental tax-policy changes directly related to natural resources and (2) bills materially affecting the French language or the French culture that failed to obtain a double majority, consisting of a majority of all senators voting and a majority of all francophone senators voting. The Senate would have had the power to initiate bills other than money bills. In addition, Senate ratification would have been required for certain key federal appointments.

In terms of the composition of the Senate, the Charlottetown agreement, by contrast with the federal proposals of September 1991, the Calgary conference of January 1992, and the Beaudoin-Dobbie report of February 1992, adopted a provincially equal Senate rather than an equitable composition, thus going further to meet the claims of the Triple-E advocates. It was able to do so by building in guarantees for the representation of Quebec, where Canada's official language minority is concentrated, in the House of Commons. This resolution was the product of three factors: (1) a more cohesive and determined stand by the coalition of leaders advocating a Triple-E Senate than among those advocating an equitable Senate; (2) the absence of Quebec from the negotiations until a very late stage; and (3) Quebec's insistence upon a veto on future constitutional amendments relating to central institutions, a provision that would have required unanimous agreement of the provinces and that, therefore, enabled Premiers Getty and Wells to insist upon provincial equality in the Senate as the price for that veto.

But many proponents of the Triple-E Senate subsequently expressed concern that the powers of the Senate as proposed in the Charlottetown agreement would make it ineffective. This view was based on the premise that only if the Senate has absolute veto powers over most matters can it be effective, and was derived from a failure to distinguish between the appropriate role of a second chamber in a system involving the separation of powers, as in the United States, and in a parliamentary cabinet system.

In fact a number of factors would have contributed significantly to the influence of the Senate proposed in the Charlottetown agreement. The fact that most senators would have been directly elected and would have represented larger constituencies than members of the House of Commons would have given them much greater political legitimacy than current senators and made them real political rivals to elected MPs. Moreover, even though senators would have been elected at the same time as members of the House of Commons, the prospect of split voting (not uncommon where there is concurrent voting in the United States) and the employment of a different electoral system from that in the House of Commons would have been likely to produce a significantly different party composition in the Senate. The proposed joint-sitting process for resolving deadlocks between the two houses would not have been unique in parliamentary federations; indeed it is the ultimate deadlock-breaking mechanism in both Australia and India. While the larger size of the House of Commons would have given the Commons predominance in joint sittings, thus recognizing the role of the Commons as the confidence chamber, nevertheless the Senate could have been able to wield significant influence and power where the government had only a small majority or was in a minority situation.[7] Moreover, the influence of the Senate would have come not just from the number of votes it won in joint sittings but from its role in the preceding reconciliation-committee process in which the Senate and House of Commons would have been equally represented and from its impact upon government action taken to avoid delays caused by anticipated possible Senate action. What this process would have done, above all, was to avoid stalemates and deadlocks by establishing a process for reconciliation between the two houses through the work of reconciliation committees and an ultimate deadlock-breaking mechanism. Such a process is more consistent with parliamentary traditions than the balancing of deadlocks upon which the U.S. congressional system is based.

In addition to these sources of power and influence the Senate would have had the power to initiate legislation (except money bills), an absolute veto over Commons legislation in a few specified areas, and the power of ratifying certain federal appointments, the latter an unprecedented power for a non-confidence chamber in any parliamentary system. All in all, it could have become an extremely influential counter to the majoritarian dominance of Ontario and Quebec in the House of Commons.

In one respect the contribution of the Senate to providing such a counter-balance to central Canada was weakened, however, by the insistence of the Triple-E advocates that senators be ineligible for cabinet appointments. It was their view that by prohibiting cabinet membership, party leverage and hence partisanship would be reduced in the Senate, thereby strengthening it through its greater independence. But at the same time this ineligibility would have weakened Senate influence in another aspect. This prohibition would have destroyed the opportunity to use elected senators to bring into the cabinet, the central organ in any parliamentary system, a stronger and more effective representation of regional views.[8] Furthermore, this prohibition would have meant that smaller provinces that fail to elect MPs for the governing party would be denied regional cabinet ministers, even non-elected ones. If such a provision had been in place during the period 1980–4 the three westernmost provinces would have been totally unrepresented in the Trudeau cabinet. In any case, the prohibition from cabinet membership is unlikely in practice to reduce seriously party dependency, since candidates competing in province-wide constituencies would require party support and resources to have any realistic chance of election.

THE HOUSE OF COMMONS

The federal proposals of September 1991 identified a number of proposals for making the House of Commons less partisan and for improving the openness and visibility of parliamentary procedures. The Beaudoin-Dobbie Committee recommended, however, that these matters simply be dealt with by Parliament rather than being included in the package of constitutional reforms. In the subsequent intergovernmental negotiations that began in March 1992 the same approach as that of the Beaudoin-Dobbie Committee was taken. It was recognized that since section 44 of the Constitution Act, 1982 placed the responsibility for such amendments in the hands of Parliament alone without provincial assent, these matters should be left to Parliament. It was also noted that Parliament already had before it the issue of Aboriginal representation in the House of Commons as a result of the report of the Royal Commission on Electoral Reform and Party Financing (Lortie) and so that issue too was left to Parliament. As a result, the only matters specifically relating to the House of Commons dealt with in the Charlottetown agreement were (1) the relative powers of the Senate and the House of Commons in relation to each other and the deadlock-breaking mechanism in cases where the two houses disagreed (discussed in the preceding section on the Senate) and (2) adjustments to the composition of the House of Commons to balance the provincially equal representation in the proposed Senate.

There were two thrusts to the proposed adjustments of representation in the House of Commons. The first was to improve representation by population in the House of Commons, which under current arrangements moderates representation by population to the considerable disadvantage of the more populous provinces, particularly Ontario. This was to be achieved by a progressive approach in the future redistributions of seats towards more accurately reflecting representation by population. The Lortie Commission had already noted that the various floors for representation of smaller provinces in the House of Commons have meant that larger provinces such as Ontario and British Columbia are seriously underrepresented in the current House of Commons, in the case of Ontario by as much as 10 per cent.[9] Early in the MMC process, Ontario raised the issue that if the larger provinces were to be reduced to equal provincial representation in the Senate, then the underrepresentation of Ontario in the House of Commons should be corrected by more fully realizing the principle of representation by population in the House of Commons. The Charlottetown Consensus Report did not go as far in this direction as the Lortie Commission had recommended for a situation where there would be a provincially equal Senate. It did provide, nevertheless, for adjustments in the House of Commons composition to better reflect representation by population in progressive stages.[10] There was a commitment that the cumulative effect of adjustments following the 1991 and 1996 census results would be to add 21 seats for Ontario, 18 for Quebec, 7 for British Columbia, and 4 for Alberta, so that no province would have less than 95 per cent of the Commons seats that it would have been entitled to by a strict application of representation by population.

The second thrust of the Charlottetown Consensus Report in relation to the composition of the House of Commons was to provide protection for the representation within the federal Parliament of Quebec, with its francophone concentration, not through provisions relating to the Senate but through a guarantee of 25 per cent of the seats in the House of Commons. The 25 per cent guarantee was based on the fact that for some time the Quebec population has been around 25 per cent of the federal population and that demographic projections do not foresee a radical change in that proportion. This guarantee was intended to reassure Quebec, and particularly its French-speaking majority, in view of the fact that the adoption of a provincially equal Senate would have reduced its Senate representation from twenty-four to six senators and the voice of francophone senators to less than 9 per cent even though they represent a quarter of the population.

THE SUPREME COURT

Ensuring the independence of the Supreme Court and entrenching its composition and the method of appointing its members was an important issue for two reasons: first, the traditional role of the Supreme Court as an umpire in jurisdictional disputes between the federal and provincial governments meant that it should not be the creature of one order of government alone; and, second, the increased role of the Supreme Court since 1982, derived from its responsibility to interpret the Charter, has added the functions of defining not only the constitutional relationships between governments but also those between governments and citizens.

During the constitutional deliberations and negotiations three issues relating to the Supreme Court were addressed:

- Entrenchment of the Supreme Court in the Constitution to replace its present situation, where it is a creature of federal law.
- Defining the composition of the Supreme Court to constitutionalize the long-established practice that three of the nine justices should come from the Quebec civil-law bar.
- Altering the method for appointing justices to give the provinces a role in the process. Currently, appointments to the Supreme Court are legally the sole responsibility of the federal government, although in practice there may be considerable consultation before the federal government exercises that responsibility.

It should be noted that a constitutional amendment relating to either of the first two issues would have required the assent of all the provincial legislatures,[11] but that specifying in the Constitution the method of appointment would have required endorsement of only seven provinces representing at least 50 per cent of the federal population.[12]

These issues were addressed in the federal proposals of September 1991 and in the Beaudoin-Dobbie report of 28 February 1992.[13] The Ministerial Meeting on the Constitution fairly quickly reached agreement on these three issues, and indeed by 30 April 1992 had tentatively approved a draft legal text that was incorporated with little change into the official draft legal text of 9 October 1992.[14] On the first two issues, entrenchment of the Supreme Court and its composition, the required unanimous agreement was obtained within the MMC. On the method of appointment, which for constitutional amendment would have required only endorsement by seven provinces representing at least 50 per cent of the population, all the government representatives except Newfoundland agreed to a system of federal appointments from lists of provincial and territorial nominees. This solution constituted a modified version of the Meech Lake Accord proposals, adding a role for territorial governments, for appointment of interim judges where necessary, and through a political accord Aboriginal input into the appointment process.

FIRST MINISTERS' CONFERENCES

An important aspect of any federation is the establishment of institutions and processes facilitating effective relations between governments. The federal proposals of September 1991 therefore included proposals for a new intergovernmental body, a Council of the Federation, to deal with issues relating to (1) proposed federal legislation to enhance the functioning of the economic union, (2) the establishment of guidelines for fiscal harmonization and coordination, and (3) decisions to use the federal spending power for new Canada-wide shared-cost programs and conditional transfers in areas of exclusive provincial jurisdiction.[15] As it turned out, although this proposal would have made the exercise of federal authority in these areas dependent upon the consent of at least seven provinces representing at least 50 per cent of the population, the proposal was fiercely attacked from some quarters as a 'federal power grab' and from others as an attempt to implement a conservative economic agenda.[16] In addition, other critics, failing to recognize that an elected Senate representing provincial electorates and not governments cannot negotiate for or commit provincial governments, wondered whether a reformed Senate would make a Council of the Federation unnecessary. As a result, by the time the Beaudoin-Dobbie Committee made its report this federal proposal had to all intents and purposes been abandoned, and that report contained only a proposal for entrenching in the Constitution annual meetings of the first ministers' conference.[17]

There is an interesting irony here, however. In Australia, which has had a powerful Triple-E Senate since its inception in 1901, a Labour federal government together with the states decided in May 1992 to adapt to its own uses the original Canadian proposal for a Council of the Federation by establishing a Council of Australian Governments that has as its primary objective the strengthening of its economic union.[18]

In the end, what the Charlottetown Consensus Report did provide for in relation to first ministers' conferences was the following:

• annual first ministers' conferences, constitutionalizing in more summary form an arrangement that had existed by intergovernmental agreement from 1985 to 1990, but with provision in certain cases for territorial and Aboriginal participation;[19]
• establishment by the first ministers' conference of a mechanism for monitoring the operation of the Social and Economic Union, and of an independent dispute resolution agency relating to the Canadian Common Market.[20]

CONCLUSION

The Charlottetown Consensus Report proposed a substantial modification to the character of Canada's federal institutions, most notably in relation to the Senate. Those proposals included a creative approach to the reconciliation of parliamentary and federal institutions and to the accommodation within a bicameral federal legislature of a fuller realization of the principles of representation by population in the House of Commons, an added voice for smaller provinces through equal representation in the Senate, and an adequate representation of Canada's major linguistic minority through guaranteed Quebec representation in the House of Commons.

For a full understanding of the factors underlying the rejection of the Consensus Report we shall need to await the results of forthcoming detailed scholarly analyses of the campaign and of the shifts of public opinion during it. Clearly many factors affected the result, including the unpopularity of Prime Minister Mulroney and of politicians in general. There seems to be some evidence too that the voting divided fairly consistently along socio-economic lines, with those less well off in economic and educational terms voting No more heavily. Thus, we have the paradox that those who were suffering most under the status quo were the strongest opponents of change, largely because they did not trust the politicians who were advocating those changes. There appears also to have been a general presumption among voters that, when faced with a complicated document that included some specific provisions which had been criticized, the safest and least risky vote was No. Furthermore, the publication of frequent public-opinion polls indicating a trend in favour of a No vote both in Quebec and in the West may also have contributed to the result, for it left voters free to vote No without the fear that they would thereby be rejecting and isolating other groups.

The contradictory motivations for voting No in the referendum illustrate vividly the continued polarization of views within Canada. The majority in Quebec, including many federalists who would prefer not to separate from Canada, voted No because the Charlottetown agreement did not give Quebec enough. Many in the rest of Canada, and particularly in the West, voted No because in their view it involved too much in the way of special arrangements for Quebec. Many Aboriginal people voted No or abstained because the agreement did not go far enough in recognizing their claims. Many non-Aboriginal people voted No because they felt that the recognition in the agreement of an inherent Aboriginal right to self-government was too sweeping and would be too costly. Many voted No from fear that the particular rights of a specific group were not adequately reinforced. Efforts to reduce disaffection in one region or for one group seemed only to increase disaffection elsewhere. Thus, the attempt to aggregate support by an inclusive 'Canada Round' instead fragmented support. In the crucible of the referendum the will of the electorate to accept the concessions and compromises necessary for constitutional change seemed to leak away.

During the campaign there was little controversy over the proposals relating to the Supreme Court and the first ministers' conferences, but those relating to the Senate and the House of Commons did occasion debate. Within Quebec, the reduced voice of francophone Quebec within a provincially equal Senate, which provoked such a sharp reaction to the earlier premiers' proposal of 7 July, was somewhat mitigated by the later compensating adjustments for Quebec's representation in the House of Commons. Although these proposals relating to federal institutions did not arouse enthusiasm in Quebec, the negative majority in the referendum in Quebec was probably not so much related to this aspect of the agreement as to a feeling that Premier Bourassa had obtained insufficient concessions in the powers transferred to Quebec. Elsewhere in Canada, the 25 per cent guarantee to Quebec in the House of Commons came under considerable attack, particularly in British Columbia with its fast-growing population, which saw that guarantee to Quebec as limiting its own ability to achieve full representation by population in the House of Commons. There seemed little understanding or sympathy for this concession to Quebec for accepting a drastically reduced representation in the Senate. Elsewhere in the West, the most ardent supporters of a Triple-E Senate, instead of taking encouragement from the extent to which their objectives had been incorporated in the Charlottetown agreement, were critical of the lack of absolute veto powers for the proposed Senate and of the reinforcement of Ontario and Quebec representation in the House of Commons. They saw this as undermining their objective of curtailing the predominance of central Canada within the federal institutions. The National Action Committee on the Status of Women, for its part, saw the failure to enshrine proportional representation and gender equality in the constitutional provisions for the Senate (the latter left to provincial discretion) as a betrayal of the principles of representation they had pressed for at the Calgary conference.

What of the prospects for the future? The problems that the Charlottetown agreement was attempting to address remain unresolved and the contradictory positions of the different advocates of a No vote provide no clear coherent or positive direction for the future. Given that the Charlottetown agreement was the product of the most extensive, exhaustive, and exhausting process of prior public constitutional discussion to have occurred in any country in this century, that in the intergovernmental negotiations the great variety of views to be reconciled made resolution so difficult, and that a consensus was reached only after a great variety of possible solutions were considered and after compromises and concessions were made on all sides, the prospects for producing another resolution in the near future seem remote. In some areas, such as progress towards Aboriginal self-government and rebalancing the roles of the federal and provincial governments, the preferred path now will be to proceed by non-constitutional adjustments and arrangements, as Canadians often had to do in the 115 years before the adoption of a constitutional-amendment process in 1982. Whether enough can be achieved by such means to enable the country to hold together remains to be seen. As far as federal institutions are concerned, this pragmatic approach may be applicable to the improvement of the consultation process for Supreme Court appointments, the evolution of first ministers' conferences, and some reforms in the House of Commons. But entrenchment of the Supreme Court and significant Senate reform is not possible without formal constitutional amendment. Thus, major progress on those fronts would regrettably appear to be blocked for the foreseeable future.

NOTES

1 Donald G. Lenihan, *Is There a Vision? Looking for the Philosophy Behind the Reforms*, Network Analyses, Analysis no. 7 (Ottawa: Network on the Constitution, September 1992)

2 Government of Canada, *Shaping Canada's Future Together: Proposals* (Ottawa: Minister of Supply and Services Canada 1991), 18–19, and Proposals 9 and 10, pp. 23–4. Canada West Foundation, *Renewal of Canada: Institutional Reform* (Calgary: Canada West Foundation 1992), 10. On the composition of the Calgary conference, see David Milne, 'Innovative Constitutional Process: Renewal of Canada Conferences, January–March 1992,' in D.M. Brown and R. Young, eds, *Canada: The State of the Federation, 1992* (Kingston: Institute of Intergovernmental Relations 1992), 31–7, 40

3 *Report of the Special Joint Committee on a Renewed Canada* (Ottawa: Supply and Services Canada 1992), 49–52

4 Multilateral meeting on the Constitution, *Report to MMC: The Equal Group Equal Senate Model* (Document 830-447/004, 09-10.06, 1992) and *Addendum to Report to MMC: Equal Senate Model* (Document 830-447/007, 09-10.06, 1992)

5 Working Group II Progress Report to the Multilateral Meeting on the Constitution, Senate Models (Document 840-647/010, Montreal, 20–22 May 1992), 11–17

6 Ibid., 18–19

7 David Elton's analysis in this volume indicates that, based on the last 47 years, the

government has had a 60 per cent majority in the House of Commons in 20 of those years. But it should be noted that, since 1968, in only 4 of the last 24 years has a government had such a majority, and current indications suggest that minority governments may be more common in the future.

8 Herman Bakvis, *Regional Ministers: Power and Influence in the Canadian Cabinet* (Toronto: University of Toronto Press 1991), 300–2, makes a good case for membership of elected senators in the cabinet.

9 Royal Commission on Electoral Reform and Party Financing, *Reforming Electoral Democracy* (Ottawa: 1992), chap. 4

10 Ibid., 135

11 *Constitution Act, 1982*, s. 41(d)

12 Ibid., ss. 38(1) and 42(d)

13 *Shaping Canada's Future Together: Proposals*, 21–2, 24–5, Proposal 12; *Report of the Special Joint Committee on a Renewed Canada*, 59–60

14 This agreement was embodied in the *Consensus Report on the Constitution, Charlottetown, August 28, 1992, Final Text*, ss. 17–20, p. 7, and in the *Draft Legal Text, October 9, 1992*, s. 15, pp. 24–6, setting out ss. 101A–F.

15 *Shaping Canada's Future Together: Proposals*, 41–2, and Proposal 28, p. 47

16 C.D. Howe Institute and Institute for Research on Public Policy, *Renewal of Canada: Economic Union: Conference Report* (Toronto and Ottawa, 10 February 1992), 10–16, 19–22

17 *Report of the Special Joint Committee on a Renewed Canada*, 89–90, 124

18 Heads of Government Meeting, Canberra, 11 May 1992, *Communique*, 1–2

19 *Consensus Report*, s. 23, p. 10; *Draft Legal Text*, p. 47

20 *Consensus Report*, s. 4, p. 3, and s. 5, p. 4; *Draft Legal Text*, p. 46

2

The Charlottetown Accord Senate: Effective or Emasculated?

DAVID ELTON

The proposal for Senate reform contained in the Charlottetown Accord met with mixed reviews from long-time advocates of Senate reform within hours of its creation. The premiers of Alberta, Manitoba, and Newfoundland, all committed Senate-reform advocates and proponents of a 'Triple-E Senate,' argued that the proposal created, in essence if not in fact, a Triple-E Senate (that is, Elected, Equal in terms of representation by province, and Effective). Many constitutional experts and Senate-reform advocates disagreed with the premiers' assessment, arguing that the first ministers' proposal would create a partially elected Senate, with formally equal provincial representation but de facto special powers for Quebec senators, and an effectively emasculated Senate. In addition, the first ministers' proposed changes to the House of Commons to accommodate equal representation for each province in the Senate were seen to exacerbate further the domination of the House of Commons by Canada's two largest provinces.

That Canadians did not like the content of the Charlottetown Accord is now a matter of record.[1] Whether the first ministers' proposal for Senate reform did or did not represent meaningful Senate reform is a matter over which there has been, and probably will continue to be, considerable disagreement. What is clear is that the first ministers' proposed Senate differed dramatically from any previous proposals. Given that Senate reform will be advocated and perhaps undertaken in the future, a review of specific details contained in the first ministers' Senate-reform proposal and the debate over the merits and flaws of the proposals are both necessary and instructive.

PLACING THE PROPOSAL IN CONTEXT

In an effort to understand why there were so many differing opinions among Senate-reform proponents about the first ministers' Senate proposals, this essay will compare the first ministers' Senate proposal with the models for a re-formed Senate put forward in a report published by the Canada West Founda-tion, entitled *A Blueprint for Senate Reform*, and two legislative-committee reports submitted to the Alberta government model of 1985 and revised in early 1992.[2] The Senate Blueprint report is based upon a review of Senate-reform literature and discussions held in 1990 among constitutional experts and Senate-reform supporters. The Alberta government reports are based upon the work of two special committees of the Alberta legislature that held exten-sive public hearings and examined second chambers throughout the world. These two reports are used because they represent the key ideas underpinning Triple-E Senate proposals.

For purposes of analysis, thirteen separate aspects of the first ministers' Senate-reform proposal are examined. Each dimension of the proposal is dis-cussed and contrasted with the ideas put forward in the two models discussed above.

ELECTION

The first ministers' Senate proposal called for the election of senators, 'either by the population of the provinces and territories of Canada or by the members of their provincial or territorial assemblies.' Given that almost every report written on institutional reform over the past decade has advocated the direct election of senators, the provision for indirect election by provincial legislatures was a substantial departure from the election principle.[3] Both the Senate Blue-print report and the Alberta government reports explicitly reject the idea of provincial-government appointments to the Senate.

The idea of having provincial governments indirectly elect senators was advocated by a wide range of people in the late 1970s – most notably by the Pepin-Robarts Task Force on Canadian Unity and the Government of British Columbia. The decision to combine the two methods was clearly a compromise that reduced the democratic legitimacy that only direct election can provide.[4] While the option of direct election or indirect election was agreed upon to accommodate the Quebec government, the premiers of Prince Edward Island and British Columbia were also known to be sympathetic to the idea of provincial-government appointments to the Senate.

The impact of the indirect-election option is clearly a substantial departure from the direct-election preference stated by nearly all reports on institutional reform. A Senate with a mixture of directly elected and indirectly elected provincial-government representatives would cause serious problems on a number of fronts.

Federal elections that would have allowed new senators to be appointed

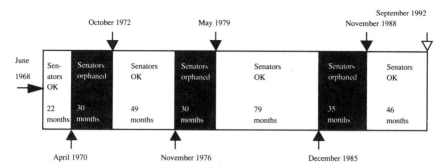

Figure 1
The appointment of senators and the 'orphan effect'

First, the mandates of directly elected senators would be considerably different than the mandates of indirectly elected senators. The directly elected senators would be representatives of citizens, the indirectly elected senators representatives of the provincial government that elected them.

A second problem with mixing directly elected and indirectly elected senators is that provincial and federal elections are never held at the same time. There is thus a good chance that indirectly elected senators could become 'lame duck senators' because of the different dates upon which provincial and federal elections are held. Should the provincial government that elected the senators following a federal election be defeated at the next provincial election, which sometimes happens within weeks of the federal election, then the senators would be without a mandate. Figure 1 provides an example of what would have happened had such a procedure been in place over the past twenty-four years in the province of Quebec. For one-third of the time (95 of 291 months) indirectly elected senators from Quebec would have been representing a party that was defeated in the most recent provincial election. For example, at the time of the 1984 federal election, the PQ-dominated Quebec legislature would have elected the Quebec senators. These senators would have served until November 1988, even though the Quebec Liberal party was elected in 1985. Thus, for three of the four years, the Quebec senators would have represented the opposition party in Quebec rather than the Quebec Liberal government of the day.

Just exactly how much more credible these 'lame duck' senators would be than the currently appointed senators is hard to determine. Given that Senate effectiveness is dependent upon the credibility of senators, there is every likelihood that the indirect-election option would reduce the effectiveness of the new Senate.

Timing of Elections

The first ministers' Senate proposal called for Senate elections to take place at the same time as elections to the House of Commons. The main reason given for opting for simultaneous elections was that the cost of stand-alone elections was prohibitive. The simultaneous elections would effectively intermarry Senate and House of Commons elections and thus increase the likelihood that federal parties would dominate or even effectively control Senate nominations and election campaigns. This tendency would substantially decrease the likelihood of Senate independence from the prime minister and the governing party.

The models developed in both the Senate Blueprint report and the Alberta Special Committee reports placed considerable emphasis upon holding elections at a different time. The Alberta government argued that holding elections at the same time as provincial elections would do two important things. First, it would help ensure that senators were more in tune with provincial issues and thus better able to represent their province in Ottawa. Second, it would increase the independence of senators from federal parties and thus increase the likelihood that they would feel more loyalty to their province than to the party they represented.

The Senate Blueprint report argued that the impact of both federal and provincial parties could be reduced by having the senators elected at stand-alone elections every three years on a fixed date. The weaknesses of this method of election (that is, the risk of creating voter fatigue through the large number of elections, and the costs of electing senators) were seen to be outweighed by the degree of independence provided to senators.

Electoral System

The first ministers' proposal called for the election of senators under rules established by federal legislation. There was no commitment to proportional representation or Single Transferable Ballots as was the case in the 7 July consensus reached by Joe Clark and the nine premiers.[5] The first ministers would have left it up to the House of Commons to draft the appropriate legislation. Whether there would be any provisions that would distinguish Senate elections from regular House of Commons elections was to be determined by Parliament at a later date.

Both the Alberta Special Committee reports and the Senate Blueprint report argued for separate electoral systems for the Senate.[6] They argued that the primary purpose for reforming the Senate was to ensure that senators would place the concerns and aspirations of those who elected them before the needs of the party of which they were a member. In addition, it was pointed out that using a separate electoral system would both differentiate Senate elections from House of Commons elections in the mind of the voters and increase the likelihood that representation in the Parliament of Canada would better reflect the wishes of the electorate.

Having federal election rules for Senate elections and holding simultaneous House and Senate elections would also substantially increase the likelihood that Senate elections would be controlled by federal party-discipline considerations. These two provisions would weaken a senator's ability to become an effective regional spokesperson. For example, an existing federal election rule requires national party leaders to sign the nomination papers of candidates for the House of Commons. Extending this rule to Senate elections would mean that senators would have to worry not only about whether they had so annoyed the voters as to make re-election difficult, but also about whether they had so annoyed their national party leader as to make re-nomination impossible.

Gender Representation

One of the unique aspects of the first ministers' proposal was the provision that would have permitted provincial legislatures to pass legislation requiring gender quotas for Senate seats. Neither the Senate Blueprint report nor the Alberta Special Committee reports provided for special representation of women in the Senate. Better representation of women in the Parliament of Canada was deemed to be better handled through changes to the electoral processes (that is, proportional representation and modified nomination procedures) rather than through a formal quota system.

The first ministers' proposal to provide for a possible gender quota system obtained the support of a number of women's lobby groups and several provincial governments. Opposition to the idea was widespread, and in British Columbia the opposition was so intense that it was used time and again to generate substantial opposition to the entire accord.

EQUAL REPRESENTATION BY PROVINCE

The first ministers' proposal for equal representation for each province was identical to one of the central elements of both the Blueprint report and the Alberta Special Committee reports. This decision to accept equal representation by province was very contentious for many Canadians, and in particular for the Governments of Ontario and Quebec. Equal representation of provinces regardless of size could not be accepted by Ontario and Quebec unless there were offsetting arrangements to limit the powers of such a Senate. Not surprisingly, the subsequent alterations made to the House of Commons to accommodate the objections of Ontario and Quebec made the House of Commons proposals equally contentious.

Given that the proposed Senate would be dominated by representatives from Canada's eight small provinces, the opportunity for representatives from these provinces to influence control of the Senate's agenda and proceedings would be considerably enhanced. While this aspect of the proposal appealed to those who felt that Canada's existing parliament was subject to the tyranny of the central Canadian majority, it also generated considerable consternation in Quebec. For Quebec, such a parliament would substantially reduce the number and influence of Quebec representatives in Ottawa.

In order to offset the Quebec objection to a Triple-E Senate, the first ministers decided to make three basic changes in the House of Commons to compensate Quebec and Ontario for the reduction in their representation in the Senate. First, Ontario and Quebec would be given eighteen additional seats each – exactly the same number they were to lose in the Senate. Second, Quebec would be given a constitutional guarantee that its representation in the House of Commons would never drop below 25 per cent. Third, legislation rejected by the Senate could be overridden by a majority vote in a joint sitting, where members of the House of Commons would outnumber senators by more than five to one. These three proposals, while seen by the first ministers as being a reasonable means of compensating Ontario and Quebec for equal provincial representation in the Senate, became the focal point of opposition to the institutional-reform elements of the Charlottetown Accord in Western Canada. The fact that the proposals came from New Brunswick Premier Frank McKenna and Saskatchewan's Roy Romanow did little to deflect their rejection.

HOUSE OF COMMONS REPRESENTATION

The first ministers' proposal to increase Ontario's and Quebec's representation in the House of Commons was necessitated by the creation of an equal Senate, not by any perceived need to reform the House of Commons. The eighteen additional members for Ontario and Quebec, plus four for British Columbia and two for Alberta, were created simply as a means of compensating larger provinces for the real/imaginary losses in numbers of parliamentarians brought

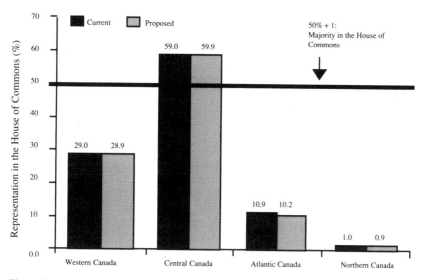

Figure 2
First ministers' proposal: Representation in the House of Commons (%)

about by the proposed creation of a Senate with six senators from each province. No previous proposals for Senate reform had argued that representation in the House of Commons would have to be altered to accommodate Senate reform.

The first ministers were either unaware of, or underestimated, the amount of opposition that would develop to their reforms of House of Commons representation. Rather than being seen as a necessary compromise in return for the creation of a Senate with equal representation from each province, their proposal was seen to perpetuate, even exacerbate, Central Canada's dominance and control of Canada's national government. That this interpretation would be made is evident from the data in figure 2. Whereas 'outer Canada' currently makes up 40.9 per cent of the House of Commons, under the first ministers' proposal, 'outer Canada' would make up 38 per cent of the new House – an absolute reduction of nearly 3 per cent. Given that major disagreements would be settled in joint sessions, it was argued that the real voting 'power' of the proposed parliament needed to be assessed in light of the House of Commons and Senate seats combined. Even in the joint sessions, as indicated in figure 3, the voting power of 'outer Canada' increases marginally from 40.9 to 44.4 per cent – an increase of 3.5 per cent. This increase in representation from 'outer Canada' in joint sessions fell far short of the kind of counterbalance to Central

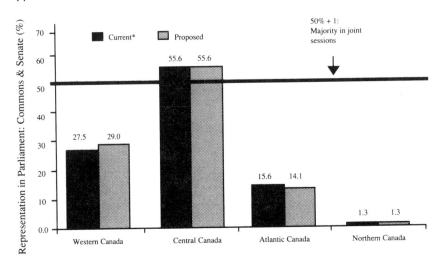

Figure 3
First ministers' proposal: Representation in joint sessions (%)

Canada's dominance in the House of Commons that Senate reform was intended to generate.

No matter how one calculates the House of Commons and Senate seat allocations proposed in the first ministers' proposal, it is hard to see how the votes
of senators from 'outer Canada' would effectively influence the outcome of a
joint session with a government that enjoyed a majority in the House of Commons. The size of a government's majority is every bit as important as regional
seat allocations when determining the potential effectiveness of the new Senate
in confronting a government willing to override the concerns of a regionally
equitable Senate.

Figure 4 (pp. 46–7) provides an assessment of the frequency and size of
government majorities since the Second World War and indicates the size of
the Senate majorities required to resist a governing party's majority. In twenty
of the forty-seven years the Senate, even if unanimously opposed to the
Government's intentions, would have had no effect on the outcome of a vote in
joint sessions. In seventeen of forty-seven years it would have taken 65 per
cent or more of the senators to effectively challenge the Government. Only in
ten of the past forty-seven years, when Canada was governed by a minority
party, would the proposed Senate have been able to affect the outcome of a
joint-session vote.

THE 25 PER CENT GUARANTEE FOR QUEBEC

In addition to providing for substantial additional representation for Ontario and Quebec, the first ministers proposed that Quebec be given a constitutional guarantee that its representation in the Senate would never fall below 25 per cent. This was another unique aspect of their proposal.

The 25 per cent guarantee for Quebec addressed one of the key objections Quebec had regarding Senate reform – the absolute reduction in the number of parliamentarians from Quebec in Ottawa. It also provided de facto recognition to the 'two-nation' concept that is a fundamental principle for many Québécois in the sense that it provided Quebec with a special status not given any other province. While it is true that all provinces have been guaranteed a certain number of seats, no province has ever been guaranteed a fixed percentage of seats in the House of Commons.

The guarantee was based upon the fact that Quebec has always had more than 25 per cent of the population, and that its percentage of the population over the foreseeable future (the next 10–20 years) is, according to a Statistics Canada projection, unlikely to drop much below this figure. None of these facts deflected the near visceral opposition to this element of the accord, particularly in British Columbia.[7]

Opposition to the 25 per cent guarantee for Quebec in British Columbia was based primarily upon two things: (1) the belief that the provision violates the principle of representation by population; (2) the expectation that existing and future population growth in British Columbia would not be adequately represented in the House of Commons because of the Quebec guarantee. Even the first ministers' commitment to redistribute seats in the House of Commons based upon the 1996 census, and the commitment that each province would obtain at least 95 per cent of the seats for which it would be eligible under strict representation by population, did little to decrease opposition to the proposal.

POWERS OF THE SENATE

The first ministers' proposal regarding the legislative powers of the Senate was based upon four categories of legislation. The Senate was to be given the following powers:

• Supply bills – 30-day suspensive vote
• French language and culture – absolute veto
• Natural-resource taxation – absolute veto
• Ordinary legislation – reconciliation, joint session

Figure 4
Joint-session voting patterns, 1945–92: Theoretical outcomes

Governments with 60% majority +

1949–53: Louis St Laurent (Lib.)
  • 71% majority in House of Commons
  • 100%+ senators needed to defeat bill

1953–7: Louis St Laurent (Lib.)
  • 63% majority in House of Commons
  • 100%+ senators needed to defeat bill

1958–62 John Diefenbaker (PC)
  • 79% majority in House of Commons
  • 100%+ senators needed to defeat bill

1968–72 Pierre Trudeau (Lib.)
  • 60% majority in House of Commons
  • 100%+ senators needed to defeat bill

1984–8 Brian Mulroney (PC)
  • 75% majority in House of Commons
  • 100%+ senators needed to defeat bill

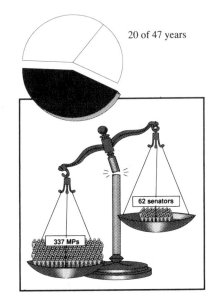

20 of 47 years

Governments with 51–60% majority

1945–9: Mackenzie King (Lib.)
  • 53% majority in House of Commons
  • 64.5% (40) senators needed to defeat bill
Govt. needs 37.1% (23) senators to pass bill

1974–9: Pierre Trudeau (Lib.)
  • 53% majority in House of Commons
  • 67.7% (42) senators needed to defeat bill
Govt. needs 33.9% (21) senators to pass bill

1980–4: Pierre Trudeau/John Turner (Lib.)
  • 53% majority in House of Commons
  • 64.5% (40) senators needed to defeat bill
Govt. needs 37.1% (23) senators to pass bill

1988 – Present: Brian Mulroney (PC)
  • 58% majority in House of Commons
  • 95.2% (59) senators needed to defeat bill
Govt. needs 6.5% (4) senators to pass bill

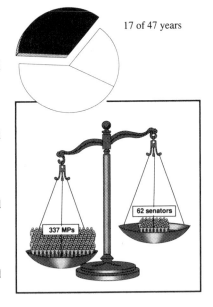

17 of 47 years

Figure 4 (continued)
Joint-session voting patterns, 1945–92: Theoretical outcomes*

Minority governments 49% >

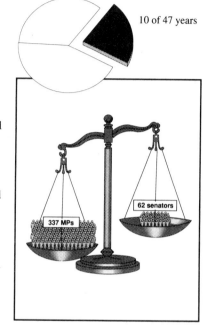

10 of 47 years

1957–8: John Diefenbaker (PC)
 • 42% majority in House of Commons
 • 9.7% (6) senators needed to defeat bill
Govt. needs 91.9% (57) senators to pass bill

1962–3: John Diefenbaker (PC)
 • 49% majority in House of Commons
 • 45.2% (28) senators needed to defeat bill
Govt. needs 56.5% (35) senators to pass bill

1963–5: Lester B. Pearson (Lib.)
 • 49% majority in House of Commons
 • 45.2% (28) senators needed to defeat bill
Govt. needs 56.5% (35) senators to pass bill

1965–8: Lester B. Pearson (Lib.)
 • 50% majority in House of Commons
 • 48.4% (30) senators needed to defeat bill
Govt. needs 53.2% (33) senators to pass bill

1972–4: Pierre Trudeau (Lib.)
 • 41% majority in House of Commons
 • 1.6% (1) senator needed to defeat bill
Govt. needs 100% (62) senators to pass bill

1979–80: Joe Clark (PC)
 • 48% majority in House of Commons
 • 40.3% (25) senators needed to defeat bill
Govt. needs 61.3% (38) senators to pass bill

* The data were computed by multiplying the election results by a ratio that accounts
  for the August 1992 proposed changes to the House of Commons. The election
  results for Quebec, Ontario, Alberta, and British Columbia were increased to
  represent their increased representation in the proposed House (18, 18, 2, and 4 extra
  seats respectively). The results from the other provinces were entered unchanged.

In addition to the legislative powers outlined above, the first ministers proposed that the Senate be given the responsibility of reviewing and accepting or rejecting the Government's appointment of the governor of the Bank of Canada. Provision was also made for Parliament to expand the list of appointments reviewable by the Senate to cover whatever appointments Parliament deemed appropriate.

Supply and Revenue Bills

The first ministers' new Senate provided for a thirty-day suspensive veto over 'the raising of revenue and appropriation as well as matters subordinate to these issues.' This proposal was in accordance with the proposals put forward by both the Alberta government and the Blueprint report.

The key issue related to money bills was the number and kind of bills that would be classified in this manner. A narrow definition would limit money bills to ordinary budgetary matters. A broad definition of money bills would mean that the Government could effectively 'Senate proof' any legislation by simply providing an expenditure clause to make it appear to be a money bill. The narrow definition would enhance the role of the Senate by placing a larger portion of legislation in the 'ordinary' category, while a broad definition would effectively emasculate the Senate by increasing the kind and amount of legislation that the Senate could only delay for thirty days.

The legal draft spelled out in some detail the definition of a money bill, and narrowly defined money bills as appropriations, the raising of revenues (but not fundamental changes to the tax system), and borrowing for public debt.[8] This aspect of the first ministers' proposal was seen as being a reasonable compromise and never became a matter of contention.

Natural-Resource Legislation

One of the areas in which the new Senate was to have unquestioned legislative power was on natural-resource taxation. Whether this 'power' would be significant or not would depend upon how often the national government dealt with natural-resource taxation.[9] An analysis of the past eleven years indicates that in fact natural-resource taxation issues seldom come before Parliament. Over the eleven-year period fewer than 3 per cent of the acts passed by Parliament dealt with natural-resource taxation.

Simply determining that natural-resource taxation legislation is seldom passed by Parliament does not deal with the potential impact of even one piece of legislation upon the economy of a region and the lives of its residents. To have a Senate that could modify or block a future piece of legislation like the National Energy Program (NEP) is probably reason enough for the creation of the new Senate in the minds and hearts of those who believe their dreams were shattered and businesses destroyed through the NEP of 1980. The emphasis placed upon this power by Alberta Premier Don Getty is indicative of this point of view. The potential value of the Senate's absolute power over natural-resource taxation did little to offset opposition to the limitations placed upon the Senate's ability to amend or reject ordinary legislation, however.

FRENCH LANGUAGE AND CULTURE LEGISLATION

Just as the special legislative powers for the Senate over natural resources were recommended to meet the concerns of Western Canada, the first ministers proposed that French-speaking senators be given the ability to veto any language or cultural legislation that they deemed not in the best interests of the francophone linguistic communities of Canada. Senators would be designated as French-speaking if they identified themselves to the Speaker of the Senate as such on first taking their seats in the Senate.[10] The first ministers' proposals on this issue paralleled those found in both the Alberta Special Committee reports and the Senate Blueprint report.

Whether Quebec senators would sometimes, often, or always make up a majority of French-speaking senators was never clear, nor was it a major issue in the debate. Those who opposed this proposal did so on the grounds that it created two different classes of senators by giving French-speaking senators a stranglehold over future changes to language legislation.

The fact that no one knew how much legislation would be subject to the approval of the French-speaking senators raised considerable concern. A review of the acts of Parliament passed from April 1980 to December 1991 suggests that the amount of legislation would be small. Only two of 491 acts over this eleven-year period had a *direct* impact on French language or culture (Canadian Multiculturalism Act, Official Languages Act). On ten occasions, acts were passed that could affect language or culture *indirectly* and in eleven instances an impact could be detected but was *questionable*. Even if all these acts were taken to affect language and culture, they would still represent only 4.7 per cent of all acts passed by Parliament during this period. If, however, communication issues are deemed to be 'cultural,' then the amount of legislation requiring a double majority in the Senate could be considerable. This interpretation would tend to make francophone senators very influential and give credence to the concern that francophone senators would become much more significant actors on Parliament Hill than their English-speaking counterparts. The possibility of this latter development generated yet another reason for people to oppose the first ministers' Senate proposals.[11]

Ordinary Legislation

The first ministers' proposals regarding the Senate's role in handling ordinary legislation was a radical departure from both the status quo and the ideas expressed in the Senate Blueprint and Alberta Committee reports. While senators were to be given the right to amend or reject House of Commons legislation, the first ministers' proposals provided that Senate amendments or rejection of a bill could be overturned in a joint session of the House and the Senate. This deadlock-breaking mechanism was chosen primarily for two reasons: (1) it dramatically increased the likelihood that the will of the House of Commons would prevail over Senate opposition to ordinary government legislation; (2) it provided the Senate with an opportunity to focus public attention on what the Senate considers to be deficiencies in the House of Commons legislation. Given the data in figure 4, there is little doubt but that the will of the House of Commons would prevail over the Senate's when a majority government was in power. Whether the joint sessions would provide the Senate with an opportunity to focus public attention on their concerns about the Government's legislation would be a function of the rules and procedures under which joint sessions were held.

Reconciliation Committee and Joint Sessions

One of the most innovative aspects of the first ministers' Senate proposals were those dealing with a joint House and Senate reconciliation committee and the holding of joint sessions to resolve seemingly irreconcilable differences. These proposals went far beyond anything that had been proposed in previous models of Senate reform. Relatively few Canadians became involved in discussing the merits or limitations of these proposals, in part because the details were not made public until the publication of the legal draft text just nineteen days before the referendum vote, and in part because other aspects of the package were considered so repugnant by those opposing the proposal that they felt it irrelevant to assess the fine print.

The debate over a parallel/mirror rule provision regarding joint sessions was at the heart of the debate regarding the Senate's independence from the House and therefore its effectiveness in influencing the legislative process. If, as some critiques of the first ministers' Senate suggested, joint sessions would be nothing more than a perfunctory counting of votes, it is hard to see how the Senate would be anything more than a minor irritant to the House of Commons – a small speed bump on the Government's freeway. If, however, joint sessions turned out to be meaningful opportunities for careful public scrutiny of Government legislation, it is possible that Government ministers would be hesitant to trigger a joint session and therefore would work diligently to reconcile the concerns of a majority of the senators at the reconciliation-committee stage.[12] Had the latter scenario been realized, then a good case could be made for the effectiveness of the first ministers' Senate package. Had joint sessions turned out to be nothing more than a perfunctory counting of votes, the argument that this Senate would be ineffective in dealing with ordinary legislation would have been valid.

While the work done in specifying the scope of activity, timetables, membership, and so on of the reconciliation committee and the joint session did not figure prominently in the referendum debate, it will affect future discussions on Senate reform. No matter what kind of Senate reform is actually undertaken (the one exception being abolition of the Senate), the issue of coordinating House and Senate work on legislation will be critical to a successful reform package. The work done by the governments on this matter provides an important baseline for future discussions on this aspect of Senate reform.[13]

CABINET APPOINTMENTS

The first ministers' proposal to bar senators from serving in the cabinet concurred with the positions taken in both the Senate Blueprint and Alberta Committee reports. The barring of senators from cabinet was based upon two key considerations. First, it would increase the senators' independence of the prime minister and the cabinet because it partially removes the Senate from the not-so-gentle chains of 'perk' and 'privilege' that tie MPs to party authority. Senators would not sit anxiously by the phone during a cabinet shuffle, or feel called upon to vote or to speak so as to curry prime-ministerial favour. Second, it would reduce the extent to which Government business would dominate the Senate agenda and thus reduce the tendency for the Government/Opposition confrontations that dominate the House of Commons to be re-enacted in the Senate. Both of these factors would in turn increase the likelihood that the Senate could act as an initiator of non-money legislation of concern to its electorates.

While the issue of Senate appointments to cabinet was not a key factor in the referendum debate, it was considered a crucial element in the creation of an effective Senate by many Senate-reform advocates. The first ministers' decision to insert this provision in their package was one of the reasons their package received as much support as it did from Senate-reform supporters in Western Canada.

SENATE OFFICERS, RULES, AND SUPPLY

The Charlottetown Accord was vague on Senate rules, officers, and access to funds to carry out their responsibilities. The first ministers' proposal, while specifying in detail how the reconciliation committee and joint sessions would work, did not address the issue of the Senate's internal structure or supply, except to provide for the election of the Senate Speaker by the members of the Senate.[14]

Both the Senate Blueprint report and the Alberta Special Committee reports dealt with this matter in considerable detail. They considered the matter of Senate rules, officers, and independence to be one of the crucial elements in the creation of an effective Senate. Party discipline, which tends to dictate the rules of the House of Commons, is considered by many Senate-reform advocates as one of the primary factors that must be diminished if a reformed Senate is to represent effectively regional aspirations and concerns. Sitting arrangements, caucusing procedures, membership on committees, and so on are all seen as factors that determine the extent of party control over a legislative body.

By not dealing with any of the specific details of Senate organization in their proposal, the first ministers effectively removed discussion of Senate rules and procedures from the debate. This left both options open – the perpetuation of the existing system or the creation of an alternative system of rules that could reduce party discipline.

CONCLUSION

An overview of the proposals contained in the Charlottetown Accord and those put forward in the Blueprint report and the reports of the Special Committees of the Alberta government is provided in table 1. The differences between these proposals indicate that the first ministers' Senate was not intended to be a powerful legislative chamber in the traditional sense. The Senate Blueprint report, by contrast, envisaged a substantially more powerful and independent Senate. The Senate conceived by both Alberta government reports falls somewhere between the other two Senate proposals: it emphasizes independence, but limits the formal legislative powers of the Senate.

Compared to the United States Senate, or even the Australian Senate, the first ministers' Senate would have had far fewer absolute levers of power to pull when it disagreed with proposed government legislation and programs.

TABLE 1

The first ministers' Senate proposal compared

Senate provisions	First ministers' Senate (28 Aug. 1992)	Alberta government reports (1985–92)	CWF Senate Blueprint report
Method of election	Directly elected by the people of a given province or elected by the legislature of a province	Directly elected by the people of a province	Directly elected by the people of a province
Timing of election	Elections to be held at the same time as federal elections	Elections to be held at the same time as provincial elections	Stand-alone, fixed-date elections
Electoral system	Until Parliament designates otherwise, first-past-the-post system	Provincial decision: either first-past-the-post or some form of proportional representation	Proportional representation with provisions for the Single Transferable Vote
Gender representation	Provisions for gender-representation require-ments at the discretion of the individual provinces	Not mentioned	Not mentioned
Provincial representation	Equal number of senators; i.e., 6 per province	Equal number of senators; i.e., 6 per province	Equal number of senators; i.e., 10 per province
House of Commons representation	New seats allocated: 18 each for ON & PQ, 4 for BC, and 2 for AB 25% guaranteed repre-sentation for PQ	Not mentioned	Not mentioned
Supply/revenue bills	Suspensive veto only	Suspensive veto only	Suspensive veto only
Natural-resource bills	Fundamental tax-policy changes to natural resources are subject to an absolute veto.	Senate given an absolute veto over matters pertaining to natural-resource development.	Not specifically men-tioned, but assumed that the Senate would have amendment/veto powers dependent upon the nature of the bill; i.e., ordinary or money bill.

TABLE 1 (continued)
The first ministers' Senate proposal compared

Senate provisions	First ministers' Senate (28 Aug. 1992)	Alberta government reports (1985–92)	CWF Senate Blueprint report
French language and culture bills	Measures affecting Fr./Eng. language and Fr. culture require a majority of both groups of senators.	Measures affecting Fr./Eng. languages require a majority of: a) Combined Senate and b) a majority of Fr. or Eng. senators depending on issue.	Measures affecting Fr./Eng. language and culture require a majority of both groups of senators.
Ordinary legislation	Ordinary legislation can be vetoed/ amended (in most cases a maximum 72-day suspensive veto).	Absolute veto on matters exclusively affecting a provincial jurisdiction Special (sliding majority) veto for matters of concurrent jurisdiction A suspensive veto for matters exclusively affecting a federal jurisdiction	Ordinary legislation can be amended/vetoed.
Dispute resolution	Joint session of House (337 members) and the Senate (62 members) Session to last a maximum of 10 sitting days	Simple majority House override for money and tax bills Sliding majority House override of all other bills; i.e., pass by a greater % than bill was defeated in the Senate	The House of Commons could override the Senate with an unusual majority vote; or by a vote of members from 2/3 of the provinces with at least 1/2 the population
Cabinet appointments	Senators not eligible to be members of the cabinet	Senators not eligible to be members of the cabinet	Senators not eligible to be members of the cabinet

TABLE 1 (continued)

The first ministers' Senate proposal compared

Senate provisions	First ministers' Senate (28 Aug. 1992)	Alberta government reports (1985–92)	CWF Senate Blueprint report
Senate officers, rules, and supply	Rules of the Senate are to mirror the House of Commons.	Senators to be seated by province rather than party. Ten provincial chairmen will constitute the 'executive council' rather than Govt./Opposition roles. Speaker elected by a 2/3 vote of the Senate for 4-year term. Executive council to determine the order of business of the Senate.	Senators to be seated by province rather than party. Ten provincial chairmen will constitute the 'executive council' rather than Govt./Opposition roles.

Even so, the first ministers were convinced that their Senate could be an influential legislative body with adequate independence from the House of Commons.

The departures of the first ministers' model from those developed in other reports were, in the final analysis, too substantial. Senate-reform supporters believe Canada needs a federal system of government in which the regional communities of the federation – that is, provincial communities – regardless of population, have the ability to influence directly national-government decision making. The first ministers' proposals were seen as a creative way to perpetuate the status quo rather than a fundamental restructuring of Canada's national institutions. For many Senate reformers, rejection of the Charlottetown Accord sends a clear message that only fundamental reform of national decision making that clearly strengthens the role of the smaller provinces is acceptable. For supporters of the Charlottetown Accord, its rejection puts Senate reform on the shelf for years, perhaps decades, or perhaps even longer. Whichever point of view one may have had on the merits or weaknesses of the first ministers' proposals, they injected into the Senate-reform debate a new set of ideas for Canadians to ponder when they again set themselves to the task of reforming Canada's national institutions.

PART TWO

Mind and Unity

3

Speaking for Ourselves

SHELAGH DAY

Women cannot become powerful or expressive by being spoken to, by being
spoken for, or especially by being spoken about. It is by being heard that women
are empowered.
Betty-Ann Lloyd[1]

Throughout the recent constitutional discussions, the National Action Committee on the Status of Women (NAC) waged a campaign for more inclusive decision-making processes.[2] Some of this campaign was located within the confines of the Senate debate; some of it was centred on support for the formal
inclusion of the Native Women's Association of Canada in the constitutional
talks; and some of it was reflected in the general effort to have NAC's concerns
incorporated into the constitutional debate.

At its narrowest, this campaign was a fight for a formula that would improve
the representation of women and minorities[3] in a new elected Senate. But at its
broadest, it was a fight about the inclusion of the least powerful groups in
society in decision making that affects our lives; it was a challenge to the
adequacy of Canadian democratic processes and institutions.

The referendum campaign and its outcome have made it evident that the
sense of alienation from the current process of political decision-making, which
is felt strongly in the ranks of the organized women's movement, is more
widely shared. When NAC women said we did not feel represented by our
politicians, there was an echoing response. When we said we wanted more
involvement, and more honest and sophisticated political debate about the
issues that affect our futures, we found we were not alone.

Since the Senate debate provided an entrance into the discussion of democracy, representativeness, and process from the perspective of women and other
marginalized groups, this article will describe the dimensions of that debate.
However, it will also discuss the broader issue of adequate democratic process,

and reflect on what lessons about process can be drawn from this constitutional round and the referendum experience.

THE MEANING OF EQUALITY: SAME TREATMENT FOR THE PROVINCES OR INCLUSION FOR MARGINALIZED GROUPS

For the Triple-E Senate proponents, the first E of the three meant equality of the provinces. For women and others, however, that E meant equality for those groups who are currently marginalized with respect to political power. Women currently hold approximately 14 per cent of the seats in both the House of Commons and the Senate. The representation of people of colour, Aboriginal people, lesbians and gay men, people with disabilities, and poor people is minimal or non-existent. The majority of seats in the institutions of government are held by white professional men, though in the Canadian population this group is a small minority.

In February 1992, at the Constitutional Conference on Institutional Reform, NAC contended that at a moment in history when a new institution of government was being designed,[4] perhaps for the only time in a century, there was a significant opportunity to address not just the claims of the regions of 'outer Canada' to a stronger voice in government, but also the claims of Canada's 'out' groups.[5] We also contended that dealing with these claims in the context of Senate reform should be merely a step towards reform of the House of Commons, and democratic process in general.

For the Calgary conference, however, equality had already been narrowly defined by the agenda makers as regional equality, or, more specifically, as same treatment for the provinces. Cracking open the discussion to let in other, in our view, more important, dimensions of equality was not easy. The materials for the conference made it clear that 'representation' meant representation for provinces. No other aspect of representation was on the agenda.[6]

When women and minorities, speaking from the floor, insisted that the issue of our underrepresentation in institutions of government become part of the discussion of Senate reform, some media commentators accused us of hijacking the agenda.[7]

This response was instructive. The reaction revealed assumptions about the democratic process and the place of 'out' groups in it (or rather out of it). The marginalized could, apparently, comment on an agenda set by the power-holders, but only if our comments were confined within the parameters established by them. If we suggested that the agenda itself was too narrow, that the questions being asked were not the only, or the most pertinent, ones, this was considered subversive, violent, and essentially undemocratic.

Despite the initial difficulty of injecting another dimension of equality into the discussion, and despite the revealing accusations it engendered, we were initially successful in obtaining some recognition for the issue. The idea of broadening the meaning of equality when designing a new Senate was embraced by the Calgary conference, by subsequent constitutional conferences, and by the Beaudoin-Dobbie report.[8] Inclusiveness became one of the principles on which it was widely assumed reforms would be based.

At the multilateral meetings this concern with inclusiveness turned into an endorsement of a formula for election to the Senate. That formula was election by proportional representation, rather than by the current first-past-the-post system, and, more specifically, by a system of proportional representation designed to promote gender equality and minority representation.[9] This one-liner appeared in the status reports and rolling drafts until the first ministers entered the discussions in August 1992. Then it disappeared, to be replaced by a provision which allowed provinces to determine their own electoral methods, and to provide for gender equality if they wished. The post-accord legal text stated:

Subject to this Act, the legislature of any province or the legislative authority of any territory may provide for

(a) the indirect election of senators for the province or territory by the legislative assembly of that province or legislative authority of that territory, and all matters relating thereto;
(b) any special measures to provide for equal representation of male and female persons;
(c) the determination of electoral districts and the boundaries thereof in relation to the election of senators.[10]

The reason for dropping the national formula for Senate elections was that Quebec wanted the option of electing senators indirectly from its National Assembly rather than directly by the people. Since the first ministers had adopted the fundamentally wrong-headed principle of same treatment for all the provinces, allowing room for Quebec's desires meant every province must be given the same right to determine its own method of election.[11] The result was that the previously endorsed national formula for increasing the representation of women and minorities was lost.

This outcome was unsatisfactory for a number of reasons. First, the final language was merely permissive. It allowed special measures to ensure equal representation for women but did not require them. Second, reference to increased representation of minorities disappeared; only gender equality stayed in.[12] Third, with no comprehensive formula, women would have to lobby province by province to obtain a method of election likely to increase their representation. In the provinces where representation of women is the poorest and government sexism the strongest women would be least likely to obtain change. Fourth, by constitutionalizing the provinces' right to determine the method of election, no future improvements would be likely since amendments to constitutional provisions regarding institutions require unanimous consent.

THE DEBATE ON METHODOLOGY

After the Charlottetown Accord was concluded, Ontario and Nova Scotia announced that they would provide for gender parity in their Senate elections. British Columbia said it would too, then a few days later, after an outcry from BC columnists, editorial writers, and Opposition politicians, recanted.[13] The columnists called such a provision 'undemocratic,' 'dogmatic,' 'far-left,' 'a restriction on voters' choices,' 'feminist flag-waving,' or – take your pick – 'not feminist at all.' Pat Carney denounced the idea as repugnant and a quota system. BC Liberal leader Gordon Wilson, making the most interesting comment, said, 'it is patent nonsense which undermines traditional democracy and the belief that everyone is equal.'

This was the second time in six months that women's efforts to make institutions of government more representative of the Canadian people caused incensed charges of undemocratic behaviour.

One aspect of this debate was its focus on methodology, which created the impression at times that our adversaries' real objection was to the means of implementing equality in the political realm, not to equality itself. Though we believed that methodological concerns were being used to disguise a basic unwillingness to address the fundamental challenges to current democratic practice that women were articulating, it was none the less important for us to respond to these concerns and to decide what might be workable methods for achieving a more inclusive Senate.[14]

NAC's initial position was simply that there should be equality for women, and better representation for other marginalized groups, in the Senate. Before the debate began we had not embraced any one method of achieving this goal.

One simple way to ensure strictly equal representation of women would be dual-member ridings. All voters would have two votes and could elect one man and one woman in a traditional first-past-the-post system.[15] Though British Columbia did not say how it would create gender parity, since it did say equal numbers of men and women, perhaps it contemplated a system of this kind. Some BC commentators, however, found the suggestion that a voter might be required to vote for women as well as men an outrageous interference with voter freedom. How this system would restrict the choice of voters more than our current one, where voters can choose only one candidate pre-selected by a riding association, and often cannot choose a woman if they want to, is not clear. Nor is it evident how this could be considered a quota system more offensive than providing the same six seats to Prince Edward Island as to Ontario, or than entrenching a double majority for francophone senators to allow them to, quite properly, protect cultural and linguistic interests. It appeared that virtually any method of addressing the claims of underrepresented regions was unexceptionable, while addressing the underrepresentation of women and others was exceptionable to some no matter how logical or fair the method.

This led some women to suggest that we should get create a women's province. Perhaps then the fact that 52 per cent of the population is represented by 14 per cent of the government members might be understood to be an important failure of democracy.[16] Given the accord's formula for resolving provincial underrepresentation, a women's province would only get six Senate seats, but could look forward to being compensated for that by having close to 52 per cent of the seats in the House of Commons.

However, the alternative to the two-seat, two-gender riding, or any method that would require voters to vote for a designated number of women and men, is contained in the formula for national Senate elections that was lost at the Charlottetown bargaining table: that is, election by proportional representation (PR) through a system designed to ensure gender equality and increased minority representation.

Though there are many different forms that election by proportional representation can take, it appears that a party-list system, which requires parties to put up gender-balanced and representative lists, would be preferable.[17] While the party-list system would not guarantee 50 per cent representation of women or any particular percentage for minorities, if designed with this goal in mind, it could greatly increase representation of these groups. In Northern European and Scandinavian countries, where PR systems are used, the representation of women is close to 40 per cent. As this discussion indicates, NAC has been concerned from the beginning that institutions of government be inclusive of women in all our diversity, as well as of men of colour, men with disabilities, gay men, and poor men. We would prefer to see an inclusive institution with 40 per cent women than a perfectly gender-balanced institution that is still dominated by those who are white, able-bodied, heterosexual, and professional.

If in a new Senate six senators were to be elected from each province, a PR system could give each voter six votes and each political party could put up a list of six candidates. Parties could be required to ensure that their lists were gender-balanced *and* representative of regional, racial, and other diversity. If parties can put forward more than one candidate, there are incentives for providing a representative list, and party performance on equity issues is evident to the voters.

PR has the benefit of ensuring that the popular vote for different political parties translates more directly into seats held. However, if every party had to put forward representative lists, no matter what the party outcome, election by this PR system would produce an institution more directly representative of the population by sex, race, disability, sexual orientation, and class. Again, democratic principles and voter choice can hardly be said to be undermined by such a system.

What is acknowledged if such electoral methods are introduced, however, is that the system is not fair now. Acknowledging this fact is difficult for some. However, the truth is that women and minorities do not enjoy equality of opportunity in the competition for political power. The assertion that women could have more political power if we would just vote for each other is false. The Royal Commission on Electoral Reform concluded that the origins of women's underrepresentation do not lie in the voting booth, but earlier in the political process. It found that there are procedural and financial obstacles to equal participation for women and minorities in the current system.[18] These include the lack of spending limits, the lack of public financial assistance, and old-boy party networks. In the first-past-the-post system that allows riding associations to nominate only one candidate, there is intense pressure to choose a winner. In a society in which white men are dominant, white male candidates are favoured. Changes are clearly needed just to make the electoral system gender-, race-, and class-neutral.

THE DEEPER RESISTANCE

The reluctance of those at the constitutional table to deal with inequities in the electoral system and the hostility that characterized the response of some commentators indicated that the issue hit a tender spot. Quibbles about methodology disguised a deeper resistance.

Women's challenge is a fundamental one. We do not agree that Canadian institutions of government, and the between-election processes that they generate, are democratic or that their results are representative of the interests of most of the people.

The simplest idea of democracy is government *by* the people. When government institutions do not reflect the composition of the population, especially when major groups are marginalized in terms of power, there is a failure of democracy. The fact that almost all positions of power in Canada are currently held by members of a small and privileged minority group is a serious problem. As Lynn Smith says, 'in a democracy those who are subject to the laws should be represented in their diversity in the institutions that formulate, enact and enforce the laws.'[19]

Part of what is experienced as threatening by current power-holders is that many women do not agree that a democracy based on the idea of the supremacy of the individual reflects reality. The notion that each of us is an individual first and most importantly does not satisfactorily describe the experiences of women, or of men who belong to marginalized groups. Historically, and still, we are perceived first as members of groups. Because of this we experience our groupness. We have been excluded, discriminated against, abused because we are members of the group 'women' and/or because we are Aboriginal, or of colour, or gay or lesbian, or disabled, or poor. As a consequence, we have different experiences of our society.

Women also have different experiences because we are the child-bearing sex; because we are more likely to be child-raisers and to care for the elderly; because we are more likely to be single parents and to be poor; and because we are, overwhelmingly, the victims of sexual assault and domestic violence.

This is not to say that we do not experience ourselves as individuals, very different from each other, or that women do not value this individuality and the liberty necessary to express it. We do, but we know that our individualness will only be allowed full social expression when our group identities,[20] that is, our identities as women, or women of colour, or lesbians, do not attract negative consequences.

The point, however, when considering the adequacy of Canada's democratic system, is that because members of marginalized and disadvantaged groups have different life experiences and different experiences of our society, we have different knowledge, different perspectives, and different needs; in a democracy these different needs must be represented and must be taken into account.[21] This will only happen if people from these groups are present, in numbers, in the institutions of governance, and in the key decision-making fora.

The idea that all individuals are the same and that the individual is the unit on which democracy is built merely reinforces the privilege of those who currently hold power in Canada. In the political realm these ideas make it possible to offer the political candidate as 'the universal man,'[22] an individual with a universal human likeness to all other individuals, who can therefore represent the interests of everyone. According to this theory, the fact that he is white and male does not in any way limit a politician's ability to represent the interests of, for example, poor Aboriginal women. (This, apparently, is Gordon

Wilson's view and the basis for his statement that efforts to ensure increased representation of women in the Senate undermine the belief that 'everyone is equal.')

Though we reject the idea of the universal man as an adequate foundation for modern democracy, this does not mean that women, when present, can only represent women or that men can never represent women's interests.[23] It does mean, however, that women and minorities, in numbers, must be involved in governing to reflect the diversity of the experiences and needs of the Canadian people. The policies and laws that emerge from more diversely composed bodies will have more legitimacy, and will be more representative of the interests of the body politic as a whole.

WHO SPEAKS: WHO DECIDES

There is another crucial aspect of this issue. Women have something different to say; but in addition to having something different to say, women and minorities want to speak for themselves, not be spoken for. Speaking for themselves is a requirement of equality, a dimension of full political personhood. Being spoken for diminishes us; full participation in our society is still denied.

The issue of speaking for ourselves was raised directly by the Native Women's Association of Canada (NWAC) during the constitutional process. NWAC claimed a right to participate in the constitutional process because the rights and lives of Aboriginal women would be affected directly by any decisions about Aboriginal self-government. NWAC had reason to believe that the other Aboriginal organizations at the table would not put forward its perspective.[24] Scorned by politicians, NWAC went to court to claim that its exclusion violated the sex-equality guarantees in the Charter. While the NWAC legal challenge was not completely successful, on 20 August the Federal Court of Appeal issued a declaration that NWAC's right to freedom of expression without discrimination based on sex was violated when it was excluded from participation.[25] The court agreed that the perspective of the Aboriginal women who are represented by NWAC would not be put forward by any other organization at the table. That this decision was ignored by first ministers and officials, who continued to meet, talk, and make decisions about Aboriginal issues, and continued to exclude NWAC even after the decision was handed down,[26] shocked and angered many women. The message was that whether lobbied in the political arena or challenged in the legal forum, power holders would continue to spurn women's legitimate claims for inclusion.

There is a final point that was made clear to women by the constitutional process this time. Consultation is important, but it is not enough. Politicians claimed that this was the most participatory round of constitutional talks ever, that citizens were thoroughly consulted – through the Spicer Commission, the constitutional conferences, and the Beaudoin-Dobbie Committee. NAC participated in every way that was open to it, but our experience shows that the only place it matters to be is in the room where the decisions are being made.

For women this process was Meech Lake II. When the consultations were over, the doors closed again, key results of the consultations were ignored, and the interests of the players in the room dominated. Though we know that some delegations made efforts to argue for women's interests and those of minorities, there was none the less no participation by these groups in the decision-making process, and little reflection of our concerns in the resulting accord.

The presence of Rosemary Kuptana and Nellie Cournoyea as heads of the delegations for the Inuit Tapirisat and the Northwest Territories, and of Alexa McDonough as an adviser to Donald Cameron, the premier of Nova Scotia, while new and welcome, did not solve the problem for women of lack of representation in the decision-making. Ms Kuptana's mandate was to represent the interests of the Inuit people, and Ms Cournoyea's was to represent the regional interests of the Northwest Territories. As an adviser, Ms McDonough had no official mandate, though she was influential in her delegation. The presence of two women leaders at a table of seventeen, and the presence of a feminist political leader as an adviser to one first minister, could not be expected to change the dynamics, or the agenda, of a traditional, male-dominated forum of political leaders with, principally, region-based mandates, and it did not.[27] No one was there specifically carrying the brief of women and minorities. The assumption is that no one should be, or needs to be. Despite the fact that the interests of women and minorities are different from those of white professional men, it is assumed by the structure of the decision-making process that those interests will, none the less, be represented effectively by the white professional men who are present.

The results of the constitutional deliberations, however, show that this assumption is false. Although, for example, the issue of women's representation in the Senate did make it from the constitutional conferences to the constitutional table, when the chips were down,[28] it was treated as marginal; the 'real stuff' was securing the same seats for each province, and trading lost seats in the Senate for new seats in the House of Commons. It is no accident that the accord did not reflect the priorities, perspectives, and needs of women and minorities, and that we were among the most critical of the deal.

POST-REFERENDUM THOUGHTS

All three major political parties said 'yes' to the accord; the majority of Canadians said 'no.' It must be acknowledged that when the three major political parties *together* do not represent the majority of Canadians, the political system is in crisis.

From NAC's perspective the process of negotiating the accord demonstrated that representative democracy was not working. The referendum campaign and the 'no' outcome endorse this conclusion. In this round, Canadian politicians took the steps that are traditional to our system – consultation, then decision-making by elected first ministers. They produced an accord supported by all three political parties. If representative democracy were working, public support for the accord should have been overwhelming.

Instead, none of it worked. Many members of the public, including NAC representatives, experienced the constitutional process as negative. What the public contributed at the constitutional conferences was, in large part, ignored; decisions were made in closed rooms by an unrepresentative group of politicians; the concerns of women and many other groups were trivialized and discounted; the accord was presented as a fait accompli; and Canadians were told to vote 'yes.' In response, the majority of Canadian voters rejected the accord, rejected their political leaders, and rejected the process.

Far from being reassured by all three major political parties lining up together in support of the accord, many Canadians were alienated. They felt abandoned, unrepresented. The lack of a difference in views among the parties was experienced as a ganging-up of political élites on the citizenry, not as a rare and welcome agreement among adversaries. The Canadian form of democracy assumes that the spectrum of political opinion will be represented by the spectrum of political parties, and that debate among the parties will serve to inform the public. In this case, Canadians wanted information, wanted to hear different points of view, and could not get this from political leaders.

The referendum had a positive side. It engaged Canadians in political debate in an unprecedented way. Given a vote on constitutional amendment, Canadians took their votes seriously, studied, read the accord, lit up the hotlines, wrote to newspapers, and came out to community meetings in numbers. Canadians also rejected threats, flag-waving, and intellectual pap, clearly demonstrating an appetite for more thoughtful political debate. More Canadians know more about the Constitution than ever before. This cannot be anything but good.

However, a referendum is a blunt instrument. Either yes or no was too simple an answer to the Charlottetown Accord, and being offered only a choice of a yes or no response to this complex political package was not politically productive. Yes would put in place some elements that many Canadians had serious problems with. No could be interpreted as slamming the door on any constitutional reform. Few people could make a happy choice.

It is possible that some version of a referendum, with a series of questions on different parts of the accord, followed by an opportunity to engage in further constitutional discussions, could have been helpful. However, in general, putting a complex package to a yes/no vote is no answer to the need to make decision-making more participatory. In an essential way, voting on a referendum question is not participatory at all; it limits political participation to one rudimentary act.

In conclusion, the Charlottetown round and the referendum experience reveals the following important problems in the Canadian democratic system:

1. Representative government in Canada is not representative. Government by a privileged minority, namely, white professional men, is not representative, not democratic, and does not serve the needs of all (or indeed the majority) of the people.

2. Many Canadians, many women among them, are not content to have political leaders make crucial decisions for them on the understanding that the leaders are representative, and that, therefore, by definition, everyone's interests are served. New ways must be found to share decision-making; consultation is not enough.

3. Referenda do not adequately answer the need for increased participation. They do not allow complex contributions or responses. They are crude political tools and open to abuse.

4. The parameters of Canadian political debate are set by the structures of decision making. When the most important pan-Canadian political forum is the first ministers' conference, competitive regional interests are a controlling and shaping force. This focus distorts the capacity of the Canadian political system to deal with the inequality of major groups in the society, and with the environment, poverty, social programs, and other vital matters that transcend regional interests.

It is time for a major debate regarding the reform of Canada's democratic system. This constitutional round has revealed the flaws and limits of our democratic system. It is time to change it; it is time to make the Canadian political system more representative, more participatory, and more democratic.

NOTES

1 From an article by Lloyd, cited in *Keyes v. Pandora Publishing Assn. (No. 2)*, 16 C.H.R.R. 1992 D/148

2 Over the last year I have been a participant in innumerable conversations with women on the NAC executive, women in NAC member groups, and other women about the issue of democratic process and women's participation in Canadian

political life. This article owes everything to those discussions, particularly to discussions with members of the NAC executive and NAC Constitution Committee. In particular I wish to acknowledge Judy Rebick, Barbara Cameron, and Sandra Delaronde. Also I have benefited from a recent discussion among the NAC Table Officers about the referendum campaign. The officers are Judy Rebick, Monique Simard, Sandra Delaronde, Maureen Leyland, Joan Meister, Carolann Wright, and Sunera Thobani. I have attempted here to capture NAC analysis and positions taken during the constitutional process; this does not mean that every observation or conclusion is a reflection of NAC policy.

My thinking on this subject has also been influenced by Lynn Smith's unpublished paper 'Women, the Canadian Constitution and Citizenship' and by Susan Jackel's article 'Rethinking Equality and Citizenship' in *Conversations among Friends: Women and Constitutional Reform* (Edmonton: Centre for Constitutional Studies, University of Alberta, 1992). Some of the comments about electoral methods appeared first in an op-ed piece prepared jointly by Judy Rebick and I in September 1992. Though the piece was submitted under both names, it was published in the *Toronto Star* under Judy Rebick's name and in the *Vancouver Sun* under mine.

3 This was the phrase that NAC used publicly. It is very unsatisfactory shorthand. The difficulty is that it seems to treat women and minorities as mutually exclusive groups. What we wish to convey is that NAC is committed to the inclusion of women in all our diversity, and particularly to the inclusion of Aboriginal women, women of colour, women with disabilities, lesbians, older women, and poor women. We are also committed to the inclusion of men who have been excluded from institutions of government because of race, sexual orientation, disability, poverty, or other similar bars.

4 Even though Canada has a Senate, the changes being proposed were extensive enough that most participants in constitutional discussions treated the proposed Senate as an entirely new creature.

5 I mean 'out groups' as opposed to 'in groups,' not as opposed to those in the closet.

6 A request to the Conference organizers (the Canada West Foundation) to allow ten minutes for a presentation on the issue of equality for underrepresented groups, was refused. Instead, the women who made the request were told that Gordon Gibson would address this issue in the speech he was already scheduled to give on representation. He did so, by dismissing the issue of equality for women and others in government institutions as trivial, on the one hand, and too complex to solve, on the other. Mr Gibson argued that there are too many groups who would claim a need for representation in an elected Senate: women, the old, the young, labour, business, linguistic minorities, Indians, scientists, artists, racial minorities, the handicapped, and cities; even copyright law would want its own senator. Most

important, in his view, considerations of other dimensions of representation were a distraction from the real task, which was reaching a decision on the number of seats that should be allotted to each region or province.

7 See, for example, 'Arrogance of Agenda Grab,' *Vancouver Sun*, 4 Feb. 1992; 'Hijacker Surprised,' *Vancouver Courier*, 9 Feb. 1992; 'Groups Seek Senate Voice,' *Ottawa Citizen*, 27 Jan. 1992.

8 See Canada West Foundation, *Renewal of Canada: Institutional Reform* (Calgary: Canada West Foundation 1992); *Compendium of Reports* (Ottawa 1992), 5, 10; *Report of the Special Joint Committee on a Renewed Canada* (Ottawa: Supply and Services Canada 1992), xv–xvi, 45–6.

9 See, for example, *Status Report of the Multilateral Meetings on the Constitution* (11 June 1992).

10 *Draft Legal Text*, s. 23(2)

11 This is merely one of a number of examples of the negative impact caused by embracing the principle of equality of (meaning: same treatment for) the provinces. In general, endorsing this principle in the accord meant that Quebec did not have its legitimate demands met, and neither did the rest of Canada. Quebec's distinctiveness was recognized on the one hand, but denied on the other by entrenching the principle of equality of the provinces. Its desires to have more powers devolved directly to it and to put limits on the federal government's ability to spend money in Quebec on matters within provincial jurisdiction were addressed inadequately, and only by giving the same things to all the provinces. With respect to the Senate, embracing the equality of the provinces meant that it was impossible to allow Quebec to have indirect elections and still maintain a coherent formula for Senate elections in Canada outside of Quebec. In the accord as a whole it meant that it was necessary to accept a fundamental decentralizing thrust with the consequent lack of coherence in social policy and the threat to national social programs which that would entail. NAC maintains that only an asymmetrical division of powers can satisfy the different needs and desires of Quebec and the rest of Canada.

12 This change was not inadvertent. Conversations with participants at the talks indicated that even agreement to a merely permissive reference to gender equality was not easily obtained, and that politicians were even more uncomfortable with giving any sign that the lack of representation of people of colour, people with disabilities, lesbians and gay men, and poor people in institutions of government was a legitimate problem to be addressed.

13 The final pre-referendum position of the BC government was that this matter would be considered further after the referendum. BC voters were instructed not to assume, when considering their vote in the referendum, that three of BC's new elected senators would be required to be women.

14 As noted above, some commentary that appears here also appeared in an article prepared by Judy Rebick and myself that was published in various Canadian newspapers during the referendum period. It appeared in the *Toronto Star* under Judy Rebick's name, in the *Ottawa Citizen* (11 Sept. 1992) under both names, and in the *Vancouver Sun* (22 Sept. 1992) under my name.

15 Lynn Smith offers this model in her paper 'Women, the Canadian Constitution and Citizenship,' prepared for the Institute for Research on Public Policy, and argues persuasively for its fairness. To date, this is an unpublished paper.

16 Ibid., 12. Smith quotes Christine Boyle, who wrote on this subject in an article entitled 'Home Rule for Women: Power-Sharing Between Men and Women' (1983) *Dalhousie Law Journal* 7 (1983): 790.

17 Lisa Young has written a helpful article on proportional representation for the Canadian Advisory Council on the Status of Women, entitled 'Electoral Systems and Representative Legislatures: Consideration of Alternative Electoral Systems.'

18 See, for example, Communiqués no. 11 and 13 from the Royal Commission on Electoral Reform, Ottawa, February 1992.

19 'Women, the Canadian Constitution and Citizenship,' 13

20 By group identities I mean our identities as women, women of colour, Aboriginal women, women with disabilities, lesbians, and so on.

21 See Smith, 14.

22 I use 'man' deliberately. Because of discrimination, 'universal woman' does not have the same meaning. We do not assume that any woman can represent all men.

23 See Smith on this point, p. 14.

24 The Aboriginal organizations that participated in the talks were the Assembly of First Nations, the Native Council of Canada, the Inuit Tapirisat, and the Métis National Council.

25 The court found that though men could represent women, in this case the organizations at the table, in particular the Assembly of First Nations, were not representing the views of Aboriginal women. The NWAC was recognized by the court as a bona fide and established representative of Aboriginal women.

26 Decisions on Aboriginal issues were being made up until the time of the release of the legal text on 20 September. In fact, changes to the text relating to equality protection for Aboriginal women, made in what appeared to be a last-minute attempt to appease NWAC, were announced in mid-September after the referendum had been called, and without any consultation with NWAC.

27 I refer to the region-based mandates of the first ministers. Three of the Aboriginal organizations – the Assembly of First Nations, the Inuit Tapirisat, and the Métis National Council – may be said to have regional interests, because their peoples have a land base, or claims to a land base. However, their mandates also include

another dimension that is shared with non-Aboriginal women and minorities, that is, their interest in overcoming historical oppression and establishing equality for their peoples.

28 The presence of Rosemary Kuptana and Nellie Cournoyea was held out many times as an answer to women's complaints about our lack of representation at the constitutional table. This claim was made without any examination of what real latitude these women had in the constitutional forum to speak for the interests of Canadian women, or of what it would take to overcome the sexist assumptions and behaviour of the male leaders who dominated the forum. These women are remarkable politicians, but alone, with the mandates they have, they cannot reasonably be expected to address all the concerns that women have or to overcome deeply entrenched sexist traditions.

29 I use this phrase on purpose. Like the Meech Lake round, once the doors were closed, the constitutional talks again had the macho ambiance of a high-stakes poker game, or a high-pressure collective-bargaining session.

4

The Charlottetown Accord and Central Institutions

GÉRALD-A. BEAUDOIN

On 28 August 1992 our political leaders agreed to the Charlottetown Accord. The accord was put into legal form on 9 October 1992. On 26 October this new social contract was rejected by a majority of Canadians (54–46 per cent) and by six provinces and one territory. It was the first time in the history of the Canadian federation that such an important and fundamental constitutional-amendment proposal had been the subject of a referendum. Such a reform happens only once in a century.

The purpose of my chapter is, first, to present an analysis of the Charlottetown Accord provisions concerning the Senate, the Supreme Court, the House of Commons, and the amending procedure. Second, I will draw some conclusions about the rejection of the accord by the Canadian people on 26 October 1992.

ANALYSIS OF THE ACCORD

The Senate

Many states, be they unitary or federal, have bicameral parliaments. It is well known that an upper chamber, or second chamber, has a raison d'être in federal systems.

Everybody in Canada agrees on one point: we must reform the Senate. We have been trying to do so for decades. The Charlottetown Accord was a major proposal for reforming our parliamentary system.

The proposed Senate would have been very different from the current one. It would have been elected instead of appointed. Senators would have been elected at the same time and for the same period as the members of the House of Commons. Parliament was supposed to adopt an electoral statute to that effect. However, it was stipulated in the accord that Quebec (and other provinces that wished to do so) would have been able to elect their senators by their legislative assembly; elsewhere, the senators would have probably been directly elected by the people of their province. The electoral system could have been the same as the one in force in the House of Commons. However, the election of senators on the basis of proportional representation was not excluded, although some premiers were opposed to it. It is the federal Parliament that would have ultimately decided this aspect after consultation with the provinces.

The new Senate would have been composed of an equal number of senators per province (six), and one senator for each territory. The functioning of the Senate would have respected the principle of equality between House and Senate in two domains: for the ratification of the appointment of the governor of the Bank of Canada, and for fiscal measures concerning natural resources. In other domains, if the Senate opposed a bill adopted by the House of Commons, the bill would have been subject to a joint sitting of the Senate and Commons where a simple majority could approve it. The reform touched also the House of Commons. The provinces of Ontario and Quebec would have had eighteen more members in the House of Commons to compensate for the senators lost in the new Senate; British Columbia would have had four more members and Alberta two. Moreover, Quebec would have had a constitutionally guaranteed floor of 25 per cent of the members of the House of Commons.

Would an elected and equal Senate have diminished the role of the premiers, especially if the senators were appointed by the provincial legislatures? In the event that a constitutional conference of the first ministers would have been held annually, I do not believe that their influence would have diminished.

The powers of the proposed Senate would have been different from those of the current one. Bills would have been divided into four categories:

1.   supply bills (suspensive veto of thirty days)
2.   bills related to French language and culture (double majority and absolute veto)
3.   bills related to the taxation of natural resources (absolute veto)
4.   ordinary bills (joint sitting when a bill is rejected or amended)

All bills except those related to the financial estimates (supply bills) would have to be passed or rejected by the Senate within thirty sitting days of approval by the House of Commons. The rejection, by the Senate, of an ordinary bill would trigger a joint sitting of the two houses, where a simple majority vote would have disposed of the bill.

The Senate's suspensive veto respecting constitutional amendments specified in section 47 of the Constitution Act, 1982 remained unchanged. The right of initiative stayed intact. The government could not be forced to resign if defeated in the Senate and senators would not be eligible for membership in the cabinet. The Senate would have also had the power to ratify major appointments made by the federal government within thirty sitting days of the House of Commons, including that of the governor of the Bank of Canada. Other appointments subject to Senate approval would have been specified in federal law.

There would have been a double majority required, not only a majority of all the senators present but also of the French-speaking senators, for bills materially affecting French language and culture. This is a case where the Senate veto would have been absolute. Each senator would have declared, at the beginning of a new Parliament, whether he or she was francophone or anglophone. If the question was controverted, the Speaker of the Senate would have settled the issue with a right of appeal to the full Senate itself.

The representation of the Aboriginal peoples in the Senate and the related questions (number, distribution, selection process) would have been discussed later in the fall of 1992. This representation would have also been constitutionally guaranteed.

In reading the Charlottetown Accord, we notice that the reformed Senate would have had relatively few decisive powers. This was the choice of the political leaders.

What were those decisive powers?

The Senate would have been able to reject by a simple majority a bill that fundamentally changed the taxation of natural resources.

Bills significantly related to the French language and culture would have required the consent of French-speaking senators by way of the double-majority clause: a majority of the senators present and a majority of French-speaking senators. For ordinary bills the effectiveness of the Senate would have been proportional to the size of the government majority in the House of Commons. It is obvious that a thin majority in the House of Commons would have increased the role of the Senate at the time of joint sittings. The Senate's role would have been greater with a minority government in the House of Commons. In any event, Senate legitimacy would have increased because of the direct or indirect election of its members. The influence of senators, some of them representing more than one million persons, would not have been negligible.

Would such a new Senate have rendered our country more difficult to govern? It would have certainly possessed a power to delay legislation, but that is not always a bad thing. The decisive power would have clearly remained in the House of Commons and especially in the cabinet, from which senators would have been excluded. Only the passage of time would have given us the measure of the efficiency of the new Senate. This new Senate would have, of course, developed its own dynamic.

Some new constitutional conventions would have been created to ensure the functioning and working of the Senate. Everything cannot be written in the Constitution, so flexibility supposes the creation of conventions. For instance, our written Constitution does not expressly deal with confidence votes. This is a constitutional convention solidly established for more than a century. Could the confidence of the government be put in jeopardy at the time of a joint sitting of the House of Commons and the Senate? As we have seen earlier, the confidence of the government is not at issue in the Senate. When the government has a huge majority in the House of Commons, the question is theoretical. It is when the government majority is thin, or when we have a minority government, that the question may become critical. It is well established, according to a constitutional convention that is more than a century old, that only the House of Commons, the only elected house that represents the whole population and from which are drawn almost all ministers, is able to vote on the confidence or the non-confidence of the government.

In my opinion, the Charlottetown Accord did not change anything in this regard. The confidence vote would have remained the privilege of the House of Commons sitting alone, reflecting a well-balanced parliamentary regime. The Charlottetown Accord clearly stated that the reformed Senate, like the current one, could not vote on the confidence of the government. It could not have done indirectly (vote on the confidence of the government at the time of a joint sitting) what it could not do directly (vote on the confidence of the government sitting alone).

About thirty proposals for reforming the Senate were studied by the 'Committee of the 17' between March and August. Only one was finally retained on 28 August 1992. The proposal was workable. Quebec would have been adequately protected, all the more since it would have had, along with the other provinces, a right of veto over any amendment to the constitutional provisions affecting the Senate.

The Supreme Court of Canada

The Supreme Court of Canada rules on conflicts between the two orders of government and interprets the Canadian Charter of Rights and Freedoms and other statutes submitted for its examination. The Charlottetown Accord constitutionalized the very existence of the Supreme Court of Canada. There have been ongoing discussions about that matter at least since 1949 when our Supreme Court became truly supreme. It is one of the points on which all governments have always agreed. The existence of the Supreme Court, which was created in 1875, depends only on federal statute. As is the case for other federal constitutions, it was suitable to enshrine the court's existence in the fundamental law of our country. The Charlottetown Accord clearly did this.

The constitutionalization of the 'civilian' composition of the Supreme Court was specified in the accord. This is normal in a federation that encompasses two systems of law and a general court of appeal of last resort. But this was the first time that we were unequivocally entrenching the civilian composition of the Supreme Court. The text of section 41 of the Constitution Act, 1982 is not clear enough on that point. Quebec would have been guaranteed three judges out of nine. Section 6 of the Supreme Court Act, which was amended in 1949 in order to increase the number of judges from seven to nine, would have been constitutionalized. The numbers '3' and '9' would have been mentioned in section 41.

Our Supreme Court judges are appointed by the federal government. For decades, we have been thinking about a formula of appointment that would be more respectful of the principles of federalism and that would enshrine the participation of the provinces; this is normal in a federation. The current practice, followed since 1875, is not respectful of the principle of federalism because it is unilateral.

Many formulae have been put forward: (1) mandatory consultation with the provinces; (2) ratification of the appointments made by the federal executive either by the second chamber or by the provinces; (3) alternative provincial and federal lists; (4) provincial lists and a double veto. The Charlottetown Accord favoured the last formula.

In the United States, the president appoints the judges but, according to the Constitution, his choices must be ratified by the Senate, which is representing the States. The Senate has a right of veto that it has used more than twenty times, most recently in 1987. This system works well for the Americans, but Canada should not borrow it. In a federation such as ours, where the review of the constitutionality of laws is rigorous, the highest court of the land strongly affects federalism. This is another reason for respecting the principles of federalism at the time of the appointment of judges.

According to the Charlottetown Accord, the federal authority would appoint judges from a list made by the provinces and the territories and, for Quebec, from its own provincial list. This procedure is a form of concurrent veto, since it would be mandatory for the two orders of government to participate in the appointment process. After its constitutionalization, this part of the accord would have been subject to the '7/50' rule of amendment, requiring approval by seven provinces representing 50 per cent of the population.

In case of a deadlock in the appointment process, the accord provided that the Supreme Court Chief Justice would have been able to ask, by a written request, a judge from a superior federal, provincial, or territorial court to sit as an ad hoc judge for the time of the vacancy. This provision represented an important improvement; there was no such formula in the Meech Lake Accord.

The question of the role of the Aboriginal peoples in relation to the Supreme Court was raised during the negotiations. It was decided to put the question on the agenda of a future first ministers' conference on Aboriginal issues. Nevertheless, the provincial and territorial governments reached a political accord that would have established a reasonable consultation process with representatives of the Aboriginal peoples to draw up lists of candidates for the Supreme Court. The Aboriginal groups retained none the less the right to make suggestions to the federal government at the time a vacancy must be filled. There was also a political accord concluded between the federal government and the Aboriginal groups dealing with the rights of elders to intervene before the court when a conflict raises Aboriginal issues.

It is normal that the last word be given to the federal authority when appointing judges to the Supreme Court. None the less, the least that can be accorded to the provinces is the right to be consulted. In fact, they should be involved more in the appointment process, as the Charlottetown Accord proposed to do. In any event, the Charlottetown formula is preferable to the current one, which sanctions unilateralism on the part of federal authorities.

Finally, it should be noted that, as with the Meech Lake Accord, Parliament retained, by a special clause to that effect, its powers stipulated in section 101 of the Constitution Act, 1867 to bring up to date the Supreme Court Act, with the exception of the existence of the court, its civilian composition, the removal of judges, and the appointment process.

The House of Commons

According to the Charlottetown Accord, Quebec would have enjoyed forever a minimum of 25 per cent of the seats in the House of Commons. This protection would have been enshrined in section 41 of the Constitution Act, 1982 which stipulates those matters where unanimity is required. Quebec would thus have had a right of veto over its minimal representation in the House of Commons.

As soon as Senate reform would have come into force, Quebec and Ontario would have seen their representation in the House of Commons increased by eighteen in order to compensate for the loss of their members in the Senate. British Columbia would have had four more MPs and Alberta two more. The House of Commons would have been composed of 337 members. Section 41(b) of the Constitution Act, 1982 would have been maintained, while section 51A of the Constitution Act, 1867 would have been abrogated. A permanent formula would have been established in section 51 of the Constitution Act, 1867 in order to ensure that Commons representation kept pace with Canada's demographic evolution. The question of Aboriginal representation in the House of Commons would remain under study.

The Amending Procedure

What about constitutional amendments related to central institutions? Section 41 of the Constitution Act, 1982 would have been amended in order to put under the amendment procedure requiring unanimity: the election of senators, their numbers and powers, the joint sittings of the two houses, the independence of the Supreme Court, the number of its judges, its civilian composition, and the minimum of 25 per cent of members of the House of Commons for Quebec.

CONSEQUENCES OF THE 26 OCTOBER 1992 REFERENDUM

No Canada-wide referendum was more important than the one of 26 October 1992. We have had only three such referenda since 1867. We must not forget that our Constitution was not ratified by a referendum in 1867.

The 26 October referendum was not mandatory under our Constitution. A referendum does not bind the government and is not part of our amending procedure. In short, it has no legal consequences. Politically speaking, however, it is of the utmost importance. We will talk about that referendum for years. Nobody can ignore its significance. Moreover, the 26 October referendum may create a precedent. In spite of the fact that the Constitution is silent on referenda, some will suggest that a referendum be used at the occasion of the next constitutional amendment.

Of course, the Constitution's amending procedure will not now be used to put into force the Charlottetown Accord rejected by Canadians. Political leaders declared before the referendum that a 'no' in any one province would be tantamount to a rejection of the accord. Nova Scotia, Quebec, and the four western provinces have said 'no.' A nation-wide majority said 'no.' The 'yes' or the 'no' was global. It encompassed the constitutional proposal in its entirety, and this was the perspective from which citizens voted. Thus, we cannot put into force those parts requiring the agreement of seven provinces representing 50 per cent of the population and forget the remaining parts of the accord.

Political analysts will write many articles on the interpretation and meaning of the referendum. The 'no' side included a wide range of different opinions, many of which were opposed to each other. How odd, for example, to see people like Jacques Parizeau, Preston Manning, and Pierre Elliott Trudeau in the same boat! Those kinds of things happen when a referendum is held.

The 26 October 1992 referendum closes an eventful chapter of constitutional reform. Henceforth, we enter a period that for now will be more political than constitutional. So, the status quo remains on the constitutional plan. The Charlottetown Accord is now a failure, as were the Meech Lake Accord (23 June 1990) and the Victoria Charter (16 June 1971). Will Charlottetown be another Victoria? Premier Bourassa did not hesitate to raise the question a few days before the referendum. After Victoria, he said, Quebec did not get back the powers that were offered; they are gone without return.

A moratorium begins. How long will it last? Until the next mandatory constitutional conference of the first ministers in 1997, which is designed, according to section 49 of the Constitution Act, 1982 to review the amending procedure (a review that will not necessarily lead to a constitutional amendment)? It is too soon to say so. We cannot make predictions for a period beyond two years. In 1993, there will be federal elections. In 1994, Quebec and some other provinces will hold elections. Those too will have important consequences.

What will the future look like?

The Aboriginal peoples have lost a lot. Since 1867, Parliament has had the power, according to paragraph 91.24 of the Constitution Act, 1867, exclusively to make laws regarding Indians and lands reserved for Indians. Parliament may make laws in relation to the rights of the Aboriginal peoples and any associated administrative structures. The federal houses and the provincial legislative assemblies may enshrine those rights and structures into the Constitution. The report within two or three years of the Royal Commission on the Aboriginal Peoples (Dussault-Erasmus) will be of the utmost importance in this regard.

Also, administrative agreements between the federal government and the provinces could be concluded regarding the division of powers. Premier Bourassa has already committed himself in that regard. Those agreements make the Constitution more flexible. The provinces could also conclude agreements with Aboriginal peoples.

So, it will take us a certain period of time to get used to the status quo. But this state of affairs is not without virtue. Federalism, especially ours, is never completely static. We can continue to live in a federal state and let the system evolve by itself; Quebec has a lot of influence so long as it knows how to use it. The constitutional amendments that one day will be necessary will come in due course. Will they involve federalism made to measure? asymmetrical federalism? That remains to be seen.

In the end, this referendum inspired in me some reflections:

1. Machiavelli was right when he affirmed that nothing is so unsure, nothing more risky, than constitutional reform. However, I would add that, in any event, this is not a good reason for never attempting it.

2. In a parliamentary regime of British inspiration, a referendum is not equivalent to a vote of confidence or non-confidence. Defeated in the 20 May 1980 referendum, Premier René Lévesque stayed in power and even got re-elected in the Spring of 1981.

3   Nothing is more democratic than a referendum. The people's verdict reflects a popular wisdom.

4. A referendum is global, without nuance. It is always possible to find one or many flaws in such a substantial proposal as the Charlottetown Accord.

5. Canadians are charter-minded, especially since 1982. I understand the fancy for such charters. Canada and Quebec among others have charters of rights and freedoms. I am myself a partisan of the Jefferson school of thought. The illustrious Jefferson was very favourable to the constitutionalization of rights and freedoms. However, we must distinguish between charters and political institutions. It is an error to constitutionalize everything. We must stop that tendency in Canada. Many problems can be best resolved at the political level.

6. New Brunswick could go forward in enshrining in the Constitution the equality of its two linguistic communities by using section 43 of the Constitution Act, 1982. (It did so in March 1993.)

7. In a federation like ours, the Supreme Court plays an important role in shaping the Constitution. By its judgments it contributes to the evolution of the Constitution. We can rely on its continued essential contribution.

8. In a system like ours, the creation of constitutional conventions renders more flexible the functioning of the parliamentary system and of the federal regime. New conventions will continue to see the light of day.

CONCLUSION

Federalism is a rich and flexible form of government. We must continue to seek solutions, and it would not be a bad thing to demonstrate creative imagination in this regard. At the right time, we may resume efforts at constitutional reform. It cannot but come one day. A new chapter of our collective history begins. It will be of the utmost importance.

The Division of Powers in the Charlottetown Accord

5

Division of Powers in the Charlottetown Accord

PETER W. HOGG

THE ISSUE

Quebec's constitutional objectives have always included an increase in the powers of the Quebec National Assembly. This objective is driven by the fact that the Quebec National Assembly is unlike every other legislative body in Canada in that it consists of a majority of French speakers. It is the only legislative body in which French speakers are not in a minority. Naturally, therefore, at Charlottetown, Premier Bourassa of Quebec attempted to secure more powers for his province.

None of the other provinces shared Quebec's aspirations for more power. The smaller provinces lack the resources to expand their responsibilities, and would indeed be damaged by the diminution in the fiscal and protective capacity of the federal government that would follow from any significant decentralization of powers. The larger provinces, which could develop the capacity to increase their responsibilities, have never tried to accomplish this goal in any serious way, and did not try to do so at Charlottetown. The main reason for this forbearance, I think, is that public opinion outside Quebec would be opposed to any significant weakening of the federal government. For British Columbia and Alberta, the preferred constitutional solution at Charlottetown was not more provincial powers but more influence in the institutions of the federal government, especially an effective Senate. For Ontario, the principal goal of the New Democratic Party government seems to have been a social charter. (Ontario did not even show much interest in the federal proposals for a stronger economic union, although Ontario would be the major beneficiary of a stronger economic union.)

SPECIAL POWERS FOR QUEBEC

The obvious solution to this problem is to give new powers to Quebec, which alone wants the new powers, and not to give them to the other provinces, which do not want them. This solution is usually described as 'asymmetrical federalism' or 'special status' for Quebec. Asymmetrical federalism raises questions about the role of the members of Parliament from Quebec in the federal Parliament. Would they vote on measures that did not apply to Quebec? And if one answers 'no,' what happens if the federal government's majority depends on the votes of the members from Quebec? These kinds of problems have never been adequately resolved, and they have led most political scientists to conclude that there are serious limits to the degree to which federalism can be made asymmetrical.

However, the Meech Lake debate and all the public consultation that followed it revealed an even more serious objection to the idea of asymmetrical federalism: the idea was massively unpopular. Nothing was more damaging to the Meech Lake proposals than the suggestion that the new distinct-society clause conferred 'special status' on the province of Quebec. It became clear that outside Quebec there was a very strong belief in the equality of the provinces. Any constitutional settlement that seriously challenged that belief could not possibly receive widespread support.

In the Charlottetown Accord, there was a distinct-society clause, but it was buried in the Canada Clause, which also affirmed 'the principle of the equality of the provinces.' There were two other special provisions for Quebec. One was a guarantee of three judges on the Supreme Court (item 18); this carryover from Meech Lake has never been particularly controversial, because it is already required by statute. The other special provision for Quebec was a guarantee of 25 per cent of the seats in the House of Commons (item 21); this idea was new to Charlottetown and proved to be one of the most controversial of the accord's provisions. But the Charlottetown Accord contained no new powers for Quebec alone. The first ministers, accurately reading the sentiment of their constituents, could not possibly agree to a set of special powers for the province of Quebec alone.

DELEGATION

Delegation is a device that would enable the province of Quebec to acquire powers that were not possessed by the other provinces. If the Parliament of Canada could delegate powers to the provinces, it could delegate some federal powers to the province of Quebec (and to any other province that wanted the powers), but make no delegation to those provinces that did not want the new powers. The end result of the process of delegation would obviously be a de facto asymmetrical federalism, but because the facility of delegation would be legally available in respect of all provinces, not just Quebec, the Constitution itself would not offend the principle of the equality of the provinces.

The delegation of federal powers to a province, or the delegation of provincial powers to Parliament, is not now permitted by the Constitution of Canada, because the Supreme Court of Canada held that the practice was unconstitutional in the *Nova Scotia Inter-delegation* case (1950).[1] A number of techniques have been found to get around this decision, and there is already a good deal of delegation from one level of government to another, for example, in interprovincial trucking, agricultural marketing, and fisheries.[2] What is not possible is the direct transfer of legislative powers from Parliament to the legislatures or vice versa. The federal proposals of September 1991 recommended (proposal 25) that the constitutional package should include a power of legislative inter-delegation, and the Beaudoin-Dobbie report of February 1992 (p. 68) made the same recommendation.

The inclusion of a new power of legislative inter-delegation in the Constitution was an important item of discussion in the meetings of officials, ministers, and first ministers that followed the release of the Beaudoin-Dobbie report. However, when the first phase of those discussions (before Quebec joined in) ended on 7 July 1992, the first ministers and Aboriginal leaders had decided 'not to pursue' the topic of 'legislative inter-delegation,'[3] and this decision was affirmed (after Quebec joined the talks) in the Charlottetown Accord itself.[4] There is no record of why the decision was taken to drop the delegation proposal. From anecdotal evidence of what took place in those talks, it seems that the first ministers were concerned that the power of delegation could lead to de facto asymmetrical federalism, that radical de facto changes in the Constitution would be possible simply by bilateral arrangements between the federal government and Quebec (or any other two governments), and that it was difficult to design effective limits on the powers of delegation. It cannot be denied that these are legitimate concerns.

RESTRICTIONS ON FEDERAL SPENDING POWER

If special powers could not be granted to the province of Quebec alone, and if a general power of legislative inter-delegation was unacceptable, how could Quebec's request for more powers be accommodated? In answering that question, a first step was to recognize that under the distribution of powers now contained in the Constitution Quebec already possessed nearly all powers needed to protect its language and culture and to regulate its social and economic development. However, in many fields of provincial jurisdiction, there was a strong federal presence that was authorized not by any federal legislative power but by the federal spending power, which authorizes programs that can be accomplished by the spending of money and other activity that does not require the enactment of federal regulatory laws.[5] Much of what Quebec was concerned about was simply the federal presence in fields that the Constitution had allocated to the provinces.

The Meech Lake Accord of 1987 had contained a modest (but nevertheless controversial) limit on the federal power to spend in areas of exclusive jurisdiction; it had provided that in any future national shared-cost program that was established in an area of exclusive provincial jurisdiction, there would have to be provision for a province to opt out, and if the opting-out province established a program of its own that was compatible with the national objectives of the shared-cost program, the opting-out province would have to receive reasonable compensation from the Government of Canada for the additional expense of running the program without receiving the federal share of the program's cost. This restriction on the spending power of the federal Parliament died along with the Meech Lake Accord when the three-year deadline for ratification expired. However, it was revived in the Charlottetown Accord (item 25).

As well as the restriction on the establishment of new national shared-cost programs, the Charlottetown Accord stipulated (also in item 25) that 'a framework should be developed to guide the use of the federal spending power in all areas of exclusive provincial jurisdiction.' This framework was intended to '(a) contribute to the pursuit of national objectives; (b) reduce overlap and duplication; (c) not distort [but] respect provincial priorities; and (d) ensure equality of treatment of the provinces, while recognizing their different needs and circumstances.' The framework would be developed by first ministers at a future conference, and would not form part of the Constitution; the first ministers would keep the framework and its implementation under review.

INTERGOVERNMENTAL AGREEMENTS

The Meech Lake Accord of 1987 had made provision for the entering into of federal-provincial agreements relating to immigration. Such agreements would define the way in which responsibilities would be shared between the federal government and the agreeing province in this area of concurrent jurisdiction.

(Section 95 of the Constitution Act, 1867 confers concurrent powers over immigration on the federal Parliament and the provincial legislatures, but does not specify how the powers are to be exercised compatibly.) The agreements would have constitutional status so as not to be subject to unilateral revocation or amendment, even by the action of Parliament. This proposal was carried forward into the Charlottetown Accord (item 27).

The Charlottetown Accord went beyond the Meech Lake Accord's immigration provisions in that the Charlottetown Accord (item 26) proposed a more general provision in the Constitution that would give constitutional status to 'designated agreements between governments' so that they are 'protected from unilateral change.' The constitutional protection would occur when Parliament and the legislatures enacted laws approving the agreement. The accord in other places contemplated the entering into of intergovernmental agreements on the Canada Assistance Plan (item 26), immigration (item 27), labour-market development and training (item 28), forestry (item 30), mining (item 31), tourism (item 32), housing (item 33), recreation (item 34), municipal and urban affairs (item 35), regional development (item 36), and telecommunications (item 37).

The reason for the proposal for the entrenchment of intergovernmental agreements is to be discerned from the last sentence of the section of the Charlottetown Accord that makes the following recommendation (item 26): 'It is the intention of governments to apply this mechanism to future agreements related to the Canada Assistance Plan.' Ontario, Alberta, and British Columbia were still smarting from the action of the Parliament of Canada in placing a ceiling of 5 per cent on the rate of increase of federal expenditures for income support and social services supplied by those three provinces (the wealthiest provinces – the 'have' provinces) under the Canada Assistance Plan, which is the last true national shared-cost program in existence. (The other programs have moved to block funding under which federal contributions are no longer tied to the amount of provincial expenditures; in other words, costs are no longer shared, and the provinces reap the full benefit of any cost savings, but bear the full burden of any cost overruns.) The three 'have' provinces (and, inexplicably, Manitoba) challenged the validity of the unilateral restriction on the increase in federal contributions, and lost the case in the Supreme Court of Canada.[6] The new constitutional proposal would have reversed that decision by rendering certain kinds of federal-provincial agreements invulnerable to unilateral legislative change.

Occasionally a government makes a foolish agreement. The Canada Assistance Plan agreements are in this category. Those agreements have caused federal expenditures on welfare and social assistance to rise from $151 million in 1967–8 to $5.5 billion in 1989–90, all entirely outside the control of the federal government! Even agreements that were wise at the time they were entered into may become very unfavourable to one side after the passage of time. The Charlottetown Accord recognized that a total bar on unilateral amendment or rescission would be far too inflexible. The accord proposed that the constitutional bar on unilateral amendment or rescission was to last for a period of only five years, after which readoption of legislation by the agreeing governments would be required to continue the bar for another five years (item 26).

ADDITIONS TO PROVINCIAL POWERS

The Charlottetown Accord identified a number of fields not now specifically mentioned in the Constitution, and proposed that they be 'identified' or 'recognized' as coming within exclusive provincial jurisdiction. These were:

- 'labour market development and training' (item 28);
- 'culture' (item 29);
- 'forestry' (item 30);
- 'mining' (item 31);
- 'tourism' (item 32);
- 'housing' (item 33);
- 'recreation' (item 34); and
- 'municipal and urban affairs' (item 35).

Each of these fields is now wholly or mainly within provincial jurisdiction, so that their identification or recognition as provincial matters would have made little or no change in the existing distribution of powers. The point of their specification was to invite provinces to enter into agreements with the federal government providing for the withdrawal of the federal government from programs in those fields in the province. Any such withdrawal was to be accompanied by compensation in the form of cash or tax points to enable the province to assume the vacated federal responsibility. These federal-provincial agreements could be constitutionalized under the provision for the constitutionalization of intergovernmental agreements (item 26, discussed above).

The specification of the eight fields of exclusive provincial jurisdiction was really an elaboration of the more general project of constraining the exercise of federal spending programs in areas of exclusive provincial jurisdiction. In the case of 'labour market development and training,' where it seems obvious that national programs would be more effective than provincial ones in opening up job opportunities across the country, it was recognized that there would be 'an ongoing federal role in the establishment of national policy objectives for the national aspects of labour market development' (item 28). In the case of 'culture,' it was not proposed to abandon the CBC or the Canada Council, or even to break them up and turn them over to the provinces. It was proposed that there be 'an explicit constitutional amendment that also recognizes the continuing responsibility of the federal government in Canadian cultural matters,' and that 'the federal government should retain responsibility for national cultural institutions' (item 29). These references to a federal role were vague, and it is not clear whether the accord would have caused any diminution of the federal role in respect of culture.

It is worth mentioning at this point that culture was also mentioned in the powers of the new Senate, which was to have special powers over bills 'materially affecting French language or French culture' (item 11). Those bills would have had to pass the Senate by a double majority, that is, 'by a majority of [all] Senators voting and by a majority of the Francophone Senators voting' (item 12). The defeat in the Senate of a bill materially affecting French language or French culture would not trigger a joint sitting with the House of Commons, but would cause the defeat of the bill. Thus, the senators from Quebec, who were bound to constitute a majority of the francophone senators, would have had a veto over federal legislation materially affecting French language or culture.

How would one determine whether a bill materially affects French language or culture? The initial designation was to be made by the originator of the bill, and there was to be an appeal to the Speaker of the Senate, who would have the final say (item 14). How would one determine whether a senator was a francophone? On taking up a seat in the Senate, a senator would declare whether or not he or she was a francophone; the Senate rules would establish the procedure for challenging a declaration (item 14).

FEDERAL DECLARATORY POWER

The Charlottetown Accord called for the amendment of section 92(10)(a), which is the provision that enables the federal Parliament to declare a local work to be for the general advantage of Canada. Such a declaration brings the work into the legislative jurisdiction of the federal Parliament. This is an anomalous power, because it enables the federal Parliament unilaterally to expand its powers at the expense of the provinces. The accord would have required that any new declaration, or the repeal of any old declaration, be made only with the consent of the province in which the work is situated (item 39).

CONCLUSION

The division-of-powers provisions of the Charlottetown Accord were, in my view, the least satisfactory part of the accord. They would have made very little significant change to the division of powers; most of what the accord contemplated can proceed under the present Constitution through federal restraint in the exercise of the spending power and through federal-provincial agreements. Although the accord's changes were quite insignificant in substance, they would have contributed a host of complexities to the Constitution of Canada. Indeed, the *Draft Legal Text* looked more like an amendment to the Income Tax Act than an amendment to the Constitution. While I deeply regret the defeat of the accord, as a generous attempt to secure a reconciliation with Quebec (and the West and the Aboriginal peoples), I am not sorry to see the end of the division-of-powers provisions.

NOTES

1 *A.G. N. S. v. A.G. Can.*, [1951] s.c.r. 31
2 P.W. Hogg, *Constitutional Law of Canada*, 3rd ed. (Toronto: Carswell 1992), chap. 14
3 Status Report on the Multilateral Meetings on the Constitution, typescript version, 16 July 1992, p. 20
4 Consensus Report on the Constitution, typescript version, 28 August 1992, p. 20
5 Hogg, *Constitutional Law*, chap. 6
6 *Re Canada Assistance Plan*, [1991] 2 s.c.r. 525

6

The Charlottetown Accord and the End of the Exclusiveness of Provincial Jurisdictions

JACQUES FRÉMONT

Examined through Québec eyes, part III of the Charlottetown Consensus, enti-tled 'Roles and Responsibilities'[1] was, to say the least, puzzling. It is difficult to assess what the impact of these measures would have been upon the workings of the Canadian federal system if they had been adopted. However, an analysis of the main elements of the consensus shows that its proposed changes to the distribution of powers were not only insufficient for Québec, but also danger-ous, especially, as we shall see, on the question of the federal spending power.

In this short examination of part III of the Charlottetown Consensus, I will first examine the more traditional issue of the distribution of powers, not in a systematic and detailed way, but rather in attempting to identify the character-istics of the proposed reform. I will demonstrate that these proposals can only be properly understood and assessed in the light of the question of the federal spending power, which was also part of the consensus and which will be discussed in the second part of this paper.

THE DISTRIBUTION OF POWERS: CONFIRMING THE STATUS QUO

In the light of the Allaire[2] and Bélanger-Campeau[3] reports, and following decades of requests from Québec for a major revision and decentralization of the distribution of powers within the Canadian federation, it was clearly on Québec's agenda during this latest round of negotiations to provoke a major shift in the way the Canadian federal system actually works by obtaining more autonomy. The results gained in Charlottetown had to be assessed on their own value, but also in the light of Québec's traditional requests.

A. Québec's Traditional Requests

Is it necessary to stress that, over the years, Québec's positions with regard to a reshuffling of the distribution of powers within the Canadian federation has been remarkably consistent? From Duplessis to Bourassa – through Jean Lesage, Daniel Johnson, Jean-Jacques Bertrand, Robert Bourassa's first reign, René Lévesque, and Pierre-Marc Johnson – a consensus has always existed, whatever the party in power and whoever the persons in place. These traditional requests concerned matters that, in one way or another, touched upon or affected the distinctive character of Québec and of its people. They mainly bore upon linguistic, education, cultural, and communication matters, as well as marriage and divorce; all these issues were seen as essential to the protection and development of the Québec people.

But there was more in terms of Québec's traditional requests for a new constitutional arrangement: all jurisdictions relating to the Québec culture (in the largest sense of that word) also had to be 'returned' to Québec in the form of exclusive legislative powers. These included such fields as manpower and labour training, social programs generally, and some form of official input into foreign relations that would constitute the extension of exclusive internal powers. In fact, history shows that Québec has constantly, over the years, claimed these jurisdictions and, more recently, others, including environment.

In the meantime, Québec has seized every opportunity to obtain all the autonomy the federal system could offer. In the fifties, it 'repatriated' the income-tax system, while the sixties saw the setting up of the Caisse de dépôt and of the corresponding Régie des rentes du Québec; many agreements conferring on Québec a distinct fiscal status within the Canadian federal system were then negotiated. In the seventies – and despite adverse political conditions with the Trudeau government in power – Québec managed to negotiate other agreements, including the Couture/Cullen agreement in the field of immigration.

It must be stressed that most of these agreements were achieved in a context where the rest of Canada did not really care about what was allowed to Québec, providing it did not 'hurt' basic Canadian values. It is as if Canadians did not really believe in the legal as well as symbolic importance of a constitution. Of course, matters have changed considerably, especially since 1982, when the Canadian Constitution, after being a purely legalistic document, became a legal instrument placed directly in the hands of citizens. The Charlottetown Consensus reflected this new approach.

B. The Charlottetown Consensus

One could argue that the Charlottetown Consensus offered a sort of smokescreen in terms of the distribution of powers within the Canadian federation. On the face of the document, many exclusive powers were to be recognized explicitly as accruing to the provinces; these would have included fields as important as labour-market development and training, and culture, as well as forestry, mining, tourism, housing, recreation, and municipal affairs. However, one must stress – and the consensus did not deny it – that these fields of proposed 'exclusive' provincial jurisdiction were already sectors where, by and large, the provinces effectively exercise their jurisdiction.

In strict terms, the addition of these new heads of jurisdiction to the list of enumerated powers of section 92 of the Constitution Act, 1867 would not in all likelihood have had any substantial or immediate effect; at best, these new enumerated heads would have eventually helped the provinces to establish their jurisdiction in these fields on a stronger footing.

As far as Québec's traditional requests are concerned, the consensus undoubtedly fell short of what has been seen over the years as minimally necessary for Québec's survival and development as a francophone society. The problem in this respect was not so much with the eight fields where exclusive jurisdictions were to be recognized for the provinces, but rather with those that were not included in the list. For instance, without falling into the Allaire report's excessive demands (in federal terms), it is striking to note that all social sectors were excluded from the list of fields granted to the provinces. The list of other issues that were not pursued under this round of negotiations[4] is even more puzzling, since it seems that it was not even possible to agree on relatively 'easy' sectors such as inland fisheries, marriage and divorce, residual power, or the question of the appointment of judges (s. 96).

Seen under this light, and despite the considerable recent reinforcement of federal economic powers through court decisions,[5] the Charlottetown agreement was, on the issue of the distribution of powers, definitely disappointing for Québec. One would have thought that while Québec's distinct character was finally accepted by its Canadian partners, the consequences in terms of powers necessary to assert this distinctiveness would have followed; this was not to be the case.

The federal Parliament would not have been deprived of any substantial field of jurisdiction under this proposal; in fact, the proposed modifications to the list of the distribution of powers seem quite neutral and confirmed the status quo for most purposes. The Charlottetown Consensus was, however, far more significant as far as the federal spending power was concerned.

THE FEDERAL SPENDING POWER: DOING AWAY WITH THE PRINCIPLE OF
THE EXCLUSIVENESS OF PROVINCIAL POWERS

The provisions of the Charlottetown Consensus dealing with the federal spending power were by far the most significant section of part III of the document, since they would have, if they had materialized, profoundly modified the functioning of the Canadian federation. The consensus would have affected the federal spending power in three respects: (1) the new Canada-wide shared-costs programs, (2) some fields of exclusive provincial jurisdiction that the consensus attributed exclusively to the provinces, and (3) the future establishment of a 'framework' to guide the use of federal spending power in all areas of exclusive provincial jurisdiction.

(1) Under the new Canada-wide shared-costs-programs provision, compensation would have been provided by the Government of Canada to any province that would have chosen to opt out of any new Canada-wide shared-cost federal program established within an area of exclusive provincial jurisdiction, providing that the province had carried on a program 'that is compatible with the national objectives'; such compensation would have had to be 'reasonable.' This part of the Charlottetown Consensus was identical to the Meech Lake agreement, which proposed a modification of section 106A of the Constitution Act, 1867 to that effect. The important problems raised by this provision will be discussed subsequently.

(2) The most significant part of the consensus on the question of federal spending was probably the provisions that, while recognizing the exclusiveness of provincial powers in some fields, would at the same time have allowed the provinces to force the federal government to constrain the exercise of any spending that is 'directly related' to these fields of exclusive provincial jurisdiction. Such fields would have included labour-market development and training, forestry, mining, tourism, housing, and recreation, as well as municipal and urban affairs.

In these fields, it would therefore have been possible for the provinces effectively to get rid of any distorting influence of the federal spending power. This conclusion is by no means trivial, but the number of jurisdictional fields in which it would have been possible to constrain federal spending in that way would have remained limited, since in all other fields of exclusive provincial jurisdiction any restriction to the exercise of the federal spending power would only have been subject to a 'political framework' that was yet to be defined.

(3) The Charlottetown Consensus effectively remained fairly evasive about how federal spending would have been restricted in all other fields of exclusive provincial jurisdiction. It said that a 'framework' would have to be developed 'to guide the use of the federal spending power' and that this framework would eventually receive some form of constitutional protection through a five-year protection device that would have the effect of 'freezing' the multilateral agreement. The consensus specified that

[t]he framework should ensure that when the federal spending power is used in areas of exclusive provincial jurisdiction, it should:
  (a) contribute to the pursuit of national objectives;
  (b) reduce overlap and duplication;
  (c) not distort and should respect provincial priorities; and
  (d) ensure equality of treatment of the provinces, while recognizing their different needs and circumstances.[6]

I would submit that the spending provisions of the consensus were danger-ous for the principle of the exclusiveness of provincial powers as well as for provincial autonomy generally (A). Other and different conditions must be present if federal spending is to be effectively 'framed' (B).

A. The Exclusive Character of Provincial Powers

It is clear that, since the very early days of the Canadian federation, Parliament has been authorized to spend money for the exercise of responsibilities granted by the Constitution. The problem with the federal spending power does not come from the fact that Parliament spends money in areas of federal responsi-bility or, it must be added, in areas of exclusive provincial responsibilities, providing that no conditions are attached to the obtainment of these amounts by provincial or local authorities.

The problem essentially lies with the imposition on provincial authorities of priorities and standards if they wish to obtain money for fields over which the Constitution attributes to the provinces full and exclusive responsibility. Fed-eral authorities thus find themselves in a position where they can indirectly impose their own norms and priorities in areas where Parliament has no corre-sponding constitutional responsibilities.

Some will object that this is already the case and that the consensus merely reflects an *état de fait*. The fact is, they are both right and wrong. Federal spending within areas of exclusive provincial responsibilities is indeed a reality of today's so-called cooperative federalism; it is accomplished in a grand scale, and it is probably true to say that very few areas of provincial responsibilities currently escape the influence of federal spending priorities.

Legally, however, the situation remains very different. The power of Parlia-ment and the federal government to spend conditionally within spheres of provincial constitutional jurisdiction has never, to my knowledge, been directly examined by the courts of this country, at least in recent years. In two recent cases before the Supreme Court of Canada, we were left with no clues as to the validity of the conditional federal spending power or, if it does exist, of its scope of intervention within spheres of exclusive provincial powers.[7]

I would submit that the effective result of the Charlottetown Consensus would have been the explicit recognition of the constitutional foundations of conditional spending within all spheres of exclusive provincial powers. This result, far from trivial, would in turn have had the effect of profoundly affecting the way the federation functions, as well as of setting aside the basic principle of exclusiveness of powers that, I like to believe, still lies at the core of the Canadian constitutional system.

Exclusiveness for its own sake is certainly not a sufficient reason to oppose such a result of the Charlottetown Consensus. I would submit that the explicit recognition of conditional federal spending would strike at the very heart of our federal system, since it would allow the setting up of a body of explicit federal norms bearing on the spending power, norms directly aimed at intervening within fields of exclusive provincial jurisdiction. Not only would the principle of provincial autonomy be affected, but there could eventually result in some fields a 'municipalization' of provincial powers.

Thus, in fields such as post-secondary education, provinces would have constantly, in the establishment of their priorities towards the accomplishment of their constitutional responsibilities, to conform to federal norms that by their nature are bound to have a flattening effect. Such an indirect effect upon the exercise of provincial powers (which Parliament could not affect directly) strikes us as strange within a constitutional system where the respect of values entrenched within the Constitution is seen as essential by all actors, including the courts. Finally, it should be remembered that if, in the past, the spending power has been used by federal authorities to develop and consolidate the Canadian welfare system within spheres of provincial exclusive jurisdiction, the same spending power could very well in the future be used to dismantle this same system.

A second consequence to the recognition of conditional spending power would have been the entrenchment, within our constitutional and political systems, of a very curious principle, that of taxation without matching constitutional responsibilities. The money spent by federal authorities within fields of exclusive provincial responsibility is not raised for the pursuit of a federal objective; these sums are raised by Parliament for the exercise of provincial jurisdictions. The principle of no taxation without effective imputability would have been set aside in a very systematic way.

These two remarks concerning the effects of any explicit recognition of the federal spending power demonstrate that the Charlottetown Consensus's recognition of the constitutional foundations of the conditional federal spending power could have constituted the Trojan horse of the federal system as we have conceived it and as it has been interpreted by the courts over the years.

B. Towards an Effective 'Framing' of the Federal Spending Power?

Of course, as I have already pointed out, the Charlottetown Consensus proposed a mechanism aimed at 'framing' the federal spending power. Under that proposal, the details of which still were to be negotiated, federal spending power within spheres of provincial jurisdiction would have had to respect a certain number of principles enunciated in section 25 of the consensus.

I would submit that these principles ran contrary to the principle of the exclusiveness of provincial powers: it is, for instance, difficult to understand that, on the one hand, federal spending should contribute to the pursuit of national objectives (principle A) while, on the other, the same spending should not distort and should respect provincial priorities (principle C). One must conclude that any province that would choose, within its own area of exclusive jurisdiction, to follow priorities of its own and not to respect national objectives, would necessarily be penalized. Furthermore, the respect of the principle of equality of treatment of the provinces (principle D) would inevitably have forced the various provinces to respect, again within their respective exclusive jurisdiction, federal spending priorities that would have had to be articulated by taking into account these equalitarian values; the end result could undoubtedly have been a considerable flattening of provincial priorities within their own fields of responsibilities. In fact, one can hardly see how the acceptance of conditional spending can reduce 'overlap and duplication' (principle B); the only genuine such reduction would have been to suppress all federal spending within areas of provincial jurisdiction.

I fail to see how the spending provisions of the Charlottetown Consensus could do otherwise than have accelerated federal interventions within sectors of exclusive provincial jurisdiction, thus seriously undermining the true federal character of the Canadian constitution. This is a far cry from Québec's traditional requests for a greater sphere of provincial autonomy, free from capricious federal interference.

In this respect, and from a Québec perspective, any acceptable solution aiming at effectively restricting duplication and overlapping with regard to federal spending would have to at least involve

- the explicit recognition of more fields of exclusive provincial jurisdiction (including social matters);
- the obligation for the federal government to withdraw formally from all sectors of exclusive provincial jurisdiction (and, accordingly, to stop exercising conditional and unconditional spending); and
- the corresponding obligation to compensate provinces in tax points in order to respect the principle of provincial taxation for provincial jurisdictions.

Such a scheme would probably appear unacceptable to many Canadians outside Québec, who would fear a radical departure from the actual situation, where Parliament plays a strong centralist role. I would submit that the disappearance of the federal spending power and a return to a state of things where provinces are truly responsible for the exercise of their jurisdictions would definitely effect a major downsizing of the federal bureaucracy and an overnight diminution of program overlap, as well as making provincial politicians more reposnsible for their jurisdictions. At the same time, the vast tendency to centralization of general federal powers confirmed by recent Supreme Court decisions such as the peace, order and good government clause and the general trade and commerce clause (s. 91(2)),[8] as well as the principle of paramountcy, are amply sufficient to maintain an effective federal leadership where it is really needed.

In this context, it would not have been unacceptable and indeed would be quite logical, at least from a Québec perspective, to consider a further formal transfer of power from the provinces to the federal Parliament in sectors considered as crucial for Canada's standing and international competitiveness; of course, Québec would then have been justified in some cases in withdrawing from such formal centralization when necessary to protect its cultural distinctiveness.

CONCLUSION

The results of the Charlottetown discussions concerning the distribution of powers and the federal spending power were not entirely surprising in the actual context. While the federal deficit continues to accumulate at an incredible pace, federal transfer payments through spending are being reduced in relative terms in many sectors, thus diminishing the legitimacy of effective conditional spending on the part of federal authorities in fields of exclusive provincial jurisdiction.

In this context, the spending provisions of the Charlottetown Consensus must be understood (with the proposed Social Charter and the reinforcement of section 36 of the Constitution Act, 1982) as a means of re-establishing the legitimacy as well as the legality of this technique of federal intervention in fields of exclusive provincial powers. In the likelihood that courts would be called upon to rule on the constitutionality of this technique of intervention, the explicit recognition of the validity of federal spending would have been a major achievement from a federal perspective. From a provincialist and certainly from a Québec perspective, it would have been a major step backwards.

In fact, a hundred years after the landmark Liquidators of the Maritime

Bank,[9] Quebeckers still would like to believe that Canada basically functions as a federal country; the Charlottetown Consensus demonstrated that this might by no means be true.

It has probably been Québec's mistake, over the years, to seek again and again to obtain the recognition, within the Canadian constitution, of new formal heads of exclusive jurisdiction. The nationalist discourse has never been adjusted to the effective reality of a Canadian state where economic and not constitutional levers are most relevant in explaining the dynamics of the federation. Even very recently, the Allaire and Bélanger-Campeau reports have fallen into the trap of claiming more jurisdictions for Québec, when they should instead have insisted on being able to exercise effectively, and without any interference, as fully and completely as possible, the jurisdictions recognized by the Constitution Act, 1867 and its subsequent judicial interpretation. If Québec did not put forward the right requests, it is not surprising they were not met by the Charlottetown Consensus.

NOTES

1 Canada, *Consensus Report on the Constitution, Charlottetown, Final Text, August 28, 1992*

2 Parti Libéral du Québec, *Un Québec libre de ses choix*, Rapport du Comité constitutionnel du parti libéral du Québec, Montréal, Québec, 28 Jan. 1991

3 Québec, Assemblée nationale, *L'avenir politique et constitutionnel du Québec*, Commission sur l'avenir politique et constitutionnel du Québec, Québec, 27 March 1991

4 Contained at p. 20 of the Charlottetown Consensus document.

5 *General Motors of Canada v. City National Leasing*, [1989] 1 S.C.R. 641; *R. v. Crown Zellerbach Canada Ltd.*, [1988] 1 S.C.R. 401

6 See *Consensus Report*, p. 9.

7 *YMHA Jewish Community Centre of Winnipeg Inc. v. Brown*, [1989] 1 S.C.R. 1532; *Re: Canada Assistance Plan (B.-C.)*, [1991] 2 S.C.R. 525

8 See note 5 above.

9 *Liquidators of the Maritime Bank of Canada v. Rec. Gen. N.-B.*, [1892] A.C. 437

7

The Charlottetown Accord:
A Faulty Framework and
a Wrong-headed Compromise

JUDY REBICK

[The following is an edited version of a speech presented by Judy Rebick as part of a panel on the division of powers.]

I will begin where other panelists have begun – the different visions of Canada. The vision from Quebec sees Canada as two nations: a French-Canadian nation, the majority of which lives in Quebec, and an English-Canadian nation, the majority of which lives in the rest of Canada. Then we have a rather new vision of Canada popularized by Clyde Wells during the Meech Lake Accord, called the equality of the provinces. This vision says that Canada is composed of ten equal provinces – what one gets, the others should also get. Some panelists have suggested that the Charlottetown Accord marries these two visions successfully. I believe that the Charlottetown Accord, in fact, accepts the framework of equality of the provinces and only pays lip-service to the notion of two nations, through the distinct-society clause.

   I think both of these frameworks are fundamentally flawed. The two-nations vision ignores, of course, the third founding nation, Aboriginal, but also ignores the evolution that has taken place in Canada with the entry of many diverse groups – races, ethnic groups, and so on. The equality of the provinces is a notion of the equality of the governments, not the people, of the provinces, and it is a model of formal or same treatment equality that has been rejected by the Supreme Court of Canada and by most Canadian human-rights experts.

   Another framework emerged somewhat implicitly from the popular constitutional conferences held last year, but explicitly in Gordon Robertson's speech to the Toronto conference. That different vision is of a country composed of three founding nations, which have now developed into three national communities. These national communities – Quebec, the rest of Canada, and Aboriginal people – each have racial and regional diversities and their own national aspirations.

Now that may sound strange, especially for the rest of Canada, but as people have pointed out, the demands of Quebec in Confederation have been very different than the demands of other provinces. Quebec has for many years wanted more power for its National Assembly. In the rest of Canada two things have emerged.

First of all, there has been a desire right across the country outside Quebec for a strong federal government to protect social programs, promote regional equalization, and defend national standards. If you look at the Spicer Commission, the constitutional conferences, or any poll, you will find very strong sentiment in the rest of Canada for a strong central government. Second, from the West, and increasingly from the Atlantic provinces, there has been a desire for more say in the central government, as expressed in the demand for a Triple-E Senate.

What we have in the Charlottetown Accord is a proposal where Quebec does not get very many more powers for its National Assembly. By contrast, the other provinces get more powers than they wanted. Quebec gets more power in the central government through the 25 per cent guarantee – power that it didn't want. And I would suggest that the West has not really gotten very much out of this new Senate.

What happened at the Halifax conference is that people came with their regional hats on. Many people were angry at Quebec. Their feeling was that Quebec wants to take something away from the rest of us. That was the problem with Meech Lake, which said that if Quebec wants more power, we all have to accept the devolution of power or the 'opt out' on social programs.

I'll tell you a story about my workshop at Halifax. There was a woman named Hilda from Moncton in my workshop. The first day of the workshop, she said, 'Get away from me. I am sick of hearing about Quebec.' But, as she listened to Senator Beaudoin and other delegates from Quebec, she realized that it was possible to find a solution – asymmetrical federalism, whereby Quebec could get what it wanted (which was more power), and those of us in the rest of Canada could get what we wanted (a strong central government). She said, 'Well, I don't mind if Quebec gets what they want, as long we in New Brunswick can get what we want.'

That was the result of a dialogue among Canadians – the kind of dialogue that I am afraid this referendum won't permit because we have to choose 'yes' or 'no.' We don't have a chance to meet together from different regions of the country. I went into those constitutional conferences, personally, as an abolitionist on the Senate. It's easy to be an abolitionist on the Senate if you live in Ontario. When I heard people from the Atlantic provinces and the West talking about how much it meant to them to have more of a voice in the central government, I changed my mind. I have been active in politics for a long time.

I travel the country, but that dialogue helped me to change my mind.

This idea of asymmetrical federalism, which is unpopular in the rest of country, is, in our view, the only long-lasting federalist solution for Canada. It is the solution that corresponds to the notion of substantive equality – different treatment to achieve equal results. The solution we have in this accord will not give Quebec what it wants and will not give us in the rest of Canada what we want. The result will be continuing anger, alienation, and regional splintering.

Instead of meeting the demands of the different regions of the country, we have an accord that does not meet anyone's demands. There is a lot of unhappiness with this accord. Despite Mr Bouchard's eloquent speech, the fact is that the majority right now in Quebec are opposed to the accord, including federalists. I have just been out West and I can tell you there is a lot of anger about this accord there. In my view, far from unifying the country, the agreements that the first ministers have made will further divide us, further set region against region. I would like to explain why.

What's wrong with the notion of equality of the provinces? First of all, it is a notion of equality of the governments, not of the people. We see this confusion repeated and repeated throughout the accord, especially in the Canada Clause. Second, it is a 'same treatment' notion of equality – a notion of equality that says that if you treat everyone the same, they will be equal. In an unequal society, if you treat everyone the same, the people with resources do the best. The people with privilege do the best. In the case of federalism, you might say that Ontario would do the best. In the case of men and women, if you treat everyone the same, men continue to do better than women and the gap increases.

The easiest example here concerns people with disabilities. If you treated everyone the same, you wouldn't build a ramp for a person who uses a wheelchair to get into a building. That's 'special treatment,' different treatment, but it's different treatment to enable that person to participate fully. Similarly with women and racial minorities, we have pay equity and employment equity because we recognize that generations of discrimination have meant that women and minorities and people with disabilities are so far behind, they need special measures to catch up and overcome that discrimination.

The people who will suffer the most from this accord are the most disadvantaged people. What the premiers have done is to develop a patchwork quilt in which they have stitched together the component parts, but left the most disadvantaged people on the cutting-room floor. That's what this Charlottetown Accord represents.

The most important question concerning division of power in this accord, in terms of division of power, is that of spending power. The spending power of the federal government has been the central instrument for the development of universal social programs in Canada.

At the time medicare was founded, for example, the Province of Ontario preferred a private insurance plan. If the 'opt out' clause that was in Meech Lake, and that is in this agreement, had been in effect then, the Province of Ontario could have opted out of medicare with compensation and maintained its private health-insurance system. I would suggest to you that we would not have medicare today in this country if the most populous, richest province had opted out.

Both M. Beaudoin and Professor Hogg talk about national standards, but there is nothing about national standards for social programs in this accord. The accord talks about national objectives. Further, it is not the federal government that will set these national objectives – but the first ministers – behind closed doors, in the most inaccessible form of government there is.

In the Meech Lake debate, M. Bourassa argued that his family policy to promote women having more children would be compatible with the objectives of a federal child-care policy. No one challenged that claim because nobody knows what 'compatible with national objectives' means. We're not going to know what it means when we vote on this accord. Maybe we will know somewhere down the road, after the first ministers negotiate it.

Let's say that in the next federal election the women's movement was successful in making child care a central issue. Child care is the most important social reform of the next period in terms of equality for women. Let's say that we were successful in electing a national government committed to publicly funded child care, that they were elected on that platform. They would be unable to implement such a reform under this agreement because as a national government they would be unable to set the standard for public child care. The Government would have to go to the first ministers and try to negotiate it. Even if it were negotiated, Alberta or Ontario could opt out with compensation and say that its program was compatible with national objectives. They could claim that private day care (in Alberta day care is entirely private right now), babysitting, and even the payment of women to stay home to take care of their children were compatible with national objectives.

That's our worry. But there is a new clause that is even more worrisome. It refers to a framework that gives the first ministers a blank cheque to restrict the federal spending power in the future in all areas of provincial jurisdiction – medicare, education, and community and social services. One of the criteria of this framework is a respect for provincial priorities. Well, that sounds okay, but when we asked officials, Would extra billing be considered a provincial priority? They said yes. Would user fees be considered a provincial priority? They said yes. In 1984, the federal government used the spending power to stop provinces from permitting extra billing. If this accord were in effect, that could not have happened.

What we have here is a compromise that doesn't give anyone what they want. Therefore, it is a mistaken compromise, one that gives the premiers what they want, but does not give the people what they want. There is a grave threat in it to social programs, as well as a significant devolution of powers. The argument that only Quebec will take advantage of this devolution is not true. Having talked to officials in Ontario and British Columbia, we know they have the idea that they can opt out or devolve powers, get the money from the federal government, and do a better job themselves.

This position is short-sighted and mean-spirited. How long are these governments going to be in power? What happens to the poorer provinces? Well, we have section 36 on equalization, but we haven't seen the legal language yet. We don't know how much force it will have. Why would the federal government, for example, be willing to initiate a national social program if it wouldn't get any credit for it in the populous provinces? What motivation would there be? On top of that, how long are people in the rich provinces going to be willing to pay equalization if they're not getting any services from the federal government? They'll just see it as charity. So the whole way in which this country has worked, although not very well in recent times – the whole creative tension between the federal government and the provinces that has enabled the people to get better programs from their provincial government and to look to the federal government to protect universality – will be gone under this agreement. It is easy to understand, given the policies of the current federal government, why some provincial governments believe that a devolution of power to the provinces on social programs will produce better social programs. But it is a very risky proposition to throw out the national system that has provided us with universal social programs until now. We have only to look south of the border to see how decentralized governments compete with each other for investment. The accord's social and economic union, because it is toothless, does not provide the necessary guarantees.

This is why the National Action Committee on the Status of Women believes that, in fact, a 'no' vote is a vote for Canada. We believe the Charlottetown Accord will lead to a dismantling of national social programs and more division and disunity over the years.

8

The Dog That Never Barked:
Who Killed Asymmetrical Federalism?

REG WHITAKER

I wish to address a murder mystery: Who killed asymmetrical federalism? Less than a year before the 26 October referendum, asymmetrical federalism (or 'special status' for Quebec, to use an unfashionable phrase) was apparently alive and well, discussed in the highest circles, an idea whose time had come. It is now dead.

The failed Charlottetown Accord bore scarcely a trace of asymmetrical federalism. The distinct-society clause might, to stretch a point, be considered a relative of asymmetrical federalism. But the essential definition of asymmetrical federalism is that exclusive powers would be devolved asymmetrically to Quebec alone among the provinces. Charlottetown slammed the door shut against this idea.

Asymmetrical federalism had some friends. The Halifax conference on the division of powers generated some spontaneous support for the idea. At this conference, held on the eve of the referendum, many participants expressed regret at the passing of asymmetrical federalism. Even former Alberta Premier Peter Lougheed revealed that he has always been a closet asymmetrical federalist.

As many have pointed out, actually existing federalism has always been asymmetrical in practice. But resistance to any formal constitutionalization of the practice has been fierce. Three main arguments have been advanced against it. First is the counter-principle of the equality of the provinces. Since this argument is stated most often by premiers, it has a resonance quite out of keeping with its actual historical or constitutional justification, which is slight. As a self-serving ideological construction employed by relatively powerful actors, it has far greater reach than an idea whose major proponents have been academics and groups existing outside parliamentary institutions. None of this means that it could not, and should not, be contested as unsound and unwise.

The second objection is one that, as Peter Hogg has suggested, is of greater concern to political scientists and academic lawyers than to the general public. This is the objection that asymmetry in powers must require asymmetry in representation in the central institutions of government. If Quebec has a much greater degree of autonomy than other provinces it can hardly be fair that Quebeckers should have 'rep by pop' in Parliament – and even less fair that they should continue to enjoy some of the vestiges of dualism that persist in the various forms of élite accommodation in Ottawa. The political-science objection to asymmetrical representation is its alleged unworkability in a British parliamentary form of government.

This is a technical objection – one to which I myself have given voice in the past – but it rather flies in the face of one of the central realities of the current constitutional debate. The demand of the smaller provinces for equal representation in the upper chamber has collided with the reluctance of Quebec to give up any of its power in Parliament. *A golden opportunity existed for bargaining asymmetry in the division of powers against asymmetry in representation at the centre.* This opportunity was never seized, and instead a messy compromise was worked out whereby an equal and (mainly) elected Senate was balanced against its possible ineffectiveness, with an extremely unpopular guarantee in the House of Commons of representation for Quebec that might in future *exceed* its proportion of the population.

The third objection to asymmetrical federalism is its straightforward unpopularity outside Quebec. No one, not even strong supporters, denies that the idea of 'special status' or 'special treatment' for Quebec is generally unpopular. Indeed, this sentiment was probably the strongest single factor leading to the downfall of the Meech Lake Accord. To leave it at that is, however, to assume that public opinion is a fixed and immutable thing. The case for asymmetrical federalism would be that everyone gains and no one loses: Quebec gets exclusive powers that no other province wants or needs, while the rest of Canada gains an effective national government that is not resisted by Quebec. Since this case was never seriously put before the court of public opinion, we are hardly in a position to declare that it has been firmly rejected.

Strange to say, this same constitutional round witnessed the proposed recognition of the inherent right to self-government of Aboriginal peoples and the proposal of mechanisms to achieve self-determination. I say strange, not because there was anything wrong with this. On the contrary, this recognition was long overdue and constituted, in my mind at least, one of the better arguments for voting Yes to the Charlottetown Accord. But it is strange that this breakthrough with regard to Aboriginal 'special status' (including the clear designation of a new, third order of government in the Canada Clause) should have been matched by a stonewall against any concrete recognition of Quebec's difference in the form of exclusive powers for that province alone. It is stranger yet when one considers that the actual working out of specific Aboriginal self-government agreements would have inevitably resulted in a degree of practical asymmetry that will put any plan for Quebec-driven asymmetry to shame. There would probably be hundreds of such agreements negotiated, each different in detail, many in substance.

The objections to asymmetrical federalism are thus formidable, but not definitive. The mystery remains as to its sudden demise. For Sherlock Holmes, the key to unravelling a certain mystery was an unusual clue: a dog that did *not* bark. The threat of Quebec sovereignty has been the dog that did not bark. It is my contention that a refusal to think seriously about the idea of Quebec sovereignty led inexorably to a refusal to consider autonomy or special status within Confederation, that is to say, formal asymmetrical federalism.

The present constitutional crisis was inspired in the first instance by Quebec's threat to seek sovereignty. The all-party Bélanger-Campeau Commission recommended sovereignty; for the first time a party appeared from Quebec in the federal parliament dedicated to sovereignty; the Liberal Allaire report insisted on virtual sovereignty as the price for remaining formally in Canada; the Liberal premier of Quebec spoke of a sovereign Quebec within a kind of Eurofederalism; and a referendum on sovereignty was planned by the Quebec National Assembly for October 1992.

What a contrast to the situation at the moment of the referendum! Bélanger-Campeau had become a dead letter. In place of the sovereignty referendum, a chastened premier of Quebec campaigned for assent to a deal that ignored even the shrunken replica of Allaire presented so diffidently by Quebec to the first ministers' meeting in August. Not only was sovereignty, *tout court*, off the table, but so too was asymmetrical federalism.

Given the build-up in Bélanger-Campeau, Allaire, the opinion polls in Quebec, and the exhortations of the PQ and the BQ, what happened to the power of the threat of separation? Why did it apparently diminish so far that the premiers could cooly reject Bourassa's last-ditch plea for even a few exclusive powers?

This silence is even odder when one considers that this time – unlike during the 1980 referendum struggle – there was an initial indication of some positive response in English Canada for the idea of Quebec sovereignty. During the 1980 campaign, there was a certain limited amount of English-Canadian sympathy expressed for the sovereignty-association option. This, however, came exclusively from the usual suspects among the left-nationalist intelligentsia and was moreover expressed almost entirely in terms of an affirmation of Quebec's right to national self-determination and of English Canada's moral obligations to respect that right.

After the failure of Meech Lake, a new note was sounded in some quarters in English Canada: Quebec's separation might be of positive benefit to the rest of Canada, allowing a potential *déblocage* of political, social, and economic agendas log-jammed by the obstinate Quebec conundrum. This point of view, however tentatively articulated, did not come from one particular side of the ideological spectrum, but was heard from both left and right (indicating some conflicting wishful hopes!). There was thus a moment when a new terrain appeared to be opening up on which both Quebec and English Canada might negotiate a new and perhaps mutually beneficial relationship.

That moment vanished as quickly as it appeared. Once serious efforts at post-Meech constitutional reforms were initiated by the politicians, Quebec sovereignty was firmly removed from the table. Of course the idea haunted the proceedings, but only as a spectre, *to be avoided at all costs.*

Perhaps this result is not all that surprising. Politically, there were powerful vested interests in keeping the sovereignty option out of sight. The governing Conservative party under Quebecker Brian Mulroney was obviously now tied decisively to its Quebec support. The same applies to the Liberals under Chrétien. The NDP for its part has never been able to articulate a Quebec policy significantly at variance with the National Unity themes expounded by its bigger counterparts. Only the Reform party – free of the demands of the élite accommodation that entangles the established parties – was able to articulate a two-track policy premised on the option of Quebec either staying or going. But Reform was also cut out of the process (which left it free to lead the No side on 26 October, but this is another story). For the political establishment, National Unity is like all ideology: it makes a virtue of necessity. And like all establishment ideology, it actively discourages dissent as contrary to the national interest.

As a result, 'responsible' political leaders simply refused to even discuss the possibility of Quebec leaving, or to countenance the sketching of scenarios of what might happen after separation. I can speak with some familiarity about the premier of Ontario and I can report that he steadfastly, as a matter of principle, refused to contemplate Quebec sovereignty, since he had begun by defining that option as the worst possible outcome. Moreover, it was widely believed that talking about sovereignty could legitimize an outcome that was to be avoided at all costs. These attitudes lend themselves to a certain negotiating strategy, a point to which I will return shortly.

The avalanche of economic arguments that descended from business, economists, think-tanks, and the financial press on the economics of sovereignty were almost entirely negative, if not alarmist. While it is undoubtedly true that separation would exact considerable short-term transition costs, it is less clear that long-term costs need be high, *if suitable means were chosen by both sides to minimize such costs in working out the terms of separation.* Even though this approach would be in the interests of all parties, it is curious that the majority of economic commentators tended either to assume that short-term costs would become long-term costs, or to put forward worst-case scenarios as the probable if not inevitable outcomes. No doubt business people and economists are not above wrapping their own strongly held policy preferences in the aura of scientific objectivity (I will even admit that political scientists have been known to do this from time to time). Badly wanting Quebec *not* to go, they used economics as a weapon to discourage this outcome.

For business, of course, even short-term costs are serious, especially in the midst of the worst postwar recession. It is perfectly true that the economic context for a political adventure in pursuit of sovereignty could not have been worse. It is also true that much of the impetus in Quebec for sovereignty was derived from the dubious belief that the grip of the prolonged recession on Quebec was somehow attributable to federalism and could be alleviated almost magically by the accession to the Quebec state of the instruments of political sovereignty. However much this mythology may have initially captivated certain nationalistically inclined Quebec capitalists, it has rather quickly worn off as the frightening prospect of even short-term flights of nervous foreign capital has taken hold. By the summer of 1992 it was evident that much of the francophone Quebec business community had become thoroughly spooked by the prospect of a sovereignty adventure, *at this time* at least. And this sense of fear was reflected in the softening support for the sovereignty option in Quebec public opinion.

It is within this context that one must understand the failure of the Quebec bargaining strategy to achieve a Meech Plus. The threat of separation was initially seen by the Quebec government and the Quebec intelligentsia as the 'knife at the throat' of English Canada (to use Professor Léon Dion's delicate phrase). Such a strategy must be premised upon credibility: the target must believe that the assailant is capable of acting upon the threat ('your money or your life'). A threat to slit one's own throat ('your money or *my* life') is obviously less convincing.

Premier Bourassa had a second line of tactics, a time-honoured approach of Quebec provincial politicians in federal-provincial bargaining. Bourassa was really the friend of English Canada who wanted desperately to find a handle on a deal that could save Canada, but was being pushed by the extremists in his own backyard for major concessions. Premiers, especially the veterans of Meech, would speak warmly, both publicly and privately, of 'Robert' as the best hope for Canada. I do not for one moment wish to suggest that this stance is not sincere on the part of Mr Bourassa; undoubtedly, he does want to save Canada-with-Quebec. Unfortunately for Mr Bourassa, however, as the credibility of the knife at the throat waned, so did the credibility of the requirement for major concessions on Canada's part.

Bourassa's weakness (and thus Quebec's weakness) was further exacerbated by what now appear as two interrelated strategic blunders. First, Quebec's refusal to take formal part in negotiations until the very end of the process meant that Joe Clark and the English Canadian premiers were dancing in the dark. Phone calls out to Quebec City – which did take place – were no substitute for Quebec's direct presence at the table. Indeed, it later became apparent that indirect understandings of what Quebec would and would not accept could turn out to be misunderstandings (as with Ontario's mistaken belief that its concessions on the Senate had Quebec's tacit approval).

If this had been purely and simply a Quebec round, the absence of Quebec would have been a problem. But since this was emphatically a Canada Round, with strongly interested parties with agendas that had nothing whatever to do with Quebec (although sometimes a negative connection), Quebec's absence tended to mean that its agenda fell off the table. Serious compromises were being worked out in which Quebec was uninvolved, but which had sometimes serious consequences for Quebec's position.

The second strategic error was the institutionalization of the knife at the throat in the form of the Quebec referendum legislation requiring a vote no later than 26 October. As a knife at the throat, the referendum was to be on sovereignty, and the deadline was presumably meant to force the pace of a response. But the more it became apparent that the knife of the referendum was actually at *Bourassa's* throat, the pressure on him to come up with any alternative to sovereignty to put on the ballot became overwhelming. Even though the package did not have a great deal in it specifically for Quebec, worked out as it had been in Quebec's absence according to a logic that did not give high priority to Quebec, Bourassa had little choice at the end but to swallow his doubts and go with whatever deal he could get – given that the alternative was a vote on sovereignty that he could hardly campaign against in the absence of any federalist option.

Because sovereignty lost credibility, either as a promise or a threat, the Canada Round developed its own internal dynamic. Because Bourassa became a hostage to his own strategic errors, that dynamic effectively overwhelmed the Quebec agenda.

Here we return to the mystery to which the silent dog was a clue. Asymmetrical federalism was never a real option because the English-Canadian actors in the process did not conclude that there was a disease requiring such a remedy. No longer taking the threat of separation seriously, and in the absence of Mr Bourassa, the premiers saw little reason to treat Quebec as anything but a province *comme les autres*. The distinct-society clause was a partial exception to this rule, but even this was watered down from the Meech Mark I version, according to the strictures of Clyde Wells.

Rigorously applying the relatively newly minted and dubious 'principle' of the equality of the provinces, the premiers did what premiers will do when given the opportunity: they aggrandized provincial power.

Even in instances where the argument for Quebec distinctiveness seems overwhelming – culture and immigration come to mind – the tendency was to negotiate as if Quebec were like all the others, or all the others like Quebec. Thus, Charlottetown featured a devolution of culture to the provinces as if it were a jurisdiction like forestry or mines. Yet this is itself curiously asymmetrical: there *is* a Quebec culture, but there is hardly a Prince Edward Island or a Manitoba culture, while there certainly is a Canadian culture. To salve the feelings of Canadian nationalists, a clause was added protecting existing national cultural institutions like the CBC, the NFB, and the Canada Council. Canadian cultural nationalists were little mollified by this grandparent clause; at the same time, Quebec nationalists were incensed at the continued presence of Ottawa in Quebec culture.

When Quebec did come to the table and presented, somewhat half-heartedly by all reports, a pared-down version of Allaire's list of powers to be transferred to Quebec's exclusive jurisdiction, they were met by the argument that any further movement in this direction would weaken the national government. This is no doubt true – when such a shopping list is understood as applicable to all the provinces.

An asymmetrical distribution of powers, by contrast, would not deny English Canada a central government effective for national purposes, at the same time as it recognized Quebec's special 'national,' as opposed to provincial, requirements. Moreover, asymmetry in powers could have been bargained against asymmetry in representation at the national level, thus balancing a Triple-E Senate against Quebec's partial opting out of full national participation. Asymmetry could have represented a settlement between peoples and societies, in much the same way that the provisions on Aboriginal self-government represented a historic agreement, albeit now aborted, between Aboriginal and non-native peoples.

All this, however, now resides firmly in that favoured travel-spot of academics, Neverneverland. In the real world of politics, it was the first ministers who held the high-rent properties on the constitutional Monopoly board. And they, as is their custom, worked out a compromise not between Quebec and English-Canadian societies, but between governments. In this transaction, Quebec was reduced from being one of three national groups making up the Canadian community, or even from being a 'distinct society,' to being just another province – and one that refused to negotiate until the deals had been cut between the other actors.

If a constituent assembly had been employed, the case for asymmetrical federalism might have had a hearing. Indeed, at the Halifax conference it was very seriously entertained. But as soon as things returned to a negotiation between governments, that option was lost. It is my contention that only a serious threat of Quebec separation could have driven the first ministers back towards the exploration of asymmetry. The dog that did not bark is thus the decisive clue to the strange death of asymmetrical federalism.

We are dealing here in perceptions and images. The dog was not *heard* to bark. As a result, a deal innocent of asymmetrical federalism was put to the voters. This deal in turn was rejected in Quebec as insufficient and in much of English Canada as too generous.* The result of the No vote on 26 October is that the counterweight that has existed in the past against the sovereignty option in Quebec (the 'renewed federalism' of Claude Ryan and Pierre Trudeau in 1980 and Bourassa in 1992) is now unequivocally dead. The choice in the future will be between sovereignty and the status quo. The death of asymmetrical federalism may then become a clue to the mystery of the dog that suddenly began barking again – very loudly.

---

* According to a post-referendum survey by Decima, 'Quebec got too much' was the most favoured reason for voting No (27%) on the part of those outside Quebec, while 44% of Quebeckers voting No did so because they believed Quebec got too few concessions: 'The Meaning of No,' *Maclean's*, 2 Nov. 1992.

PART THREE

Distinct Society, Aboriginal Rights, and Fundamental Canadian Values

9

The Charlottetown Discord and Aboriginal Peoples' Struggle for Fundamental Political Change

MARY ELLEN TURPEL

One of the things we have to do as First Nations peoples is to create a balance in our relationships with the other governments and the Canadian people. We cannot find balance if we are dominated by the other society. We cannot find harmony when we are threatened with choices like 'take this policy or nothing else.' No balance can be found unless we can do it as equals. The constitutional amendments could require that we be treated as equals; to tip the scales toward a more balanced relationship. Only then will we be able to build relationships with the other governments and the Canadian people based on respect, recognition of our inherent and collective right of self-government and our identity as distinct peoples.
National Chief Ovide Mercredi[1]

There are two impressions or conclusions that seem fairly clear from my vantage point at the end of 1992.[2] The first is that the Charlottetown Accord[3] is as dead as any constitutional agreement has ever been in the history of Canadian constitutional politics, and the prospects for its complete or partial resurrection are remote short of a major constitutional crisis (that is, a clear 'yes' vote in Quebec on full sovereignty).[4] Canadian politicians have distanced themselves from constitutional-reform discussion or debate after the clear rejection of the accord in the 26 October referendum, even though the meaning of the No vote is highly ambiguous.[5] As individuals interested in a future in elected office, their attitude makes political sense; this attitude is also not likely to be reversed for some considerable time to come given the riskiness of ongoing constitutional reform. The second conclusion that seems even clearer to me, and many others,[6] is that the status quo is utterly unacceptable for Aboriginal peoples.[7]

It is difficult to square these two conclusions because Aboriginal peoples, and particularly four of the national Aboriginal organizations – the Assembly of First Nations, the Native Council of Canada, the Inuit Tapirisat of Canada, and the Métis National Council[8] – all looked to the multilateral constitutional process and the Charlottetown Accord for fundamental changes in the status-quo relationship with the governments of Canada in order to improve the Aboriginal situation; a situation that has been described as nothing short of a 'national tragedy.'[9] For many, the Charlottetown Accord was simply the culmination of a long struggle for constitutional reform for Aboriginal peoples that can be traced back to the Trudeau repatriation effort in the late 1970s and even prior to that debate.[10]

After repatriation in 1982, considerable attention was focused by Aboriginal organizations and leaders on constitutional reform. The inclusion of several new provisions in the 1982 Constitution Act, such as the recognition of Aboriginal and treaty rights and the protection of these rights from state wrongdoing in section 35. These new provisions represented a paradigm shift from an era of dispute over the very existence of Aboriginal and treaty rights into the constitutional recognition of a doctrine of Aboriginal and treaty rights.[11] While the concept of Aboriginal and treaty rights was entrenched in the Canadian constitution in 1982, it was seen as nascent and abstract. Intense debate ensued over what these rights entailed, for whom, and how they impacted upon the governance of Canada. This debate has, for the most part, been challenged through litigation; however, this is largely because governments are unwilling to discuss change, implement reforms, or recognize Aboriginal peoples and their governments as distinctive in Canada.

Political intransigence became apparent during the four unsuccessful first ministers' conferences in the 1980s that examined Aboriginal constitutional reform and attempted to give fuller meaning to the abstract recognition of Aboriginal and treaty rights.[12] It was through the vehicle of these conferences and the officials-level preparatory sessions that a more focused agenda was established by the Aboriginal leadership around certain key political issues, like self-government, treaty implementation, gender equality, and equity of rights for all Aboriginal peoples. While these conferences assisted in defining an Aboriginal-driven agenda, and solidified Aboriginal political alliances,[13] they were still abysmal failures in terms of effecting actual change.

The bitterness that resulted from the four failed conferences, the last of which was held in the Spring of 1987 (just months before the Meech Lake Accord 'breakthrough'), left a resolve on the part of the Aboriginal leadership to resist further opposition to Aboriginal and treaty rights and to assert Aboriginal interests strongly in all forums and on every issue. Particularly, on the constitutional front, there was a sense that Aboriginal peoples' constitutional objectives were insignificant national political matters. This perception changed rather abruptly, and some would say effectively,[14] with the Aboriginal campaign against the Meech Lake Accord. The Assembly of Manitoba Chiefs, with the assistance of MLA Elijah Harper, masterminded the now well-known campaign of opposition to the accord's passage through the Manitoba Legislature. This opposition campaign united many Aboriginal people, who saw Elijah Harper, and the chiefs with him, as well positioned to demand that the constitutional reform agenda be expanded to include Aboriginal issues and leaders.

Analysing the Meech Lake experience is critical for an appreciation of what ensued with the Charlottetown round, not only because of the prominence given to Aboriginal issues, but also because of the significant political lessons regarding Aboriginal solidarity and the impact this campaign had on Canadian political leaders. As Chief Louis Stevenson of the Pequis Band in Manitoba had pointed out regarding the impact of Meech Lake on the first ministers, it was 'a humbling experience for the First Ministers because it created an acute awareness that First Nations' concerns in the constitutional process were serious and legitimate.'[15] Unfortunately, a full analysis of these events is beyond my scope here; however, some key impressions emerge from this period. First, from a national-constitutional-reform perspective, Aboriginal peoples and their leadership cannot be left out of the reform process, nor can Aboriginal issues be put aside. Second, in terms of Aboriginal solidarity, Meech Lake demonstrated that campaigns in opposition to Canadian government policies unite Aboriginal people; the Charlottetown Accord demonstrated the opposite – campaigns in tandem with government are difficult to win support for and potentially divisive because of the history of betrayal by the Canadian state. Herein lies a curious double bind that set the stage for interesting intra-Aboriginal political debate during the referendum.

It is important to reflect, and our vision will undoubtedly be clearer with the fullness of time, on Aboriginal participation in the multilateral discussion process, the Aboriginal provisions of the Charlottetown Accord, and the details of the accord's demise. This paper is an attempt at an early analysis of these dimensions of the Charlottetown Accord experience. The process of reflection, and realistic proposals for change, is pressing because it is so clear that the status quo is unacceptable and hurtful for Aboriginal peoples. However, we first have to step back from the Charlottetown round and examine critically the accord and the impact of the 'No' vote. I leave prescriptive analysis of the options post-Charlottetown to others better suited and positioned.[16] My interest here is on situating the accord and its demise within the struggle by Aboriginal peoples for fundamental political change in Canada.

STATUS-QUO RELATIONSHIP

Why are there grave social, economic, and political problems for Aboriginal peoples in Canada? While most Canadians might be familiar with the problems, an understanding of the source or reasons for these problems has not been engendered. One way of understanding matters is to realize that the current situation for Aboriginal peoples in Canada is one of imbalance. This is certainly true at the structural level, when one examines the political relationship between Aboriginal peoples and the Canadian state. As the prefatory quotation from National Chief Ovide Mercredi indicates, First Nations do not have a balance in their relations with Canadian governments or the Canadian people. This imbalance is echoed in Aboriginal communities, where social harmony, a key objective of community life, has deteriorated. It is not only the First Nations that suffer this imbalance; this seems true also for the Métis and for the Inuit. Aboriginal peoples have never been full partners in nation building in Canada. The current relationship envisioned by the Canadian constitution is one of denial of Aboriginal peoples' historical and ongoing presence as distinct peoples in what is now known as Canada.

Aboriginal peoples have been consistently excluded from the nation-building experience in Canada, and have been seen as subject to the authority of the federal government as a head of jurisdiction along with other responsibilities like the postal services and national defence. At the time of Confederation there was no independent recognition of the status or jurisdiction of Aboriginal governments, despite the existence in 1867 of many such governments and of treaties that presumed recognition.[17] Instead of viewing Aboriginal peoples as distinct political entities with the capacity to have a relationship with the Crown and as pre-existing governments in Canada, the Constitution has fundamentally only envisioned the inferiority or wardship of Aboriginal peoples and the superior wisdom and guardianship of the Crown. This imbalance is the very premise of the Indian Act, the comprehensive federal legislation that aims to regulate all aspects of 'Indian' life in Canada. This scheme of administration of 'Indians' in Canada[18] sees the all-powerful minister of Indian Affairs as having final authority over all aspects of the life of 'Indians' – from birth to the disposition of an estate.

Disentangling the unbalanced relationship between Aboriginal peoples and the Canadian state cannot be done unilaterally – the state cannot simply propose change without appreciating that state-driven change is more of the same; that is, more all-knowing Crown control over the lives of Aboriginal peoples. In my view, there is a direct connection between this imbalance and the social, economic, and political problems that Aboriginal peoples face. The Charlottetown Accord round of discussions was the first opportunity, outside of the early treaties,[19] in the history of Canada where change was discussed with Aboriginal peoples, based on Aboriginal ideas for a new relationship. The power imbalance was still there during the Charlottetown round in that Aboriginal organizations were not consenting players in terms of the current constitutional amending formula; however, the act of meeting as equals around a multilateral negotiation table was no small breakthrough when seen against the uniform history of exclusion.

INCLUSION IN THE PROCESS FOR CHANGE

The invitation of Aboriginal representatives to the constitutional-reform discussions in 1992 is a precedent that will stand for years to come. Aboriginal peoples were excluded in the discussions leading up to the passage of the British North America Act; they were excluded during the 1981 negotiations, as well as during the Meech Lake round. Hints of a break from the past were evident in July 1991 when the minister responsible for constitutional affairs, Joe Clark, met with First Nations leaders in Morley, Alberta, and assured them that they would receive funding for their own study of constitutional priorities and options for reform.

Later, when Mr Clark convened a meeting on how to proceed with the constitutional file, on 12 March 1992, his agenda was to canvass his counterparts, the provincial ministers for constitutional affairs, regarding the identifiable options for a consensus-building process geared towards the inclusion of Quebec in the constitutional fabric of Canadian society. The national chief, Ovide Mercredi, and other national Aboriginal leaders had been campaigning vigorously, leading up to 12 March, for the identification of Aboriginal issues in any constitutional-reform process, and for the inclusion of national Aboriginal leaders as direct participants in whatever process was devised. Their arguments were compelling; Aboriginal peoples as the first peoples of Canada should not be excluded from the discussions on the future of their country. Apart from the moral argument, Mr Clark no doubt realized that it was more valuable to have Aboriginal peoples supporting a process than replaying the Meech Lake scenario, with Aboriginal peoples attacking the process, especially in light of opinion polls to this effect.[20] He decided that a different, more inclusive, process was in order, and to that end, he invited the representatives of the territorial governments and those of the four national Aboriginal organizations to the 12 March 1992 meeting in Ottawa.

Following the 12 March meeting, a process was established to attempt to reach a consensus on constitutional reform by early summer 1992. The four

national Aboriginal organizations were full partners in this process and participated in all meetings, at every level, with the exception of two meetings of the
first ministers convened by the prime minister in July at Harrington Lake,[21]
ostensibly to break the impasse on Senate reform and smooth the path for the
entrance of Quebec into the discussions. The officials-level meetings, and the
ministerial and first ministers meetings, were attended by Aboriginal representatives, as were the coordinating meetings of senior government deputies
that set the agenda for the process and reviewed pace and progress weekly.

The access to the multilateral forum for the discussion and resolution of
outstanding Aboriginal grievances was extremely significant. During the six-
teen-week process, the acceptance of Aboriginal and treaty rights developed a
momentum that was played off strategically against the enthusiasm of the
ministers and first ministers for an agreement. The Aboriginal leadership stick-
handled this opening brilliantly by coming up the middle and insisting on the
redress of the long-standing grievances that Aboriginal peoples have against
the Canadian state. The only concern, in hindsight, is that the frenetic pace of
the process with intense media attention on every advance towards consensus
on Aboriginal issues may have saturated public interest in the agenda or acted
as a catharsis, purging the concern that, according to the opinion polls, Canadians felt about Aboriginal peoples. This possibility is worrisome, because all the
efforts have led, at this point, to no political change, and public concern and
political interest are required to move forward in the months and years ahead
with the Charlottetown lesson behind us.

One other significant structural advance in the multilateral process was the
appointment of an Aboriginal co-chair in Working Group III – the multilateral
working group of officials assigned to develop positions and draft amendments
on Aboriginal issues. Neil Sterrit, a Gitskan hereditary chief and well-known
First Nations leader from British Columbia, acted as co-chair of Working
Group III along with a federal and provincial chair. His participation at this
level was an important symbolic statement of inclusion. Moreover, his insights
into moving the process ahead and working towards consensus were important
for the ultimate agreement that was reached in the process.

The structure of the multilateral process allowed for Aboriginal participation
in the organizational and coordinating functions that increased the profile of
Aboriginal issues and a familiarity with a process heretofore alien to the Aboriginal organizations. Another remarkable aspect of this new participation was
the extent to which Aboriginal organizations quickly became immersed in the
process and were able to work within it as if they had been participating in
these kinds of discussions all along. Their adaptability to the process and its
vicissitudes demonstrated that these organizations can indeed function in intergovernmental forums like their provincial and federal counterparts. After all,

familiarity with intertribal alliances and processes has made these organizations adept in complex multiparty discussions like the Charlottetown round. However, to say they 'adapted' to the process is to downplay and shortchange their contributions in making this round of discussions different from other ones.[22] The Aboriginal leadership spoke for Canada, their homeland, and they spoke from a perspective of living close to the land. This introduced a different vision in a process that was preoccupied with power and money.

One further point is worthy of note, because it was pivotal to the success of Aboriginal organizations in advancing the agenda as far as they were able. Several months into the mulitlateral process, the discussions at the working-group level were becoming stagnated with fairly rigid and irreconcilable extreme positions playing themselves out repeatedly. The representatives of the Aboriginal delegations felt that many of the bureaucrats assigned to the working groups were overly cautious, conservative, and unsympathetic to our aspirations. They appeared to be assigned the 'dirty work' of opposing Aboriginal and treaty rights, which the politicians wanted little part of in the ministerial-level meetings. Of course, not all officials were in this camp. There were certainly exceptions from those provinces that had publicly supported Aboriginal peoples' demands for the recognition of the inherent right of self-government.[23]

The frustration over the working group's intransigence reared its head at the political level when the ministers met in Edmonton in April.[24] As a result of an intervention by Ovide Mercredi, who expressed his frustrations to the chair about working-group-level difficulties, it was agreed that the discussions at that level would shift to Aboriginal-proposed drafts and Aboriginal-driven priorities. This was a turning-point in the multilateral process, because after April, Aboriginal delegations were able to redirect the attention of the working group, and in turn the ministers, to their priorities, drafts, and approaches. This allowed for a change in orientation of the officials' meetings and the eventual consensus around Aboriginal drafts and concepts, which would have otherwise been discarded, overlooked, or filibustered out of the working group. In my opinion, this reclaiming of the process in the interests of Aboriginal priorities and drafts was central for the relative success of the Charlottetown round in embracing many fundamental principles for a new relationship between governments and Aboriginal peoples in Canada.

While inclusion had a price for Aboriginal political organizations in terms of the suspicion of the constituents of those organizations who looked with concern to any agreement reached with government, it was pivotal in achieving the acceptance of many ideas that would have been flatly rejected had the organizations not been there to insist the ideas be kept on the table or to protest their elimination from the agenda. The inherent right of self-government, treaties, and many other issues were kept alive in the process through the sheer will of the Aboriginal representatives, who refused to allow them to fall off the agenda and controlled the agenda by turning around the process at critical points, such as at the Edmonton meeting. I can attest to the fact that many issues that we raised in the process were the subject of outright ridicule when they were introduced as agenda items.[25] Yet the fact that they survived the arduous battle of negotiation to emerge, albeit transformed in significant ways, in the consensus document is a testament to the successes that Aboriginal organizations achieved in making the process work for them.

THE CHARLOTTETOWN ACCORD: ITS VISION FOR CHANGE

The Charlottetown Accord is a vast document. As a participant in the development of the accord at all stages from early debate through to the drafting of the legal text, I have at times found myself unable to keep track of its contents, which seemed to branch out into so many aspects of the Canadian political structure. This complexity was identified by some as one of the accord's fatal flaws during the referendum campaign: it was too much, too fast, for Canadians, who are fundamentally conservative and measured in their disposition towards new political concepts and change. It is certainly true that the accord was too large. However, this is the nature of constitutional bargain making after Meech Lake, where the criticism was that Quebec cannot be accommodated to the exclusion of other provinces, peoples, and issues. Just the Aboriginal portion of the Charlottetown Accord was itself broad and far-sweeping. It was the largest package of proposals for reform on Aboriginal issues in the history of Canada. Its scope reflected the fact that so much had been neglected for so long, that to begin to reverse the situation required considerable amendment and agreement, and the charting of a different course.

I want to touch upon the key elements of the accord, because I believe these elements will remain the benchmark for some time to come, if not the bottom line for future discussions. While many criticized the accord, including Aboriginal peoples, its vision for change largely reflected the proposals that Aboriginal peoples had been advancing in Canada for twenty years, and thus it deserves serious attention. The problems with the accord, at least for Aboriginal peoples, stemmed from the concessions that the federal and provincial governments insisted upon during the final stages of the process for the sake of agreement. These concessions were painful during the negotiation process and were often motivated by what I could only describe as mean-spirited objections to self-government, based on stereotypes about Aboriginal peoples as peoples without the sophistication to govern themselves.[26] The Aboriginal leadership –

despite their indefatigable will and political savvy in the process – were only able to advance the agenda to a certain point in the face of enormous opposition and reluctance to move forward on the part of many Canadian politicians. The question for Aboriginal leaders became, then, whether the gains made in Charlottetown were enough for Aboriginal peoples or whether they were too restricted.

For the sake of my analysis, I want to review four main areas that formed the basis of the Aboriginal package: (a) the inherent right of self-government; (b) treaty rights; (c) recognition of the status and rights of Aboriginal peoples; and (d) Aboriginal consent and amending-formula changes. I can only provide an overview here of the contents of the accord and the dynamics of its formation and emphasize that more careful evaluation is needed to address our real and ongoing problems.

Inherent Right of Self-government

The proposal to entrench a provision that would recognize the inherent right of self-government within Canada was the main breakthrough in the Consensus agreement and the entire Charlottetown round. Leading up to the consensus on the accord, there was much debate over whether or not the right of self-government should be recognized as inherent (pre-existing and not granted by the Constitution) and also whether it should be specifically limited in the text or by subsequent negotiation. In February 1992, the Royal Commission on Aboriginal Peoples released a report on self-government[27] that bolstered the suggestions by Aboriginal organizations that the right be recognized as an inherent one. The Commission suggested:

[T]he term 'inherent' has important practical implications. By clearly identifying the source and nature of the right, it gives courts and other interested parties a strong mandate to implement the right and significant guidance on how to interpret it. The term indicates that the right does not consist of something 'granted' by the Federal and Provincial government, as such it minimizes the significance of governmental intentions as a guide to interpretation. It also highlights the fact that the right of self-government should be understood in the light of the living cultures and traditions of Aboriginal peoples, as well as their contemporary outlooks. Since these traditions are multiple and diverse, the right may well assume different shapes in the various Aboriginal nations.[28]

While this statement was helpful, the battle for the acknowledgment of the right as an inherent one was fought at every meeting, either through explicit rejection of the idea of a pre-existing right or through the demand for limits to be placed on the recognition of the right to suit provincial governments. In the end, the consensus agreement embraced the notion of inherency, but made the inherent right of self-government subject to three key limitations: it was to be 'within Canada,' subject to federal and provincial laws in the interest of peace, order, and good government, and subject to a provision that no new land rights would be created by implication. These demands were insisted upon, respectively, by the premiers of Alberta, Newfoundland, and Quebec.

The breakthrough on the inherent right of self-government came with these limitations because the Aboriginal leadership could push the politicians no further than this point. Each of these limitations was debated extensively, with repeated pleas by the Aboriginal leadership to eliminate such restrictions. The leadership knew these limitations would prove to be troublesome to their members, who were already suspicious of governmental goodwill given the trickery of the past. They had continually to evaluate how worthwhile the Aboriginal package was in potentially recommending it to their constituency. This process of ongoing evaluation was difficult, given that trade-offs were not attractive, yet the accord represented a moment of acceptance, albeit partial, of Aboriginal rights that the leadership saw would not soon be repeated in Canada. The question the leadership faced, like that faced by all social reformers, was whether significant although incomplete change was better than none.

For example, one area that caused First Nations grave concern was the restriction on self-government to the effect that these provisions were not to be construed as creating new land rights. This provision was added at the request of the premier of Quebec, who believed self-government in Quebec would not 'sell' because Quebeckers are nervous about the status of Cree and Inuit territories in northern Quebec; specifically, Quebec did not want to act to bolster Aboriginal territorial claims. While this might not be a profound restriction from a crafty legal viewpoint, because it recognizes existing land rights that are arguably extensive, politically it was hard for Aboriginal leaders to endorse. For Aboriginal peoples who are stuck on undersized reserves, have no land base, or are without access to their traditional territories, the notion of a provision explicitly stating there would be no new land rights was enough for an immediate rejection of the package.

Another practical limitation placed on the inherent right of self-government by the Canadian politicians concerned financing. The Aboriginal organizations, and the Assembly of First Nations particularly, advocated a financing provision modelled on section 36 of the Constitution Act, 1982, which provides for equalization payments. A constitutionalized standard for funding was considered essential because otherwise Aboriginal governments would not be able to function. When one looks at the deficiencies in basic infrastructure in Aboriginal communities (such as sewers, water, roads), one can see why the leadership had to press hard for a constitutionalized standard; self-government on paper is no advance without the resources to make it a reality. The leadership was worried that, without resources, self-government could simply mean the Aboriginal peoples administering their own misery in the same manner as under the Indian Act. Despite four lengthy and heated pleas for a constitutional standard for financing, the Aboriginal leadership, spearheaded by National Chief Ovide Mercredi, could not get the federal government or the provinces to budge on financing. This failure was particularly ironic because, on one occasion at least, the item was raised for discussion just after section 36 had been strengthened to assure 'have-not' provinces that the standards for equalization payments could be reviewed to ensure they were fair. Yet when the discussion turned to Aboriginal financing – for those who are the poorest of the poor in Canada – governments advocating stronger protection for their interests as 'have-not' provinces had no time for the notion of financing Aboriginal governments to protect against poverty and disadvantage.[29]

In addition to recognizing the inherent right of self-government, the Charlottetown Accord included what was called a 'contextual statement,' which set out to define or situate the right in terms of its purposes. This statement, which was developed by the Assembly of First Nations, was a compromise position that was accepted instead of either conceding that the right was unlimited in terms of the scope of powers Aboriginal governments enjoy or agreeing on a restrictive list of powers for the right that may not be suitable for all Aboriginal peoples. Neither of these options was feasible in light of the negotiations, and a contextual statement was devised to mediate the two extremes and effect an agreement.

It is worth reproducing the contextual statement in its entirety because it captures the spirit of the aspirations of Aboriginal peoples for the recognition of their identity and governments as distinctive within Canada:

35.1
(3) The exercise of the [inherent] right [of self-government] includes the authority of duly constituted legislative bodies of the Aboriginal peoples, each within its own jurisdiction,
  (a) to safeguard and develop their languages, cultures, economies, identities, institutions and traditions, and
  (b) to develop, maintain and strengthen their relationship with their lands, waters and environment,
so as to determine and control their development as peoples according to their own values and priorities and to ensure the integrity of their societies.[30]

The contextual statement was an interesting compromise provision because it was potentially expansive for Aboriginal peoples, yet provided a framework for the negotiation of agreements on self-government with particular Aboriginal peoples that could be sensitive to their situation. This was a key challenge: designing provisions that would meet the varied needs of Aboriginal peoples without restricting the rights of some Aboriginal peoples at the expense of others. A mechanism for flexibility was required, yet complete open-endedness in the recognition of the right was not politically possible.[31] The fact that this contextual statement would be used for negotiating specific agreements, or treaties, with Aboriginal peoples was emphasized through the addition of a five-year delay period before the contextual statement or the inherent right would become justiciable.

The Charlottetown Accord also proposed to recognize Aboriginal governments as one of three orders of government in Canada. This was another important advance, championed by the Inuit leadership, because it recognized that Aboriginal governments were sovereign in their spheres of jurisdiction and not simply subject to the federal or provincial governments. This recognition was difficult for many governments because they believed that the creation of a 'third level'[32] of government in Canada meant too much government in an era of reducing bureaucracy and circumscribing state structures. However, what many neglected to realize was that Aboriginal governments are already one of three orders of government, although unrecognized in the formal constitutional structure of Canada. Recognizing three orders of government served to ensure that the Indian Act style of domination would be left behind, not retrenched.

The Interpretation of Treaties and Treaty Rights

A significant problem for First Nations stems in particular from the fact that many treaty grievances have accumulated since the seventeenth century that have never been honourably addressed by the Crown. There are several hundred treaties with First Nations from before Confederation up to more recent agreements on land claims (such as the Inuvialuit Final Agreement in the Western Arctic or, more recently, Nunavut). Treaty grievances are numerous and diverse, from outright fraud in the negotiation process to failure to implement the terms of the treaties. It was extremely difficult to advance new concepts and foster a new relationship between Aboriginal peoples and the Canadian state during the Charlottetown process when the history of such relations, as demonstrated through the treaty-making process, was shameful. The Canadian government has seldom acted honourably with respect to its treaty responsibilities and the First Nations are all too aware of the track record on this front.

The Assembly of First Nations insisted upon and eventually obtained a commitment to include a provision requiring that treaty rights be interpreted in a 'just, broad and liberal manner taking into account the spirit and intent of the treaties.' Along with this provision was a commitment to establish a process with the Crown to clarify, implement, or rectify the terms of the treaties when requested to do so by the treaty First Nation concerned. This was to be a bilateral process, with provincial involvement only when invited by both parties. The treaty provisions could have extended to new treaties entered into on the basis of the self-government provisions, depending on the specific terms of those treaties.

The treaty provisions can be seen as a way of dealing with historic problems before embarking on new relations that are premised on the inherent right of self-government. Also, for many First Nations, their treaties are seen as the basis for self-government discussions. These treaty provisions invoke complex political issues internal to Aboriginal organizations like the Assembly of First Nations; many First Nations rightly maintain that the treaties are premised on a nation-to-nation relationship with the federal government and that the entrenchment of the right to self-government in the Constitution should not undermine or compromise the spirit or nature of that relationship. The difficulty is that, while the treaties were entered into with the federal Crown (or the Crown in right of Great Britain), the treaty grievances cannot be resolved now without some provincial involvement. For example, section 109 of the Constitution Act, 1867 gives responsibility to the provinces for lands and many treaty grievances stem from promised land transfers that have never been realized. It is not politically, or even constitutionally, possible, in a decentralized Canadian state in 1992, to deal with these issues without the provinces, unless First Nations are prepared to limit negotiations to inadequate reserve lands rather than their expansive traditional territories, which have now been transferred to the provinces. Provincial involvement was optional in the proposed provisions, but clearly there were political problems brewing because of the suggestion that this could even be an option.

Moreover, there was a concern on the part of some First Nations that the provisions would 'domesticate' the treaties or take them out of an international dimension. This is another complex aspect of First Nations treaties that is not well understood. The treaties, as currently determined by Canadian courts, are not recognized as international treaties. Instead they are viewed as being somewhere between contracts and international treaties, with a status that is termed 'sui generis.' First Nations maintain that they are international in character. However, little careful analysis has been done on the consequences of formal recognition of the treaties as international; for instance, they might be easily voided under international legal instruments like the Vienna Convention on the

Law of Treaties and could benefit from additional safeguards in Canada's constitution.[33] The Charlottetown Accord provisions called for the recognition of unique rules in Canada for the interpretation of treaties to avoid such consequences and to elevate treaty rights to a higher standard of recognition in Canadian law.

Recognition of the Status and Rights of Aboriginal Peoples

The Canada Clause included a recognition that the Aboriginal peoples, as 'the first peoples to govern this land, have the right to promote their languages, cultures and traditions and to ensure the integrity of their societies, and their governments constitute one of three orders of government in Canada.' This statement, coupled with the recognition in the contextual clause of Aboriginal peoples' right to 'determine and control their development as peoples according to their own values and priorities and ensure the integrity of their societies,' represented, in my opinion, a significant break with the past recognition of the status of Aboriginal peoples and their rights. The Canada Clause was largely symbolic – despite the enormous attention it attracted during the referendum campaign – and, comparatively, of lesser legal consequence as simply an interpretive provision. Nevertheless, this acknowledgment that Aboriginal peoples were the first to govern Canada and have the right to ensure the integrity of their societies is a recognition that Aboriginal peoples themselves have a power and authority in their hands to ensure their identity is preserved and their status as distinct peoples accepted as part of Canada without expecting them to assimilate.[34] While many suggest this is a pre-existing historical situation, the formal recognition was clearly pathbreaking.

The parallel recognition, in the Canada Clause, of respect for the individual and collective rights of all people was also critical for Aboriginal peoples, whose rights are essentially collective in nature: they are the rights of peoples. In addition, the Canada Clause included protection from any negative impact the distinct-society provision for Quebec could have on Aboriginal peoples in the Province of Quebec.[35] These provisions, taken together, would have had the effect of elevating the status and rights of Aboriginal peoples in Canadian society because they are relevant to the whole of the Constitution of Canada.

Aboriginal Consent and the Amending Formula

The amending formula introduced in the Constitution Act, 1982 did not require Aboriginal consent. It did call for the four 1980s constitutional conferences on

Aboriginal rights, but not for Aboriginal consent to reform the Canadian constitution.[36] One of the key demands made by the Aboriginal organizations was for their consent to be required for future amendments to provisions that referred to Aboriginal peoples or for the addition of new provisions affecting these sections. Gaining the amending-formula position was a long shot, because it required unanimity among all parties and hence could easily be weakened or dropped off the table. However, Aboriginal leaders were successful in obtaining a commitment for devising a formula for Aboriginal consent and then having this made part of the Charlottetown package.

It would make perfect sense that as a third order of government, Aboriginal peoples should consent to amendments that affect or mention them. Otherwise, the old wardship notion is continued, whereby it is presumed that another level of government can act for you, or that you are for some reason unable to act for yourself. The inclusion of Aboriginal consent in the amending formula, although complex in its details, would have truly completed the circle of Confederation by appropriately recognizing that Aboriginal peoples are full partners in the federal structure of Canada and not simply 'minorities' or 'special interest groups.'[37]

Other Provisions of the Accord

There are a few other provisions of the Charlottetown Accord that are important to note. The recognition of seats for Aboriginal senators, the acceptance of 'equity of access' or the equal access to Aboriginal rights by all Aboriginal peoples, and the provision for the conclusion of a Métis accord to deal with the historical grievances of the Métis people were all important facets of the accord. In addition, the fascinating proposal that the federal government examine with Aboriginal groups an Aboriginal Council of Elders, which could make submissions to the Supreme Court of Canada when it considers Aboriginal issues, could greatly assist in the dominant society's understanding of Aboriginal peoples' conflicts with the Canadian state.

The final truly critical breakthrough, I believe, was the acceptance of a provision[38] that would ensure that any redistributions of power between the federal and provincial governments could not diminish Aboriginal or treaty rights, the federal fiduciary responsibility for Aboriginal peoples, or the jurisdictions or rights of Aboriginal governments. This provision also allowed for protection from redistributions that could affect language, culture, or traditions, and so would safeguard First Nations from the transfer of responsibility for culture to the provinces, especially where cultural policies could undermine Aboriginal practices and traditions.

OPPOSITION TO THE ABORIGINAL PACKAGE OF
THE CHARLOTTETOWN ACCORD

The opposition to the Aboriginal package, and in particular to the inherent right of self-government, was arguably minor in relation to the sum total of issues the 'No campaign' targeted during the referendum debate on the Charlottetown Accord. [39] However, Aboriginal issues were seized upon by the print and electronic media, which had been accused of being too uncritical regarding Aboriginal aspirations in the period leading up to the accord.[40] For the purposes of my analysis, I want to review the areas of opposition and assess how significant they were, and why, and what messages they convey for future discussions regarding Aboriginal and treaty rights.

One can characterize the opposition to the Aboriginal package as gravitating around four more or less distinct themes, although these cut across party and other allegiances into a strange conglomerate of opponents.[41] These four themes are (a) the exclusion of Native Women's Association of Canada and gender-equality concerns; (b) the hostility to collective rights in a liberal conception of Canadian society; (c) the fear of ongoing constitutional negotiation with and financing for a third level of government; and (d) Aboriginal distrust of Canadian governments and Aboriginal nationalism. I want to consider each theme in turn, then revisit the entire opposition and its significance for future discussions of the options for changing the political status quo for Aboriginal peoples.

*Exclusion of Native Women's Association of Canada and
Gender-Equality Concerns*

The Native Women's Association of Canada, supported by some First Nations women[42] and non-Aboriginal women and men, raised an objection early in the process to the fact that the Native Women's Association of Canada was not invited by the prime minister or the minister for constitutional affairs to join the four national Aboriginal organizations at the table. The Native Women's Association of Canada waged a high-profile campaign of opposition to the Accord, including litigation to stop funding to Aboriginal organizations and to stop the referendum, because they argued that they had been excluded and their rights were threatened. It is important to note here that none of the national-level Aboriginal women's associations was invited by the prime minister, including the other three – the Inuit Women's Association (Pauktutit), the Métis Women's Association, and the Professional Native Women's Association.[43] Many did not realize that the Native Women's Association is not the only national Aboriginal women's organization.

While the Native Women's Association protested its absence from the invitation list, it had participated through the Assembly of First Nations' and the Native Council of Canada's internal political and technical processes. It is accurate to say that they did not participate directly by speaking in their own seat at the table. The Inuit Women's Association participated through the Inuit Tapirisat of Canada and the Métis women through the Métis National Council. The Native Women's Association suggested that the four national organizations did not represent the interests of women, and they were successful in bringing arguments before the Federal Court of Appeal to the effect that their freedom-of-expression rights under the Canadian Charter of Rights and Freedoms were compromised by the fact that they were not invited to the table.[44] The Court did not agree that their gender-equality rights were infringed through their absence at the table. They were not joined in their litigation efforts by the other three Aboriginal women's organizations.

The opposition campaign by the Native Women's Association of Canada was interesting because it garnered support from non-Aboriginal women's organizations, like the National Action Committee and the leaders of the Women's Legal Education Action Fund (LEAF). It also gathered support from unlikely sources, like Preston Manning of the Reform party. While this campaign was initially waged as expressing a concern for gender equality and self-government, its key point was that without the Native Women's Association of Canada at the table, Aboriginal women's interests would be compromised. Although it is clear that the Native Women's Association of Canada did have a particular approach to self-government that differed from other organizations, they are not the only organization to represent Aboriginal women. Moreover, it is not clear that the four national Aboriginal organizations would simply act in a hostile fashion towards the interests of women.

Given that the Inuit Tapirisat of Canada is headed by two Inuit women known for their advocacy for Aboriginal women,[45] this latter belief is somewhat difficult to accept. Moreover, the Assembly of First Nations, with prominent women like Vice-Chief Wendy Grant of British Columbia in their delegation, also felt they could speak for the Aboriginal women they represent through their chiefs and councils. The issue was not whether Aboriginal women participated in the process, but whether those who participated represented the views that the Native Women's Association advocated. On this latter point, they probably did not. The views of the Native Women's Association of Canada are legitimate and should have been included as one of many perspectives offered from the Aboriginal side of the table. However, the Native Women's Association cannot be said to have the monopoly on representing the views of Aboriginal women; they are just one of the national organizations and some of their own sister organizations, like the Ontario Native Women's Association (their largest affiliate), did support the accord and the multilateral process.

With respect to gender equality, there were concerns raised by the Native Women's Association of Canada about drafts of the self-government provisions in the accord leaked to them. They viewed these drafts as allowing Aboriginal governments to operate outside the Charter of Rights and Freedoms and as a licence to undermine the rights of women. This argument was again a complex one, although it proved to be based on incomplete texts and particular interpretations of worst-case scenarios. The final text did include a provision on gender equality providing that all Aboriginal and treaty rights, including the right of self-government, would be guaranteed equally to male and female persons. In addition, the Charter was to be specifically amended to apply to the governments of Aboriginal peoples. However, the fear raised of Aboriginal governments acting to undermine the rights of women were just what many opponents of self-government loved to hear, especially coming directly from Aboriginal people.

Aboriginal women in Canada have been discriminated against by the Canadian state through the Indian Act, and in some cases this treatment has been carried over into Aboriginal communities, which have continued a practice imposed upon them by the federal government.[46] However, getting out from under these discriminatory practices may only be possible through a transition to self-government. It is the Canadian state that has attempted to inculcate in Aboriginal peoples that patriarchy is the ideology of the civilized. Not the other way around. Gender-equality concerns are legitimate, but they are interwoven with cultural and racial oppression that has been imposed upon Aboriginal peoples. To see only the gender aspect is, unfortunately, to miss the bigger picture of just how do we get out of this oppression that has been the legacy of Canadian dominance of Aboriginal peoples. Also, to insist on the same ideas of gender equality in Aboriginal society as may pertain in Canadian society is another form of dominance, in my view, when many Aboriginal systems demand a much more central role for women than in mainstream government.[47]

The gender issues are aspects of inter-Aboriginal disputes that have been fostered by the federal government but obviously have to be resolved through more internal discussion, cooperation, and change. However, the extent to which gender-equality concerns were focused upon by non-Aboriginal people during the campaign raises a different point for me. The level of scrutiny of Aboriginal governments and the expectations of perfection by non-Aboriginals in all aspects of governance is so outrageous that no Aboriginal government would ever satisfy these expectations; expectations that are based in many instances on non-Aboriginal views of the relations between men and women in Aboriginal communities.

Beyond this, the problem is simply that to address gender-equality issues properly, Aboriginal authority over community relations is required. For example, Band councils can do little about the unfairness in matrimonial property distribution issues caused by the Indian Act, which primarily recognizes male occupation of the home on an Indian reserve. First Nations authority, in a self-government context, could address this issue. Nevertheless, the referendum debate suggests that Aboriginal communities are being told they cannot have that authority until they prove they can conform to the dominant society's ideals. This is a clear double standard, since Canadian governments govern despite the fact that the ideals of gender equality, Charter protection, and social justice for all are far from realized in the dominant society. Underlying this opposition to self-government is an expectation that Aboriginal peoples must perfect their societies before they will be 'permitted' to govern and that, prior to that point, the far-from-perfect dominant society is entitled to control Aboriginal communities.

Hostility to Collective Rights in the Liberal Concept of Canadian Society

The second front of attack on the Aboriginal package in the accord, which dovetails with the first to a large extent, was rooted in a rejection of any possible differences in the operation of the Canadian Charter of Rights and Freedoms vis-à-vis Aboriginal peoples' governments based on presumptions about the equality of everyone in Canadian society. Aboriginal organizations, and especially First Nations leaders, had argued for some time that the Charter does not represent their value systems because it does not embrace social and economic justice, nor does the litigation style of rights redress suit their history and traditions. The Charter, with its preface recognizing the supremacy of God and its emphasis on individual rights instead of individual responsibilities (a First Nations approach) was always rejected by First Nations. It was developed without First Nations input in 1981 and over objections to concepts and principles that were either too limited for Aboriginal communities or just outside their traditions and cultures (for instance, the model of taking human-rights disputes to court instead of to Elders or using other dispute-resolution processes that are traditionally part of an Aboriginal community).

However, First Nations concerns about the Charter were summarily dismissed by those with little apparent familiarity with Aboriginal peoples, their traditions, or their cultures, who, from their vantage points in Toronto and other major urban centres, believed they knew what was best for Aboriginal peoples. They opposed the accord because they interpreted it as potentially allowing Aboriginal governments to operate under standards different than those of the Charter.[48] As Professor Lorraine Weinrib of the University of Toronto Faculty of Law boldly suggested: 'We reject the idea, put forward by some members of the Aboriginal community, that the *Charter* would impose foreign ideas on the new Aboriginal order of governments. The *Charter* reflects ideas of individual dignity now accepted by a large variety of countries, many of which are neither Western nor white.'[49] To say that the Charter accepts or reinforces individual dignity and is the only way this principle is assured is hardly supportable, and is indeed ignorant of the customs, traditions, and approaches that Aboriginal peoples bring to self-governance.

Professor Weinrib gives no indication of why the Charter is other than culturally foreign, or why imposing such a law on Aboriginal peoples without their consent should be accepted as legitimate. One would presume that she, and others who advanced this argument, would oppose male-imposed views of how women should behave; yet she does not oppose non-Aboriginal peoples imposing their views on Aboriginal peoples as to how they should behave. Indeed, her point on non-Western and non-white acceptance of Charter ideas is simply untrue, given that many non-Western countries and peoples have advocated very different human-rights standards and that specific instruments to this effect have been adopted (for instance, the Banjul Charter on African and Peoples' Rights).[50]

The Charter-based opposition focused on a variety of issues, including gender equality, democratic rights, and the potential use by Aboriginal governments of the notwithstanding clause to except certain legislative acts from Charter scrutiny. On the latter point, the double standard was again present – non-Aboriginal governments could have a notwithstanding clause, but Aboriginal governments could not because they couldn't be trusted with it. In my view, much of this opposition to the Aboriginal package was premised on an unworkable liberal conception of equality in a pluralistic democratic society. It was argued, rather vehemently, that any 'special' rights for Aboriginal peoples would undermine the basic equality of all persons in society. As former prime minister Trudeau suggested in his Maison du Egg Roll speech on 1 October 1992, 'When each citizen is not equal to all other citizens in the state, we are faced with a dictatorship, which arranges citizens in a hierarchy according to their beliefs.'[51] The problem with Mr Trudeau's conception is that all individuals are not in fact equal in Canadian society; there is a hierarchy of privilege that has been created precisely because of this concept of equality. Moreover, if equality is the goal, what or who is the benchmark for that equality – the white English-speaking Christian male? Must we all be equal to this standard?

This concept of equality is not worthy of support. As Justice Rosalie Abella observed in her capacity as commissioner in *Equality in Employment: A Royal Commission Report*:

Sometimes equality means treating people the same, despite their differences, and sometimes it means treating them as equals by accommodating their differences. Formerly, we thought that equality only meant sameness and that treating persons as equals meant treating everyone the same. We now know that to treat everyone the same may be to offend the notion of equality ... Ignoring differences and refusing to accommodate them is a denial of equal access and opportunity. It is discrimination ... To create equality of opportunity we have to do different things for different people. We have to systematically eradicate the impediments to these options according to the actual needs of the different groups, not according to what we think their needs should be.[52]

For Aboriginal peoples, it is the imposition of policies based on what others believed the needs of Aboriginal peoples were that has caused such intolerable oppression and abuse. Whether it was the government bureaucrat who decides Aboriginal peoples need education at residential schools, or the politician who decides Aboriginal peoples should assimilate, this has been the basic approach of the Canadian state. This is an experience we want to end, not retrench.

The hostility that people like Trudeau, and those who share his views,[53] demonstrated to collective rights is also worthy of note. They suggested that any acceptance of collective rights could eventually lead to the tyranny of the majority and the elimination of individual rights. He stated that 'the theory of collective rights is a dangerous one. Larger and smaller collectivities confront each other in the heart of one and the same country, and that can lead eventually to civil wars. That's what collective rights are all about.'[54] The distinction between collective and individual is erroneous. We participate in social life as part of collectivities *and* as individuals – these are abstract categories that do not capture the rich texture of social existence; they are metaphors manipulated to frighten people into opposing the accord.

I can write this paper because we share a collective language that allows me to express myself – this is not tyrannical, but a fact of social life. I may have other languages in addition that would exclude this audience but include another collectivity. This is part of being different – experiencing different cultural and linguistic realities and world-views. The pleas for collective rights by Aboriginal peoples are about allowing for decision-making power in the hands of Aboriginal peoples over their own lives instead of subjecting them as 'equal Canadians' to a Canadian state that will not represent their interests, either because of their small numbers or because of the differences in language, culture, and traditions. Interestingly, Trudeau suggested that he had already identified the answer to Aboriginal peoples' problems when, in 1969, he introduced a white paper calling for the end to the Indian Act and the assimilation of Aboriginal peoples as equals into the Canadian state.[55] It was this paper, and the Aboriginal outrage that it unleashed, that led to the formation of national Aboriginal political organizations. So Trudeau can only take credit for shocking Aboriginal peoples into action years ago – not for finding answers.

The equality-for-all argument, coupled with concerns about hierarchies of rights, are, in my view, empty yet troubling strains of opposition to Aboriginal peoples' status and rights in Canadian society. They were powerfully appealing to the public, as suspicion that some Canadians would not be equal to others was effective for the opposition campaign during the referendum debate. These concerns will endure because a discourse was created during the referendum campaign that will be with us for some time to come. This is a worrisome after-effect of the referendum.

Ongoing Negotiation and Financing of a Third Order
of Aboriginal Governments

A third line of opposition to the Aboriginal package stressed the fact that the framework put in place by the accord did not define the right of self-government sufficiently and that ongoing negotiations would be required. Those in the Reform party especially seized upon this fact and suggested that the accord would lead to an endless series of negotiations and meetings, and be a drain on taxpayers' money. This final point was surprising, because many concerns were raised about how much self-government would cost, yet there was not even a guarantee of funding in the accord itself. Nevertheless, these concerns were successfully brought forward and appealed to many who worried about the expense of the Charlottetown round and the future costs of what they were told would be an undefined 'new' order of government.

What was not mentioned in this opposition was the fact that Aboriginal self-government is pre-existing, even if it has been unrecognized in the Canadian Constitution since Confederation. Of course implementation of the right to self-government is complicated and will take time to work out through negotiations. Canada includes many different Aboriginal peoples who have not been made full partners in the governance of the nation. Constitutional negotiations on funding agreements and transfers of responsibility are conducted every year between federal and provincial governments on many matters. Full Aboriginal self-government cannot happen overnight. Moreover, on the issue of financing, it is disturbing to hear suggestions that Aboriginal self-government is too expensive when Canada itself is the Aboriginal peoples' homeland, and Aboriginal lands have for the most part been taken through outright theft, sharp dealings, and exploitation. To turn around and suggest that self-government would be too expensive, when Canada's wealth as a nation has been made on the backs of Aboriginal peoples, is historical denial hardly worthy of a response.

Aboriginal Distrust of Canadian Governments and Aboriginal Nationalism

The final kind of opposition to the Charlottetown Accord was perhaps the most difficult for Canadians to understand. Within Aboriginal organizations, particularly the Native Council of Canada and the Assembly of First Nations, there were pockets of concern about the generosity of the Charlottetown Accord. Even though these concerns may have been those of a minority of the total Aboriginal population in Canada, or even of the participants who had been part of the Aboriginal delegations, they were substantial factors in affecting both the Aboriginal and non-Aboriginal attitude towards the accord. These concerns will be reviewed below as they pertain to the actual referendum; however, politically they are more deeply rooted than simply being a reaction to the accord.

There is a vicious circle in the experience of Aboriginal peoples with the Canadian state. The state cannot be trusted because of the wrongdoings of the past and present, yet it is the state that must change its orientation before Aboriginal communities can assume greater responsibility for their lives and peoples. However, the state cannot be turned around overnight. How much change is needed, in what areas, and through what mechanisms? These issues are so basic to the movement for political change, yet they have been the subject of national debate and attention only recently in the Aboriginal community. Even still, the pressing immediate problems of daily survival are such that little concentrated attention can be placed on such large (and often abstract) questions like constitutional reform.

Alongside these developments stands a discourse of Aboriginal nationalism that is significant in shaping the Aboriginal reaction to political change. Aboriginal peoples have developed, since 1969, stronger movements in opposition to government policies, actions, and proposals. However, the level of rapprochement between the government and Aboriginal peoples is minimal. In many instances, there is no trust of Canadian governments, so there can be no real bridges built and no policies jointly supported. Discussions are barely possible, let alone useful. This situation has even spilled over into Aboriginal communities where the Indian Act governs; Aboriginal peoples have no trust or faith in their governments set up under this act. This makes for a vicious circle of conflict out of which it is difficult to break. When Aboriginal peoples examined the accord and considered some of the restrictions on self-government, they rejected the proposals because they felt it did not offer them enough. The promising aspects of the accord were viewed with suspicion, because Aboriginal peoples are aware of the government's poor track record.

This situation is compounded by the fact that Aboriginal peoples are diverse and are not politically organized into a system of party discipline where one approach or philosophy predominates. In fact, consensus decision making is such that many views are expressed, without censure, and the final direction arises from a long and patient process of expressing different viewpoints.

Indeed, consensus decision making encourages opposing viewpoints. The process is even more involved when one considers that there are so many different peoples and languages that must figure into the national discussion process on Aboriginal political change. These factors were relevant during the Charlottetown process, because many failed to realize that the Aboriginal leadership and decision-making process does not operate in the same way as do provincial premiers or the prime minister, in closed discussions with their cabinet colleagues and assembly representatives. Many expected Aboriginal peoples to be of one view on the accord, but this expectation was impossible and not reasonable. Canadians did not fully understand that there is a diversity of views in the Aboriginal community in Canada and that these are expressed openly without party discipline.

In addition, a movement surfaced in the debate during the Charlottetown round that could be called the movement for Aboriginal nationalism. There are First Nations in Canada who are not interested in recognition in the Canadian Constitution. They view themselves as independent from the Canadian state and have decided to exercise their right of self-determination in a manner that allows for the greatest possible separateness from the institutions of Canadian society, if not complete autonomy.[56] The discourse of independence and sovereignty has been based upon a relationship with the federal Crown (or the Crown in right of Her Majesty) articulated through treaties and has not included the quest for legal status as part of the federal state. This discourse arose from the treaty-making period, pre-Confederation and in the early post-Confederation years, and is still a significant factor in shaping reaction to political change. The Aboriginal nationalism movement, which exists on a First Nation by First Nation basis, would not be receptive to any constitutional amendments that described First Nations as partners in Confederation or as an order of government. This is antithetical to their aspirations politically and to their historical identity.

This position is understandable historically. First Nations have never seen themselves as being within the Canadian state, and they resent the notion of being invited to join the state when this is their original homeland. The right of self-determination includes more fully autonomous options, and it is for those First Nations to decide on their futures. However, at this point it is difficult to envision how an actual relationship could be worked out according to these aspirations, which are secessionist.[57] It is unlikely that such fully autonomous claims would garner support among Canadian politicians or in the international community, unless they are expressed in the context of Quebec secession.[58] This discourse of nationalism is intriguing because those engaged in it are nevertheless intertwined in the apparatus of the Canadian state – for instance, they still hold band-council elections under the Indian Act and follow Indian Act rules on band monies, land use, and occupancy. This may be seen as a transitional state of affairs. The significant point regarding the nationalist movement is that none of the Charlottetown Accord would be acceptable based on this discourse of total autonomy. Those aspirations would have to be promoted and realized in a forum other than the forum for constitutional reform. Perhaps that is one of the next developments post-Charlottetown.

The No vote in the 26 October referendum was decisive. What it meant or means for Canadian politics and constitutional reform is much more uncertain. An empirical analysis of voter preference and the rationale for voting patterns defies my analysis. Some speculative thoughts are in order, but I leave the detailed analysis of these matters to those more schooled in predicting and interpreting voter behaviour and attitudes, if such predictions are ever more than lies, damn lies ... First, it is evident that political reaction to the No vote was swift and fairly decisive, tending towards no progress on any of the items in the accord. Only the government of New Brunswick dared to proceed on certain issues flowing from the accord, such as French-language protection for Acadians in the province. On this issue, their attempts at bilateral constitutional reform were opposed vigorously when a resolution was introduced in the House of Commons that would have allowed for constitutional recognition of bilingualism in that province.

Aboriginal Vote

While I would prefer to leave aside an analysis of Canadian voter preference and the referendum results, some comments on the Aboriginal vote are in order. What was the Aboriginal vote and how do we interpret it? As with the Canadian vote, the referendum results for Aboriginal voters are difficult to interpret, especially since at the time of this writing they are still unofficial and disputed. The (unofficial) results of the Aboriginal vote in the referendum, as reported by Elections Canada,[59] are outlined in table 1.

The actual number of Aboriginal voters is still in question. While the table reproduced above indicates some 111,015 votes were cast, some organizations, like the Assembly of First Nations, have challenged the unofficial figures as

TABLE 1
Aboriginal vote in the 26 October 1992 referendum vote

Province	Total votes	Total Yes	Total Yes (%)	Total No	Total No (%)	Total rejected
Newfoundland	317	235	74.1	82	25.9	0
Nova Scotia	2,537	986	38.9	1,542	60.8	9
PEI	415	285	68.7	127	30.6	3
Ontario	12,986	4,161	32.0	8,731	67.2	3
Manitoba	10,554	1,876	17.8	8,609	81.6	94
Saskatchewan	12,182	5,660	46.5	6,464	53.1	58
Alberta	7,263	1,487	20.5	5,744	79.1	32
British Columbia	41,447	12,279	29.6	29,020	70.0	148
Yukon	3,049	1,406	46.1	1,626	53.3	12
NWT	16,981	11,236	66.2	5,598	33.0	147
Total	111,015	41,503	37.4	68,906	62.1	606

Note: Results do not appear for Quebec, since in that province the referendum was administered under Quebec law rather than by Elections Canada.

inaccurate, suggesting they included non-Aboriginal voters who voted at Aboriginal polling stations, thus distorting the results.[60]

Despite this conflict with Elections Canada, which has yet to be resolved before final results are released, there are some significant points to be noted from the referendum results. First, even with the disputed figures, the Aboriginal voter turnout was very small, with less than 8 per cent of the estimated Aboriginal population of approximately 1.5 million people voting. The poor turnout can be attributed to a variety of factors. Some Aboriginal communities opted not to participate in the referendum because this process was seen as contrary to their traditions.[61]

Other communities, especially in the Province of Quebec, did not wish to participate as they did not want there to be any implication that they might be bound by the referendum results and create a precedent for future referenda, which could be highly prejudicial to their interests.[62] A small number of Aboriginal communities opted not to participate in the referendum because their chiefs or band councils did not like the contents of the Charlottetown Accord. Overall, the voter turnout was extremely low.

The main problem in assessing the Aboriginal vote is the fact that the majority of Aboriginal people do not live in identifiable Aboriginal communities. They live in urban centres or away from their communities. These people were not able to have their ballot identified as being that of an Aboriginal voter.

Elections Canada would not permit the identification of the voter's status on the referendum ballot, as this was seen as contrary to the Canadian Human Rights Act. Some organizations, such as the Assembly of First Nations, argued for such identification in order to gauge the Aboriginal opinion on the accord; however, this was not considered possible by Elections Canada. For the Native Council of Canada and the Métis National Council (whose membership resides largely outside of identifiable Aboriginal communities),[63] and to a lesser extent the Assembly of First Nations, this means that the Aboriginal vote will never be known. Consequently, speculating about or analysing the Aboriginal vote results is exceedingly problematic. Only the Newfoundland, Prince Edward Island, and Northwest Territories Aboriginal communities voted 'yes' on the accord; a slight majority in Saskatchewan and the Yukon voted 'no'; the others issued a resounding 'no,' with Manitoba leading with an 81.6 per cent No vote.

The No vote in Manitoba was interesting but perhaps unsurprising, because this was the locus of opposition to Meech Lake spearheaded by Elijah Harper and the Manitoba Chiefs. Harper's role in the days preceding the referendum no doubt influenced many voters to either not vote or to vote 'no' – his two suggestions based on his view that there was not enough time to analyse the accord. Nor was participation in the vote in keeping with First Nations traditions.[64] The Manitoba Chiefs came out fairly strongly against the accord in the last few weeks before the referendum, because they saw it as insufficient to meet their constitutional demands. This stance evidently influenced voters in Aboriginal communities in that province and, because of the Chiefs' role during Meech Lake, beyond Manitoba as well.

From my own vantage point, as someone closely involved in disseminating information about the Charlottetown Accord and meeting with Aboriginal people[65] to discuss the contents of the accord and its implications, I have some impressions of the Aboriginal opposition to the accord that have not been highlighted above. Aboriginal support for the accord at the national level was clear and relatively strong. The four national Aboriginal organizations felt comfortable enough with the accord's provisions to be able to endorse it and take it to their membership for further discussion. However, the Aboriginal organizations had, in my view, one major difficulty to address in discussing the accord with their members: given the history of dealings in bad faith on the part of the Crown on every issue from the Indian Act through to treaties, how could any agreement unanimously reached by thirteen governments be seen as fair for Aboriginal peoples?

Aboriginal people, communities, and leaders were justifiably suspicious of a deal reached with governments. Their suspicion mounted when they were faced with the compressed time frame of the referendum – a referendum that was not a First Nations–designed process. The compressed time frame meant that Aboriginal peoples only received information about the Charlottetown Accord, especially information translated into their languages, a few weeks before the vote. At the same time, there was a lack of consensus, at least among the chiefs across Canada, as to the method of ratifying the accord. Some were of the view that Canadians should decide on 26 October 1992, while First Nations should set up their own ratification processes, allowing for extensive community consultation.

The Inuit, by contrast, were in support of the accord and delivered a Yes vote in their communities in the Northwest Territories, Quebec, and Labrador. The Métis vote is not known because of their residence largely outside identifiable communities, although there was no vocal opposition from within the Métis societies during the referendum campaign.

THE FUTURE OF CONSTITUTIONAL REFORM AND ABORIGINAL PEOPLES

What are the options for change after the Charlottetown Accord? More specifically, what is the future, if any, of constitutional reform in Canada on Aboriginal and treaty-rights issues? These are complex questions and cannot be fully answered here. There are questions we need to focus on in the post-Charlottetown period, although perhaps the momentum for further action will not be there until after a federal election. However, on the issue of constitutional reform, at this stage, it is difficult to envision constitutional-reform discussions for some time to come. Given the reaction of Canadian politicians to the referendum results, I would say it is fairly evident that they will not touch the issue with a proverbial 'ten-foot pole.' It is true that there is a constitutional requirement for a national review of the amending formula in 1996. However, this is simply a review with no consequences attached that would compel larger reform discussions or amendments touching upon Aboriginal peoples.[66]

My impression at this point is, as I stated at the outset, that there will be no further constitutional-reform discussions in Canada unless we are on the brink of Quebec secession. This situation would require more than a proposed vote or provincial referendum – it would require, in my view, a provincial decision to chart an independent course from Canada. Beyond this, I find it highly doubtful that there could be constitutional reform on specific issues, like Aboriginal peoples, given the nature of the amending formula and the kind of constitutional politics in which first ministers have engaged since repatriation. The breadth of the Charlottetown Accord can be attributed to the political nature of deal-making in Canadian federalism. With the current amending formula, there must be a give-and-take, all-or-nothing, bargain in order for there to be an agreement.

To be direct about the prospects for future constitutional discussions based on the Charlottetown experience, the nature of these processes is such that there will be no explicit recognition of the inherent right of Aboriginal peoples to self-government without many other constitutional objectives being achieved for provinces, such as an elected Senate, redistribution of powers, and so on. However, the Supreme Court of Canada may clarify the constitutional status of self-government prior to the resumption of further discussions.[67] With our model of constitutional reform in Canada, advances on issues like Aboriginal and treaty rights are achieved only when other changes the provinces deserve can be offset against compromises that they must make. The style of constitutional reform championed by former prime minister Trudeau is not politically possible in Canada today. It was the kind of action possible in a centrist, almost unitarian state, but impossible in a federal state that is as highly decentralized as Canada is with the amending formula we now have after 1982. Since the amending formula cannot be changed short of unanimous agreement, it will not likely change for some time to come.

CONCLUSION

The Charlottetown Accord experience was complex for Aboriginal peoples and for Canada. The Aboriginal package that formed part of the Consensus Report requires detailed examination by Aboriginal communities and organizations to determine what aspects were or were not acceptable to Aboriginal peoples, and why. This is itself a long and arduous process, which is difficult to embark upon when one does not know the likelihood of revisiting the accord politically. There are always options for implementing or advancing on the Aboriginal package other than through constitutional amendment. Political accords, the treaty-making processes, and many other options are available if the political will is there for reform. One troubling reminder post-Charlottetown is the fact that governments did not easily embrace many of the ideas in the Aboriginal package; they were cajoled into doing so in the context of a negotiated bargain where other assurances were given to them on their agenda items. The political will may have evaporated after Charlottetown, or at least will have to be kick-started to address the profound problems that Aboriginal peoples have in Canadian society.

One concluding point: I have an overwhelming sense that significant education is required in Canadian society regarding Aboriginal peoples' history, grievances, and aspirations. The Charlottetown Accord process, and even the Meech Lake and Oka experiences, have not been sufficient to educate Canadians properly regarding Aboriginal peoples' contexts and problems. Canadians are also very confused about Aboriginal divisions and differences, and have difficulty understanding why the past is so important to Aboriginal peoples. The profile of Aboriginal peoples' issues, and their leaders, has been raised. This is an important first step towards broader education. In and of itself, however, it is not enough to accomplish fundamental political change on complex issues in a society that seems at times not terribly interested in its past and how this shapes its future. Other strategies for educating Canadians will have to be found and, along with this, the political will reharnessed so that fundamental changes can be achieved to ensure that the rights of Aboriginal peoples are fully respected in Canada.

NOTES

1 National Chief Ovide Mercredi to the Huron people at Huron Wendat Village, Quebec, 18 Oct. 1992 (unpublished remarks, on file with author)
2 During the multilateral discussions on constitutional renewal in 1992 (the Charlottetown Round), I had the privilege of heading the Assembly of First Nations' legal team. I acknowledge all those who worked with the assembly on this effort from the political leadership and legal team to the superb support staff who co-ordinated our hectic efforts. Working alongside this dedicated group was a wonderful learning experience.
3 By 'Charlottetown Accord' I mean both the final text of the *Consensus Report on the Constitution* of 28 August 1992 and the *Draft Legal Text* of 9 October 1992. More specific distinctions between these two documents will be drawn, where required, in this paper.
4 I mean a genuine crisis that would involve Quebec secession (not simply anticipation of a vote for secession, and an actual Yes vote in that direction in the Province of Quebec). It seems to be fairly evident that politicians have been stung by the No result of the referendum. Many resignations, leadership changes, and the retrenchment of 'old' positions (e.g., on the Senate) would seem to flow from the sting of No.
5 It was only partially a No to the priority of constitutional reform; the No seemed to be more of a rejection of certain aspects of the accord rather than of constitutional discussions per se. However, for the political leaders of the nation, the No was a signal to get off the subject of constitutional reform and get back to something that is more popular publically and in tune with the electorate's will.
6 See R. Jhappan, 'Inherency, Three Nations and Collective Rights: The Evolution of Aboriginal Constitutional Discourse from 1982 to the Charlottetown Accord' (29 Oct. 1992, unpublished essay on file with author)
7 I use the expression Aboriginal peoples as a catch-all to refer to the First Nations,

Métis, and Inuit peoples, who are diverse culturally, geographically, and politically.

8 The Native Women's Association of Canada did not, as a national organization, share this view, although many of its constituent organizations did, such as the Ontario Native Women's Association, the Yukon Indian Women's Association, and others. This issue will be addressed further in the paper when questions of gender equality are canvassed.

9 Canadian Human Rights Commission Annual Report, 1988. See also the findings for 1989 and 1990, which further underscore the tragedy and urgency of the situation for Aboriginal peoples.

10 The First Nations protested and made appeals to the Monarch during the colonial and early years of the Dominion of Canada. These focused on the terms of union, treaties and the respect of treaty rights, and the relationship between the governments of the First Nations and the Crown.

11 The evidence of this shift can be found in the decision of Chief Justice Dickson in *R. v. Sparrow*, [1990] I S.C.R. 1075. For a more general review of the doctrine of Aboriginal rights and its legal treatment, see B. Slatttery, 'Understanding Aboriginal Rights,' *Canadian Bar Review* 66 (1987): 727.

12 For an analysis of these conferences and the issues raised, see Bryan Schwartz, *First Principles, Second Thoughts: Aboriginal Peoples, Constitutional Reform and Canadian Statecraft* (Montreal: Institute for Research on Public Policy 1986).

13 These have always been very unstable. In my view, the scarcity of governmental resources for Aboriginal peoples, and the effective government strategy of reserving for itself the role of official judge of who is or is not an 'Indian' have made the possibilities for alliances quite difficult.

14 See, for example, D.C. Hawkes and M. Devine, 'Meech Lake and Elijah Harper: Native-State Relations in the 1990s,' in Frances Abele, ed., *How Ottawa Spends: The Politics of Fragmentation, 1991–92* (Ottawa: Carleton University Press 1991), 55.

15 Assembly of First Nations Report of the Constitutional Circle, *To the Source* (Ottawa: Assembly of First Nations 1992), 25

16 Such as the Aboriginal political leadership or the Royal Commission on Aboriginal Peoples, which has been given a mandate to make recommendations for changing the Aboriginal situation in Canada.

17 The Maritime Treaties, such as the Treaty of 1752 between the British and the Mikmaq Grand Council Chiefs, are examples of treaties that establish a political alliance based on respect for the independence of an Aboriginal people and that of the British Sovereign.

18 Métis and Inuit are, of course, excluded from the scheme because the definition section does not embrace them, although similar policies of assimilation and bureaucratic control have been imposed on the Inuit and the Métis.

19 I make a distinction between the early treaties and later treaties because with most

of the post-Confederation treaties, the Crown came with a prepared text. The opportunity for balanced discussion or genuine negotiation is not possible when one side controls the process and the text.

20 For example, an Angus Reid poll conducted during May and June 1992 found widespread support and goodwill towards the recognition of Aboriginal rights and self-government in particular. Support for self-government was approximately 65%. *Canadians and Aboriginal Peoples 1992: A Syndicated National Public Opinion Research Study* (Angus Reid Group 1992)

21 Inuit representative Zebedee Nungak made some comical comments about the exclusion from the Harrington Lake meetings and the fact that Aboriginal consent was not part of the amending formula. He said that Aboriginal peoples had made it to the executive bathroom, and maybe someday they will be allowed into the boardroom.

22 I was not involved in other rounds of constitutional-reform discussions, so I can only comment on this point based on what I have read and learned about those processes from the players who were involved in the Charlottetown round.

23 The four provinces that come immediately to mind are Saskatchewan, British Columbia, Ontario, and Prince Edward Island.

24 29, 30 April 1992

25 For example, I can recall the scorn that Mr Paul Tellier, Clerk of the Privy Council, expressed towards the Assembly of First Nations when we introduced the idea of changing the amending formula to require Aboriginal consent in the future to amendments affecting Aboriginal and treaty rights. Despite his initial protestations, this idea did survive and found a place in the Consensus Report, though not without a battle at every level.

26 The requirement that Aboriginal laws be consistent with federal and provincial laws essential for peace, order, and good government was such a restriction. However, even this was a compromise from what the provinces of Quebec and especially Newfoundland wanted, namely, the right to override Aboriginal governments when they deemed it was in the public interest. Such a broad power of override is only justifiable if you believe Aboriginal government will not be able to do things properly, or if you want to continue in the mode of control.

27 *The Right of Self-Government and the Constitution: A Commentary* (Ottawa: Royal Commission on Aboriginal Peoples, 13 Feb. 1992)

28 Ibid., 19

29 This was especially the position of the Government of Newfoundland, which would not accept anything short of an absolute federal commitment for financing before discussing the financing of Aboriginal governments.

30 *Draft Legal Text* (9 Oct. 1992), 37–8

31 Even the royal commission report (p. 20) recommended that the right be limited or circumscribed in its scope if recognized in the Canadian constitution.

32 Critics referred to it as a third *level* of government, suggesting more government for Canadians. What was envisioned was in fact a third *order* of governments of the Aboriginal peoples. It was not a level, subordinate to the federal and provincial order, but an order of government, one component of the Canadian federation.

33 It is unlikely that many First Nations will alter their position on international recognition of treaties since this is entirely consistent with their history as sovereign nations and their current aspirations to be treated as subjects of international law, with full access to international complaint, and other, fora. It may be that distinctive rules for indigenous treaties could be developed at the international level.

34 The policies of the Canadian government have been geared towards assimilation since the first Indian Act was passed in 1876. Assimilation has had devastating effects. The recent public discussion about residential schools and their after-effects on Aboriginal peoples is an indication of how devastating and indefensible the assimilation approach has been in Canada.

35 See *Consensus Report*, 2.

36 It also requires that the prime minister hold a conference with Aboriginal representatives should amendments to certain sections on Aboriginal and treaty rights be proposed. This does not imply Aboriginal consent, but is simply a requirement to hold a conference.

37 For further discussion on this point, and some international-law implications, see M.E. Turpel, 'Indigenous Peoples' Rights of Political Participation and Self-Determination,' *Cornell International Law Journal* 25 (1992): 579.

38 See *Legal Text*, s. 127, p. 29.

39 The special edition of *Maclean's* dedicated to referendum analysis, 28 Oct. 1992, suggested that only 4% of the No vote was because of the Aboriginal package – a profoundly small percentage.

40 This criticism was articulated repeatedly in Jeffrey Simpson's columns in the *Globe and Mail.*

41 Admittedly no more strange than the conglomerate of advocates of the Charlottetown Accord

42 It is important to say 'some' because the situation was a complex one, and certainly not all First Nations women opposed the Charlottetown Accord. The largest organization of First Nations women, the Ontario Native Women's Association, the Métis Women's Association, and the Inuit Women's Association supported the accord.

43 None of these national groups is represented by the Native Women's Association of Canada.

44 See *Native Women's Association of Canada v. Canada*, [1992] 4 C.N.L.R. 71.

45 Rosemarie Kuptana and Mary Simon

46 See my article 'Patriarchy and Paternalism: The Legacy of the Canadian State for Aboriginal Women,' *Canadian Journal of Women and the Law* 6 (1993).

47 See ibid.

48 Of course it is worth noting that nothing in the Charter is terribly certain, given that the Supreme Court of Canada is deeply divided on almost every significant Charter issue, from freedom of expression to fundamental justice.

49 Professor Weinrib's legal analysis of the Charlottetown Accord, signed by thirteen other lawyers, prepared on 12 Oct. 1992 and released to the press (on file with author)

50 This is what indigenous peoples are advocating in the form of a United Nations Declaration on Indigenous Peoples' Rights (in drafting stages at the United Nations Working Group on Indigenous Peoples). See Draft Declaration, E/CN.4/Sub.2/1992/28, 23 June 1992.

51 P.E. Trudeau, *A Mess That Deserves a Big No* (Toronto: Robert Davies Publishing 1992), 12

52 *Equality in Employment: A Royal Commission Report*, October 1984, pp. 3, 4

53 Like Deborah Coyne and Sharon Carstairs and many others

54 *A Mess*, 57

55 Ibid., 72

56 The Iroquois Confederacy is an example of this movement and it has always maintained this position. After the Charlottetown experience it has been restructuring itself along traditional lines.

57 To describe the aspirations as secessionist is a little ironic when in fact some First Nations are basing their political goals on the fact that Canada is their homeland, not that they want to separate from it.

58 See M.E. Turpel, 'Does the Road to Quebec Sovereignty Run Through Aboriginal Territory?' in D. Drace and R. Perron, eds, *Negotiating with a Sovereign Quebec* (Toronto: Lorimer 1992), 93.

59 Elections Canada unofficial results, 28 October 1992

60 The Assembly of First Nations has estimated that only approximately 75,000 Aboriginal votes were cast. They are engaged in ongoing discussions with Elections Canada over the official results.

61 The examples here are many, but the Mohawk communities of Kanawake and Kanestake come to mind; they are prominent opponents of a referendum as contrary to their traditional decision-making processes.

62 This view was carefully outlined in correspondence with the federal government and the Quebec government from the National Chief of the Assembly of First Nations and from the Crees and Mohawks of Quebec.

63 An exception for the Métis occurs in the Province of Alberta with the Alberta Métis Settlements, which are officially recognized and enumerated.

64 This was somewhat ironic given that Elijah Harper is himself a member of the provincial legislative assembly, a rather non-traditional Ojibwa-Cree institution.

65 Arguably too closely involved to form any reliable conclusions, although I will hazard some speculation anyway.

66 Of course the amending-formula concerns that Aboriginal peoples brought to the table during the Charlottetown round can be raised again in 1996.

67 Many leading scholars, such as Brian Slattery, *supra*, already believe it is part of section 35.

10

Québec, a Nation Divided

RAYMOND GIROUX

When *you* talk about a nation divided, you mean Canada. When *I* talk about a nation divided, I mean Québec. We can take for granted that the political organization called Canada is dead in its present form. The 1867 Confederation was a compromise that satisfied almost everybody 125 years ago. Canadians gained a territorial government that, in the long run, would be their most powerful tool in building a distinct society. For their part, English-speaking people started building a new nation that for almost a century would be able to accommodate its backward, French-speaking, priest-ridden minority. For us – and I use the word 'us' knowing full well that I will confirm Mordecai Richler's appreciation of Québec as a tribal society – this new Canadian nation was a foreign country. Our Canada was born in 1534, not in 1867. Therein lies the deep Canadian misunderstanding. There lies, also, the source of the division in Québec, torn between its old continental nationalism and its more recent, narrower, territorial nationalism.

Do not forget that our ancestors roamed the Prairies, were the first among the European explorers to see the Rockies and travel the Mississippi River, wrote *O Canada*, and used the maple leaf as a national symbol. It is not an easy task to eradicate a few centuries of national history. So even in a time of real political turmoil, Québécois still consider themselves Canadians and are not ready for what they see as a shameful retreat to the present boundaries of Québec. Public-opinion polls give a series of different figures regarding the strength of the pro-sovereignty movement. I submit that the response may vary depending on the exact wording of the question asked and that the wording of the question will vary according to the political stripe of those who pay for the poll. Political scientists might hate to be reminded of that, but it is too often true to be forgotten.

At the moment, one person out of three in Québec is a committed federalist.

This group encompasses the English-speaking minority, most of the cultural minorities, people over fifty-five years of age, and big business. Another third has made its choice and will vote for sovereignty on any day, rain or shine – white collars, intellectuals, students, educated people, trade unionists, and so on. The pro-sovereignty faction includes the most vocal and the most active part of our society. Then there is the final third, those who totally reject the status quo, but would be happy with a real re-confederation that recognizes Québec as a really distinct society and gives real power to its national government. If, however, the choice is to be between a vague national sovereignty for Québec and the familiar, but unworkable and no longer acceptable federalism, they will choose sovereignty – if they ever find a leader they can have faith in. Robert Bourassa, for one, would carry the day if he ever chose to go for a kind of national sovereignty 'à l'européenne.'

This divided Québec has survived for a long time as a component of Canada, but Canada itself has changed so fast and so deeply that the main complaint you hear these days from Newfoundland to Vancouver Island is, We do not recognize our own country any more. Canada is no longer a British country. Toronto and Vancouver are international cities, not Canadian cities. Even in Montréal you can hear people whining. According to the last census, the non-British ethnic population in Montréal almost equals in number the English-speaking minority, and two-thirds of them still choose English as their language of everyday communication. Fifteen years after Bill 101, Quebec's language-rights legislation, this picture is quite disturbing to the French-speaking majority.

People have come to Canada from all over the world during the past forty years, an immigration pattern that has changed this country's complexion. Pierre Trudeau's philosophy of the priority of individual rights over collective or social rights, combined with the newcomers' deep ignorance of their new country's history, has destroyed the old Canadian compact. This new Canada has matured through the 1982 Charter of Rights. The former prime minister wanted only one Canada, not two nations.

A majority of Canadians agreed to Trudeau's appeal because, according to political scientist Kenneth McRoberts,[1] it was the best way to avoid, and then eliminate, the Québec question. The Charlottetown Agreement gives a perfect snapshot of this new Canada. Québec's distinct society is being reduced to the bare bones of language, culture, and civil law. Even then, the accord did not recognize marriage, divorce, and property rights as civil-law issues. As for the really important issue, a new federal-provincial division of powers, it is no-where to be seen. In this context, Québec is just one of ten provinces and two territories asking for undue privileges. According to the equality principle,

Ottawa has to give every province what it is ready to concede to Québec. Such a huge devolution of powers would make Canada unmanageable.

This tentative deal is a negation of our national identity. What is a national identity? Pierre Trudeau likes to despise any nationalism, especially Québec nationalism, but he may have been the foremost promoter of a new Canadian nationalism. Remember 1968, when he gave the CBC and Radio-Canada a mandate to promote national unity at the same time he was trying to entrench a Charter of Rights that recognized freedom of expression. The journalists at the networks did their best meandering through these contradictory statements of principle, but he was the one who decided that a nationalism of his own choice was worth fighting for.

The Quiet Revolution in Québec has been quiet, indeed. So quiet that a large majority of Canadians did not understand that while there was a process of nation building going on in English-speaking Canada – whose peak was, from my point of view, the No vote to the free-trade agreement that was overwhelmed by a Yes vote in Québec – Québec was living through a nation-building process of its own. A study by McGill University's Maurice Pinard published in the *Journal of International Affairs*[2] describes the whole process.

Reviewing a series of polls carried out between 1970 and 1990, Pinard noticed a real fundamental change in ethnic self-identification in Québec. As he writes, a set of socio-psychological forces contributed to a massive transfer of national allegiance. Look at the figures: in 1970, 34 per cent of the French-speaking Quebeckers described themselves as Canadians, 44 per cent as French Canadians, and only 21 per cent as Québécois.

Twenty years later, in 1990, there was a dramatic change. Only 9 per cent still saw themselves as Canadians, 28 per cent as French Canadians, and 59 per cent as Québécois. There is no definition of national identity. I submit that a willingness to live together on a given territory rich enough in human and natural resources is sufficient to create a national identity. The important word here is willingness. There is a Swiss national identity, but there was no Yugoslav national identity. As soon as the dictatorship ended, the country began to crumble. The Belgian identity is a very fragile one because both sides in the Belgian debate, Flemish and Walloon, seem ready to trade their Belgian identity for a new European one.

Then is not also a new Québec faced with similar challenges? Are there not Natives in Québec? Are there not cultural minorities in Québec? I answer yes to all three questions. We, in Québec, have to tackle these issues very seriously and the Charlottetown deal is both helpful and dangerous.

Dangerous because you can already hear voices from the fringe, some lunatics or extremists from the Société Saint-Jean Baptiste (even if not all of them are xenophobic) demanding that a Yes vote in the Charlottetown referendum requires a majority of francophone votes to be politically binding. Statistically speaking, such a demand moves the goal post to 60 per cent. This is nonsense. We live in a democracy and every single vote has the same value. There is no such thing as a French vote, an Anglophone vote, a Jewish vote, or an Italian one. No one will leave a voting booth with a red maple leaf, a blue fleur-de-lys, or a yellow star on his jacket.

Dangerous, yes, but helpful. We have to come to terms with the fact that the 'pure laine' will never be more than 80–82 per cent of the overall population of Québec. We do not lose because there are minorities in Québec. The presence of several cultures is, generally speaking, a gain for society, but their presence causes a problem. Historically, and up until the present, their allegiance has been to Canada, not to Québec. There is a deep mistrust of Québec nationalism on the part of multicultural communities. At the same time, I like to think that Québec's new version of nationalism is quite progressive and open to the world. The French-speaking majority has the responsibility to build bridges towards the ethnocultural minorities. We forced their children into French schools under Bill 101 a dozen years ago, but now it appears that we resent their presence. In 1980, only 37.2 per cent of the 'allophone' children were enrolled in the French school system. This figure has now climbed to 71.9 per cent according to the latest statistics.[3]

Are racism and xenophobia more entrenched in Québec than elsewhere in Canada? No, absolutely not, if we refer to a survey submitted to Employment and Immigration Canada last February.[4] The authors debunk what they call the myth of Québec racism: 'The study shows that Quebeckers, in general, and Montrealers, in particular, are amongst the least racially intolerant of Canadians.' This is not to deny the existence of racism in Québec, but only to put it in perspective.

Let's talk about the Native issue. It is the general consensus that Natives won a lot within the framework of the constitutional negotiations, and I am happy about that. But the outcome of this deal might be a fight between Québec nationalists and Natives. It would be easy for any demagogue to pit the two minorities against each other. We must not let that happen.

On their side, Natives fear that the distinct-society concept might trample their rights. They also fear that sovereignty might be worse for them, and they threaten to secede from Québec and keep their territories within the borders of the Canadian realm. Many of them do not know our history or political background. We can see here a phenomenon of mutual ignorance, but when we heard Ovide Mercredi saying in front of the National Assembly that Quebeckers do not have national rights, we thought he was either a member of APEC (the Association for the Preservation of English in Canada) or a reader of Pierre Trudeau's early works. Neither Natives nor Quebeckers have anything to gain from such battles.

Let us face reality. Natives don't trust us, but if you refer to Professor Brad Morse's study prepared for the Québec National Assembly last February,[5] Québec is in the forefront of the fight for Aboriginal rights. Let us cite a few notable sentences from his study: 'The amount of land recognized as belonging exclusively to Aboriginal people in Quebec is much higher than in any province.' 'No other provincial government has made the limited yet relatively concerted effort to support the survival of Aboriginal languages on a par with Quebec.' 'The Government has in general been far more supportive of educational initiatives, particularly for the Cree and Inuit, than any other provincial government.' '[Quebec] authorized the Mohawks of Kahnawake to construct a hospital and to receive provincial funds for its operation as a private establishment completely administered by the Mohawks. To the best of my knowledge, this legislation and arrangement is unique in Canada.' 'Quebec has been a leader among provinces in sponsoring economic development within Aboriginal communities and First Nations.' 'The Province of Quebec was the first in Canada to accept the continued existence of aboriginal title and to respond to this recognition through seeking to negotiate land claims settlements.' 'The Government of Quebec has also been the provincial leader in fostering the desires of Aboriginal people to exercise greater control over their lives and the affairs of their communities.'

If Natives do not trust Quebeckers, it is also true that we do not trust them. The reciprocity factor is hard at work. The Indian summer of 1990, the sad events of Knesatake and Kahnawake, provoked a catastrophic reaction in Québec from which we have not yet recovered. One should add to these significant sources of discord such minor irritations as some Natives' bad habit of taking a ten-day head start on hunting season! Aside from the Hurons, Natives have decided to opt out of the Québec referendum. As of this writing, they have decided to hold a consultation in keeping with their traditional customs. This is seen as the ultimate example of mistrust, because most of the Natives living outside Québec will take part in the Canadian referendum even if its legal constraints are softer and more open to financial abuse than the provisions of the Québec referendum law.

We must try to end this mistrust between Natives and Quebeckers. Here are a few provisional reflections on this issue whose legal implications are partly based upon an international study commissioned by Québec's National Assembly:[6]

1. According to the Canadian constitution, there is no way Natives can secede from Québec.
2. According to international law, if Québec votes for its sovereignty, its borders will stay the same.
3. The Natives cannot lose any rights if there is a transfer of sovereignty.
4. Québec will have to accommodate its minorities before getting any international recognition.
5. There are so many questions left open by the recognition of self-government for Natives that turning the issue over to the courts after a five-year delay is almost a denial of justice. We must accelerate the present process of land-claims negotiation that has become a denial of Natives' elementary rights, but we cannot correct a wrong by another wrong.

Following these parameters, I submit that whatever happens to the Charlottetown deal and whatever the subsequent political status of Québec will be, there should be some kind of constituent assembly in this province to deal with issues concerning Native and multicultural communities. The failure of the Charlottetown Accord should not be interpreted as a rejection of Native peoples. Quebeckers know very well the meaning of rejection, having lived through that experience twice, once after the patriation deal of 1982 and then again when the Meech Lake Accord failed in 1990. They have absolutely no interest in inflicting the same treatment on anyone else. Sooner rather than later, we'll have to find a made-in-Québec solution for the Aboriginal issue. That implies a new state of mind on the part of both national communities, not an easy endeavour in this troubled period.

NOTES

1 McRoberts, *English Canada and Quebec: Avoiding the Issue*. 6th annual Robarts Lecture (North York: Robarts Centre for Canadian Studies 1991)
2 'The Dramatic Reemergence of the Quebec Independence Movement,' *Journal of International Affairs* 45, no. 2 (Winter 1992): 471–97
3 Conseil de la langue français, *Indicateurs de la situation linguistique au Québec* (Gouvernement du Québec, avril 1991)

4 Ekos Research Associates Inc. Final Report. *National Opinion Study on Changes to Immigration Policy.* Submitted to Public Affairs, Employment and Immigration Canada, Ottawa, 21 Feb. 1991

5 *Comparative Assessments of Indigenous Peoples in Québec, Canada and Abroad.* Report prepared for La Commission d'étude sur toute offre d'un nouveau partenariat de nature constitutionnelle and La Commission d'étude des questions afférentes à l'accession du Québec à la souveraineté. University of Ottawa, Faculty of Law, February 1992 (version préliminaire)

6 *L'Intégrité territoriale du Québec dans l'hypothèse de l'accession à la souveraineté.* Étude présentée à la Commission d'étude des questions afférentes à l'accession du Québec à la souveraineté par les professeurs Thomas M. Franck (New York), Rosalyn Higgins (Londres), Alain Pellet (Paris), Malcolm N. Shaw (Leicester) et Christian Tomuschat (Bonn). Québec, mai 1992

11

The Referendum and Democracy

MAUDE BARLOW

Much of the constitutional debate of the last several years has come down to a fundamental disagreement over the nature of Canada. Are we a federation of equal provinces – a geographical and political territorial base for a second level of government – or an association of equal nations: the three national communities of French, English, and Aboriginal peoples that make up the historical national cultural communities of this country? While one vision is based in geography and constitutionally assigned authority, the other is a social and cultural concept that transcends both geographical and often legal definitions, but is no less real.

Usually, the debate is cast as if these definitions were mutually exclusive and Canadians must choose one vision over the other. The fact is, however, that Canada is a complicated mixture of both, sitting under an increasingly multicultural and multiracial national umbrella. In fact, we are a multinational nation-state and it is important to recognize that the First Nations and the French have never voluntarily surrendered their language or cultures anywhere in the country.

Across the great divide of the referendum, many in English Canada seemed unable to understand the central concern of francophone Quebeckers about the Charlottetown Accord, that the deal emphasized Canada's identity as a federation of provinces and territories at the expense of the idea of Canada as an association of three nations. The fact that the concept of nationhood for Native peoples was accepted in the proposed accord, but that this recognition was not extended to Quebec, was a bitter pill for many francophones. The majority of Quebeckers believed that the distinct-society clause was symbolic in nature only and that, in fact, Quebec was offered no more than the other provinces and under the new arrangement would have in effect been drawn deeper into Canadian Confederation. The irony, of course, is that many in English Canada rejected the deal because they saw it as entrenching special powers for Quebec and confirming the equal-nation model sought by Quebec. Two communities looked at the same package and rejected it for different reasons. This tension remains unresolved.

The Charlottetown Accord was the result of a process driven by itself and was not a framework or vision towards which all were working. The constitutional proposal was the result of horse trading and it showed. In the end, it was rejected for as many reasons as there were differing agendas in its creation.

For the Council of Canadians, which is deeply concerned about the destruction of national institutions, our manufacturing base, and our political sovereignty under the Canada-U.S. Free Trade Agreement, our concerns centred around the decentralizing nature of the deal and the limits it placed on federal spending powers. Among jurisdictions offered exclusively to the provinces were forestry and mining, and the Council questioned if this meant that Canada could ever sign an international environmental treaty on forestry or mining practices as a nation again. We shared with environmental groups strong concerns about how national environmental and trade rules would be set.

Labour-market training and development were also to be turned over to the provinces, and the Council argued that, with the impending further loss of jobs sure to come as companies take advantage of NAFTA and move south, this was the worst possible time to be doing such a thing. As well, there seemed to be conflicting opinions about whether unemployment insurance would remain in federal hands, and this greatly concerned us, as we believe that Canada needs a strong, coherent national labour plan to take us into the next century.

Although our organization did not take a formal position on the referendum, leaving the decision up to individual members, most in our group are relieved that the accord was rejected. We believe that a different model for constitutional reform will be needed in the future, albeit after a long rest from constitutional wrangling.

The Council of Canadians is perhaps the best-known nationalist group in the country. The expectation of many is that we would have a uniform definition of what constitutes Canadian citizenship, a single vision of our country to which all must adhere. In fact, we understand the drive to self-determination of Quebec and the First Nations, and we celebrate the diversity that these distinct cultures bring to Canada. We seek the recognition and celebration of Canada as a distinct society in North America and would choose to have Canada play a strong role in finding a new definition of democracy and nationalism in our increasingly interdependent world now dominated by anti-democratic, nation-destroying transnational corporations. We believe that English Canada has much to learn from both cultures on the protection of our democracy and heritage.

Months before this constitutional proposal was announced, we warned that the offer would be based on the devolution to the provinces of what are now national jurisdictions and on a refusal to recognize Quebec's different relationship to Canada in any meaningful way. We called for a new social contract based on the fundamental principle that the country of Canada is made up of three national communities, each with inalienable rights to protect its sovereignty, historical roots, and culture. We called for an option that would permit Quebec to define the level of autonomy it requires to feel safe and welcome in the Canada of the twenty-first century. We argued that English Canadians had to accept that most French Quebeckers define themselves as Québécois first and Canadians second. We said that this fact did not mean that the majority would opt to leave Canada and argued that these differences enriched the country. We stand by this vision of Canada as providing the best model for its future.

Meanwhile, much healing will have to be done and we will have to examine the concepts and words that come between us, English and French. One has only to look to the dictionaries of the two languages to show that we in English Canada often misinterpret the meaning of Quebec's concerns. In French, in my *Petit Larousse*, the word 'nation' is defined as a 'grande communauté humaine,' one that possesses a common history, language, and culture. It does not necessarily denote a geographic entity, as does the English term, which my *Concise Oxford* defines as 'congeries of people ... inhabiting a territory bounded by defined limits.' Sovereignty is defined in *Petit Larousse* as the supremacy of the people and comes from a principle of French common law established after the French Revolution, whereby authority, once held by the king, is now in the hands of the people. In English, again from the *Concise Oxford*, the word means 'supreme, as power ... supreme ruler, especially monarch.'

No wonder we looked at the same constitutional offer and came to totally different conclusions as to its meaning. We have not yet even agreed on the nature of the debate, but all Canadians do share one thing coming out of this referendum process. We decided that our country and its future belonged to us and we took direct responsibility for it instead of trusting our elected leaders to make the decisions for us. This process signalled that we are maturing as a people and that our system is emerging from one of representative democracy, whereby we elect a government to represent us and make decisions for us, to one of participatory democracy, whereby we demand direct influence in the decisions affecting our lives. The referendum showed that, for better or for worse, and perhaps for the first time, Canadians have decided to claim direct democracy as our preferred system, and we will never be the same again. All Canadians, regardless of ethnic origin, language, or region, share this new-found power.

Whatever happens, we must not give up on Canada or brook any talk about the end of our country. Every time we feel weary with our constitutional wrangling, we can turn our televisions on to remind us how such decisions are being made in other parts of the world, then try one more time ourselves.

12

Sinking Again into the Quagmire of Conflicting Visions, Groups, Under-inclusion, and Death by Referendum

ERROL P. MENDES

The constitutional process that has aroused, angered, and perhaps ultimately bored Canadians since the death of the Meech Lake Accord on 23 June 1990 should above all teach us that we have evolved a unique form of democracy in the community of nations.

The Charlottetown Accord of 1992 was the result of negotiations between the federal government, the ten premiers, the territorial leaders, and the leaders of the four Aboriginal groups. The minister for constitutional affairs, Joe Clark, had insisted that other groups looking for guarantees within the Constitution, but not seeking status as governments themselves, would not be included in the multilateral talks. These talks began on 12 March 1992 and ended thirty-six negotiating days later in Charlottetown, on 28 August 1992. Examples of groups that were excluded from the multilateral process were francophone groups outside Quebec, women's groups (including Aboriginal women concerned about their equality rights under Native self-government), ethnocultural groups, and an array of groups classified as disadvantaged in our society, such as the disabled. These groups monitored the process closely and many even managed to obtain what could be regarded as observer status by membership in the monitoring committee of the Native Council of Canada, one of the four official Native delegations.

The aim of this paper is to examine whether the present practitioners of what has been termed executive federalism have learned the lesson of the Meech Lake débâcle, especially in their reformulation of the fundamental values and identity of Canada found in the Charlottetown Accord of 1992. We can begin by accepting as historical fact that the Meech Lake Accord perished because many of the groups described above insisted that the accord had ignored and indeed imperilled their vital concerns.[1] We can also begin by accepting that the constitutional consciousness of these groups was uncorked by the 1982 constitutional repatriation process, in particular by their participation in the formulation of the Canadian Charter of Rights and Freedoms.

These groups now feel such a sense of ownership concerning the Constitution in general, and the Charter in particular, that one political scientist, Allan Cairns, has assigned the somewhat unidimensional title of 'Charter Canadians' to them.[2] I have always felt that such a term is somewhat insulting, because it implies that these groups' quest for social justice and substantive equality may be a narrow-minded quest at odds with the general welfare. If the Constitution is designed to profess the dream of social and political justice that Canadians desire, then all Canadians should be Charter Canadians.

In the aftermath of the Meech Lake crisis, the federal and provincial governments made great efforts to encourage not just public participation, but interest-group participation in the 'political segment' of the constitutional process. Huge amounts of democratic coinage, both fiscal and political, were spent on hearings before the Spicer Commission, the two federal parliamentary committees,[3] many provincial committees on the Constitution, and the constitutional conferences sponsored by the federal government.[4]

There began a growing suspicion among many of the groups described above that what took place in these public fora was a 'harvesting'[5] of public and group opinion primarily to satisfy the demands of group democracy in Canada. The thirty-six days of multilateral negotiations leading up to the Charlottetown Accord, however, represented a swing back to traditional executive federalism, with one major exception. At the insistence of the premier most responsive to group politics, namely Bob Rae of Ontario, the four major Aboriginal groups were finally officially brought into the real decision-making process, a truly historic milestone in Canadian constitutional development.[6]

The package that finally emerged from the multilateral negotiating sessions represented, inter alia:[7]

- the traditional forms of élite accommodation, especially as regards provincial demands for institutional reforms, in particular of the Senate, the division of powers, the spending power, the amending formula, and other federal-provincial concerns;
- the concrete results of letting one major set of groups, the Aboriginal organizations, into the decision-making process, as opposed to merely 'harvesting' their opinions; and
- the incorporation of other politically powerful group concerns, very imperfectly 'harvested.'

The reaction to the Charlottetown Accord was tremendously varied. It ranged from a description of the accord being the most historic reformulation of the

Canadian constitution since 1867, in the great traditions of national compromise and reconciliation, to its being a dog's breakfast that equalizes unhappiness across the country.

The opposition that became focused against the accord seemed to come yet again from the same groups and parties that dance around the dialectic of group politics in Canada. The one exception were the leaders of the four main Aboriginal organizations, who were allowed into the real decision-making process. Ironically, the people whom at least one of the aboriginal leaders represented, namely the on-reserve Aboriginal communities, voted by a large majority against the accord in the referendum.

The organized opposition to the accord was to be found in one of three camps: first, opinion leaders of the only group that really has the power and potential to break up the nation, namely the francophone majority in Quebec. The sovereignist or ultra-nationalist opinion leaders of this group desire either a de facto associate-state status for Quebec (the general thrust of the Allaire report)[8] or a fully independent state, and nothing less will satisfy them. The Charlottetown Accord provided for substantially less than either option. What the accord did provide was bureaucratic disengagement of the federal government from vital areas of provincial jurisdiction with compensation. The real objective of the accord in the area of division of powers was administrative and fiscal autonomy in existing and vital areas of provincial jurisdiction.

The distinct-society clauses in the Canada Clause, the guarantee of seats in the House of Commons and the Supreme Court, and the veto for all provinces over future changes to federal institutions[9] were designed to compensate those Quebec nationalists and federalists who could accept Quebec within the Canadian federation. However, while such segments of the body politic in Quebec could accept their province as one among ten or potentially more provinces, for them, Quebec must have sufficient armour-plating against linguistic, cultural, political, and economic assimilation. These segments of the francophone collectivity in Quebec did not have sufficient numbers to form a majority, together with other parts of Quebec society, to keep the Charlottetown Accord alive on 26 October 1992.

The second camp of opposition to the accord included the inevitable opposition from outside Quebec to even the minimal demands of moderate Quebec leaders such as Premier Robert Bourassa. Such opponents rejected the granting of constitutional group armour-plating to moderate Quebec federalists and nationalists. This was the role played by the strange alliance of the Reform party, Pierre Trudeau and his hard-core anti-collective-rights followers across Canada, and finally perhaps the majority of Western Canadians. The Western Canadian opposition had concluded that the increased representation of Central Canada in the House of Commons, the guaranteed 25 per cent representation of Quebec in the House of Commons, the perceived underrepresentation of British Columbia in the same House, and the perceived lack of an effective reformed Senate were unacceptable.

Third, we saw the opposition, in varying degrees of forcefulness, of the other groups in our democratic polity who had concluded that either their vital concerns were imperfectly harvested from the political segment of the constitutional process or, worse still, were left unharvested, to wither away outside the Charlottetown Accord in general and the Canada Clause in particular. It is on these groups and their concerns about the statement of fundamental values contained in the Canada Clause that I wish to concentrate for the rest of this paper.

The Canada Clause was proposed as an amendment to section 2 of the Constitution Act, 1867. It would have served as a mandatory interpretative clause for the entire Constitution, including the Canadian Charter of Rights and Freedoms. It read as follows:

2. (1) The Constitution of Canada, including the *Canadian Charter of Rights and Freedoms*, shall be interpreted in a manner consistent with the following fundamental characteristics:

(a) Canada is a democracy committed to a parliamentary and federal system of government and to the rule of law;

(b) the Aboriginal peoples of Canada, being the first peoples to govern this land, have the right to promote their languages, cultures and traditions and to ensure the integrity of their societies, and their governments constitute one of the three orders of government in Canada;

(c) Quebec constitutes within Canada a distinct society, which includes a French-speaking majority, a unique culture and a civil law tradition;

(d) Canadians and their governments are committed to the vitality and development of official language minority communities throughout Canada;

(e) Canadians are committed to racial and ethnic equality in a society that includes citizens from many lands who have contributed, and continue to contribute, to the building of a strong Canada that reflects its cultural and racial diversity;

(f) Canadians are committed to a respect for individual and collective rights and freedoms of all people;

(g) Canadians are committed to the equality of male and female persons; and

(h) Canadians confirm the principle of the equality of the provinces at the same time as recognizing their diverse characteristics.

(2) The role of the legislature and Government of Quebec to preserve and promote the distinct society of Quebec is affirmed.

(3) Nothing in this section derogates from the powers, rights or privileges of the Parliament or of the Government of Canada, or of the legislatures or governments of the provinces, or of the legislative bodies or governments of the Aboriginal peoples of Canada, including any powers, rights or privileges relating to language and, for greater certainty, nothing in this section derogates from the aboriginal and treaty rights of the Aboriginal peoples of Canada.

A constitution without an interpretative vision of a nation's past, present, and future is like an artist who possesses the tools of her trade, but has lost or, worse still, never had the creative vision that drives the artistic process. Had Canada obtained through the Canada Clause the truly inclusive and inspiring creative vision of its nationhood, as demanded by its citizens before the Spicer Commission, the Dobbie-Beaudoin Parliamentary Committee, the various provincial constitutional committees, and the public constitutional conferences? The clause was as inspiring as anything that is written by a committee can be, but was it even inclusive enough to meet the rigorous demands of the group-based democracy in Canada?

The answer is that it was inclusive enough to meet the demands of the representatives of groups that were able to be part of the real constitutional decision-making process. Thus, the distinct-society provisions, the Aboriginal-peoples provisions, and the equality-of-provinces provisions satisfied those collectivities directly involved in the decision-making process. It should be noted that the Native Womens' Association felt that the Aboriginal womens' concerns had been excluded, and pursued a comprehensive legal strategy to remedy this exclusion.

Premier Clyde Wells of Newfoundland attempted to explain away his reversal of position on the distinct-society provisions, which are for the most part identical to those found in the Meech Lake constitutional accord. He dreamed up a new equality to add to his fundamental federal principles of equality of provinces and citizens, which he titled 'the equality of the founding peoples of Canada.' The First Nations and ethnocultural groups may have problems with this new Wellsian equality.

The Canada Clause was also substantially inclusive enough for one set of groups who were sufficiently organized through the political segment of the process, and as observers at the multilateral negotiations through the generosity of the Native Council of Canada, to achieve substantially what they wanted. These groups were the various francophone groups organized outside Quebec, who lobbied extremely hard for wording that would commit governments to the vitality and development of official language minority communities. Many governments, in particular the federal and Quebec governments, desired initially only a weak reference to the preservation of such minorities. This position was vehemently opposed by the francophone groups, who argued that such wording would guarantee only the 'pickling' of their threatened communities.

The major groups who felt their vital concerns were not completely incorporated into the Canada Clause were ethnocultural groups, women's groups, disabled groups, and other disadvantaged groups. Their objections can be summarized as follows.

The ethnocultural groups were not impressed that clause (f) of the Canada Clause, coming immediately after the linguistic-minority clause, dropped the reference that governments in Canada are also committed to racial and ethnic equality. The same could also be said of the gender-equality clause in clause (g), which caused the National Action Committee on the Status of Women to conclude that there was a danger that a hierarchy of rights was being created, with racial and ethnic equality and gender equality lower down on the rights totem-pole. In addition, NAC was also concerned that the wording of the gender-equality clause would promote the concept of formal equality. This concept was rejected in the context of the section 15(1) equality guarantee in the Charter by the Supreme Court, in *Andrews v. Law Society of British Columbia*,[10] in favour of the richer concept of substantive equality for disadvantaged groups and persons in our society. Fearful that the wording and structure of the Canada Clause would thus endanger already hard-won gains by women, NAC decided, partly on these grounds, to officially oppose ratification of the Charlottetown Accord.

The Canadian Ethnocultural Council, the main umbrella organization for thousands of ethnocultural community organizations across the country, decided not to oppose the accord as a whole in the interests of national unity, but registered its disapproval of the wording of the Canada Clause. The CEC also recommended changes that would in its opinion prevent a hierarchy of rights being created.

The concern of the disabled groups centred on the fact that they had been completely left out of the Canada Clause, again reinforcing the possibility that a hierarchy of rights was being created by the wording and structure of the clause. They were particularly incensed that the original shopping list for the Canada Clause suggested by the federal government in September 1991 included a reference to the disabled and other disadvantaged groups. This reference was dropped during the multilateral negotiations. After a very public and intense protest by these groups, Constitutional Affairs Minister Joe Clark indicated it might be possible to meet their concerns after the 26 October 1992 referendum. The disabled groups ultimately rejected this offer and came out against the accord.

The reaction of many commentators, that such 'special interest' demands are stifling democracy in Canada and perhaps even threatening its continued existence, was inevitable. When do interests cease to be 'special' and become democratic? Perhaps when they do not need to organize into groups because they already control the economic and political levers of our society. Then they can be premiers or party bosses, captains of industry and opinion leaders, but never 'special interests' who fight for recognition in the Canada Clause.

Moreover the condemnatory attitude towards some of the so-called special-interest groups has often ignored the unifying actions of such groups. One prime example was the Canadian Ethnocultural Council, which decided to support the Charlottetown Accord in the interests of national unity, even though it felt that the accord had not achieved, potentially to the detriment of its communities, a truly inclusive and inspiring vision of this country that mandates equal concern and respect for all.

Finally, I registered my strong support for the Charlottetown Accord for the following reasons.

The structural and legal flaws in the Canada Clause were capable of being remedied.

The Aboriginal package was an essential beginning to the restoration of group dignity to the Aboriginal peoples of the land. Those who opposed the accord and draw comfort from the fact that the on-reserve vote was heavily against the accord ignore one fact. The on-reserve populations voted against the accord because, from their perspective, the Aboriginal package offered, inter alia, too little in the way of safeguarding and promoting treaty rights and too little detail on the financing of self-government. It is very uncertain that governments will offer more or even the same in future constitutional rounds. I feel a deep sorrow for the missed historic opportunity to build a base of constitutional justice for our Aboriginal peoples.

Next, the acceptance of an armour-plated Quebec within Confederation is infinitely better than the potential for an Associate-State of Quebec or an independent Quebec that would stand as a testament to the failure of Canadians to appreciate the country's transcendent and terrifyingly beautiful diversity.

The failure of Canadians to approve the Charlottetown Accord now puts the burden on those who have to rule under the status quo to recognize, in non-constitutional ways, the value of diversity and substantive equality in our society or to turn ugly and deny such diversity and equality – until the next constitutional reform battle. But can such a quagmire be avoided?

NOTES

1 For the most extensive historical account of the fate of the Meech Lake Constitu-

tional Accord, see Patrick J. Monahan, *Meech Lake: The Inside Story* (Toronto: University of Toronto Press 1991).

2 See Cairns, *Disruptions: Constitutional Struggles from the Charter to Meech Lake* (Toronto: McClelland and Stewart 1991).

3 The Beaudoin-Edwards Committee on the Amending Formula and the Beaudoin-Dobbie Committee on a Renewed Canada

4 These were public fora hastily arranged by Constitutional Affairs Minister Joe Clark at the time that the Castonguay-Dobbie Committee seemed near to collapse. The fora involved consultation on various aspects of the Constitution with experts, advocacy groups, and citizens at six televised national conferences that took place between January and March 1992. A compendium of reports from these conferences, titled 'Renewal of Canada Conferences,' can be obtained from the Privy Council Office, Government of Canada.

5 A word coined by Mary Eberts in her presentation to the Beaudoin-Dobbie Committee; see the Minutes of the Proceedings and Evidence before the Committee, 22 Apr. 1991.

6 See the *Globe and Mail*, 28 March 1992, A6.

7 See the *Consensus Report on the Constitution, Charlottetown, August 28, 1992.*

8 It became inevitable that the author of the report himself would oppose the Charlottetown Accord; see *Le Devoir*, 28 aout 1992, 1.

9 See articles 1, 18, 21, 25–39, and 57–59 of the Charlottetown Accord.

10 [1989] 1 S.C.R. 143

13

The Charlottetown Accord: A Canadian Compromise*

PETER LOUGHEED

I propose to address four issues. First, how did we get into this constitutional crisis? Second, what pressures are involved in creating agreement among eleven first ministers? Third, how does the Charlottetown August 1992 agreement meet Canada's needs today? And finally, what are the implications of a 'yes' vote on 26 October of this year?

At the outset, let me confess that this is my first focused address on the Charlottetown agreement. I think with some wry amusement, whether it's true or not, that I am speaking on this first occasion in what is perceived to be, in some parts of the country, the core of centralist thinking in Canada. Now, not all of you would agree with that, but there would be a number of you who would. But I thought, 'Well, this is probably the place for Peter to start.'

Let me start with the first question: 'How did we get into this constitutional crisis?' And it *is* a crisis that we are in!

Ever since 1931 there remained one last vestige of colonialism – the fact that the constitution of our country still resided with the mother of parliaments in the United Kingdom. We Canadians could not agree on an amending formula that would allow us to bring back, or 'patriate,' the Constitution. And this situation continued for many years, as you know, on into the mid-1960s, when a partriation effort, known as the Fulton-Favreau formula, was made. But none of these efforts was ever accepted. It should be kept in mind that throughout all these years there was never the slightest question that, when the Canadian government presented a proposed constitutional change to the Parliament in Westminster, regarding unemployment insurance or whatever, it would be accepted by Britain.

Then we moved, in 1971, to the attempts in Victoria to develop an amending

* Delivered as Pierre Genest Memorial Lecture, York University, 23 September 1992.

formula. The Victoria formula essentially allowed for a veto by the larger provinces of Québec and Ontario, along with only two of the four Western provinces and only two of the Atlantic provinces. I was then an aspiring opposition leader, about two months from being elected. I took issue with the Victoria formula on the basis that it meant that the other eight were made second-class provinces. I think you have heard similar phrases recently. They started at that point. As you know, Mr Bourassa, for other reasons, turned aside from what was agreed to in Victoria. The formula, as with the other elements of the Victoria Charter, then collapsed. The issue did not arise again until 1976 when Prime Minister Trudeau wrote to me in my capacity as chair of the annual Premiers' Conference, to raise again the question of a constitutional amending formula and other matters.

Within not too many months, the Parti Québécois was elected in Québec. As a result, there was a waiting period with regard to the constitutional issue. Over the period 1971–80, the constitutional issue was not on the front burner, so to speak, of the national agenda. But it has certainly been on the front burner since that time.

In 1980 we had the referendum in Québec. Although the view is controversial, there are many who felt that the 'no' vote represented an undertaking to respond to the distinct society of Québec in some way. (The phrase 'distinct society,' from my recollection, was not used in precisely those terms, but that was the meaning.) But others take the view that that undertaking was not given.

Then we had the constitutional conference in September 1980, in which an effort was made to deal with many of the issues. It resulted in a lack of agreement. Finally, on 2 October 1980, the federal government and the prime minister moved ahead with a unilateral package on the Constitution. That was the start of the process that brings us to today.

The dramatic year was 1981, starting with parliamentary hearings in the House of Commons, and then the procedural wrangle that involved the ringing of the bells in the House by the Opposition, led by Joe Clark. That was followed by the undertaking by the federal government to not proceed with the matter until the Supreme Court of Canada rendered its decision on the issue. The Court's decision, in September 1981, found that what was proposed by the federal government was legal but not constitutional. At the first ministers' conference in November 1981, the ultimately agreed-upon elements were patriation, an amending formula proposed by Alberta that involved the opting-out provisions, the Charter of Rights with the notwithstanding clause, and the Saskatchewan taxation resource initiative. That really was it.

But, as you all know, we ended that fateful day in November with Mr Lévesque walking out of the room and refusing to sign. I tried, as others did, to have him stay by broadening the compensation on the opting-out provision, beyond education or other cultural matters, to all elements. That, by the way, is proposed today in the Charlottetown agreement. But he walked, and so it became a very difficult matter.

I have two observations with the benefit of hindsight. First of all, it was a bad time to attempt constitutional change. We were dealing with a government in Québec that was committed to sovereignty. A second observation I hold today, that I did not hold then because of the nature of the environment, is that perhaps under any circumstances Mr Lévesque was caught within party politics and could not have signed any constitutional document.

In any event, we move to 1986. The premiers of Canada (I was no longer there, having been succeeded by Mr Getty) met in Edmonton – just the premiers. They discussed with Mr Bourassa the question of what should be done. I believe at that point that the vast majority of Canadians were of the view that to have a constitution in a federal system without the signature (and I want to emphasize that word 'signature') of the Government and the National Assembly of Québec really impacts the credibility of that constitution and its legitimacy. My belief is that it was incomplete and some action had to be taken to make sure that Québec was in fact a full participant in our Canadian constitution.

Out of that declaration by the premiers in Edmonton in 1986 came the 1987–90 period of Meech Lake and the failure of that accord. The Québec response, which you are very familiar with, involved the Bélanger-Campeau Commission and the Québec Liberal document, the Allaire report. Joe Clark was appointed unity minister for the federal government in 1991. His document in September of that year was followed by the six constitutional conferences that were held with citizens. That consultation led to very extensive negotiations with ministers and officials, culminating this past month with the first ministers' meetings in Harrington Lake and the Pearson Building in Ottawa and, finally, with the Charlottetown agreement.

I believe it is important to remember why all this occurred. In essence, it happened because the Constitution of 1982 was signed without the legitimacy that it needed to have from the province representing one of the founding nations of Canada – Québec.

Not as an aside, but directly, I want to take a moment to describe the pressures to create a unanimous first ministers' agreement, and the circumstances under which it must be achieved. It is important for people to understand these factors, and not many do. There is, first, the realization of the consequences of failure to reach an agreement. Added to this are the expectations citizens have for the conference or meeting, the cooperation required between all involved, and, of course, the subject-matter. When the subject is the Constitution the consequences of failure are significant. In November 1981 we tried hard. There were many compromises made. From the Alberta side, we thought that it was a very good day, in the sense that we had the amending formula we proposed with the opting-out provision, we had the notwithstanding clause, and we had Saskatchewan's tax resource provision. But none of us was happy with the incomplete result.

A sense of the consequences of failure played a key role in August 1992, at the first ministers' meeting at Harrington Lake. They discussed the enormity of the consequences, in their view, of 'no deal'; this discussion itself provoked compromise.

A second set of circumstances surrounding these meetings is something that I believe most of you know, but it needs to be underlined. When you go to one of these meetings as a first minister, you can be parochial, but only up to a point, because your own voters look on themselves as (to use my terminology) 'Canadians first and Albertans second.' You recognize that politics *is* the art of the possible and it is truly an art form.

Another element of these gatherings is the personal chemistry between the people. Few observers understand the importance of this factor. There are three groups: the eleven first ministers, the senior ministers of the Government, and the senior officials. In 1981 we had good chemistry between Mr Davis and Mr Trudeau, between Mr Blakeney and myself, between Mr McMurtry of Ontario and Mr Romanow of Saskatchewan, between the officials Peter Meekison of Alberta and Mel Smith of British Columbia, and between many others.

Then there is the matter of the political realities of the people around that table. The degree of support they have within their province and the scope they have for compromise are all-important. One thing I never found in my fourteen years as premier at these events was a party dogma that demanded, 'We can't do this because of the Party.' (The Parti Québécois was an exception.) There was always a feeling of trying to resolve the issues for the nation and your province. For example, I lived through a period of time in which there were three NDP premiers in Western Canada, and yet we accomplished a lot together.

Yes, Québec is recognized as distinct. Throughout these last negotiations I have thought, 'I hope they'll come with something new, something different that will be helpful to the Premier of Québec,' and they did. It was something that's a hard sell in the West, but it's there – the 25 per cent floor for House of Commons seats for Québec and Québec alone.

The political realities in August 1992 created – for me and I believe for you – some very unexpected, even some strange, compromises and results. I have reflected upon these events, and I now sense how the first ministers achieved the results they did. They had the intensity that was required to make a deal – the pressure from the prime minister and Mr Clark – and it worked in a unanimous way. If you ask me today what I thought at that time the chances were that they would make such a deal, I would have said no better than fifty-fifty. But I am pleased, deeply pleased, that they did.

Let me move next to how this final unanimous agreement meets Canada's needs today. Here I admit with candour to you that I am an advocate. I think it is important to note that Parliament supports the Charlottetown agreement – all major parties with negligible dissent. The agreement is also supported by the two territorial leaders and the four Aboriginal leaders that were involved. Everybody knows (but it needs to be restated) that in these situations nobody gets all they seek. And that's obviously because everyone starts with a negotiating position. We took that approach in 1981, wanting curtailment of federal-government spending power in Alberta. We didn't get that provision in the 1981 agreement. Mr Trudeau clearly did not want a notwithstanding clause with his Charter of Rights and he didn't want the Alberta amending formula. But we reached a compromise.

In 1992, quite clearly, Québec did not get what it set out to get in terms of the division of powers, as in the Allaire report – that was, in my view, a negotiating position. Newfoundland did, at the end of the day, accept the concept of a distinct-society clause.

So let me assess quickly for you some of the segments of this arrangement from the perspective I have, both from the West and from my background. I'll deal first with the division of powers, then with Québec as a distinct society, then quickly with Aboriginal self-government, and then with the central institutions, particularly the Senate. I will pass over the other elements because of limited time.

Let me start with the division of powers. In my judgment a balance is needed in this country between a strong central government and strong provincial governments. I've spent my lifetime on that issue. We hold different views here. In Toronto, I recognize, the inclination is more to the centralist point of view. If I was making the same remarks in Calgary, there would be a different reaction and the reasons are obvious.

The reality is that Canada is a federal system, both historically and necessarily, not a unitary one. The existing constitutional amending formula requiring the consent of seven provinces with 50 per cent of the population is a reflection of that reality. We have a huge country with varied resources – a thinly spread population with diverse opportunities. We have as well the distinctiveness of Québec.

I want to pause here and tell you about a tough issue I have had to ponder, and maybe some of you have as well. It's called 'asymmetry' – the idea of giving a particular power to the province of Québec and not to the other provinces. I'll probably surprise you with this, but when I saw what they did in Halifax in early January 1992, I was pleased. The idea would be a very hard sell in Alberta, but I was pleased with it. I thought there was scope for such an approach and that's what the people thought in Halifax as well. But, then, I guess I'm not facing voters and so perhaps I couldn't have sold it myself. In any event, the first ministers concluded that it couldn't be sold in other parts of Canada.

But leaving this issue aside, I believe the first ministers struck a sound balance between conflicting perceptions of the division of powers as they tried to move towards less duplication and overlap. The first element, and a very fundamental one, is the curtailment of the federal spending power. That curtailment is very important. The text reads: 'A provision should be added to the Constitution stipulating that the Government of Canada must provide reasonable compensation to the government of a province that chooses not to participate in a new Canada-wide shared-cost program that is established by the federal government in an area of exclusive provincial jurisdiction, if that province carries on a program or initiative that is compatible with the national objectives.'

That statement is important, very important, to Québec in view of its desire to control its own destiny. The key phrases are 'new' programs and respect for provincial priorities. I am aware that many in this room will disagree with this conclusion. I also sense that if I were in Vancouver or Montréal there would be a different view – that's the nature of Canada.

The second element is the immigration agreements, which are key in terms of the provinces and for Québec in particular. More and more these agreements are a factor in meeting provincial priorities and providing job opportunities. But then came the additional compromise – bilateral or multilateral federal-provincial agreements were to be protected from unilateral change. Many had said, What's the use of these agreements if they can be unilaterally changed? I thought they made a very important compromise by stating: 'The Constitution should be amended to provide a mechanism to ensure that designated agreements between governments are protected from unilateral change. This would occur when Parliament and the legislature(s) enact laws approving the agreement.' The agreements can be renegotiated after a sunset period of five years. I believe it was a good compromise, a very important one, because it means these agreements have a much stronger meaning and significance in the political arena.

The next major section of the agreement, in my judgment, is labour-market development and training. This is now to become an exclusive provincial jurisdiction. To me, this is very positive and very meaningful for change. I say that because of the degree of overlap and cross purposes between the federal and provincial governments in programs in the labour and training area. I want to take a moment here to focus on this issue, which is tied to the post-secondary education system, and relates to Canadian competitiveness. I worked as premier on pulling together community colleges and technical schools and apprenticeship programs. They fit, and have to fit, the job opportunities in the province of Alberta not, say, those in the province of Nova Scotia. There are very different needs province by province, according to the local business input, in what is required. What is important is building on these local strengths. So this was a key provision – for Québec, British Columbia, and for others. I realize that from a centralist point of view, there are concerns that this change would weaken national economic strategy. It will, to a degree. But if you balance that with the federal government's strength in control over trade and investment, in spheres such as the GATT or the North American Free Trade Agreement, and over monetary policy and tax policy, we still have in our Canadian federal system a very strong central government control on economic matters.

Now I go to a more difficult area, for me at least – culture. This was the most difficult and controversial issue that I saw on the list. When I became involved with the free-trade-agreement debate a few years back, we made it a condition that culture should be clearly excluded from the Canada-U.S. Free Trade Agreement and the North American Free Trade Agreement.

Let me deal with the issue by way of a reference, because the reference is important in terms of the question of culture: 'Provinces should have exclusive jurisdiction over cultural matters within the provinces. This should be recognized through an explicit constitutional amendment that also recognizes the continuing responsibility of the federal government in Canadian cultural matters. The federal government should retain responsibility for national cultural institutions ... The Government of Canada commits to negotiate cultural agreements with provinces in recognition of their lead responsibility for cultural matters within the province and to ensure that the federal government and the province work in harmony.' Of all the provisions in the agreement this one causes me the most anxiety. I believe the federal role in culture is important. But I believe it can be worked out with goodwill, ensuring that those national cultural institutions such as the CBC are sustained and that there is in fact harmony.

I won't deal here with the other areas of the agreement in terms of the division of powers – forestry, mining, housing, tourism, recreation, and municipal affairs. My conclusion is that a good balance was struck. It fits the realities of the nineties, certainly the fiscal realities. There has been major waste, and the agreement offers a real prospect for reducing that waste.

The second segment of the Constitution that I want to deal with today is Québec's distinct society. The text of the agreement basically refers to the responsibility of the province of Québec to preserve and protect the French language and culture.

Now this issue has been controversial, but this is what Canada *is*. Whether one likes it or not, Québec is a distinct society in our midst. I believe this is an essential constitutional provision, and I take the view that it will be very meaningful. I take objection with the view that when somebody gains, the others lose. Yes, this provision is a gain for Québec. But I do not see it as a loss for the West or for other parts of the country. It doesn't always follow that a gain for one region of the country results in a loss or a decline for another. I believe that the courts will interpret 'distinct society' in a meaningful way, but with balance. I have confidence that they will do so based on a review of the history of decided cases in matters of this nature.

I mention a supplement to this provision – the 25 per cent seat guarantee for Québec in the House of Commons. This was a key concern of Québec regarding Senate reform. Québec has always had more than 25 per cent of the population and that is unlikely to drop much. But if I were the premier of Québec I would want that provision very much in order to sell the agreement in my province.

Now a short reference to Aboriginal self-government. Simply put, we *must* respond in fairness to this issue. Yes, I share the concern of many that there are many diverse groups involved and it will be difficult to reach an understanding. I agree that it is a leap of faith, but I for one am prepared to take it.

Let me move, finally, in this segment of my evaluation to the issue of the central institutions and the Senate. The question is, and it rages in my province and in British Columbia, Does the compromise regarding the Senate give the proponents of Senate reform (essentially the West and Atlantic Canada) what they wanted? What they wanted was an institution in the centre that can balance what has been called the tyranny of the majority in central Canada.

The compromise reached on the Senate is not as much as I would have wanted, but it is as much as I expected. The issue is effectiveness. Why do I believe the Senate would be effective? Because I believe the senators will be influential. And I believe that on the basis of some hard political realities. Number one, they will be elected. Number two, a senator will represent a larger constituency than the average MP. And here's the one that I like the best: it has to do with the pressures around being selected for the cabinet. You've got the new Senator X from Alberta. The Prime Minister's Office can't phone him and say, 'Now look, Henry, if you don't behave you'll never get in the cabinet.' Because Henry can say, 'Look, haven't you read, I can *never* be in the cabinet.' Don't underrate that factor. It can have a considerable bearing on the independence and thinking and attitude of the senators in this process. I can go on here, but I would just emphasize that I believe the Senate will be, in fact, very effective. It will be fascinating to see how it will work out.

Let me give my overall evaluation of the agreement. I am going to do something here that some people told me I shouldn't do. As a Westerner, I will attempt to assess this deal from a Québec point of view. I'm told that's dangerous. Well, looking at it from a Québec point of view, I say there are some very important gains. The agreement responds to the implied or express promises in 1980 about recognizing the special position of Québec in Canada. I wanted so much for Mr Lévesque to sign on that morning. As I mentioned, I now feel he was trapped by party politics. I don't think there is legitimacy without the signature of the Government and National Assembly of Québec on our Constitution.

What have Quebeckers gained? I believe they gain in a very meaningful way the provisions for a distinct society. They gain the double majority in the Senate to protect their distinctiveness; the joint sittings in the Senate to balance the equality of the provinces; the division of powers with regard to spending, intergovernmental agreements, labour development and training, and other matters; the 25 per cent guarantee in the House of Commons; and the opting-out, full-compensation provision in terms of the amending formula.

From the point of view of the rest of Canada, a constructive compromise keeps a strong central government, reduces duplication, and responds to provincial priorities, particularly in terms of labour development and training and spending power. It gives us a new Senate that, for those of us in the West and Atlantic Canada, will be influential, and within the cultural field still preserves national institutions. You can judge by my remarks that I don't think the deal is perfect. How could I conceivably think it's perfect? Clearly, it was reached in a process of compromise.

Let me close this way: What are the implications of a 'yes' vote on October 26th? Obviously, I feel very positive in that then we can get on with a job-creation focus. Now, two arguments have been raised against voting 'yes,' both of which I think are simply wrong. First, some have suggested that if we vote 'yes' in Québec and elsewhere, it won't end anything. Québec will be back at the national table with more demands from the nationalists. My view is this is simply wrong, and I would like to explain why.

If you go back to the period 1981–6, what was troubling Canada was that we had a country and a Constitution of which Quebeckers were not legitimately a part because they hadn't signed. The motivation to respond to Québec was not based on threats, but on the view that we really had to have a Constitution with Québec as a signed party to it. The motivation was to get them to sign up.

So if, on October 26th, there is a 'yes' vote in Québec and elsewhere, the Government of Québec, the National Assembly of Québec in its majority, will be obliged to sign up. After the signature, it's over. Yes, it's over. The Constitution won't get on the national agenda for a dozen years. I was there in 1977 and 1978, and I saw the PQ try to put it on the national agenda; they didn't even get close. After what we've gone through in this country between 1987 and 1992, it won't soon get on the agenda. So to those people who make the argument, which I believe is fallacious, that if we vote Yes we'll never satisfy the demands of Québec nationalists, I say this: yes, those demands will always be there. The nature and the history of Canada will make it so. But the notion that these demands will be on the national agenda in the period ahead of up to a dozen years is, in my opinion, false.

Now there's another view that primarily comes from the West, and it says: 'Vote "no." The deal's not perfect. We'll have a moratorium for five years, during which time the status quo will continue and then we'll negotiate again.' Well, my first problem with that point of view is it isn't very smart for us Westerners. The fact is, we did gain some important things here. The prospect that we would be able, sometime in the future, to re-establish those gains, particularly with regard to an elected Senate and control over national appointments, simply isn't in the cards. It was only because of the pressure for national unity, to make trade-offs, to have Québec 'come aboard,' that these gains for the West were achieved in this agreement. So I don't think it's very smart to say, 'We'll vote "no" and then we'll negotiate a better deal later.'

Second, what about the view that the status quo would simply continue in the face of a 'no' vote? Gee, who are we kidding? Québec is going to drift away and become more isolated. We'll have a divided country. There will be no national effort at reaching consensus on other issues, and there are lots of other issues. Now I'm not saying there aren't good grounds to have logical debate about these questions; this conference is doing just that. Is there too much decentralization, will the Senate that is proposed ever work, what are the consequences of Aboriginal self-government, and can we pull all elements of the package together? There are lots of reasons for very healthy debate over the weeks ahead.

Let me conclude this way. We haven't had much experience outside Québec with referenda. I had one experience when I was running for office. We had a plebiscite in Alberta about daylight saving. I was trying hard to convince a farmer one morning to vote for me. He said, 'Peter, I don't want to talk about that. Don't you know that we're having a plebiscite on daylight saving? And you tell me, are we going to have to get up one hour earlier every single day?' I was trying to get the subject back to voting for me, but that was in his mind.

Now referenda are funny things. My experience is pretty limited, but I'm told by those who know that it will be volatile and emotional, and that those against the proposition will turn out to vote. There will probably be people south of Calgary who will vote 'no' because they don't like the provincial law with regard to Sunday shopping. That will happen. Similar things will happen all across the country. For those who are on the Yes side, there had better be a large turnout.

Now in my world today, friends – and I'm involved in international business – in this new global reality, Canada is being passed by; by investment, by purchase of our goods, our resources, our services. I am deeply troubled that my children's generation – my four kids – will not have as good a life as mine. I fear that they won't have the same number of opportunities and they'll have a greater risk of job loss than my generation has had. It doesn't have to happen, and I think Pierre Genest, if he were here, would agree with this one. We can develop new attitudes in our country with regard to skills training and growth areas. I believe Canadians can be the best traders in the world. We can provide for young people the job opportunities that our generation had. But we have got to get on with it – and soon. We can only do that with a unified country, seeking and securing and focusing on our place in the new global reality.

PART FOUR

The Referendum

14

The October 1992 Canadian Constitutional Referendum: The Socio-Political Context

MICHAEL ADAMS

The United Nations Development Program ranked Canada first in the world for quality of life in 1992; the United States placed only sixth. Does that mean Canadians are among the luckiest people on earth? Undoubtedly, that is what many of the people wanting to emigrate to Canada think. But is that how Canadians see themselves? Are they as content, secure, and grateful as one would expect the citizens of such a fortunate land to be?

Our surveys show that most Canadians recognize they have it pretty good, compared with people in other parts of the world. Nevertheless, they have deep misgivings about the way their country is being managed, and they are increasingly pessimistic about the future. This public angst stems in part from the psychological impact of living through a two-year recession. But our data indicate that today's anxiety runs deeper than concern over the current economic situation, that it speaks to an intense frustration with the performance of the nation's political institutions.

A November 1991 Environics survey examined Canadian and American attitudes on a number of quality-of-life dimensions, and compared current data with tracking data from 1986. The 1991 survey found that large majorities of Canadians were satisfied with the environment in their area, with social and health services for the poor and elderly, and with their opportunities to get ahead. However, only one-third (34 per cent) of Canadians said that they were satisfied with the Canadian system of government. This percentage represented a huge decline of seventeen points since 1986. Six in ten (62 per cent, an increase of sixteen points since 1986) reported they were dissatisfied with their system of government.

Americans expressed a similar decline in satisfaction with their system of government. Although a slight majority of 52 per cent said they were satisfied, this percentage was down twenty-four points from 1986, and the percentage who said they were dissatisfied had more than doubled in five years to 46 per cent.

Looking further at Canadian attitudes towards their government, Environics' quarterly FOCUS CANADA survey of 2019 adult Canadians, conducted in September 1992, found that only 21 per cent were satisfied with the performance of their federal government. Even fewer, 18 per cent, approved of the performance of Prime Minister Brian Mulroney, and fewer still – just 15 per cent – said they would vote for his party if an election were held that day. Moreover, that 15 per cent somewhat overstates the case since, according to polling custom, it excludes the 23 per cent who were undecided or refused to state a preference. The Tories' actual support in September stood at an unbelievably low 11 per cent. Nor are the federal Tories alone in their low standing. As of September 1992, only two of eleven senior governments in this country enjoy the approval of a majority of their electorates.

So why have Canadians turned so sour on their government? At least part of the explanation, I believe, lies in the cumulative effect of unpopular policies. Free trade has taught people they can't trust the politicians to tell them the truth about the economy. Where are all those new jobs? And the main lesson of the Meech Lake débâcle and the imposition of the GST is that an élitist approach to governing is unacceptable to a less deferential electorate. Indeed, all forms of political élitism – from patronage at the constituency level to an appointed Senate – are now rejected by Canadians, not only as anachronistic, but as intolerable. To quote the burnt-out television newsman in the movie *Network*: 'We're mad as hell and we're not going to take it anymore!' People are looking at the activities of their nation's politicians and they're concluding that both the process and the results are sadly lacking.

Put in its simplest terms, the current mood is one of *anxiety* and *disillusionment*. We question the ability of our leaders, and our institutions, to solve the problems we see around us. In other words, Canadians are as upset by what the politicians haven't done as by what they have done.

First and foremost, Canadians are anxious about an economy that is both experiencing a cyclical recession and is in the throes of major structural change. They see the results as not only temporary unemployment, but long-term job losses – and, on a personal level, an increasingly ingrained sense of insecurity about one's future employment. Our surveys find the recession has resulted in a steady increase in anxiety over economic issues. Our quarterly FOCUS CANADA surveys show that concern about the economy and unemployment are now higher than they have been since the mid-1980s. In September, 30 per cent of Canadians cited unemployment and 21 per cent the economy as the most important problem facing Canadians today.

Among those with university degrees, we find the reverse pattern of response: 32 per cent cited the economy, while 21 per cent selected unemployment, as the country's most important issue. This difference is significant. In the past, Canadians typically focused on the symptoms of our economic problems – unemployment, inflation, and interest rates, for example. But the better-informed are becoming increasingly aware of the underlying structural factors such as public-sector debt, productivity, and the competitiveness of our industries.

Among the general public, our polling shows an increasing anxiety over the growing importance of international market forces in economics and communications. These market forces, acting in tandem with consumer demand, have eroded the ties that held Canadians together in the past. The election of a pro–free trade government in 1988 has been the most dramatic indication of the strength of these forces, reversing a century-long commitment in Canadian public policy.

Canadians are also anxious about the physical environment and the global ecology. It's hard to believe that just a few years ago concern over the environment was largely focused on aesthetics and lost recreational opportunities. Now Canadians see the deterioration of the environment as something that threatens their own health and that of future generations.

Our surveys also find a growing consensus that crime is a serious problem for society in general and for us as individuals. We are anxious about escalating violence, both inside and outside the home, and a growing underclass of youth.

We are anxious about the legacy of public debt that the current generation is leaving for the next. In the past, and especially in the years immediately following the Second World War, people took for granted that the next generation would have a higher standard of living than the preceding one. However, the era of 'presumed prosperity' has been replaced by one of 'diminishing expectations.' Our surveys find only a minority of Canadians believe today's young people will be better off than today's adults. Instead, there is a definite feeling that our children will actually be worse off, that they will not be able to look to governments for all the solutions, and that they had better start looking out for themselves. The sense of pessimism about the future – so rampant today – is perhaps greater than at any time since Europeans first set foot on North American shores.

Finally, we are anxious about living in a country that is being torn apart by powerful centrifugal forces and an overloaded constitutional agenda. There's a feeling that the Constitution is an issue for politicians, not for people, and that our leaders are wasting valuable time and resources that could be better spent on issues of greater relevance to our everyday lives. The mismatch between the priorities of the politicians and those of the general public may be wider today then at any time in our history. And if the discepancy continues, it will mean not only a series of one-term governments, but calls for fundamental changes to our system of government.

We at Environics, after examining nearly two decades of tracking data on public attitudes, have concluded that the growing crisis of confidence in to-day's politicians is indicative of an erosion of confidence in the basic elements of the country's political institutions and in the system of party politics that evolved out of British colonial rule in the nineteenth century. We have further concluded that many of the institutions and practices that have characterized the political process since 1867 are no longer suited to the values and expecta-tions of Canadians on the eve of the third millennium, and that, in the absence of democratic reforms, the Canadian political system is in danger of losing its legitimacy in the public mind.

Since the nation's founding in 1867, Canada's politics has been character-ized by a process referred to as 'élite accommodation.' If Americans have been united by their 'values,' Canadians have been divided by 'interests,' primarily linguistic and regional. It has been largely through the brokering of these competing interests by the political élites that the country has stayed together. Today, the legitimacy – not to mention the efficacy – of this process of 'élite accommodation' has come under serious strain, as international economic and cultural forces erode the ties that once bound francophones to anglophones and eastern Canadians to their compatriots in the West.

Our governing institutions presume a relatively passive electorate, one that was willing to let the political élites work out the compromises that kept the country together, developed the public infrastructure, and created the social-welfare state. The electorate's role was limited to indicating its approval when the government sought it, or to replacing the 'ins' with the 'outs' every four or five years.

However, since the early 1970s, we have seen massive changes in the socio-economic context in which Canadian governments must operate. These changes have reduced governments' ability to deliver the level of economic growth and state-sponsored services voters had come to take for granted. In the Canada of the 1980s, it became clear that governments do not have the fiscal resources needed to create the great national projects that had traditionally elicited public gratitude and support. No equivalent of a continental railroad, national broad-casting network, or system of public health insurance can now be afforded. Instead, voters are seeing the erosion of public services and ever-increasing taxes. In the 1950s, Canadians began to doubt the ability of organized religion to deliver eternal life; in the 1980s, they have recognized the inability of their governments to deliver eternal security.

Paralleling the deteriorating economic conditions in which governments must operate are radical changes in the social context over the past generation. The demographic evolution of the population has altered the structure of the Canadian family, the role and status of women, and the country's ethnic and racial composition. Complementing these demographic changes is widespread socio-cultural change – that is, changes in the values, attitudes, motivations, and lifestyles of the Canadian people. Canadian social values have changed in ways that make maintenance of the ideologies and accommodations of the past much more difficult.

One major and continuing source of diversity in Canadian society is the increasing numbers of people who are not descended from one of Canada's two founding groups, the English and the French. According to the 1871 census, 92 per cent of Canadians were of either British or French descent. By 1986, that figure had declined to 58 per cent. The British Isles and France now account for less than 5 per cent of the immigration to Canada, with most of the others coming from non-European, non-Caucasian sources.

The growth in the percentage of the population who are of neither English nor French origin has helped erode the legitimacy of the 'two charter groups' theory of Canada in favour of a perspective in which Canada is the home of unhyphenated citizens living in a federation of ten equal provinces. French Quebeckers are insecure in the face of these demographic realities and this insecurity leads to their ambivalence about their province's continuing participation in the Canadian federation. That province may well be led to a more extreme form of sovereignty than most of its citizens actually want if a new constitutional accommodation cannot be found with the rest of the country. (On the question of Quebec's status in Canada, Environics' September 1992 survey found that 42 per cent of Quebeckers favoured their province becoming an independent country; and 60 per cent want sovereignty together with economic association with the rest of Canada.)

Another source of demographic diversity is the baby-boom generation. The eight million Canadians born between 1946 and 1966 are generally better educated and more urbane than their parents. Moreover, they grew up in an era that took prosperity for granted. This generation is characterized by an orientation to the individual, a rejection of traditional roles and statuses, and a deep cynicism towards the motives of institutions. Baby-boomers are more egalitarian and less patriarchal than their parents, and they tend to question authority, rather than defer to it. This is the generation that is most disillusioned with Canada's politicians and political institutions, and most likely to support new processes for consensus building and decision making.

By the late 1980s, the new values of the baby-boom generation had moved well beyond that generation to affect Canadian society as a whole. The egalitarian ethic, for example, is reflected in the psychological affluence of minority groups once relegated to the periphery of society. Canada's Native peoples, women, ethnic and racial minorities, the disabled, the elderly, victims of domestic violence and sexual abuse – these and other traditionally powerless groups have liberated themselves from the silence and stereotyping of the past to demand recognition, social justice, and opportunities. As a result, we see the increasingly important role played by these interest groups in Canadian politics. These economic, demographic, and socio-cultural forces all combine to undermine the Canadian 'political nationality' that George-Etienne Cartier spoke of more than a century ago.

Although Canadians' disillusionment with the system seldom results in the violent demonstrations of discontent so evident elsewhere in the world, this should offer little solace to Canada's political incumbents. Our polling data lead us to conclude that Canadians have stopped believing that Parliament and the political parties represent the interests of the people. Their MPs, once elected, seem to become vassals to an alien system that has little in common with the aspirations of the average citizen who elected them. To many Canadians, MPs do not look like crusaders fighting for their constituents' interests, but rather like trained seals barking to the beat of some partisan drummer. As for the televised theatrics of Question Period, they no longer meet the demand for democratic accountability.

The image of Parliament as an unresponsive institution is further evidenced in the low level of public support found for federal-government policies over the last few years. Take, for example, the goods and services tax and the Meech Lake constitutional accord. Was either an issue in the 1988 election campaign? Was either even mentioned? In the absence of public debate, how can anyone seriously claim that the government received a popular mandate to proceed with these two important initiatives?

At the time of its introduction in January 1991, the goods and services tax had the support of only 22 per cent of Canadians. By May 1990, just weeks before the Meech Lake Accord died, an Environics survey found that only 35 per cent of Canadians approved it. In fact, the Meech Lake agreement was a prime example of politicians not reflecting the views of the people. Although all three major federal parties supported the accord, this important constitutional reform did not receive majority approval from the Canadian public. Our other polling showed people were as repulsed by the élitist approach of the negotiation and ratification process as they were by the controversial aspects of the accord itself.

How much longer can our system bear the strain of so much important public policy being rejected by the majority of the people? Is it not becoming clear that, however well intentioned recent government legislation, or however wise it may seem to certain experts or élites, the process of its development, in today's context, lacks political legitimacy? To average Canadians, the system doesn't work anymore, or at least it doesn't work for them. Canada's political institutions will need to be reformed in fundamental ways if the politicians are to win back the confidence of the people they wish to represent. Merely changing the political players will not be good enough. The rules of the game must change.

But changing the decision-making process will not solve all our problems. Governments in the 1990s – whatever their political stripe – will still find themselves faced with the twin challenges of paying the bills for past commitments and attempting to maintain as much of the public infrastructure and social safety net as possible. None of this is good news.

On the issue of public spending and public services, Canadians and their politicians are going through a difficult phase that can be likened to a person's response to the news of imminent death. Elizabeth Kubler-Ross has written that people go through five stages when faced with such information: denial, anger, bargaining, depression, and finally acceptance. I believe Canadians as a whole are going through similar stages as they grapple with the implications of the new economic paradigm for their lives and with their relationship with government.

The defeat of the Charlottetown Accord also has consequences for the public agenda. Sooner or later we will see the re-emergence of constitutional issues, whether the majority of Canadian voters and their politicians want it or not. The question is not *if* the Constitution will return as a salient topic, but *when*. Any one of three forces could push the Constitution back on the front burner: Quebec's desire for a different status, Natives' aspirations for self-rule, and Westerners' populist hopes for more representative central institutions.

Quebec is most likely to make the first really serious move in terms of Canadian federalism. An Environics poll conducted from 9–15 October, in the midst of the referendum campaign, asked what should happen next, if the Charlottetown Accord failed. Nearly two-thirds of Quebeckers either wanted talks to begin for a new constitutional agreement (36 per cent) or wished negotiations to begin for a sovereign Quebec (28 per cent).

These sentiments may subside for a period while people catch their breath, but it seems certain that the issue of Quebec's place in Confederation will figure prominently in the next provincial election in Quebec, which will happen sometime in the next eighteen months. When it does, Mr Bourassa or his successor will probably maintain a position of nuanced federalism within Confederation and Mr Parizeau or his successor will maintain a position of some sort of 'sovereignty' with economic association with the rest of Canada. No one can predict the outcome of this contest or any subsequent referendum on sovereignty in Quebec, but one can predict with virtual certainty that there is little sympathy in the rest of Canada for renewed constitutional discussions, particularly if the topic is some sort of special status for Quebec. In the 9–15 October poll, the position adopted by the plurality of Canadians outside Quebec (48 per cent) was that there should be no new constitutional discussions should the Charlottetown Accord fail.

At this stage, Canadian leaders appear to lack both a vision and a process for keeping the country together (unless we accept the status quo). As for the aspirations of the Aboriginals and the populists, these will probably be eclipsed by events in Quebec, particularly since the majority of Native Canadians rejected the Charlottetown Accord. For the foreseeable future, these and the host of other interest groups wanting a piece of the constitutional pie will be forced to concentrate their energies within the current constitutional framework.

Whatever one's position on the Charlottetown Accord, almost everyone will agree that it marks the end of the era of élite accommodation in matters constitutional and the beginning of a new era of public consultation and ratification. In fact, the one truly revolutionary change in our constitutional process to have occurred in the past decade – the referendum – has never been included in the formal Constitution. Perhaps there is a message here for Canadians, especially our politicians, lawyers, and constitutional mandarins.

15

The Referendum and Its Aftermath

JEFFREY SIMPSON

Were they soon tempted to change the Constitution by formal amendments, Canadians would be invited to experience again the joys and dangers of a national referendum. Though 'One swallow does not a summer necessarily make,' one constitutional referendum probably does. The 26 October referendum created a precedent: Canadians must be consulted directly before political leaders attempt to alter the country's basic document. By the oxymoronic creation of an instant convention, Canadians have further wrested control of the country's constitutional arrangements from politicians. A future prime minister, or set of first ministers, could decide to forego a referendum, but excellent explanations, not expedient ones, would be required for discarding the precedent.

Switzerland and Australia, of course, have had mandatory provisions for constitutional referendums. In a majority of instances, proposed constitutional changes have been defeated in referendums in those countries. Their histories ought to have put paid to any optimism that Canada's record might be different. So, too, the inherently difficult task, bordering on the impossible, that the constitutional negotiators set for themselves was momentarily obscured in the glow of the unexpected consensus among first ministers that emerged at the conferences in Ottawa and Charlottetown.

The task of fitting their consensus into the framework of the referendum was exceptionally difficult, because the rule of unanimity is never applied to serious public business in democratic societies for the obvious reason that its quest mocks pluralism. Perhaps an exception to the rule can be found in declarations of war, although even these rarely produce unanimous consent. Unanimous consent is usually found in graveyards rather than politics. None the less, Canada's constitution requires unanimous consent for particular changes. Some such items found their way into both the Meech Lake and Charlottetown accords, and this requirement then spread like a stain throughout both packages, so that the unanimity requirement for some elements of the packages became a rule for the entire package.

Those who negotiated and supported Charlottetown, therefore, faced an insuperable obstacle: securing support in every province. True, the Charlottetown consensus lulled its negotiators into believing that their unanimity would be contagious, but in this naïveté they merely forgot the lessons of constitutional referendums elsewhere, the cleavages in Canadian society they sought vainly to obscure, and a host of other factors that rendered futile the search for unanimity. It is perhaps perversely fitting for a country so preoccupied with constitutional debate – a preoccupation that has spawned a large and, until recently, burgeoning national-unity industry of scholars, journalists, and civil servants – that its rule for changing parts of the Constitution should so securely ensure deadlock and failure that the country will remain preoccupied with the issue *sine die*.

As the 26 October vote turned out, unanimity was only marginally relevant. The accord was thrashed in six provinces and barely scraped through in Ontario. By granting blocking power, however, to any one province, the rule of unanimity did encourage voters to watch developments elsewhere in the country. Some polling data and much personal observation suggest that people in one region were aware of the general drift of public opinion elsewhere. Since a single No vote sufficed to kill Charlottetown, once people who were hesitating saw the accord would be doomed elsewhere, they could vote No themselves without carrying any burden for Charlottetown's defeat.

Not since the decision to enter the Second World War had Canada's élites been so united. Four Aboriginal leaders, two territorial leaders, ten provincial premiers, three federal parties, all but two official opposition leaders in the provinces, the political arms of the large- and small-business communities, the leading trade unions, the editorial boards of all major newspapers in English-speaking Canada, the majority of women's groups, the leading mouthpieces for multicultural groups – the élite consensus outside Quebec was quite overwhelming and quite ineffective.

The élites were part of the problem rather than the solution just as they were in Denmark, where the élite support was just as overwhelming and as inconsequential for the Maastricht treaty. As in Denmark, so in Canada, people took out their anger and frustration at politicians by kicking their constitutional baby. Not often, after all, do disgruntled voters get an opportunity to kick all politicians at the same time. This urge was especially strong among those with the least economic security, as referendum voting patterns revealed. Generally speaking, those with the lowest incomes and least-attractive economic circumstances were most likely to vote No. Their preoccupations were quite different from the constitutional ones proposed by the country's political leaders.

Nor did the bulk of the Canadian electorate perceive any links between the defeat of the Charlottetown Accord and political or economic instability. Some leaders of the Yes campaign, notably Prime Minister Brian Mulroney and the organizers of the Yes side advertising, attempted to draw such links. So did the Royal Bank by publishing a study of the dire consequences for Quebec and Canada of a political divorce, but the bulk of the public remained supremely unmoved by these attempts. In fact, many voters resented them as blackmail and intimidation.

Indeed, it is the height of political incorrectness and, therefore, politically irresistible to suggest that the same gap between élite and mass preoccupations may partly explain the substantial rejection of Indian élites by their followers. True, many Indians believed the accord did not go far enough towards self-government, did not provide enough specificity in its clauses and financial commitments, and may have undermined treaty obligations. To the extent that Indians share something with non-Aboriginals, ordinary Indians may well have looked at self-government and Charlottetown as non-Aboriginals did: a power grab by those already in power, whom ordinary Indians did not especially support and whose priorities were somewhat removed from the less glamorous, but none the less urgent daily preoccupations of the majority. Clearly, anti-élitism, or at least a disaffection with political leadership, was at work across both Aboriginal and non-Aboriginal society.

Charlottetown's opponents attacked the accord like a swarm of bees from every conceivable angle and with great ferocity. In one evening debate at Simon Fraser University, opponents from the National Action Committee on the Status of Women, the Reform party, and a fiercely anti-free-trade group attacked the accord because it (a) weakened the status of Canadian women under the Charter; (b) de-centralized the country; (c) gave Ottawa too much power; (d) gave Quebec too much; (e) gave Quebec too little; (f) constituted part of a free-trade agenda to hand the country to the Americans; (g) handed over too much power to Indian chiefs; (h) did too little for Aboriginals; (i) created a hierarchy of rights; and (j) furthered the dangerous trend towards framing everything in Charter terms. While a few of these arguments were mutually reinforcing, the bulk of them were mutual contradictions.

We learned, therefore, that in a referendum campaign it is sufficient to oppose. The presentation of cohesive or even marginally reconcilable alternatives counts for nothing. Such a dynamic gave opponents a formidable advantage.

The recent European experience offered a similar pattern. Danish and French critics of Maastricht had wildly different visions for the future of the countries: in France, Maastricht was opposed by Jean-Marie Le Pen's right-wing party and the Communists, but since their mutual coherence was not at issue, they did not need to pass the test of a plausible, coherent alternative sometimes demanded by informed citizens at election time

Clearly, much criticism could be made of the tactics and strategy of the Yes side's campaign – that the campaign reflected the secular equivalent of Noah's Ark goes without saying. People of different political persuasions tried to work together with indifferent results. The advertising was uninspired when it was not wrongly inspired. The prime minister's theatrics and threats, including the ripping up of the text of the accord in Sherbrooke, did not help, nor did the intervention of the Royal Bank. The Yes campaign in Quebec was sandbagged by the Wilhelmy tapes affair and the publication in *L'Actualité* of memoranda written by civil servants that reflected their negative assessments of Premier Robert Bourassa's negotiating tactics. Former prime minister Pierre Trudeau's intervention proved an important fillip to the No side. It legitimized dissent in the rest of Canada, especially among those unfavourably disposed towards Quebec. Although isolated in his opposition from all his former political colleagues in Quebec, Trudeau still commands an important and diverse following outside his native province.

These and other myriad details of a failed campaign, however, were less consequential by way of explaining the result, I believe, than the inherent difficulties of winning any referendum on constitutional amendments. Some of these factors have been touched upon above, but the cardinal one follows.

Canadian politicians' persistence in seeking formal constitutional amendments acceptable to all governments and interest groups has been matched only by their failure. For almost three decades, prime ministers and premiers, and now Aboriginal and territorial leaders, have wrestled with the Constitution, trying to reshape it to everyone's satisfaction. Though the putative explanation was the search for unity, the practical effect was the deepening of division.

Ingenuity has not been lacking. Politicians have tried small amendments and large ones. They have tried to proceed sequentially – Meech Lake first followed by other negotiations. They have tried to proceed globally with many changes rolled into one package, as in the Charlottetown Accord. They have tried classic executive federalism. They have tried executive federalism embellished with extensive public consultation, and now they have tried a referendum.

Four prime ministers, dozens of provincial premiers, and hundreds of advisers have been engaged and sometimes consumed by these efforts. There have been intellectual titans and deadbeats, people of strong and weak character,

Liberals, Conservatives, New Democrats, Social Crediters, Péquistes. The results? Failure, in whole or in large part.

The closest Canada came to achieving formal changes to the satisfaction of all governments was Mr Trudeau's patriation package of 1981–2. This is not the place to rehash that exercise, nor to engage in the ongoing interpretations as to its desirability, wisdom, and legitimacy. All that can be said as a matter of political fact is that patriation was opposed by the Parti Québécois government, predictably in my view, but also by a majority of the Liberal members of the National Assembly. My understanding of federalism as a system of divided sovereignty means that constitutional change must be approved by both levels of government, or at least by a majority of the provinces including the large ones. (I leave the detailed debate over the precise amending formula to rest in peace.) Therefore, by this standard, adding up the massive majority of federal MPs from Quebec to the handful who agreed with them in the National Assembly to assert that Quebec as a constituent part of the federation endorsed patriation and should be forever thankful for its arrival strains my understanding of federalism. At some point, if not in 1981–2, then later, a federalist government of Quebec would demand certain changes to the constitutional fabric of Canada and these would have to be considered.

However, let us saw off the interpretive differences that still abound about 1981–2, differences that, like Mr Trudeau himself, 'haunt us still' and argue that patriation was not all that its principal architect could have wished. It was certainly not a complete success. Whole or partial failures then are the legacy of three decades of attempting to change formally the Canadian constitution.

In the wake of the referendum, two wrong conclusions commended themselves. One camp argued that if only Canadians went about formal amendments a different way, perhaps the next time they might be successful. If only this or that clause had been changed or added; if only this or that group had been present to represent additional 'interests'; if only the timing had been different; if only the personalities had been changed – the if-onlys are magnificent in their complexity and almost completely oblivious to the lessons of recent history.

The if-only school invites the country to yet another attempt to amend the Constitution formally in the hope that the next time success can replace repeated failure. The if-only school, of course, has been around for three decades in various guises, always giving the same advice. Politicians have repeatedly taken, or been tempted by, the advice and, therefore, launched fresh attempts to find a solution to Canada's tensions through formal constitutional amendments. After repeated failures, the cliché springs to life: 'Those who ignore the lessons of history are condemned to repeat them.' The most urgent lesson from the referendum, the previous constitutional failures, and the cleavages these efforts exposed is not that a new process, or this or that wording change, or some new constitutional formula, or a rehash of an old one will produce constitutional peace, but that the search itself through the venue of formal constitutional changes is too difficult, treacherous, and divisive to be attempted yet again.

Another school comprises those who counsel an extended reprieve from all constitutional debate. The most frequently heard comment following the referendum was that the issue would now be placed on the 'back burner.' This comment had the virtue of being true, but not for long. The social and economic pressures that gave rise to the constitutional debates will not disappear, nor will interest groups be silent. Western alienation, Aboriginal discontent, and Quebec restlessness will not go away simply because the Charlottetown Accord died. Pressures, therefore, will remain with us, mocking those who believe that in moving the Constitution to the 'back burner,' these pressures will likewise be shifted.

What the referendum ought to have taught the country, and especially those of us who have spent some of the best years of our lives labouring in the national-unity industry, is that these and other pressures are manifestly ill-suited for relief by formal constitutional amendments. Many of these pressures do not have their roots in the Constitution, although their relief has been wrongly described as running through the Constitution. The task, therefore, for concerned citizens is to recast the entire debate towards the alleviating of these pressures and to deal with real grievances by other means than formal constitutional amendments.

If Charlottetown and the thirty years of failure that preceded it teach the country nothing else, let it be that the practice of enlightened politics and the delivery of sound government are better responses to national tensions than formal constitutional amendments. If that is the lesson taken from the Charlottetown debate, the country will save itself future grief and direct its energies into solutions that lie in the territory of the possible rather than search for constitutional castles in the sky.

I suspect that such a conclusion would produce a polarization of debate in Quebec, a polarization that many Quebeckers do not want. The defeats of Meech Lake and Charlottetown demonstrated that the rest of Canada is not impressed by Quebec's demands to change the constitutional status quo by formal amendments, particularly since such debates summon up the demons of regional grievances and highly symbolic issues in a country without a consensus on symbols of national life.

A few intellectuals believe that asymmetrical federalism enshrined in the Constitution can satisfy everyone: Quebeckers looking for quasi-independence,

English Canadians searching for a strong central government, and Aboriginal Canadians demanding their own governments. The scarcity of common purpose upon which such a vision is built ensures that this model of federalism would not long survive and, anyway, the English-speaking part of Canada, having demonstrated its opposition to Quebec's more modest demands in Meech Lake and Charlottetown, is unlikely to accept Quebec's demands for something considerably more, up to and including asymmetrical federalism, as an operating and organizational principle of our national life. The rest of the country, having rebuffed Meech Lake and Charlottetown, is insisting that Quebec take the current constitutional arrangements and put them to the test in the confrontation with secession. It may be possible to bring administrative and pragmatic changes to the Canadian constitutional arrangements in the years before the showdown occurs, but these will not take the form of formal and sweeping constitutional changes.

The lesson from Charlottetown and Meech Lake is, therefore, that the rest of Canada would prefer Quebeckers to choose, but, of course, Quebeckers, with their innate preference for playing the angles and keeping options open, do not wish to make such a firm choice if they can avoid it.

16

The Quebec Referendum:
Quebeckers Say No

ANDRÉ BLAIS

On 26 October 1992, Quebeckers were asked to vote on a simple question:[1] 'Do you agree that the constitution of Canada should be renewed on the basis of the agreement reached on August 28th, 1992?' Fifty-seven per cent of those who voted said 'no.' I will not attempt here to offer a systematic explanation of the vote. Rather, I will limit myself to summing up what we know about the evolution of public opinion during the referendum campaign and to making a number of observations on the meaning of the vote.

This paper has two parts. In the first, I examine the dynamics of opinion during the campaign. I determine whether Quebeckers were opposed to the agreement from the very beginning of the campaign. I also indicate whether some of the major events of the campaign seem to have had any impact on the vote. In the second part, I offer preliminary thoughts on some potential interpretations of the outcome.

THE DYNAMICS OF THE CAMPAIGN

A total of twenty-nine polls were published in Quebec between the time the constitutional agreement was initially reached in Ottawa, on 22 August[2] and 26 October, the day of the referendum. The majority (20) of these polls dealt only with public opinion in Quebec, but a few (9) were Canada-wide, with specific results for Quebec. The results of these polls are shown in the appendix to this paper.

Table 1 summarizes the poll results by presenting the median No lead by periods. I use the median for each period to make sure that the pattern is unaffected by any outlier or rogue poll. I look at the difference between the No and the Yes vote in order to control for variation across survey firms in the proportion of 'don't knows' and refusals.[3]

TABLE 1
The evolution of the No lead

Period	Median no lead (percentage points)
1 End of August (surveys 1 to 5)	4
2 Early September (surveys 6 to 8)	10
3 Late September (surveys 9 to 14)	13
4 Early October surveys 15 to 21)	19
5 Late October (surveys 22 to 29)	19

Source: Appendix to this chapter

I distinguish five periods. The first corresponds to the last week of August, when the polls registered Quebeckers' initial reactions to the agreement. The second period is the first half of September. By that time, Quebeckers had come to know the exact wording of the referendum question. This period ends with the Wilhelmy 1 affair,[4] as the Quebec Superior Court granted on Monday, 14 September an injunction to prevent publication of the Wilhelmy transcript in Quebec. Excerpts of that transcript were, however, published on Tuesday the 15th in the *Globe and Mail* (but not in its Quebec edition). The two weeks following that event form the third period. That period ends with the Wilhelmy 2 affair on Wednesday, 30 September, as the injunction was lifted and the Quebec media revealed the contents of the conversation between Diane Wilhelmy and André Tremblay. The fourth period corresponds to the first twelve days of October up to the televised debate between Robert Bourassa and Jacques Parizeau. The final period covers the last two weeks of the campaign.

One can see from table 1 that the polls were predicting a No lead of around twenty percentage points by the end of the campaign. The actual lead on referendum day was only thirteen points. This difference could either indicate a late rally to the Yes side in the last days of the campaign or merely reflect a general propensity for the polls to underrepresent the Liberal or federalist vote in Quebec. All the available information points to the latter interpretation. The last two polls, carried out in the first part of the last week of the campaign (see appendix), show no late trend. Of course, something may have happened in the very last days of the campaign. That possibility is, however, extremely unlikely.

During the course of the campaign, the Institute for Social Research at York University conducted, under the supervision of our research team,[5] a rolling cross-section survey. A total of 2500 respondents were interviewed during the campaign, of whom 1000 were in Quebec. The overall sample was divided randomly into equal 'replicates' representing the thirty-two days of interviewing.[6] This design permits us to examine how opinions shifted during the course of the campaign.[7] The survey data show no sign of a surge of the Yes vote in the last week or days of the campaign.

The most plausible explanation for the difference between the polls and the actual results thus lies in a generalized bias in the polls themselves. That bias is not new. Since 1970, the Liberal vote has been systematically underestimated in Quebec provincial elections (Blais, Crête, and Lachapelle 1986). Similarly, the Yes vote in the 1980 referendum was overestimated (Blais 1980). It would seem that this bias stems mainly from the lower response rate to surveys among parts of the population, especially older people (see Blais, Crête, and Lachapelle 1986).

The presence of such a bias, however, does not prevent us from examining the movement of opinion during the campaign. Table 1 indicates that the initial reactions to the agreement were evenly divided. From early September on, support for the agreement started to erode. What strikes me the most about this erosion is how progressive and smooth it was. Most important, the movement started in early September, much before the Wilhelmy affair. It is impossible at this stage to offer a proper evaluation of the impact of that incident. We cannot even rule out the possibility that the affair had no impact, that as information about the accord improved during the course of the campaign, Quebeckers came to be more and more opposed. Finally, table 1 indicates that the leaders' televised debate did not have any impact on the vote. The polls showed that a majority of Quebeckers thought that Bourassa had won the debate, but that was not enough to move the vote. There is some indication that support for the Yes side may have increased a few percentage points in the days immediately following the debate,[8] but those small gains proved to be ephemeral.

SOME CORRELATES OF THE VOTE

Let me present some of the findings from our survey and suggest some interpretations.[9] First, as usual, Quebec was strongly divided along linguistic lines. In our survey, among those who indicated how they would vote, 72 per cent of francophones[10] and 26 per cent of non-francophone said they would vote No.[11] If we take into account the fact that the No vote is overes-timated in our study as in all polls in Quebec, we can surmise that around two-thirds of francophones and one-fifth of non-francophones voted No.[12] The 45-percent-age-point gap is similar to the one observed in the 1980 referendum (see Blais and Nadeau 1984).

Second, the vote was strongly correlated with constitutional attitudes. In our survey, 89 per cent of those who are favourable to Quebec sovereignty intended to vote No. Since around 40 per cent of our sample indicated they were very or somewhat favourable to Quebec sovereignty,[13] this means that there was a solid block of one-third of Quebeckers on the No side. In order to win, the Yes camp had to get the support of at least three-quarters of the non-sovereignist group. This was quite a challenge.

That challenge, however, was not insurmountable, at least in theory. All that was needed was for the federalists to be as solidly behind the Yes as the sovereignists were behind the No. In fact, within the non-sovereignist group,[14] 35 per cent ended up voting No. There are many reasons for that erosion. Let me mention two. First, there was the feeling that it was possible to say No to the Charlottetown Accord without saying Yes to sovereignty or independence. Only 27 per cent of those opposed to sovereignty agreed with the statement that voting No to the agreement meant saying Yes to independence. Similarly, only 32 per cent indicated they thought Quebec would separate if the No side won. As Quebec's place in the Canadian federation was not perceived to be directly at stake, many felt they could afford to vote No.

The second reason concerns the assessment of the accord as such. In our Quebec sample, 43 per cent said that in their view Quebec was a loser in the agreement, while only 26 per cent perceived Quebec to be a winner. Even among those opposed to sovereignty, 29 per cent had come to the conclusion that Quebec had lost. This perception had a powerful impact on the vote of non-sovereignists. Seventy-three per cent of those who were opposed to sovereignty, but believed Quebec had lost in the deal, intended to vote No.

It remains to be explained what led many Quebeckers, even among federalists, to the view that Quebec had been a loser in the negotiations that resulted in the Charlottetown Accord. I will limit myself to two observations. At first sight, these findings would seem to buttress the hypothesis that the Wilhelmy affair had a great impact on the outcome of the vote. Was not the main message of that affair that Bourassa had 'caved in,' that in the last round of negotiations Quebec made crucial concessions and hardly any gains, that it was, in fact, the loser? However, the available information on the evolution of public opinion (table 1) tends to suggest that concerns about Quebec having lost in the constitutional bargaining predated the Wilhelmy affair. In fact, these concerns were the basic reasons leading some prominent Liberals to campaign on the No side.

The second observation is perhaps more interesting. In our survey, we asked our respondents not only whether Quebec was a winner or loser in the agreement, but also whether the federal government, the West, and Aboriginal people were winners or losers. To my surprise, perceptions about what Quebec got out of the deal are basically uncorrelated with assessments of what was obtained by the West and by the Aboriginal people, at least among non-sovereignists. This result tends to suggest that the No vote in Quebec should not be construed as expressing frustration with the gains obtained by other groups. There is, by contrast, a moderately strong relationship (a correlation of .18) between the perception that Quebec lost and the perception that the federal government won.

CONCLUSION

This brief review of the survey evidence cannot lead to any definitive conclusion. It is possible, however, to make some observations and to point out some possible interpretations. First, the polls overestimated the No vote, in the same way as they sytematically overestimate support for the Parti Québécois and sovereignty. Second, the increase in opposition to the agreement from late August to early October seemed to be progressive, suggesting that the major campaign events such as the Wilhelmy affair may not have had as great an impact as some believe. Third, opposition to the deal among non-sovereignists stemmed from the belief that a No vote would not lead to separation and that Quebec had lost in the constitutional negotiations. That latter belief reflected the view that Quebec had lost to the federal government, not to the West or Aboriginal people.

APPENDIX
The evolution of vote intentions on the Quebec referendum

Fieldwork	Survey firm	Yes (%)	No (%)	Other	Source
1. 24 August	CROP	30	37	33	*La Presse* 25 August
2. 24–25 August	Léger & Léger	32	36	32	*Journal de Mtl.* 26 August
3. 25–28 August	CROP	37	41	22	*La Presse* 29 August
4. 25–31 August	Angus Reid	49	38	13	*Gazette* 2 September
5. 28 August – 1 September	Environics	43	39	19	*La Presse* 8 September
6. 2–6 September	SOM	34	39	27	*Le Soleil* 9 September
7. 9 September	Léger & Léger	31	41	28	*Journal de Mtl.* 11 September
8. 10–14 September	Gallup	31	48	21	*La Presse* 16 September
9. 15–16 September	Léger & Léger	25	43	32	*Journal de Mtl.* 18 September
10. 16–19 September	CROP	38	46	16	*La Presse* 21 September
11. 22–23 September	Léger & Léger	23	43	34	*Journal de Mtl.* 25 September
12. 22–23 September	Angus Reid	38	45	17	*Gazette* 26 September
13. 23–26 September	CROP	37	49	14	*La Presse* 28 September
14. 29–30 September	Léger & Léger	29	43	28	*Journal de Mtl.* 22 October
15. 29 September – 1 October	CRÉATEC	27	40	33	*Le Devoir* 5 October
16. 30 September – 3 October	CROP	34	53	13	*La Presse* 3 October
17. 1–5 October	ComQuest Research	27	54	14	*Globe and Mail* 16 October
18. 6–7 October	Léger & Léger	33	58	9	*Journal de Mtl.* 9 October
19. 6–13 October	ComQuest Research	27	53	15	*Globe and Mail* 16 October
20. 7–10 October	CROP	34	50	16	*La Presse* 11 October

APPENDIX (contd.)
The evolution of vote intentions on the Quebec referendum

Fieldwork	Survey firm	Yes (%)	No (%)	Other	Source
21. 9–15 October	Environics	29	44	27	*Toronto Star* 17 October
22. 12–15 October	Angus Reid	35	55	10	*The Gazette* 17 October
23. 14–15 October	Léger & Léger	37	57	6	*Journal de Mtl.* 16 October
24. 14–17 October	CROP	36	53	11	*La Presse* 19 October
25. 15–18 October	Multi-Réso	31	46	16	*Le Devoir* 20 October
26. 15–19 October	Gallup	30	58	12	*Gazette / La Presse* 21 October
27. 16–20 October	SOM	28	46	26	*Le Soleil* 22 October *La Presse* 23 October
28. 19–22 October	CROP	31	52	17	*La Presse* 24 October
29. 20–22 October	Léger & Léger	37	55	8	*Journal de Mtl.* 24 October

Data compiled by Edouard Cloutier, Département de science politique, Université de Montréal

NOTES

1 Note that the French question asked whether one accepted (rather than agreed) that the Constitution be renewed ... One may suppose that those who drafted the question thought that 'accept' could elicit more support than 'agree.'

2 The premiers and Native leaders met in Charlottetown the following week to finalize what came to be called the Charlottetown Accord.

3 It can be seen, in particular, that Léger et Léger polls came out with the highest percentage of 'don't knows' and refusals in August and September and with the lowest in October.

4 The affair could also be called the Wilhelmy/Tremblay affair. On Monday, 14 September the media reported that André Tremblay had allegedly told Quebec Chamber of Commerce officials that Robert Bourassa was so exhausted by the end of the negotiations that he had difficulty understanding nuances in English.

5 The team was composed of Richard Johnston (UBC), Henry Brady (Berkeley), Joseph Fletcher (Toronto), Elisabeth Gidengil (McGill), Neil Nevitte (Calgary), and myself.

6 Interviewing started on 24 September and ended on 25 October, the day before the referendum.

7 For an application to the 1988 election see Johnston, Blais, Brady, and Crête (1992).

8 See Hugh Windsor, 'Yes side gains in Quebec,' *Globe and Mail*, 16 Oct. 1992, 1.

9 For a more extensive analysis, see André Blais and Elisabeth Gidengil 1993.

10 This refers to the language first learned and still understood.

11 The results referred to here are those of the campaign-period survey. They include the responses of those who first said they did not know how they would vote, but then indicated which way they were leaning. We report unweighted data.

12 To arrive at these estimations, we assume that all the undecided among non-francophones voted Yes (for a justification of that assumption see Blais 1980), while they split equally between the Yes and the No among francophones. This gives a No vote of 21% among non-francophones and of 66% among francophones and a total of 58% No in our sample.

13 We did experiments tapping support for sovereignty through two different questions. We refer here to answers to the following question: 'What is your opinion on Quebec sovereignty, that is Quebec is no longer a part of Canada? Are you very favourable, somewhat favourable, somewhat opposed, or very opposed?' Thirty-nine per cent said they were favourable and 54% said they were opposed.

14 I consider here only those who said they were opposed to sovereignty and thus exclude the small group of undecided.

REFERENCES

Blais, André. 1980. 'Le vote: Ce que l'on en sait ... ce que l'on en sait pas.' In *Québec: Un pays incertain* (en collaboration). Montréal: Québec-Amérique

Blais, André, and Richard Nadeau. 1984. 'L'appui au OUI.' In *Le comportement électoral au Québec*, ed. Jean Crête. Chicoutimi: Gaétan Morin

– 1992. 'To Be or Not To Be Sovereignist: Quebeckers' Perennial Dilemma.' *Canadian Public Policy* 18: 89–103

Blais, André, Jean Crête, and Guy Lachapelle. 1986. 'L'élection québécoise de 1985: Un bilan des sondages.' *Revue canadienne de science politique* 19: 325–37

Blais, André, and Elisabeth Gidengil. 1993. 'The Quebec Referendum: Why Did Quebeckers Say No?' Paper presented at the annual meetings of the Canadian Political Science Association, Ottawa.

Johnston, Richard, André Blais, Henry Brady, and Jean Crête. 1992. *Letting the People Decide: Dynamics of a Canadian Election*. Montréal: McGill-Queen's University Press

PART FIVE

The Future of Canada

17

The End of Mega Constitutional Politics in Canada?

PETER H. RUSSELL

On 26 October 1992, the Canadian people, for the first time in their history as a political community, acted as Canada's ultimate constitutional authority – in effect, as a sovereign people. In the referendum conducted on that day, a majority of Canadians in a majority of provinces, said 'no' to the Charlottetown Accord proposals for constitutional change.

Though the referendum was only consultative and not legally binding, none the less the governments that supported the accord – and these include the federal government, all ten provincial governments, and the two territorial governments, plus organizations representing the four groupings of Aboriginal peoples (status and non-status Indians, Inuit, and Métis) – will not proceed with ratification of the accord in their legislative assemblies. The politicians will respect the vox populi.

The referendum may have killed more than the accord. It may also have killed one form of mega constitutional politics to which Canadian political élites seemed to have become addicted. The referendum may very well be the last time this generation of Canadians attempts a grand resolution of constitutional issues in order to prevent a national-unity crisis. If in the next few years Canada plunges once again into the constitutional maelstrom, it will be because it is confronted with an actual, not an apprehended, crisis of national unity.

MEGA CONSTITUTIONAL POLITICS

Mega constitutional politics is not exactly a household term – even among political scientists. It is a term I have coined for the peculiar and painful form of constitutional politics Canada has suffered for a quarter of a century. Virtually all the constitutional democracies are constantly engaged in low-level,

212 Peter H. Russell

piecemeal constitutional change, whether through formal constitutional amendments, informal political practice, or judicial interpretation. This is ordinary
constitutional politics. Canada, contrary to rumour, has enjoyed long periods of
low-key constitutional politics. Indeed, this is how I would describe Canada's
constitutional politics through most of its first century.

But when constitutional politics reaches the mega level, it is a horse of a
very different colour. At the mega level, constitutional politics moves well
beyond disputing the merits of specific constitutional proposals and addresses
the very nature of the political community on which the constitution is based.

Mega constitutional politics, whether directed towards comprehensive constitutional
change or not, is concerned with reaching agreement on the identity and fundamental
principles of the body politic. The second feature of mega constitutional politics flows
logically from the first. Precisely because of the fundamental nature of the issues in
dispute – their tendency to touch citizens' sense of identity and self-worth – mega
constitutional politics is exceptionally emotional and intense.[1]

You can tell that a country's constitutional politics is at the mega level when
the constitutional question in public affairs and media coverage tends to dwarf
all other issues.

Mega constitutional politics is not peculiar to Canada. The United States
knew this kind of politics last in the Civil War. Recently, much of eastern
Europe passed through mega constitutional upheavals. South Africa is now
fully engaged in constitutional politics at the mega level and western Europe
approaches such politics as it moves towards federation. Belgium has been
involved in constitutional politics of the mega variety almost as much as Canada.
But my country, Canada, must surely win the prize – and a booby prize it well
may be – for the duration and intensity of its involvement in mega constitutional politics. We were at it, almost non-stop, from 1967 to 1992.

THE PREVIOUS ROUNDS

The 26 October referendum was the final act of what the media and the players
referred to as the Canada Round of constitutional politics. The Canada Round
was the fifth round of constitutional politics since the mid-1960s. Like each of
the previous rounds, the Canada Round produced a package of constitutional
proposals, the Charlottetown Accord, whose main purpose was to provide an
alternative to Quebec sovereignty. Though the context and agenda of all five
rounds varied considerably, the fundamental objectives of the constitutional
architects were always essentially the same – to strengthen national unity and
stave off the threat of Quebec separation.

The first round began in the 1960s, when Quebec's 'quiet revolution' unleashed a surge of ethnic nationalism that suddenly widened the constitutional agenda. Although in principle Canada had been an autonomous, self-governing Dominion since 1927, it had not been able to convert its Constitution from a British statute to a constitution amendable to Canada. This was because its federal and provincial leaders, despite numerous conferences, could not agree on a formula for amending the Constitution in Canada. Finally, in the mid-1960s, just as agreement seemed in sight, Quebec raised the ante. Quebec would agree to patriation of the Constitution only if the federation was restructured to recognize Quebec's special status as the homeland of one of Canada's founding peoples.

A political struggle over the Constitution – at the mega level – was fully engaged when Quebec's demands were countered by Pierre Elliot Trudeau. Trudeau had become federal justice minister in 1967 and prime minister in 1968. Instead of making concessions to Quebec, Trudeau's strategy was to initiate constitutional proposals designed to build a stronger sense of Canadian nationhood. An intense series of federal-provincial meetings ensued. For three years, they were the country's main political preoccupation. The inter-governmental negotiations were dominated by Trudeau's agenda, with a constitutional bill of rights as its centrepiece. In June 1971, Trudeau seemed on the brink of success when the first ministers came to a tentative agreement on the Victoria Charter built around his proposals. But within days, the Quebec premier, Robert Bourassa, responding to Quebec nationalist criticisms of the Charter, withdrew his support. Although legally Trudeau could have gone ahead and asked Britain to patriate Canada's constitution on his terms, he did not at that time feel sufficiently strong or impatient enough to impose a constitutional settlement on Quebec.

This first round demonstrated the risks of waging constitutional politics at the mega level in order to strengthen national unity. Trudeau's agenda of Canadian nation-building reforms did not win the hearts and minds of a majority of his fellow Québécois, but the Trudeauian constitutional vision with its emphasis on the equal rights of the Canadian citizen rather than the powers of provinces garnered a strong following outside of Quebec. Ever since this first round, Trudeau has been English Canada's constitutional hero, but Trudeau's success rather than unifying the country gave a sharper ideological edge to its constitutional politics. When constitutional politics are élite driven, as they usually are, they may deepen rather than narrow divisions within the populace.

In round two, the agenda widened and a more complex set of cleavages opened up. In the early 1970s, the Trudeau government's energy and language policies alienated opinion in Western Canada. Western premiers became constitutional activists. Provincial leaders from 'outer Canada' began to press for a

214 Peter H. Russell

restructured Senate in which the smaller provinces could check the perceived Ontario/Quebec, central Canadian dominance of national policy. During the same period, Canada's Aboriginal peoples showed signs of entering the constitutional fray. Quebec's ethnic nationalism provided an influential demonstration effect and the infatuation of élites with wholesale constitutional revision promised opportunities for decolonization unavailable to native peoples in other countries dominated by white-settler majorities.

But the mega constitutional struggle was not resumed until 1976 when Quebec elected a separatist government, led by René Lévesque. This event unleashed another flurry of feverish constitutional activity. Federal and provincial leaders, aided and abetted by the country's chattering classes, engaged in a season of 'new constitutionalism.' The assumption was that unless a new constitutional arrangement could be worked out satisfying Quebec's demands as well as other sources of constitutional discontent in the country, the Canadian federation would break up. Another tense series of federal-provincial negotiations produced no accord and ended with the electoral defeat of the Trudeau government in 1979.

The third round began with the 1980 Quebec referendum, which produced a 60 per cent majority against the Parti Québécois's option of a sovereign Quebec in an economic association with Canada. A miraculously resurrected Pierre Trudeau aimed to take advantage of the Quebec separatists' defeat and consolidate Canadian unity by driving through his own program of constitutional reform. At the centre of that program was patriation of the Constitution with a charter of rights and freedoms. Using Gaullist techniques, Trudeau bypassed the provincial premiers to build public support for his 'People's Package,' even threatening to hold a referendum. In televised hearings in the federal Parliament, the constitutional advocates were not provincial premiers pressing for more power for their governments, but civil-liberties and public-interest groups pressing for the constitutional rights of citizens.

In the end, the Supreme Court of Canada persuaded Trudeau to negotiate with the provincial premiers before asking the British Parliament to patriate Canada's constitution. This he did, reluctantly accepting modifications to the federal proposals, the most notable of which were a stronger role for provinces in the amending process and a legislative override attached to the Charter of Rights. These concessions were enough to obtain the agreement of all the provinces except Quebec. Quebec's resistance deterred neither Trudeau nor the British Parliament. And so, in 1982, Canada at last took custody of its Constitution in its own hands, but on terms that were repudiated by one of its primary constituent elements.

For Trudeau and his supporters that should have been the end of Canada's constitutional struggle, but not all Canadians were willing to accept Trudeau's verdict that 'the federation was set to last a thousand years.'[2] To begin with, there were the Aboriginal peoples. The 1982 constitutional amendments included a vague affirmation of 'the existing rights' of Aboriginal peoples, which did not provide the explicit recognition Native peoples sought for their inherent right of self-government. Through four successive constitutional conferences, from 1983 to 1987, Aboriginal leaders failed to obtain that recognition from the federal and provincial governments. None the less, these conferences established the Aboriginal peoples' status as key players in Canada's constitutional politics.

But again, it was Quebec that brought this fourth round to the all-absorbing mega level. With Lévesque and Trudeau replaced by more conciliatory leaders, the scene was set for an attempt at reconciling Quebec to the changes made in 1982. Robert Bourassa, enjoying a second coming as Quebec premier, brought forward as Quebec's price for accepting the 1982 changes the most minimalist set of demands of any Quebec administration since the 'quiet revolution.' In Brian Mulroney, Bourassa found an eager constitutional partner.

For a year, Mulroney and Bourassa quietly negotiated a deal with the other provincial premiers whereby they would all support Quebec's conditions by obtaining the same accretions of power for themselves. The one exception was the essentially symbolic constitutional recognition of Quebec's 'distinct society.' The deal was consummated at Meech Lake on 30 April 1987, and when it was announced to a surprised and ungrateful nation, mega constitutional politics began in earnest.

The first ministers who negotiated the Meech Lake Accord failed to appreciate how much the 1982 amendments had transformed Canada's constitutional culture. They did not comprehend how much the Charter of Rights had converted a governments' constitution to a citizens' constitution,[3] or how difficult it would be to combine the traditional practice of executive federalism with the new requirement of legislative ratification. They compounded their difficulties by putting together a package that, under the new amending rules, required unanimous approval of all ten provincial legislatures plus the federal Parliament, and then announcing to the legislatures that they could debate the Meech Lake Accord all they wished so long as they did not change a word of it. Perhaps most fatally, the first ministers failed to commit themselves to any timetable and allowed the ratification debate to drag on for the three full years permitted by the Constitution.

When time ran out in the Spring of 1990, although the accord had been ratified in all but two legislatures, polling data showed that it was strongly opposed by a majority of Canadians outside of Quebec.[4] And while it may have had majority support in Quebec, it was by then a clear second choice to Quebec sovereignty. Round four ended with the country more divided than ever.

THE CANADA ROUND

The fifth round of mega constitutional politics that Canadians have just lived through has been by far the most exhausting. It felt so exhausting partly because, constitutionally speaking, Canadians were all tuckered out from the previous rounds; but add to that the fact that in this round there was far more public participation than in any previous round. Not only was there the two-month referendum campaign at the end, but over the two years leading up to the Charlottetown Accord the public, through all kinds of committees and commissions, was 'consulted' as never before.

Though relatively participatory, this pre-referendum process was fundamentally flawed. Throughout the public-consultation stage and, indeed, until the very end of the multilateral negotiations that produced the accord, there was very little interaction between Quebec and what came to be known as the 'Rest of Canada.' The Canada Round was very much a two-nation round.

Immediately following the death of the Meech Lake Accord, Premier Bourassa, smarting from the rejection of Quebec's 'minimal demands,' cranked up the constitutional machine. In collaboration with separatist leader Jacques Parizeau, he established a Quebec 'estates general' chaired by two Quebec businessmen, Michel Bélanger and Jean Campeau, to consider Quebec's future. At the same time, he encouraged a party committee chaired by Jean Allaire to consult Liberals throughout the province on constitutional options. These Quebec discussions focused entirely on the question of what Quebec needs to fulfil its national destiny. Not surprisingly, both Bélanger/Campeau and Allaire concluded with highly autonomist reports. In May 1991, Quebec's National Assembly committed itself to a referendum on 'the sovereignty of Quebec' not later than October 1992 and in the meantime to have a committee look at the 'best offer' that might be forthcoming from the Rest of Canada.

Public discussions on the Constitution got under way in the Rest of Canada just as the Quebec process was reaching its culmination and the only way the public outside Quebec could be persuaded to participate was by firm undertakings that, unlike Meech, this would not be a Quebec Round, but a Canada Round. Thus, the agenda was opened up to include all matters of constitutional discontent in the land, especially those neglected by the Meech Lake Accord – Aboriginal self-government and Senate reform. As a result, participants in the massive round of public hearings that went on at the federal and provincial levels in the Rest of Canada were playing an entirely different constitutional game from Quebec's.

It was this Rest of Canada process that created the agenda for the Charlottetown Accord. Its public-discussion phase culminated at the end of February 1992 with the release of the Beaudoin-Dobbie report by a federal parliamentary committee following five mini constituent assemblies.[5] Through the spring and summer, the Beaudoin-Dobbie proposals were modified and honed into a package of constitutional proposals through closed-door negotiations among the federal, provincial, and territorial governments and organizations representing the Aboriginal peoples. Bourassa chose not to join this negotiating process until August. By then he was faced with a fully negotiated package that, though it contained pretty well all of Meech, had little else for Quebec and a lot more for the Rest of Canada, including an elected Senate in which Quebec would have no more power than any other province. It was at this point that the idea of guaranteeing Quebec 25 per cent of the seats in the House of Commons – regardless of its population – was pulled like a rabbit out of a hat. It was the only way Bourassa could be persuaded to accept provincial equality in the upper house.

Unlike all the other components of the Charlottetown Accord, the 25 per cent guarantee had not been put before the country in the two years of public discussion leading up to the accord. It was a deal-maker, but a referendum-breaker. Guaranteeing Quebec a secure place in the institutions of a central government is, potentially, a more integrative way of recognizing Quebec's special status than giving a whole lot of extra powers to its provincial legislature, but this novel idea was one for which the public had not been prepared. In Quebec, it was not enough to serve as a surrogate for more provincial autonomy; outside Quebec, it was considered grossly unfair and was by far the accord's most objectionable feature.

THE FUTURE OF CONSTITUTIONAL POLITICS

The foregoing review of the five rounds of mega constitutional politics that Canada has experienced over the twenty-five years should make it clear why neither the people nor the politicians are in a hurry to launch a sixth round. The recent referendum may have demonstrated that Canadians are deeply divided in their sense of identity and political justice, but it has, none the less, left them united in their constitutional fatigue. Constitution just now is the 'C word' in Canada and most politicians want to avoid it like the plague.

In post-referendum Canada, there are no politicians of any consequence with any stomach for resuming the effort to fashion a grand constitutional restructuring designed to strengthen national unity and stem the tide of Quebec separatism. There are still, believe it or not, some well-meaning intellectuals and some constitutional junkies who would like to have another kick at that can, but they will find no support from political leaders or the general public.

The federal election scheduled for 1993 may well bring about a change of government in Ottawa, but this is unlikely to change the picture. The Bloc Québécois will be the only political party contesting that election on a constitutional platform. While the BQ may very well win the largest block of Quebec seats, its aim is not to restructure the Canadian federation, but to break it up.

The resumption of mega constitutional politics in Canada now depends entirely on politics within Quebec. In Quebec, the prevailing mood after the referendum is entirely different from what it was after Meech Lake. The defeat of Meech immediately gave currency in Quebec to the myth of rejection – compounding the 1982 myth of imposition.[6] In the year following Meech, Quebec was moving 'serenely' towards sovereignty. Now the mood is entirely different. The rejection of the Charlottetown Accord by majorities both in Quebec and outside Quebec obviously cannot be interpreted as English Canada's rejection of Quebec. Premier Bourassa, though he campaigned strenuously for the accord and lost, appears to have gained political strength in the process. Far from jumping on the sovereignist bandwagon, he is cleansing his party of its autonomist wing. Nor is the Parti Québécois in any position right now to stoke the *sovereigniste* fires. Throughout the campaign, the PQ was emphatic that a vote against the accord was not a vote for sovereignty.

This picture could change dramatically over the next two years. Bourassa must call an election by late 1994. In that election, the constitutional issue will be front and centre. Mega constitutional politics will resume after the next Quebec election if two conditions are met: first, the winning party is committed to obtaining more constitutional autonomy for Quebec and, second, the winning party subsequently wins a referendum in favour of some form of Quebec sovereignty. Then, Canada will be in a real crisis of national unity, not just an apprehended crisis.

In these circumstances, constitutional politics would likely take on a much more confrontational style. The long, elaborate process of public consultations and intergovernmental negotiations that had aimed at working out an accommodation of differences would be replaced by an exchange of ultimatums, threats, and counter-threats. The confrontation would not be over the right of French-speaking Quebeckers to form their own sovereign nation, but about their right to force ethnic minorities in Quebec, especially Aboriginal peoples, to be part of a sovereign Quebec. Such circumstances would pose a tremendous challenge to Canada's civilized ways: violence could supplant tedium as the central feature of our constitutional politics.

There is a good chance that Canada will avoid such an ugly turn of events. Premier Bourassa (or, if his health fails, his successor) may well duplicate René Lévesque's ironic feat of losing a referendum, but winning the subsequent election, and he may be able to pull this off without having to promise Quebeckers some sort of restructuring of the federation as an alternative to independence. Only about a third of Quebeckers support the complete, unqualified separation of Quebec from Canada. The constitutional status quo in the straight-up contest could prevail over pure independence. The danger is that both sides may fudge their options so that Quebec will elect a government committed to a constitutional restructuring of the federation that the rest of Canada has not the slightest interest in negotiating.

For Canada to foresake mega constitutional politics for a while does not mean that it will or should forsake any kind of constitutional reform. A great benefit of the country's exhaustion from dealing with big packages of constitutional reform would be to learn how to do ordinary, one-reform-at-a-time, constitutional politics.

The top priority, needing immediate attention, is the position of Canada's Aboriginal peoples. In socio-economic terms, it is the Native component of the population (roughly 4 per cent) that suffers the greatest deprivation of substantive equality and the continuing imposition of non-Aboriginal rule over the Aboriginal peoples constitutes Canada's most serious constitutional injustice. Canada's prolonged engagement with mega constitutional politics opened up an opportunity for Aboriginal peoples to force a fundamental reconsideration of their colonized status. Aboriginal leaders have taken advantage of that opportunity to raise the constitutional expectations of their own people and to win majority support within the non-Aboriginal community for the basic principle of Aboriginal self-government within Canada.

On a regional basis, constitutional action on the Aboriginal front is already under way. In November 1992, less than a month after the national referendum, another referendum in the eastern Arctic, where 85 per cent of the population are Inuit, voted in favour of a land-claims settlement under which the region will be separated from the Northwest Territories and organized as the largely self-governing territory of Nunavut.[7] In Yukon, after nearly twenty years of negotiations, agreement in principle has been reached on a land-claims settlement giving that territory's Native peoples a very large measure of self-government. Settlements of this kind are also under negotiation south of the sixtieth parallel in a number of provinces. Thanks to a 1983 constitutional amendment, provisions for Aboriginal self-government obtained through these modern treaties can be constitutionally secured.

For much of the Aboriginal leadership, achieving self-government on a piecemeal, regional basis will not suffice. There will continue to be considerable pressure for another attempt at an across-the-board settlement of Aboriginal issues. This pressure will be resisted by Canadian politicians. They will sense the inescapable linkage of the Aboriginal question, when it is dealt with on a national basis, with all the other constitutional discontents. The Aboriginal peoples themselves may have cause to question the wisdom of negotiating an omnibus constitutional settlement. Their Canada Round experience demonstrated both their own heterogeneity and the difficulty of reconciling the first ministers' negotiating style with the traditional relationship of Aboriginal leaders to their communities. A royal commission with strong Aboriginal and non-Aboriginal representation has been at work for over a year conducting a public inquiry into all aspects of the Aboriginal question.[8] Although not scheduled to give its final report until 1994, the commission will likely provide interim advice on how best to proceed with the constitutional question.[9]

Aside from the Aboriginal issue, the other major elements of the Charlottetown Accord may be left alone for quite some time. There will be pressure from Western Canada to do something about the Senate, but again, because it is virtually impossible to disentangle Senate reform from the Quebec issue, that pressure – which does not have a deep popular base – will not produce constitutional action.

There is some scope for micro constitutional reform through section 43 of the amending formula. Under this section, amendments concerning one or more provinces, but not all provinces, can be made with the agreement of the legislatures of the provinces affected and the federal Parliament. Already New Brunswick's Frank McKenna has initiated a section 43 amendment that would make New Brunswick officially bilingual.

But if Canadians have any sense, they will, for quite some time, eschew formal constitutional change as the primary means of dealing with structural or institutional problems. There are a myriad of ways in which the Canadian federation can be made to work more efficiently and responsively without risking the heavy politics of formal constitutional amendment. Political will, not constitutional change, is all that is required to remove virtually all barriers to internal free trade. Similarly, a federal prime minister enlightened and bold enough to depart from the tradition of strict party discipline in the House of Commons, and of political patronage in the selection of judges and senators, could do much to enhance the credibility of the federation's central institutions. But don't hold your breath. It will be no easier for politicians to break from these practices than for the intelligentsia to abandon its predilection for constitutional solutions to every national problem.

However, if Canadians are fortunate enough to kick their constitutional habit for a decent interval, the October referendum will have had more positive long-term results than its majority 'no' might portend. Although that 'no' means there was no popular consensus on a new set of constitutional arrangements, it may translate into a fairly long-term, grumpy acquiescence in the constitutional status quo. That may be all it is reasonable to expect by way of agreement among the sovereign people of this multinational state called Canada.

NOTES

1 Peter H. Russell, *Constitutional Odyssey: Can Canadians Become A Sovereign People?* (Toronto: University of Toronto Press 1992)
2 Trudeau used this phrase in his May 1987 newspaper article attacking the Meech Lake Accord. See Andrew Cohen, *A Deal Undone: The Making and Breaking of the Meech Lake Accord* (Vancouver: Douglas and McIntyre 1990), 165.
3 See Alan C. Cairns, *Constitutional Struggles from the Charter to Meech Lake* (Toronto: McClelland and Stewart 1991).
4 See Cohen, *A Deal Undone.*
5 *Report of the Special Joint Committee on a Renewed Canada* (Ottawa: House of Commons, 28 Feb. 1992)
6 See J. Stefan Dupré, 'Canada's Political and Constitutional Future: Reflections on the Bélanger-Campeau Report and Bill 150,' in J.L. Granatstein and Kenneth McNaught, *'English Canada' Speaks Out* (Toronto: Doubleday Canada 1991)
7 Louise Kinross, 'Inuit vote to change face of the Arctic,' *Financial Post,* 17 Nov. 1992, 23–8
8 For the results of the commission's first round of public hearings, see *Framing the Issues,* Royal Commission on Aboriginal Peoples, Ottawa, October 1992.
9 The commission rendered such advice during the Canada Round. See *The Right of Aboriginal Self-Government and the Constitution,* Royal Commission on Aboriginal Peoples, Ottawa, February 1992.

18

The Sounds of Silence

PATRICK J. MONAHAN

Last October, Canadians participated in what was universally understood to be a watershed political event. For the first time in our 125-year history, the people of Canada were given a direct voice in determining the constitutional arrangements governing the country. While constitutional experts and commentators were divided on the substantive merits of the proposed constitutional amendments, nearly everyone was agreed on the significance of the referendum itself. There seemed little doubt that the referendum exercise represented a decisive moment in Canadian politics, and that its outcome would determine the shape of the country for well into the next century.

Yet today, just months later, it is as if the referendum never happened. A quite remarkable collective silence reigns across the land. No one talks about the referendum or its outcome. There are none of the customary post-mortems analysing what happened and why. Politicians and the media, taking their cue from an exhausted public, seem to have agreed tacitly that the dreaded 'C' word should be banned from discussion. Even in Quebec, long regarded as a perpetual hotbed of constitutional motion, fatigue reigns supreme and the Constitution is off limits in polite conversation.

The inevitable question is whether this current uneasy silence is lasting or ephemeral. Is it scarcely possible that, having expended untold political energy and hundreds of millions of tax dollars developing a comprehensive set of constitutional proposals required in order to 'save the country,' only to see those proposals overwhelmingly rejected by the public, Canadians have inadvertently stumbled on a solution to an apparently endless constitutional crisis? Or has the rejection of Charlottetown merely provided us with a temporary breathing space within an ongoing constitutional crisis that, when it next erupts, will prove more intractable than ever?

Given that political events are inherently unpredictable, attempting to forecast future political outcomes is almost always foolhardy. At the same time, and perhaps for that very reason, offering such predictions is sometimes utterly irresistible. Thus, I will hazard the guess that, of the two descriptions offered above regarding the significance of the referendum outcome, the second is more likely to prove correct than the first. The constituencies that prompted the Canada Round of constitutional negotiations – namely, Quebeckers, Aboriginals, and Western Canadians – have certainly not been satisfied by the outcome of 26 October. It is difficult to imagine that these constituencies will simply resign themselves to the fact that their constitutional aspirations remain unfulfilled. One has to expect, therefore, that the constitutional issues that have so preoccupied Canadians over the past thirty years will re-emerge on the political agenda sometime before the end of this decade.

It is impossible to identify the precise catalyst that might thrust these issues back into the political spotlight. But, whatever the trigger, it also seems predictable that the next round of constitutional discussions may prove even more intractable and divisive than any that have gone before. What the Canada Round experience of 1991–2 has demonstrated is that Canada and Canadians lack a common organizing vision that might serve as the touchstone for a genuine constitutional renewal. It is the absence of this common organizing vision, rather than the details of any particular set of constitutional proposals, that explains the failures of the Meech and Canada rounds of constitutional reform.

This paper is an attempt to look back at the Canada Round experience in order to identify what we have learned about the country and about the process of constitutional reform. It is also an attempt to look forward, to ask how we might avoid repeating our past mistakes, and to ensure that we might build on our (relatively infrequent) successes.

Not surprisingly, I will suggest that most of the lessons of our recent experience are rather unhappy ones. Still, amidst the wreckage of past constitutional projects, there is always cause for guarded optimism. This is particularly true if we compare the current mood of the country with that prevailing in the immediate aftermath of the failure of the Meech Lake Accord. The collapse of Meech produced a very deep sense of rejection within the province of Quebec. This sense of rejection fuelled sovereignist sentiment in the province and made it necessary for Premier Robert Bourassa to launch a parliamentary commission to consider Quebec's future within Canada. It also prompted the Quebec Liberal party to adopt the quasi-sovereignist Allaire report as the party's official constitutional position in March 1991. The defeat of the Charlottetown Accord has not given rise to the same sense of rejection, probably because Charlottetown was voted down by Quebeckers themselves, as well as by Canadians across the country. Thus, in the months following the referendum there has been relative peace on the constitutional front in Quebec, permitting Premier Bourassa to adopt a federalist stance and to distance himself from the Allaire report.

I believe that this moment of constitutional tranquillity is unlikely to be permanent – it is more of a temporary ceasefire than a lasting constitutional peace. Still, while there will no doubt be future constitutional 'crises' to preoccupy and frustrate Canadians, and while the challenges facing the Canadian federal state should not be underestimated, neither are these challenges insurmountable. As we shall see, however, meeting those challenges may well depend less on finding permanent constitutional 'solutions' – since there are probably none to be found – and more on finding ways to divert attention away from the constitutional file. The maxim about leaving sleeping dogs well enough alone should be prominently displayed on the bulletin board of every constitutional expert and commentator prone to resurrect the constitutional issue.

Let there be no mistake about it: what the Canada Round has demonstrated most clearly is the futility of the continuing efforts to comprehensively 'renew' the Canadian constitution. Further attempts at comprehensive constitutional reform within the framework established by the Constitution Act, 1982 are virtually certain to fail. Those who are unhappy with the status quo have but two options: either work with the existing constitutional rules, or attempt to 'jump outside' the existing constitutional order and establish a completely new set of ground rules.

Of the constituencies likely to seek constitutional changes over the next five to seven years, only the province of Quebec is in a position to attempt this kind of unilateral rewriting of the constitutional order. Thus, as has been the case over the past thirty years, the fate of the constitutional file over the next decade rests ultimately in the hands of the province of Quebec. This fact will no doubt prove disquieting to many Canadians in other parts of the country, who continually complain that Quebec has received an inordinate amount of attention on the national political stage. But in the post-Charlottetown era, the pursuit of constitutional politics appears to be a negative-sum game – a form of political activity in which *everyone* is made worse off and virtually no one benefits. As this fundamental reality begins to penetrate the consciousness of those responsible for setting the political agenda in Quebec City and Ottawa, we may yet discover a way to muddle through together into the twenty-first century.

A LOOK BACK AT THE CANADA ROUND: SUCCESS OR FAILURE?

A primary focus for the opponents of the Meech Lake Accord had been the élitist and 'closed door' process that had been used to create it. Thus, in the

A0097.

While you were out

TO

DATE _____ TIME 6:45?

M _Irene Rome_

OF _____

PHONE _____
Area Code | Number | Extension

TELEPHONED ☑	PLEASE CALL ☑
WILL CALL AGAIN ☐	URGENT ☐
RETURNED YOUR CALL ☐	WANTS TO SEE YOU ☐

MESSAGE

Lee McGowan

wake of Meech's demise in June 1990, Prime Minister Mulroney committed himself to a more open and participatory process for any future constitutional discussions. Promising that 'you will not be able to get me to ever cut off debate on a constitutional resolution,' Mulroney said that, in future, the Constitution would be taken to the people: 'They can go on for as long as they want, years. I want to hear everybody. I want them recorded. I want them filmed. I want documents. I want ... and if I've missed anybody I'm going to reopen it. And then when its done, then we're going to take it and we're going to pass it.'[1]

Mulroney was as good as his word in the opening stages of the Canada Round. In November 1990, the Government established the Citizens Forum on Canada's Future, chaired by Keith Spicer. The Spicer Commission's mandate was to listen to Canadians and to ensure that their concerns were reflected in any future constitutional proposals. Despite a rocky start and considerable public scepticism, the commission claimed to have consulted over 600,000 Canadians by the time it reported in June 1991.[2] In December 1990 the Government also established a parliamentary committee, co-chaired by Senator Gérald Beaudoin and MP Jim Edwards, to examine proposals for changes to the constitutional amending formula.

The public consultations continued into 1991. In September 1991, the Government unveiled its initial package of constitutional proposals, entitled *Shaping Canada's Future Together*, and promptly established yet another parliamentary committee to consult with the public. The Castonguay-Beaudoin-Dobbie Committee was initally met by massive public scepticism and indifference and, by November 1991, appeared to be in danger of collapsing. But the Government salvaged the committee's credibility by announcing a series of five constitutional conferences to be held in early 1992 on various elements of the federal package. The conferences brought together politicians, representatives of various interest groups, and 'ordinary Canadians' chosen from respondents to newspaper advertisements. The conferences received extensive and very favourable media coverage and seemed to restore a measure of public confidence in the constitutional process.[3]

But with the publication of the Beaudoin-Dobbie Committee report on 28 February 1992, the 'public consultation' phase came to an abrupt end and a second 'intergovernmental negotiation phase' began. This intergovernmental phase bore a striking similarity to the supposedly discredited 'élite accommodation' model of constitutional negotitions. From March 1992 onward, constitutional negotiations were conducted entirely behind closed doors. The cast of players narrowed quite dramatically. While four national Aboriginal organizations and the two territorial governments remained at the table, the key participants from this point onward were the federal government and the ten provinces. The many interest-group representatives and the 'ordinary Canadians' who had played such a prominent role in the policy conferences in early 1992 were once again relegated to the sidelines. And any 'deal' that might emerge from this process would inevitably be a package of compromises and trade-offs, and thus would likely be presented to the public as a 'seamless web' that could only be accepted or rejected in its entirety.

Some critics might decry this return to the 'élite accommodation' model of constitutional negotiations in the final stages of the Canada Round. My own view is that this type of process is the only practical method of securing a constitutional amendment under our current amending forumla. The amending formula in part v of the Constitution Act, 1982 requires the consent of legislatures (and, by implication, governments). It follows that the only practical way to ensure broad governmental support for any proposed constitutional package is to ensure that governments are at the centre of the process that drafts the package. When governments are the key players in the process, they are forced to 'buy in' to any proposals that might be produced. Conversely, if governments are mere spectators or marginal participants in the process, they are unlikely to support proposals that emerge, unless those proposals match their optimal 'wish-list.'

Consider, as an illustration of this proposition, the very different reaction of the government of Quebec to three sets of constitutional proposals that appeared in the spring and summer of 1992: the Beaudoin-Dobbie report of 28 February,[4] the Pearson Accord of 7 July[5] and the Charlottetown Accord of 28 August.[6] From Quebec's perspective, none of the packages was ideal. But of the three sets of proposals, the Beaudoin-Dobbie report appeared to be the most palatable in the terms of the interests of the government of Quebec.

Quebec's 'traditional demands' have been for greater provincial autonomy. None of the three sets of proposals was particularly satisfactory in this regard: in each instance, the federal government agreed to withdraw from certain areas already under provincial jurisdiction, but there was very little 'transfer' of authority from Ottawa to the provinces. But there were other elements in these proposals that suggested that Quebec should clearly prefer the Beaudoin-Dobbie package to either the Pearson or Charlottetown accords. In particular, Beaudoin-Dobbie proposed an 'equitable' Senate in which Quebec and Ontario would have the largest numbers of seats – as opposed to the 'equal' Senate models in both Pearson and Charlottetown. Beaudoin-Dobbie also proposed that, in cases of deadlock, the House of Commons should be able to override a Senate veto, perhaps by a simple majority.[7] In addition, in terms of the recognition of Aboriginal rights (a key Quebec concern), Beaudoin-Dobbie recommended the entrenchment of the inherent right of Aboriginal self-government – but it was not clear whether this recognition could form the basis for a legal claim absent a concluded agreement involving the federal and provincial governments.[8] In both the Pearson and Charlottetown accords, the inherent right to self-government could be the basis of a legal claim by Aboriginal peoples after a specified 'delay period,' even absent a concluded agreement with Ottawa or the provinces.

Despite the obvious superiority of the Beaudoin-Dobbie package from the perspective of the Quebec government, Premier Bourassa rejected Beaudoin-Dobbie and the Pearson Accord, and then subsequently endorsed the inferior proposals in the Charlottetown Accord. How can one account for this apparent disregard of its own self-interest on the part of the Quebec government? I believe that the explanation has less to do with the content of the various proposals than with the process that generated them. While Beaudoin-Dobbie might appear to have offered more advantages (or, alternatively, fewer disadvantages) for Quebec than either of the other two packages, the Quebec government was a marginal player in the process that generated Beaudoin-Dobbie. Having played no real role in the drafting of the committee report, Quebec was much more likely to be conscious of the limitations or defects of Beaudoin-Dobbie and to believe that it could negotiate a 'better' package.

Contrast this with the role played by Quebec Premier Robert Bourassa in the drafting of the Charlottetown Accord. Following a first ministers' meeting at Harrington Lake on 4 August, Bourassa agreed to end his boycott of constitutional negotiations with the other provinces. From that point onward, Bourassa played a key role in the negotiations leading up to the Charlottetown agreement. The Quebec premier was clearly unable to achieve all of his objectives; indeed, the agreement of 28 August resembled in most of its broad outlines the earlier Pearson Accord of 7 July. What was critical, however, was the fact that Bourassa participated directly in the process of trade-offs and compromises that produced the agreement. This meant that the accord bore his own fingerprints. It also meant that the Quebec premier could be under no illusions about the possibility of negotiating a mythical 'better deal.' As one of the accord's primary authors, Bourassa could not help but actively support it.

There are important lessons to be learned here in terms of the structure of any future constitutional discussions. In the wake of the defeat of the Charlottetown Accord, some commentators have suggested that any future constitutional negotiations should be taken out of the hands of politicians and handed over to a non-partisan constituent assembly. Certainly a constituent assembly might play a helpful role in terms of shaping and defining options, in the manner of the constitutional conferences in early 1992. But if the objective is to design a package of proposals that will prove broadly acceptable to governments and legislatures, then the reality is that governments must be the key players in the final stages of any process. The Canada Round experience reinforces this fundamental principle: unless governments are at the centre of the process whereby the final, key trade-offs are made, they are unlikely to support actively any proposals that might emerge. And without active government support, constitutional proposals stand little chance of actually being enacted as part of the Constitution.

Aside from these reflections on the key role of governments and political leaders, what other general conclusions can be drawn from the Canada Round experience? An initial question that might be posed is whether the experience ought to be regarded as a success or a failure. To some, the answer to this question will appear self-evident: given the overwhelming rejection of the accord on 26 October, the whole exercise ought to be categorized as a collosal failure.

In my view, to draw this conclusion from our recent experience would be overly simplistic and misleading. Viewed from a different perspective, the Canada Round was at least partially successful. The multilateral process that began on 12 March and concluded with the Charlottetown agreement on 28 August managed to accomplish something that many thought impossible: it secured the unanimous consent of the federal, provincial, and territorial governments and four national Aboriginal organizations for a comprehensive package of constitutional amendments. This type of unanimity on a constitutional package is unprecedented. Moreover, the agreement was achieved under less-than-ideal conditions: there were seventeen parties at the table; the interests at stake, particularly in terms of Senate reform and on Aboriginal issues, were contradictory; and the sheer range and complexity of the issues under negotiation was mind-boggling, touching on virtually every aspect of the Constitution.

Given these obstacles, the fact that the parties were able to agree at all must be regarded as something of a minor miracle. Thus, in assessing the Canada Round, it is important to remember that the outcome was an ambiguous and bittersweet mixture of both success and failure. Later, I propose to attempt to explain the failure – the negative referendum result. But first I will attempt to account for how the process succeeded, against all odds, in producing a unanimous agreement amongst seventeen parties. How, given the long odds, was such an agreement even possible?

EXPLAINING SUCCESS

Any attempt to account for the partial success of the Canada Round must begin with the observation that this process differed in some significant respects from that utilized during the Meech Lake round of negotiations over the 1986–90 period. In the Meech process, the key negotiations were conducted almost entirely by the prime minister and the premiers. Federal and provincial cabinet ministers, along with their officials, played a restricted supporting role, laying the advance groundwork for the political meetings and providing indirect support and consultation during the meetings themselves. During the final marathon Meech meeting in Ottawa in June 1990, for example, the negotiations were conducted almost entirely by first ministers alone; the only other individuals regularly permitted into the room were some federal cabinet ministers and a number of federal officials. (The provinces as a whole were permitted a single 'notetaker' who was apparently to brief the remaining delegations on developments in the negotiations.)[9] The theory was that by limiting direct participation to the first-minister level, the instinct for compromise and the chances of achieving an agreement would be maximized.

The approach during the multilateral negotiations in the spring and summer of 1992 was quite different. The multilateral process relied much more heavily on the direct involvement of ministers and their advisers. The meetings from 12 March to 7 July were chaired by Constitutional Affairs Minister Joe Clark and included ministerial-level representatives from the provinces and territories, along with the heads of the Aboriginal organizations. Further, the heads of delegation, or 'MMC' (as the Multilateral Meeting on the Constitution came to be known), relied very heavily upon the direct participation of officials. The MMC created four working groups of officials to develop options and recommendations for consideration by the MMC. Issues would first be considered by the appropriate working group,[10] which would develop options and recommendations; these options would then proceed to a committee of senior officials from each delegation, the Continuing Committee on the Constitution (the 'CCC'); finally, they would proceed to the MMC, where ministers would be briefed by officials and decisions would be taken (see figure 1).[11]

During the Meech Lake Round, the assumption was that this type of complicated negotiating structure was practically unworkable and was therefore unlikely to produce general agreement. It was believed, in particular, that the extensive involvement of officials would render the process cumbersome, bureaucratic, and inefficient. It was also thought that officials were more likely to adopt and advocate fixed positions, thus reducing the development of acceptable compromise solutions.

The process was, indeed, very cumbersome and highly bureaucratic. The process was so unwieldy that the chair, Joe Clark, was constantly forced to extend the deadline for the completion of the process. Initally, the deadline was the end of May; when this passed without an agreement, the process was extended to mid-June; ultimately, the multilateral process dragged on into early

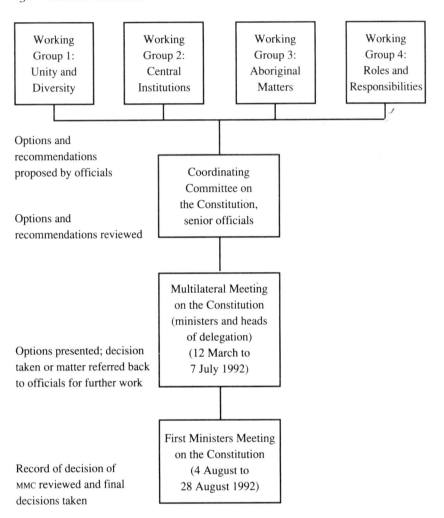

FIGURE 1
Multilateral Meetings on the Constitution: Decision Process

July. The reality was that the ministers and heads of delegation, despite meeting almost continuously from early April, required over three months to deal adequately with the numerous issues that required decisions.

Despite these obstacles, the process managed to yield a unanimous agreement involving all seventeen participants in the negotiations. The question is,

How can we account for the emergence of this consensus, in the face of the many impediments confronting the negotiators? In my view, three factors were of critical importance – the role played by the federal government, the absence of the province of Quebec from the early stages of the process, and the widespread perception that there were significant costs associated with failure. I turn now to a brief discussion of each of these factors.

The Role Played by the Federal Government

In previous constitutional discussions, the federal government had often been perceived as a master manipulator, attempting to orchestrate the participants in the process and predetermine its ultimate outcome. Certainly this was the impression left by Prime Minister Mulroney in his now-infamous description of the strategy of the federal government leading up to the week-long meeting of first ministers in June 1990: 'I asked [my advisers] to come and see me and I told them when this thing was going to take place. I told them a month ago when we were going to start meeting. It's like an election campaign, you've got to work backwards. You've got to pick your date and you work backwards from it. And that ... and I said that's the day that I'm going to roll all the dice. It's the only way to handle it.'[12]

Yet, whatever the approach of the federal government to earlier negotiations, it certainly did not undertake any such 'roll of the dice' strategy in the Canada Round in early 1992. If anything, the federal approach was to move to the opposite extreme. The federal government at many points appeared to lack any coherent strategy or any sense of 'bottom line' objectives. The main role it played was to act as a facilitator for the other parties around the table. If a proposal was found to be generally acceptable to the provinces and Aboriginal organizations, then by definition it would find favour with the federal government.

The events surrounding the establishment of the multilateral process in early March 1992 are themselves indicative of the largely facilitative and improvised role played by the federal government throughout the process. Leading up to the initial meeting of ministers and Aboriginal leaders on 12 March, federal Unity Minister Joe Clark described the purpose of that meeting as to sound out the provincial and Aboriginal reaction to the Beaudoin-Dobbie parliamentary report, which had recently been released. But the federal plan, according to Clark, was for the federal government alone to table a response to Beaudoin-Dobbie in Parliament sometime in April.[13] Clark argued that the provinces, territories, and Aboriginal organizations should not be concerned about the federal intention to draft its own proposals: 'I'd be very surprised,' Clark told reporters, 'if the government of any province would object to the ... government of Canada responding to a Parliamentary report ... What's at issue here is the presentation of a response by our government to that report.'[14] Prior to the 12 March meeting, Clark also indicated that the Aboriginal organizations were to be permitted to attend only a public morning session; the closed-door session scheduled for the afternoon was described by Clark as 'a meeting of governments.'[15]

But the meeting of 12 March was conducted according to an entirely different script, one that was apparently written by the government of Ontario rather than the Government of Canada. Ontario Premier Bob Rae reportedly came to the 12 March meeting armed with a position paper arguing for a 'multilateral' process that would place all governments and the Aboriginal organizations on an equal footing.[16] A key element of the Ontario position was the commitment of all participants that they would not put forward any 'unilateral' proposals during the continuation of the multilateral process. This effectively meant that Ottawa would have to abandon its strategy of presenting a federal-government response to Beaudoin-Dobbie in April. More significantly, the federal government was effectively ceding exclusive authorship of any future proposals; the federal, provincial, and territorial governments, along with the Aboriginal organizations (who ended up attending the private session on the afternoon of 12 March after all) would *all* jointly draft the next set of proposals.

Federal officials were reportedly 'grumbling over what they felt was Ontario's uncompromising approach to the meeting,' particularly the insistence that Ottawa not make any unilateral proposals for the duration of the multilateral process.[17] But despite this grumbling, the federal government agreed to the Ontario proposals, effectively abandoning the federal approach spelled out prior to the meeting. Clark defended what he described as a strategy of 'innovation,' comparing it favourably to that followed by Ottawa under then prime minister Pierre Trudeau in the early 1980s. 'Some of you will remember the era of the Kirby document [drafted by former Secretary to the Cabinet Michael Kirby] when everything was spelled out in advance,' Clark said. 'There was an attempt made, which failed, to try to make people conform to a script. It failed because the world doesn't work that way.'[18]

Mr Clark was no doubt correct in pointing out that any attempt to make people 'conform to a script' would certainly end in failure. But recognition of this reality should not preclude the federal government from developing a coherent strategy of its own and attempting to implement that strategy. What was disturbing about the proceedings on 12 March 1992 was the appearance that the federal government was acting in an entirely improvised and unplanned manner. In the space of a few hours, the federal government abandoned its plan to present a response to the Beaudoin-Dobbie report and instead embraced a totally different process devised by a different government. When decisions are taken in this kind of off-the-cuff fashion, it is impossible to assess in advance their longer-term implications.

This is not to suggest that the decision to opt for a multilateral process, with the provinces, territories, and Aboriginal organizations participating as equal partners, was necessarily wrong. Indeed, given the reality that the provinces must consent to any significant constitutional amendment if that amendment is to be enacted into law, the direct involvement of the provinces was inevitable. The point is simply that the way in which the federal government came to this decision suggested that decisions of fundamental importance were being taken on an immediate and ad hoc basis rather than in accordance with a long-term strategy.

The meeting of 12 March set the tone and context for the negotiations that unfolded over the subsequent four months. With the number of parties around the negotiating table increased, the agenda for the negotiations was also broadened quite dramatically. Once the multilateral process began in mid-March, a whole series of new issues that had not been part of the original federal proposals or discussed at the policy conferences in January and February found their way to the table. The new issues under discussion reportedly included such matters as a provincial role in international treaty making, strengthening the federal government's commitment to equalization in section 36 of the Constitution Act, 1982, adding a new constitutional obligation requiring the federal Parliament to make payments for regional economic development, granting the provinces power to make laws in relation to international exports of natural resources, and recognizing Aboriginal governments as one of three constitutional orders of government in Canada.[19] Significantly, these items largely involved an increase in the role and authority of the provinces, territories, or Aboriginal groups in relation to the federal government.

The federal government was able to resist some, but not all, of these demands for increased power on the part of the other parties around the table. Thus, while the federal government agreed to strengthen the commitment to equalization, agreed to a constitutional obligation to negotiate regional-development agreements, and recognized Aboriginal governments as one of three constitutional orders of government, it managed to stare down provincial demands for a role in international treaty making or increased provincial power over international exports of natural resources. At the same time, the federal government's own proposals for strengthening the economic union – proposals that had been central to the original federal package in September 1991 – ran into stiff opposition and were eventually abandoned.[20]

What is striking about this result is the fact that, as late as July 1992, Prime Minister Mulroney was still describing the federal proposals on the economic union as a 'bottom line' objective. But the fundamental reality was that the federal government saw itself as playing a facilitative role in which its primary objective was to secure agreement from the other parties. This meant that it was simply impossible for the federal government to adopt any fixed positions. Once it became apparent that there was insufficient provincial support for the federal proposals on the economic union, it was only a matter of time before these proposals would be abandoned.

While some might tend to be critical of this federal approach, it did have one significant advantage; it increased the chances of securing general agreement from the seventeen parties around the table. Because the federal government was adopting a flexible and facilitative role, both in relation to matters of process and of substance, it made it more likely that common ground could be discovered. Had the federal government taken a fixed or hard-line position in the negotiations, the chances of securing general agreement would have been much more remote. This is not to suggest that the largely passive and reactive approach adopted by the federal government was not without its own difficulties; as we will see later, one of the main criticisms of the accord during the referendum campaign was that the federal government had been unduly accommodating and had failed to defend adequately the national interest. Nevertheless, it needs to be emphasized that the accommodating attitude of the federal government was one of the key factors in explaining how the process managed to produce an agreement.

The Absence of Quebec

The second factor that increased the chances of securing a consensus during the negotiations was the absence of the province of Quebec from the early stages of the process. At first glance, this conclusion might appear to be counterintuitive and surprising. As I suggested earlier, unless governments are directly involved in constitutional negotiations, they are unlikely to buy into any proposals that eventually emerge. Thus, the fact that Quebec refused to participate in the negotiations over the March to July period made it highly unlikely that they would accept the Pearson Accord agreed to on 7 July.

At the same time, the absence of Quebec from the negotiations contributed in an indirect way to the creation of a general consensus on two of the most intractable issues confronting the participants – Senate reform and Aboriginal self-government. Had Quebec been at the table, opinion on these two key issues would have been much more divided. Because Quebec was not there,

there was a greater perception of common ground and the outlines of a general consensus began to emerge. This initial consensus crystallized in the Pearson Accord of 7 July. While Quebec initially rejected the Pearson Accord as inadequate, the accord was an important achievement – it demonstrated that the nine English-speaking provinces were capable of reaching agreement. This consensus heightened the pressure on Quebec to return to the bargaining table and increased the momentum in favour of a unanimous agreement.

To understand how this dynamic operated, it is necessary to review very briefly the positions of the various parties on the key issues of Senate reform and Aboriginal self-government. These issues were likely to be the most intractable in the negotiations because they pitted certain provinces against others (Senate reform) or required the provinces to agree to constraints on their legislative powers (Aboriginal self-government). In this sense, these issues differed from the 'division of powers' questions in which the provinces generally were able to achieve gains at the expense of the federal government.

On Senate reform, there were two main 'camps' of provinces, defined by their position on the Triple-E model proposed by Alberta. At least five provinces (Alberta, Saskatchewan, Manitoba, Nova Scotia, and Newfoundland) were strong supporters of 'Triple E' while two others (Ontario and Quebec) were strong opponents. The remaining provinces fell somewhere in between these two main groups. Had Quebec been at the table, the result might well have been a stand-off between the Triple-E supporters and opponents. But with Quebec absent, Ontario was left as the only strong opponent of Triple-E. This isolated Ontario and increased the pressure on Premier Rae to 'compromise' in favour of some variant of the Triple-E model. Eventually this pressure became unbearable. After four months of holding out against the Triple-E group, Premier Rae accepted the concept in the Pearson Accord of 7 July.

A similar dynamic developed in relation to Aboriginal self-government. Again, there were two main groups of provinces. One group included provinces who were seen as strong proponents of the inherent right (Ontario, British Columbia, Saskatchewan, Prince Edward Island, and New Brunswick), while a second group was sceptical or cautious of constitutionally entrenching the right (Alberta, Manitoba, Quebec, and Newfoundland). But the absence of Quebec from the table reduced both the number and the political weight of the sceptical provinces. Further, these sceptics faced pressure to compromise, not only from the other large provinces, such as Ontario and British Columbia, but from the four Aboriginal delegations around the table. As was the case on the Senate-reform issue, the opponents of the self-government package found themselves politically isolated. Eventually the pressure proved unbearable, as first Manitoba, then Alberta, and finally Newfoundland agreed to the proposals on

Aboriginal self-government. Thus, by the time Quebec returned to the table, the main outlines of a consensus on the self-government issue had emerged. Had Quebec been participating actively from the very beginning, it might well have added political credibility and weight to the sceptics, and stymied the development of a consensus.

Thus, the absence of Quebec had the unforeseen consequence of narrowing the differences around the table and isolating certain provinces on the key issues of Senate reform and Aboriginal self-government. Once a consensus emerged on these two key issues, an overall agreement was within reach.

The Consequences of Failure

A key factor affecting the outcome of any negotiating process is the participants' perceptions of the consequences of a failure to agree. If one or another of the players believes that the costs of failure are low or non-existent, then this will reduce the incentive for those parties to move off their preferred positions and accept compromise solutions. Conversely, a belief that the costs of failure are high will promote what Michael Stein has described as 'integrative bargaining' – a bargaining environment in which the parties attempt to take account of the other interests around the table.[21]

What was evident over the spring and summer of 1992 was the widespread belief amongst all the governments around the table that the costs of failure were very high. This perception flowed primarily from Quebec's legal requirement to hold a referendum on sovereignty by 26 October 1992.[22] Of course, it was open to the Quebec government to amend or repeal Bill 150, thus avoiding the referendum obligation. But any such amendment of Bill 150 could only take place in the context of acceptable 'offers' from the rest of Canada. Without such acceptable offers, Premier Bourassa would have been politically and legally bound by the terms of Bill 150, and would have had to proceed with the scheduled sovereignty referendum. Furthermore, in the event that there were no acceptable offers, it would have been exceedingly difficult for Bourassa to adopt a strong pro-federalist stance in any ensuing referendum. With the Quebec premier handcuffed, the uncertainty associated with any sovereignty referendum would have increased quite dramatically.

Both the federal and provincial governments wanted to avoid a sovereignty referendum if at all possible. The outcome of such a referendum was uncertain at best, particularly in the event that the rest of the country had shown itself unable to produce proposals acceptable to the Quebec government. But the only practical way to avoid such a referendum was to arrive at some kind of negotiated constitutional agreement. (The other possible alternative – a unilateral offer to Quebec from the federal government alone – would have provoked stiff provincial resistance and would have been extremely divisive.) Thus, there was considerable pressure on all the parties around the table to reach some kind of negotiated agreement. A failure to achieve agreement was seen as imposing significant costs on all the parties. This widely shared perception about the costs of failure produced a willingness from all parties to compromise, particularly on the two intractable issues of Senate reform and Aboriginal self-government.

In summary, there were at least three main factors – the facilitative role played by the federal government, the absence of the province of Quebec during the early stages, and the widely shared perception that the costs of failure were high – that together help to explain how the seventeen negotiating parties managed to agree on the Charlottetown Accord. But despite this unanimous agreement amongst governments and the Aboriginal organizations, the accord was subsequently rejected, in quite decisive fashion, by the Canadian people in the referendum of 26 October. This brings us to the next question: Is it possible to account for the negative referendum result?

EXPLAINING FAILURE: A COMPARATIVE PERSPECTIVE

While there have been relatively few published attempts to explain the referendum result on 26 October, those that have appeared have tended to argue that the result represented a rejection of the country's political élites by ordinary Canadians. In one sense, this description is completely accurate. The country's established political and business leaders were almost unanimously in favour of the accord. But this élite support could not be translated into a majority at the mass level.

The question is how to account for this divergence between élite and mass attitudes. One possibility is that Canadians were simply voting against their political leaders – that the details of the Charlottetown Accord were less important than its authors. On this view, Canadians would have voted against *any* agreement reached by their current political leaders, simply because of the massive distrust and suspicion of politicians on the part of ordinary Canadians.

But this explanation seems at odds with the experience of the referendum campaign itself. In the first place, there was initially very broad public support for the accord, despite the widespread dissatisfaction with the document's authors. Polls published at the end of August in the days immediately following the Charlottetown agreement suggested a comfortable majority in favour. This broad support must have been a central factor in persuading all governments to support the holding of a national referendum in the first place.

Second, there appeared to be a very strong desire on the part of Canadians to find out more about the substance of the actual accord. The government mailed out close to ten million copies of the accord to individuals and groups across the country during the course of the referendum campaign. Far from judging the accord on the basis of its tainted authorship, Canadians appeared genuinely interested in the details of the agreement itself.

Finally, polling data published immediately following the referendum suggested that antipathy towards the country's political leaders played a relatively minor role in the result. Asked by one pollster to identify why they voted 'no,' less than 10 per cent of respondents indicated that it was as a result of opposition to Brian Mulroney.[23] Over three-quarters of those voting 'no' responded that they had done so because of their unhappiness with particular aspects of the accord.[24]

So it would appear necessary to go beyond the 'rejection of élites' theory in attempting to explain the referendum result. In fashioning any such explanation, it would be wise to begin by raising our sights somewhat and comparing our own recent experience with that elsewhere. Placed in a comparative and historical perspective, there is nothing surprising about the result of 26 October. The international experience with constitutional change over the past thirty years suggests that fundamental constitutional reform is the exception rather than the rule. Internationally, the only instances of genuine 'reconstitutions' have been in cases where established interests had been shattered by war, revolution, external threat, or similar disruption. As Banting and Simeon put it in their seminal study of comparative constitutional change: 'while examples of demands for constitutional change abound, examples of actual change are scarce ... The predominant pattern is of frustrated demands, not wholesale renewal.'[25]

It is worth reminding ourselves precisely why fundamental constitutional change is so difficult to achieve. The international experience with constitutional reform suggests that some kind of prior consensus on the general direction of reform is a prerequisite to success.[26] In the absence of this kind of prior consensus, it is extremely difficult to mobilize the kind of special majority support that constitutional change normally requires. The international experience also indicates that fundamental constitutional change is extremely rare in those countries where the existing constitution continues to function in a tolerable fashion. Where the existing constitution continues in place, there is a tendency for all parties to prefer the status quo rather than to accept changes that are seen as inadequate or unacceptable.[27] Continuation with the status quo appears preferable because it avoids having to accept unwelcome changes, while keeping open the possibility of achieving a 'better deal' sometime in the future.

It is evident that in Canada, in late 1992, neither of these two prerequisites for a successful 'reconstitution' was present. On the one hand, there was clearly no generalized consensus on the nature of the proposed constitutional changes that which were necessary. Nor is there even any consensus on the nature of Canada and of Canadian society. One view of the country suggests that it is composed of ten equal provinces, with a strong central government, committed to the equality of all its citizens.[28] A second vision sees Canada as the product of 'two founding nations,' French and English.[29] More recently, some have argued that Canada is composed of 'three nations': English, French, and Aboriginal.[30] Each of these contradictory visions enjoys a measure of support and legitimacy in the country at present.

The fact that there was no underlying societal consensus on the desirability of constitutional change helps us to understand the very contradictory ways in which the Charlottetown Accord was perceived in different parts of the country. In Quebec, the accord was denounced because it granted no new provincial powers and represented an abandonment of the 'traditional demands' of the province; in the West, the accord was condemned on the basis that it failed to create a 'Triple E' Senate, while granting unjustified privileges to the province of Quebec; in Ontario, the accord was criticized for stripping too much power from the federal government and on the basis that it undermined Charter rights; within the Aboriginal communities, the accord was rejected on the basis that it undermined the 'nation to nation' relationship between the Crown and Aboriginal peoples and threatened treaty rights. These very contradictory visions of the accord are nothing more than a reflection of the very contradictory visions that Canadians hold of the purposes that the Constitution is designed to serve.

While there is no consensus on the nature of the country or on the proposed direction which constitutional change should follow, neither has there been a breakdown in the existing constitutional order. The Constitution Acts, 1867–1982, continue in place, functioning tolerably well. There was no political breakdown or constitutional vacuum that precipitated the Canada Round of negotiations. The existing constitution remains a going concern. While many Canadians might be unhappy with various aspects of the status quo, they were apparently not *so* unhappy as to endorse a complicated package of amendments whose effects were uncertain, at best.

During the referendum campaign, the defenders of the accord had attempted to argue that a 'no' vote would have dire consequences in terms of the future unity of the country. But these attempts backfired, particularly following Prime Minister Mulroney's Sherbrooke speech on 28 September in which he ripped up a copy of the accord in order to symbolize the consequences of a 'no' vote.

These predictions of dire consequences ran up against the fact that the existing constitution remained a going concern. People could vote 'no' on 26 October secure in the knowledge that the country would not turn into a constitutional pumpkin come midnight. On the morning of the 27th, the existing constitution would continue to function, and the country could carry on with its other business. And that is precisely what has happened, to the relief of almost everyone, perhaps even the prime minister himself.

Given these fundamental realities, it is hardly surprising that the Canada Round exercise ended in the manner it did. A successful outcome would have been all the more remarkable given the extraordinarily high level of consent that was required. Success in the referendum was defined as a majority in favour of the accord in all ten provinces. Looking once again to the international experience, it is clear that securing this kind of unanimous sub-national support in a constitutional referendum is an extremely rare event. In Australia, for example, where amendments require majority support in two-thirds of the states (as opposed to majorities in all states), a mere eight of 42 proposed amendments have been ratified through referenda since 1901.[31] The Australian experience also reflects the difficulty in securing popular support for a comprehensive 'package' of amendments, as opposed to an amendment proposing a narrow or incremental adjustment to the status quo. Those amendments ratified in Australia have been of a limited, focused, or 'stand-alone' variety, involving incremental rather than comprehensive changes.

The difficulties associated with a decision-rule requiring unanimous consent, whether through referenda or legislatively, are widely appreciated in Canada. Indeed, following the Meech Lake round of negotiations, it was recognized that one of the major reasons why Meech failed was precisely because of the requirement of unanimous provincial consent. In an attempt to avoid the same fate in any future rounds, the federal government appointed the Beaudoin-Edwards parliamentary committee in the fall of 1990, with a mandate to propose alternatives to the existing amending formula.[32] Further, when the federal government tabled its initial set of proposals in the fall of 1991, it was careful to focus on areas that could be amended under the 'general' amending formula, which requires support of just two-thirds of the provinces.[33]

Despite these attempts to avoid the straitjacket of unanimity, the country ended up in a situation where majority support in all ten provinces was required in order to ratify the Charlottetown Accord. This result was not due to political mismanagement or miscalculation, but rather was a product of two very powerful dynamics that emerged during the Canada Round. The first of these dynamics was an expansion of the constitutional agenda, particularly after the commencement of the multilateral round on 12 March. The expansion of the agenda meant that it was impossible to restrict the accord to items subject to the '7/50' general amending formula. The second dynamic was the fact that the accord emerged through a series of delicate trade-offs or compromises from all the parties around the table. As with Meech Lake, the Charlottetown Accord represented an integrated whole, a single package of amendments, rather than a series of isolated proposals. Altering any particular part of the accord (for example, by deleting those parts requiring unanimous consent) would have been a fundamental change that would have required a renegotiation of the entire package. Thus, the parties were unwilling to separate out the parts of the package that required unanimity from those requiring '7/50' support, or to permit one part of the package to proceed on its own.

In practical terms, this meant that the Charlottetown Accord would have to be passed by all ten provincial legislatures in order to become law. We can also assume that no provincial premier could possibly proceed with a constitutional resolution through his or her legislature in the face of a majority 'no' vote in a provincial referendum. Thus, in any referendum on the Charlottetown Accord, it would be necessary to obtain majorities in *any* province in which the referendum were held. A 'no' result in even a single province would effectively prevent that province's legislature from proceeding with ratification, thus denying the necessary unanimous provincial consent. For this reason, it became necessary, as a practical political matter, to secure majorities in each province in the referendum of 26 October.

Some might suggest, with the benefit of hindsight, that the decision to hold the national referendum was itself mistaken and that governments ought to have proceeded directly with legislative ratification. But there seems little reason to suppose that the final outcome would have been any different had governments proceeded in this way. Remember that at least three provinces – Quebec, Alberta, and British Columbia – were already committed to provincial referenda. The accord was defeated by wide margins in each of these provinces. It also seems difficult to imagine that Canadians in the remaining provinces would have accepted a situation where they were denied an opportunity at democratic participation that was being enjoyed by citizens in Alberta, Quebec, and British Columbia. Any attempt to proceed directly with legislative ratification in the remaining provinces, without a referendum, would undoubtedly have stimulated intense controversy and opposition. In short, it seems that there was little practical option but to proceed with a referendum following the agreement at Charlottetown.

And so there should be nothing mysterious about the failure of the Charlottetown Accord in the recent referendum. The first problem was that there was no underlying societal consensus on whether the Constitution needed change or, if so, on what changes were needed. These contradictory views of the country and of the Constitution generated contradictory views about the significance of the Charlottetown Accord. So a deal that was seen by Quebeckers as too centralizing was at the same time described in the West as granting 'special status' to Quebec. Then there was the problem presented by the continuing viability of the status quo – the existing constitution remained a going concern. This meant that people could vote against the accord secure in the knowledge that it would be business as usual on the morning of the 27th. Finally, the requirement of securing majority support in each province, as well as a national majority, represented a hurdle that could be cleared only by a very limited and uncontroversial constitutional amendment, rather than a complicated package like Charlottetown.

At the end of the day, these obstacles were so imposing that they would probably have scuppered any package of amendments, no matter who had put them forward. The fact that one of the prime architects of Charlottetown happened to be Brian Mulroney simply made this outcome all the more unavoidable, while providing the pundits with a convenient explanation and scapegoat. Had it not been for Brian Mulroney and his élitist brand of politics, we are now told, the result on 26 October might have been different. This explanation is easily understood and it is also politically soothing, since it suggests that the underlying forces that produced the Charlottetown Accord can be overcome simply by voting against the current occupant of the Prime Minister's Office in the next election. But the reality, as I will argue in the next section, is rather more complicated and unpleasant than this currently fashionable explanation might suggest.

A LOOK AHEAD: CANADA AFTER CHARLOTTETOWN

Perhaps the greatest benefit of the recent referendum campaign is the fact that it has cleared the constitutional air. This 'clearing of the air' refers not just to the fact that Canadians and their political leaders have consciously avoided talking about the Constitution in the months following 26 October. More important, the referendum has clarified for Canadians the precise nature of the choices open to them in the years ahead.

Both the Meech Lake and Canada rounds were premised on the theory that it was possible to agree on a set of constitutional amendments to bring Quebec 'back in' to the Constitution. In the Meech Lake Round from 1986–90, the strategy was to focus on a limited set of demands formulated in advance by the federalist government of Robert Bourassa. This having failed, a different strategy was employed in the Canada Round in 1991–2; the agenda was broadened to include all those with constitutional grievances so as to develop a comprehensive proposal for renewing the Canadian constitution.

Both strategies have now been exposed as failures. And it is difficult to see where a new, more successful strategy might lie. Some have suggested that the problem with the Charlottetown Accord was simply that it was a 'bad deal' and that a more carefully crafted package of amendments might meet with a better fate. But this suggestion seems implausible. The basic problem that would bedevil any comprehensive package of constitutional amendments, no matter how carefully crafted, is the lack of a constitutional consensus in Canada. Absent such an underlying consensus, any future package would likely meet the same fate as the Charlottetown proposals. This would especially be the case if the existing constitution remained in place and the choice was between the status quo and a set of proposals whose effects were controversial and unpredictable.

The difficulties facing any future package of amendments would be compounded by the important precedent set by the referendum itself. Having consulted the people directly on one occasion, it makes it practically impossible to avoid consulting them on all others. In practical political terms, the use of referenda has now become mandatory in Canada, at least for any significant package of constitutional proposals.

This is an important gain for democracy. But it further narrows the passageway through which constitutional amendments must pass in order to become law. As noted earlier, the international experience suggests that complicated packages of proposals are extremely difficult to ratify through referenda. When voters are presented with such complicated packages, they tend to focus on those parts of the package they dislike, rather than on the parts they support. Success in a referendum is more likely with a narrow and specific 'stand alone' amendment rather than with a comprehensive package.

The problem for Canada is that any future set of amendment proposals is likely to be in the form of a complicated package. The received wisdom is that it is necessary to deal with all constitutional grievances simultaneously. To propose a limited, 'stand alone' constitutional amendment would be regarded as an 'exclusion' of the other interests or concerns that were not addressed by that amendment. Thus, any future constitutional proposals will undoubtedly be of the Charlottetown variety – complicated and sprawling – and would be just as vulnerable in a referendum.

The upshot of this analysis is simply this: attempts to 'renew' the Canadian constitution through formal constitutional amendments are futile and counter-

244 Patrick J. Monahan

productive, at least over the short to medium term. Formal constitutional change based on the general amending formula in part v of the Constitution Act, 1982 has been foreclosed, for at least a generation.

This does not necessarily mean that all forms of constitutional change should be regarded as off limits. Informal constitutional change, not involving amendments to the formal constitution, certainly remain a live possibility. Many of the elements of the failed Charlottetown Accord might be acted upon in this way. In terms of Senate reform, for example, the prime minister could make future appointments on the basis of elections, similar to the procedure utilized in relation to Stan Waters. In terms of the division of powers, the federal government could agree to limitations on the exercise of the federal spending power in areas of exclusive provincial jurisdiction, similar to those contemplated in both Meech Lake and Charlottetown. On the issue of Aboriginal self-government, the federal and provincial governments could proceed with the negotiation of self-government agreements with Aboriginal communities across the country. But none of these agreements or commitments could be enshrined in the formal constitution.

This post-Charlottetown reality has important implications for the province of Quebec. Since the early 1960s, federalists in Quebec have built their constitutional strategy on a program of 'renewed federalism.' Even Pierre Trudeau felt it necessary to promise Quebeckers something called 'renewed federalism' in return for their vote in the 1980 referendum. There has been no major political party in Quebec for the past generation that has campaigned on the basis of the constitutional status quo.

What has now been made plain is that the goal of 'renewed federalism,' if it involves formal constitutional amendments, is simply not on the table. Thus, Quebeckers have essentially two political options in the decade ahead. The first is to work within the confines of the existing constitution, attempting to increase the powers of the provincial government to the extent permitted by the formal terms of the Constitution as it now stands. The second option is to attempt to unilaterally jump outside of the existing constitution, and opt for political sovereignty.

It is impossible to predict how this contest between the status quo and sovereignty will play itself out. What is certain is that the next eighteen months will be a particularly important period in the working-out of these issues, given the fact that both federal and Quebec elections must be held within that period. In the federal election, which must be called by 12 December 1993, the critical issue will be whether Canadians elect a majority government with support from all regions of the country. A broad-based majority government would mean that the party system was still capable of accommodating the many differences that exist among Canadians. Alternatively, the next election may result in a minority government (or a majority government that is not seen as sufficiently representative of all regions), combined with significant support for the Reform party and/or the Bloc Québécois. This scenario might suggest that the main-line parties are no longer capable of moderating regional cleavages. As the experience with federations elsewhere indicates, the demise of national parties and the rise of predominantly regional parties operating within federal institutions is a tell-tale indication of imminent dissolution.[34]

The second key event on the political horizon is the Quebec election, which must be held by the fall of 1994. The Charlottetown experience suggests that the outcome of this election will likely turn on the ability of the two main parties to attract support from the 'nationalist/federalist' segment of the Quebec population. This 'nationalist/federalist' group, exemplified by Jean Allaire and Mario Dumont and comprising up to 20 per cent of the Quebec population, appeared to play a decisive role in the referendum outcome in Quebec. We can expect both the Quebec Liberal party and the Parti Québécois to court these voters in the period leading up to the next election. For the Quebec Liberal party, this means continuing to position itself as the advocate of greater power and autonomy for the province within Canada. For the Parti Québécois, it means moderating or softening its advocacy of sovereignty, perhaps by promising a subsequent referendum on the issue following the election and prior to any final decisions being taken.

This focus on developments in Quebec should not be taken to mean that there are not other groups and constituencies with constitutional claims and ambitions. The Aboriginal peoples have been pressing for constitutional recognition of their right to self-government, particularly over the past decade, and will continue to do so in the future. In the West, there is widespread dissatisfaction with a lack of regional responsiveness in our national institutions, particularly in terms of the House of Commons and the Senate. It is doubtful that these constituencies will be satisfied for very long with informal adjustments to the status quo.

But despite these diverse constitutional aspirations, *only* Quebec has the capacity, as Preston Manning has put it, to 'split the Constitution wide open.' It is widely recognized in the rest of Canada that an unequivocal decision by Quebec to leave the federation would be respected. It is for this reason that the political dynamic in Quebec over the next eighteen months will be particularly important to observe.

If Quebec is to succeed in reopening the constitutional file in the short to medium term, there will have to be a very clear indication that Quebeckers are prepared to opt for sovereignty. During the Canada Round, Quebec scheduled a referendum on sovereignty and then, at the last minute, held the referendum on the Charlottetown Accord instead. That sent an important message to the rest of the country. In any future constitutional round, the Rest of Canada will undoubtedly require Quebec to go ahead and hold any planned referendum first, in advance of any serious discussions about restructuring the country.

The good news is that, had Quebeckers been asked to choose between sovereignty and federalism on 26 October, they would probably have opted for federalism. The 'no' side appears to have triumphed in Quebec only because it managed to convince the population that a rejection of the Charlottetown Accord did not imply a vote for sovereignty.[35] The bad news is that the country may have passed up a golden opportunity to resolve decisively the issue of Quebec's continued place in Canada. How and when that question will ultimately be resolved is impossible to predict. The most that can be said is that the prospects for convincing Quebeckers to remain within Canada appear significantly more promising at the end of 1992 than they did in the months immediately following the failure of the Meech Lake Accord. With goodwill, tolerance, and a little luck, the distinctive Canadian capacity to discover unity in diversity may yet succeed for a while longer.

NOTES

1 See 'It's a tough country to govern' [interview transcript with Prime Minister Mulroney], *Globe and Mail*, 20 June 1990, A13.

2 See *Citizens' Forum on Canada's Future: Report to the People and Government of Canada* (Ottawa: Minister of Supply and Services Canada 1991), 22.

3 For a review of the distinctive contribution of the constitutional conferences during the Canada Round, see David Milne, 'Innovative Constitutional Processes: Renewal of Canada Conferences, January–March 1992,' in D. Brown and R. Young, eds, *Canada: The State of the Federation 1992* (Kingston: Queen's University Institute of Intergovernmental Relations 1992).

4 *A Renewed Canada: Report of the Special Joint Committee of the Senate and House of Commons* (Senator Gerald Beaudoin and Dorothy Dobbie, MP, co-chairs) (Ottawa: Queen's Printers, 28 Feb. 1992)

5 *Status Report: The Multilateral Meetings on the Constitution* (Summary of results of the Multilateral Meetings on the Constitution, 12 March to 7 July 1992) (Final version dated 16 July 1992)

6 *Consensus Report on the Constitution: Charlottetown* (Final text, 28 Aug. 1992)

7 The committee report was ambiguous on this point, noting cryptically that '*some* members of the Committee believe the override should require a 60 per cent majority in the House of Commons' (p. 55; emphasis added). But the Committee's

formal recommendation simply stated that the House of Commons should be able to override the Senate, without specifying the precise majority required. See *A Renewed Canada*, 54–5.

8 Ibid., 29–32

9 For a more detailed analysis and discussion of the Meech Lake round, see P. Monahan, *Meech Lake: The Inside Story* (Toronto: University of Toronto Press 1991) and A. Cohen, *A Deal Undone: The Making and Breaking of the Meech Lake Accord* (Vancouver/Toronto: Douglas and McIntyre 1990).

10 The working groups were organized in the following manner: Canada Clause and Amending Formula (Group 1); Central Institutions (Group 2); Aboriginal Matters (Group 3); Division of Powers and Social and Economic Union (Group 4).

11 This description of the decision process is based on my involvement as an adviser to the delegation from the Inuit Tapirisat of Canada.

12 See 'It's a tough country to govern,' A13.

13 See Edison Stewart, 'Meech's shadow looms over talks on unity today,' *Toronto Star*, 12 March 1992, A13.

14 See Susan Delacourt, 'Today's talks for map-making, Clark says,' *Globe and Mail*, 12 March 1992, A4.

15 See Stewart, 'Meech's shadow.'

16 As reported in Graham Fraser, 'Ottawa embraces new partnership: Can't prepare constitutional offer on own, federal officials concede,' *Globe and Mail*, 14 March 1992, A1

17 See Fraser, 'Ottawa embraces new partnership.'

18 As quoted in Edison Stewart, 'How to make history in a hurry: Seat-of-pants strategy the only way to fly, Clark says,' *Toronto Star*, 14 March 1992, A8

19 These items were all reported in the extensive media coverage of the talks during the April to June 1992 period.

20 The Consensus Report of 28 August stated that there was to be a non-binding statement of the 'policy objectives' surrounding the social and economic union entrenched in a new section 36.1 of the Constitution Act, 1982; but, in contrast to the federal proposals in September 1991, this statement could not be utilized by the courts to strike down federal or provincial laws that were inconsistent with these objectives.

21 See Michael Stein, *Canadian Constitutional Renewal, 1968–81: A Case Study in Integrative Bargaining* (Kingston: Queen's University Institute of Intergovernmental Relations 1989).

22 See Bill 150, 'An Act respecting the process for determining the political and constitutional future of Quebec,' S.Q. 1991.

23 See 'Why Canadians Voted the Way They Did' (Maclean's/Decima Poll), *Maclean's*, 2 Nov. 1992, 17.

24 By far the most common reasons were: 'Quebec got too much' (27%); 'The
    agreement is a poor one' (22%); and 'The provinces should not be given more
    power' (15%). See ibid., 17. See also Richard Mackie, 'Ontario knew accord in
    trouble, polls show,' *Globe and Mail*, 11 Jan. 1993, A4 (showing that the fall in
    support for the accord during the referendum campaign coincided with an increase
    in the number of voters who said they knew what was in the accord.)

25 See K. Banting and R. Simeon, 'The Politics of Constitutional Change,' in Banting
    and Simeon, eds, *Redesigning the State: The Politics of Constitutional Change*
    (Toronto: University of Toronto Press 1985), 25.

26 See E. McWhinney, *Constitution-Making: Principles, Process, Practice* (Toronto:
    Univeristy of Toronto Press 1981), 113.

27 See Banting and Simeon, 'The Politics of Constitutional Change,' 22–6.

28 See P.E. Trudeau, *A Mess That Deserves a Big No* (Toronto: Robert Davies
    Publishers 1992).

29 This view was an underlying theme of the Meech Lake Accord, particularly the
    propsed 'distinct society' clause in section 2 of the accord.

30 See Maude Barlow, chap. 11 of this volume.

31 For a discussion see P. Monahan, L. Covello, and J. Batty, *Constituent Assemblies:
    The Canadian Debate in Comparative and Historical Context* (North York: York
    University Centre for Public Law and Public Policy 1992), 19–26.

32 See *The Process for Amending the Constitution of Canada: The Report of the
    Special Joint Committee of the Senate and the House of Commons* (Hon. Gerald
    Beaudoin and Jim Edwards, MP, joint chairs) (Ottawa: Queen's Printer, 20 June
    1991).

33 See *Shaping Canada's Future Together: Proposals* (Ottawa: Minister of Supply
    and Services 1991).

34 For a discussion, see R. Watts, 'Canada in Question, Again,' *Queens Quarterly* 99,
    no. 4 (Winter 1992): 11.

35 See the discussion by Andre Blais in chapter 16 of this volume.

19

Disagreeing on Fundamentals: English Canada and Quebec

KENNETH McROBERTS

The failure of the Charlottetown Accord, like the failure of the Meech Lake Accord before it, can best be understood in terms of the profoundly different conceptions of political community that predominate in English Canada and Quebec. Certainly, both attempts at constitutional revision were greatly hampered by such institutional factors as the need to secure full unanimity among governments, as well as such popular sentiments as deep distrust of governments in general and the Mulroney government in particular. But, in the last analysis, it was the divergence between English Canadians and Québécois over the most basic of constitutional questions, the definition and nature of the political community, that explains why the exercise ended in such abject failure.

Given that their conceptions of political community were mutually exclusive, so English Canadians and Québécois tended also to view as mutually exclusive their primary projects of constitutional change: Senate reform and recognition of Quebec's specificity. Apparently for this reason the framers of the Charlottetown Accord felt that they could not fully incorporate each project, even though formulae had been proposed whereby this might be done. They instead tried to accommodate English Canada and Quebec by draining each project of much of its content so as to make it more palatable to the other party. Thus, the 'Triple E' Senate of the 7 July accord had to be seriously diluted and recognition of Quebec's project had to be kept to an absolute minimum. In the process, there was little direct incentive left for either English Canadians or Québécois to support the accord.

CONSTITUTIONAL VISIONS

Quebec's constitutional vision has been clearly defined for close to thirty years now. The underlying principle is one of asserting the specificity of Quebec, the basic project one of expanding the powers of the Quebec government. The precise form of the project has changed from government to government: *statut particulier, associate states, souveraineté culturelle, sovereignty-association, distinct society*. But the underlying rationale has been the same: since it is only in Quebec that francophones are in the majority, Québécois are bound to see Quebec as their primary political community and will want the government of Quebec to have all the powers necessary to preserve and strengthen that society. These objectives need not lead to full sovereignty for Quebec. They might be met within the Canadian federal system – provided that Quebec's specificity is constitutionally recognized and its government is granted the necessary powers.

For its part, over the last two decades English Canada has become firmly attached to a constitutional vision of its own. Central to this vision is the ideal of Canada as the pre-eminent political community. Coupled with this is a concern to protect and strengthen the role of the federal government as the 'national' government of all Canadians. In recent years, survey after survey has demonstrated rejection among most English Canadians of any substantial decentralization of powers and responsibilities to the provinces.[1] Equally integral to this conception of Canadian political community is the principle of absolute equality among the provinces, Quebec included.

The most powerful movement for constitutional change to arise in English Canada, Senate reform, has been carefully framed within these principles. While the source of this movement is a concern with regional interest, the perennial hinterland complaint against Central Canadian dominance, the objective is resolutely conceived in 'national' terms: better incorporation within central political institutions. One finds little trace of the 1970s Western Canadian demands for greater power for provincial governments, let alone 'separatism.' As Reform party leader Preston Manning is fond of saying, 'Our whole theme is that the west wants into Confederation as a more equal partner, not out.'[2] By the same token, the most popular version of Senate reform, the 'Triple E' Senate, is directly based upon the principle of equality among the provinces.

In short, through the constitutional debate of the last few years English Canada and Quebec have pursued fundamentally different agendas, with English Canada seeking to reform and strengthen national institutions and Quebec seeking to strengthen its own political institutions.

THE 7 JULY AGREEMENT: ENGLISH CANADA'S PROJECT

The 7 July accord gave concrete form to English Canada's constitutional project. Not only did the accord have the clear agreement of the premiers of all nine predominantly English-Canadian provinces, as well as the federal government, but there is good reason to believe that if it had been submitted in a formal referendum to the populations of these provinces the accord would have passed.

First and foremost, the 7 July agreement clearly respected the desire of most English Canadians that there be no major attenuation of federal powers. By and large, any reinforcement of provincial power was in areas already under provincial jurisdiction.

Perhaps the clearest instance of enhancement of provincial power was in the 'six sisters': urban affairs, tourism, recreation, housing, mining, and forestry. There, provinces could force a total federal withdrawal. None the less, not only are these all areas of exclusive provincial jurisdiction, but they are areas in which federal activity (based upon the spending power) is in any event minimal.

With respect to labour-market development and training, provincial governments were granted the right to oblige federal withdrawal from training and labour-market development activities. However, the federal government could continue to play an important role through its responsibility for setting national objectives that the provinces would be bound to respect: 'There should be a constitutional provision for an ongoing federal role in the establishment of national policy objectives for the national aspects of labour market development. National labour market objectives would be established through a process which could be set out in the Constitution including the obligation for presentation to Parliament for debate.'[3]

Similarly in the case of cultural affairs, the agreement declared that there should be a constitutional amendment specifying that 'Provinces should have exclusive jurisdiction over cultural matters within the provinces,' but specified that the proposed amendment would also recognize 'the continuing responsibility of the federal government in Canadian cultural matters. The federal government should retain responsibility for national cultural institutions, including grants and contributions delivered by these institutions.'[4]

To be sure, the accord did incorporate the spending-power provisions of the Meech Lake Accord, setting up conditions under which provinces would have the right to establish their own programs with compensation. But these constraints apply only to *cost-shared* programs within *exclusively* provincial jurisdictions. By the same token, as many Quebec jurists have noted, the provision has the effect of giving the federal spending power a much clearer constitutional sanction than ever before.[5] Similarly, it incorporated the Meech Lake provisions regarding immigration – a concurrent jurisdiction in which the federal government remains paramount.

Second, the 7 July accord contained a proposal for Senate reform that squarely met the 'Triple E' criteria and could expect to receive the active support of the Triple-E forces. The Senate was to be composed of an equal number of elected representatives (eight) from each province, plus two from each territory and an undetermined number of Aboriginal representatives. Moreover, it had a clear promise of being 'effective': a simple majority could veto House bills 'that involve fundamental tax policy changes directly related to natural resources'; on most other bills a 60 per cent majority could force reconciliation and, if needed, a joint sitting of the House and Senate; 70 per cent could veto a bill outright.[6]

Third, just as with the Senate proposal, so all other elements of the 7 July accord are closely bound to the principle of equality among the provinces. Thus, with respect to Quebec's claims for recognition, the accord contained a 'distinct society' interpretative clause patterned after that of the Meech Lake Accord. However, just as with the Meech version, it is clear that the clause could not directly affect the division of powers. Unlike Meech, the significance of the clause is further attenuated by the fact that it is carefully inserted within a 'Canada Clause,' in which it stands as one of eight principal characteristics of Canada.[7] (At the same time, it would also be inserted in the Charter as an interpretative provision.)

In short, the 7 July agreement fell squarely within the parameters of English Canada's constitutional project. It respected the clearly stated desire of most English Canadians that the roles of the federal government not be weakened in any fundamental manner. At the same time, it offered a Senate reform that clearly met the Triple-E criteria. By the same token, it contained scarcely a nod towards Quebec's project, focused on the expansion of the Quebec government's powers. The primary reference to Quebec's specificity, the distinct-society clause, was devoid of any such notion.

Of course, the process giving rise to the 7 July agreement had virtually guaranteed such a result: Quebec was not formally a party to negotiations. Quebec's absence was perhaps understandable, born of frustration with the Meech Lake débâcle when two English-Canadian premiers failed to respect commitments made by their predecessors. None the less, it was a strategical error, since it allowed the participants to effectively impose English Canada's constitutional agenda. Quebec may have presumed that the premiers would not be able to reach an accord. (Apparently, this had been the clear assumption of Prime Minister Mulroney.) But the English-Canadian premiers were able to agree on a package of constitutional reforms – precisely because Quebec was not there.

THE CHARLOTTETOWN ACCORD AND QUEBEC

None the less, even when Quebec Premier Bourassa finally joined the negotiations, Quebec's project was not seriously incorporated. Apparently most negotiators presumed that Quebec's project was necessarily in conflict with English

Canada's. Instead of adding elements desired by Quebec, the main strategy for altering the 7 July accord to accommodate Quebec was to dilute a major element of what was already there, the Senate reform so coveted by Outer Canada. For good measure, Quebec's (and Ontario's) representation in the House of Commons was expanded. But there was no significant expansion of the powers or general status of the Quebec government.

Thus, unlike the Senate reform agreed to on 7 July, the Charlottetown version falls far short of the 'Triple E' model. Representation would indeed have been 'equal,' with the same number of representatives from each province (six), plus an indeterminate number of Aboriginal representatives. But it would not necessarily have been 'elected': to placate Quebec Premier Bourassa, provincial legislatures had the option of appointing the representatives. And on the basis of the powers to be wielded by the Senate, there was uncertainty about the extent to which it would be 'effective.' While a majority of the Senate could still veto taxation bills relating to natural resources, the Senate could no longer veto (by 70 per cent) most other measures. Bills that were rejected in the Senate would simply be submitted to joint sittings, where senators would be outnumbered by MPs five to one. To add further insult to injury, within the House Central Canadian representation would be increased by 36 seats, bringing it from 59 per cent to 62.3 per cent.[8]

At the same time, with respect to the primary focus of Quebec's demands, the division of powers, only two minor additions were made to accommodate Quebec: a commitment to establish a general framework to guide use of the federal spending power and a commitment to negotiate an agreement to coordinate and harmonize the regulation of telecommunications.[9]

In effect, Quebec had to content itself with the treatment of powers already contained in the 7 July agreement. Yet, as we have seen, these were of quite limited significance, out of deference to English Canada's concern to maintain a strong federal government. The most substantial changes, regarding the 'six sisters,' did not really respond to Quebec's list; they had been drawn up by the federal government itself. The measures with respect to manpower and culture do address concerns of Quebec; however, each had important qualifications that assured a continued federal role. Beyond that, all that remains are the provisions drawn from the Meech Lake Accord on the spending power and immigration policy.[10]

By the same token, the treatment of Quebec's status as a 'distinct society' follows the same restrictive lines as in the 7 July accord. Quebec's 'distinct society' remained one of eight enumerated 'fundamental characteristics' of Canada. This time the nature of Quebec's specificity is carefully delineated – and circumscribed. The delineation is based upon a traditional conception of

Quebec's specificity: French-language majority, distinct culture, and civil code of law. There is no reference to the distinctive economic and social institutions of contemporary Quebec. There follows a reproduction of the distinct-society clause of the Meech Lake Accord, with its provision that nothing in the clause can derogate from 'the powers, rights or privileges' of Parliament and the Government of Canada, as well as their provincial counterparts.[11]

As a matter of fact, with respect to the division of powers and the status of Quebec, both accords, 7 July and Charlottetown, fall within the same limited parameters as both the federal government's October 1991 constitutional proposals and the February 1992 report of the joint parliamentary committee (Beaudoin-Dobbie) established to assess those proposals. Premier Bourassa had felt obliged to denounce that package as nothing less than 'un fédéralisme dominateur.' Six months later, despite Quebec's new participation in negotiations, nothing had changed.

In fact, it could be argued that Quebec's clearest 'gain,' to use one of Robert Bourassa's favourite terms, was in an entirely different area from the division of powers: representation in central institutions.

Under the Charlottetown Accord, representation in the House of Commons was to be increased in numbers for Quebec (as well as Ontario), going from 75 to 93. In addition, Quebec was to be guaranteed 25 per cent of the seats of the House, in perpetuity. Beyond that, the new Senate was to require a majority of francophone senators on any matter that 'materially affects the French language or culture in Canada.' (To be sure, the senators would not necessarily come from Quebec alone.) In addition, Charlottetown incorporated the Meech Lake Accord's provision constitutionalizing Quebec's right to three of nine positions on the Supreme Court.[12]

These changes represent, moreover, perhaps the most substantial of all alterations of the 7 July agreement. Yet, representation in central institutions had not been a priority of the Quebec government. In fact, *reduced* representation might have been acceptable. The Quebec government had not even proposed the guarantee of 25 per cent of seats in the House of Commons. Apparently, it was proposed by Saskatchewan Premier Roy Romanow and New Brunswick Premier Frank McKenna.

In sum, the Charlottetown Accord appears to adopt both English Canada's and Quebec's constitutional projects, but then qualifies them very substantially in an effort to make them acceptable to the other side. Rather than a mutual accommodation of the two projects we have a mutual frustration of them. As a result, neither Quebec nor English Canada (at least outside Ontario) was left with a clear reason to support the project.

COMBINING THE TWO PROJECTS

In point of fact, it is far from clear that English Canada's and Quebec's projects could not both be accommodated within a common set of institutional reforms. After all, meeting Quebec's demands need not entail a general weakening of the federal government, as with decentralization of powers to all the provinces. Under schemes of asymmetry, any decentralization of powers could go to Quebec alone; Ottawa would continue to perform these functions in the rest of the country. In effect, English Canada could continue to have as strong a federal government as it wished.[13]

To be sure, asymmetry would raise some institutional problems. In particular, critics have wondered about the propriety of Quebec MPs voting on measures that, under asymmetry, do not apply to Quebec, and of Quebec MPs assuming cabinet portfolios that involve programs that do not function in Quebec. But the problem should not be exaggerated. After all, Quebec MPs have voted on laws dealing with the Canada Pension Plan, even though Quebec has its own Quebec Pension Plan, and two Quebec MPs have even assumed responsibility for these programs as ministers of health and welfare: Monique Bégin and Marc Lalonde.

Even then, there may be ways to alleviate these complications. For instance, Quebec MPs may simply not vote on these measures – they would not be votes of confidence. This arrangement might even be formalized in the House proceedings: measures not applying to Quebec would be reserved to certain days, when Quebec MPs would absent themselves.

Some critics have contended that 'opting out' on Quebec's part might induce other provinces to do the same, leading to a 'Checkerboard Canada,' with some provinces opting out and others not doing so, or perhaps worse, a generalized decentralization. Yet, with proper safeguards, asymmetry could be limited to Quebec alone. To be certain of this, the right to opt out might be formally restricted to Quebec. If, as would most likely happen, such a formal limitation would be politically untenable in English Canada, the right might be extended to all provinces, but with procedural requirements that would preclude it from being used frivolously: a two-third's majority in a provincial legislature or approval in a popular referendum.

Nor is the desire of Western and Atlantic Canada (Outer Canada) for more power at the centre incompatible with Quebec's desire for greater provincial autonomy. In fact, under certain assumptions these desires are highly compatible. Presuming that under asymmetry Quebec MPs would not vote on measures that do not apply to Quebec, Outer Canada would in these instances dominate the House of Commons. Without Quebec MPs voting, Outer Canada MPs would have a majority of the seats. To this extent, a Triple-E Senate might not even be necessary to accommodate Western Canadian concerns.[14]

If it were to prove necessary, a Triple-E Senate might still be made acceptable to Quebec by coupling it with a major expansion in Quebec's powers. In fact, among the documents prepared by top Quebec civil servants that were published in October 1992 in *L'actualité* there is the intimation that Senate reform might have been acceptable to Quebec if it had been accompanied by additional powers for the Quebec government: 'En raison de son caractère distinct, le Québec peut difficilement accepter une réforme du Sénat où sa représentation serait sensiblement amoindrie. Seule l'obtention d'un statut particulier – réformant au gré du Québec le partage des pouvoirs – pourrait hypothétiquement justifier une diminution sensible de sa représentation au sénat.'[15]

None the less, there appears to have been no serious discussion of these possibilities for an incorporation of Quebec's project. In effect, negotiators seem simply to have presumed that such a reform was unacceptable to English Canada. Accommodation of Quebec could only be made through diluting the concessions to English-Canadian priorities.

To be sure, there can be no guarantee that asymmetry would have done the trick. But it is clear that with the approach that the Charlottetown Accord did use, the accord was doomed from the outset. The singularity of the Charlottetown Accord is that it managed to offend *both* English Canada and Quebec.

THE REFERENDUM

A good number of handicaps plagued the 'Yes' forces and they have all been widely cited: the advertising campaign was not well-conceived; there were conflicts among the three major parties and between them and citizen activists; some political leaders did not campaign as vigorously for the cause as they might have; many voters were unable or unwilling to separate their vote from their basic antipathy towards government leaders; and so forth. But at least part of the explanation must lie with the terms of the accord itself, and its failure to meet squarely the constitutional objectives of either Quebec or English Canada, especially Outer Canada. On this basis, it is not surprising that the No vote was strongest in Quebec and Western Canada.

In Quebec, a primary focus of opposition was the failure of the accord to expand significantly the powers of the Quebec government. It was largely on this basis that Jean Allaire, the author of the Quebec Liberal party's constitutional position, called for a No vote and was joined in this by Mario Dumont, president of the Liberal youth wing, and a good number of other Liberal dissidents. By the same token, the division-of-powers issue was a major theme of the famous Wilhemy-Tremblay lament over how Bourassa 'caved in' to the English-Canadian premiers. While expressing uncertainty as to the precise impact of the latter on the Quebec referendum vote, André Blais concludes, in chapter 16 of this volume, that survey data 'would suggest that dissatisfaction with the agreement stemmed at least in part from the view that not enough powers had been devolved from the federal to the provincial level, precisely the main complaint about the accord voiced by Liberal dissidents such as Jean Allaire and Mario Dumont.'[16]

At the same time, in Western Canada a major focus of opposition was the limited powers of the Senate. Supporters of the accord could argue that the reformed Senate would have great potential influence: members would be elected, relatively few in number, and, given their exclusion from cabinet, fully focused on their Senate tasks. Moreover, in a joint sitting the Senate might prevail if it hangs together and the Government has a narrow majority in the House. But arguments like these were far too subtle for the average voter. And Quebec's expanded representation in the House could only be all the more galling to Western Canadians given the reductions in the Senate's powers.

In fact, even some experts were not impressed. Professor David Elton of the University of Lethbridge, one of the originators of the concept of the Triple-E Senate, concludes in chapter 2 of this volume that the departures from reform proposals were too substantial. In this he was joined by Professor Roger Gibbins of the University of Calgary, who declared the accord to be nothing less than a 'humiliation.' In Gibbins's words, 'it is bitterly ironic that the new agreement on Senate reform will strengthen central Canadian dominance, and more specifically Quebec's dominance, of the national political process.'[17]

It is not entirely clear what impact the Senate issue had on the average Western Canadian voter, as opposed to opinion leaders. Some analyses suggest that only a small proportion of voters were directly influenced by the issue. Yet, even if this was true, the fact remains that the Senate issue had an enormous indirect effect on the Western Canadian vote, since it was the deficiencies of the accord's Senate proposal that virtually forced the Reform party to overcome its hesitations and launch a forthright attack on the accord.

In short, the referendum campaign presented the paradox of *both* Outer Canada and Quebec claiming that they had been 'humiliated' and, moreover, claiming that they had been humiliated by each other! It would be tempting to conclude that if both sides felt that they had lost, then something must have been 'right' about the accord. It must have constituted the ideal compromise, since neither side has won too much. But the fact of that matter is that each side had won very little. And the referendum campaign made it clear that opinion leaders in both areas were very much aware of that fact.

Thus, the referendum result reflects in large part the fact that the Charlottetown Accord did not fully incorporate the two leading constitutional projects: Senate reform and expansion of the Quebec government's powers. In the vain hope of making the 7 July agreement acceptable to Quebec the framers of the Charlottetown Accord pursued a strategy, not of introducing elements that responded to Quebec's aspirations, but of diluting the component that Quebec found most objectionable, the Triple-E Senate, while at the same time introducing a notion, the 25 per cent guarantee of Commons seats, that many English Canadians were bound to find profoundly objectionable.

Yet, as we have seen, Quebec francophones might have been able to support even a Triple-E Senate if there had been a direct response to their demands for greater powers for the Quebec government. Such a response need not have undermined the strong federal role that most English Canadians desire if it were to be based upon asymmetry. Yet, most participants in the constitutional negotiations clearly were unprepared to pursue this possibility. As Reg Whitaker notes in chapter 8, only a credible threat of Quebec independence might have forced an openness to asymmetry – and this did not happen, thanks in part to the strategic errors of Robert Bourassa.

COMPETING CONCEPTIONS OF POLITICAL COMMUNITY

Why was there such resistance to formulating a constitutional package that responded directly to what Outer Canada *and* Quebec were seeking? The answer lies in the premises that underlay the constitutional projects: definitions of political community that are themselves mutually exclusive. More specifically, most constitutional proposals from English Canada were framed in terms of a conception of Canada that precluded, implicitly or explicitly, the type of differentiation between Quebec and the rest of the country upon which Quebec's project rests. Thus, for instance, no matter how useful asymmetry might be in providing a basis for reconciling the constitutional aspirations of English Canada and Quebec, it is simply unacceptable to most English Canadians because of their conception of the Canadian political community. To understand why this is true, we need to examine the origins of these two conceptions of political community.

As it happens, the conception of political community now dominant in English Canada was born directly of an effort to deny Quebec's.[18] The 1960s had seen the rise within Quebec of a new political identity focused upon the province of Quebec and its institutions. As such, it constituted the transformation of a long-standing phenomenon: French-Canadian nationalism had become Quebec nationalism. While not necessarily indépendantiste, this new Québécois nationalism did assert the pre-eminence of Quebec as a political community and the urgency of strengthening the jurisdictions and capacity of the Quebec state.

With the ascendancy of Pierre Elliott Trudeau, the federal government became committed to the dissemination of a counter-identity. The elements of this new Canadian identity can be readily established: official bilingualism, a Charter of Rights and Freedoms, multiculturalism, the absolute equality of the provinces, and the reinforcement of national institutions. Equally evident is the extent to which this new identity, and its various components, was designed to nullify any claims of Quebec to constitutional recognition of its specificity.

With official bilingualism, it was argued, Quebec could not claim distinctiveness on the basis of language. French would be present throughout the country, enjoying an equal status to English. Thus, as Trudeau declared in a memorable 1968 address, 'if minority language rights are entrenched throughout Canada then the French-Canadian nation would stretch from Maillardville in BC to the Acadia community on the Atlantic Coast ... Quebec cannot say it alone speaks for French Canadians ... Nobody will be able to say, "I need more power because I speak for the French-Canadian nation."'[19]

For the federal government, language rights also were the essential purpose of a constitutionally entrenched bill of rights. The bill would serve to further solidify the notion that French would have equal status to English throughout the country rather than just in Quebec; the rest of the country would become like Quebec. Trudeau acknowledged that the Charter was really about language rights in the fall of 1980 when, after having released his constitutional project, he addressed the Quebec City Chambre de commerce. He explained that in order to avoid the English-Canadian cries of 'French Power' that would have accompanied the entrenchment of language rights alone, the government felt it had to add other rights to the project.[20]

In committing the federal government to a policy of multiculturalism in 1971, Prime Minister Trudeau openly acknowledged that he was rejecting biculturalism, the formulation that had dominated the 1960s. Biculturalism had made him uneasy because it could be used by Quebec to argue that, on the basis of cultural distinctiveness, it should enjoy 'national' status. As Trudeau and several colleagues had argued in the pages of *Cité libre* during the 1960s, with its focus on two cultures biculturalism could lead to the notion of 'two nations': 'And what is the meaning in practice of a Confederation which "develops according to the principle of equality between the two cultures? ..." It would have been interesting to see how the Commission [on Bilingualism and

Biculturalism] intends to interpret its mandate without being led necessarily to propose the division of Canada into two national states.'[21] Multiculturalism served to avoid all that: Quebec's culture was only one of a myriad of 'official' cultures.

Firmly embedded within each of these components of the new Canadian identity was the notion that Quebec was simply 'a province like the others.' They were clearly designed to render illegitimate Quebec's claims to a distinctive status within Canadian federalism. Beyond that, however, during the Trudeau years federal officials addressed the issue head-on: all the provincial governments must have exactly the same status. On that basis they systematically rejected any constitutional recognition of Quebec's specificity beyond what already existed.

Thus, not only did the Trudeau government enshrine the principle that Quebec must be treated on the same basis as all the other provinces, it created a series of mechanisms that have been remarkably effective in entrenching that principle: a Charter of Rights and Freedoms, multiculturalism, and official bilingualism.

Even though these notions of a Canadian identity had been designed primarily with Quebec francophones in mind, intended to supplant the newly ascendant Quebec identity, their impact upon Quebec has been minimal. Most Quebec francophones have remained firmly committed to the primacy of Quebec as their political community and have largely resisted the federal government's attempts to incorporate them within the new Canadian political identity. If nothing else, the results of the Charlottetown referendum have at least demonstrated that fact.

Instead, it is in English Canada that the new Canadian identity has taken root, thanks in particular to the constitutional revision of 1982. By the same token, it is the commitment of most English Canadians to the new principles of Canadian nationality that explains their resistance to such ideas as asymmetry. Within these principles, there is no room for recognition of Quebec's specificity. Quebec *must* be a province like the others. The problem with asymmetry is not that it would complicate national institutions, as it clearly would. The problem is more profound and intractable: asymmetry is unacceptable in principle.

As a consequence, Québécois and English Canadians are more divided than ever before, separated not just by different constitutional preferences but by mutually exclusive notions of political community. As we have tried to demonstrate, their constitutional preferences might be accommodated within a common set of revisions. But it is much more difficult to accommodate their different notions of political community. Taken literally, they are mutually exclusive: within the new Canadian political identity it cannot be legitimate to place primary allegiance with a province. Because the identities are mutually exclusive, so the constitutional projects associated with them tend to be treated as mutually exclusive.

THE FUTURE

On the basis of the Charlottetown experience, as well as the Meech episode before it, there are a good many reasons to be pessimistic about the potential for a constitutional agreement in the near future.

First, the process clearly has become more complex. Thanks to the precedent set by the multilateral negotiations of last spring, any future negotiations will necessarily include a larger number of participants than was past practice: at a minimum, representatives of Aboriginal peoples and the territories will have to be included. Moreover, thanks to the precedent of the 26 October referendum, unsuccessful as it may have been from the governments' point of view, any future constitutional agreement will have to be submitted to a popular referendum.

Second, it is difficult to see how a new set of constitutional negotiations might be launched. What politicians would want to take the responsibility of initiating an exercise that is so likely to fail? Certainly not the English-Canadian premiers, and probably not even the federal prime minister. Only a Quebec premier might be impelled to do so. Even then, it is less likely to be a Quebec 'federalist' premier than the head of a Parti Québécois government, preparing the ground for a referendum on Quebec sovereignty – hardly the most propitious condition for a new round of constitutional talks.

Clearly, conditions will not again be as favourable as they were at the time of the Meech Lake negotiations, when not only did the prime minister and Quebec premier have a good working relationship and the federal government had a strong electoral interest in securing Quebec's signature to the Constitution, but the Quebec government was prepared to accept the most minimal of conditions. After the failure of Meech, Quebec public opinion resolved that any new agreement must be 'more' than Meech. Now, for an agreement to be acceptable in Quebec, it clearly must be considerably 'more' than Charlottetown.

None the less, as we have argued in this chapter, the most profound obstacle to a constitutional resolution is ideological. English Canada and Quebec are now firmly attached to notions of political community that are mutually exclusive. Inevitably, it seems, constitutional proposals are assessed in these terms. On that basis, what is acceptable to one party is highly likely to be unacceptable to the other.

There is now a great temptation simply to shelve the whole constitutional question. Since the question manifestly cannot be resolved, the argument goes, better to leave it alone and focus on more tractable problems. Yet, this can be at best a short-term strategy. One way or another, the constitutional question will come forward once again. In all likelihood, as almost invariably has happened in the past, developments in Quebec will bring this about.

The challenge next time will be to address constitutional questions more directly and to assess proposals on their merits rather than in terms of issues that by definition cannot be resolved, such as competing notions of political community. Otherwise, as recent events elsewhere suggest, English Canada and Quebec may stumble into a process of separation that, by all appearances, neither of them really wants.

NOTES

1 For instance, a 1991 survey found that 60 per cent of anglophónes outside Quebec preferred a greater *centralization*. Typically, they wanted this centralization to be combined with a Senate elected on the basis of regions. The survey was conducted by CROP for *L'actualité* and TVA over 18–23 January 1991. Conceivably some respondents may have rejected the option of decentralization since it was linked to satisfying Quebec: 'A Canada decentralized into four or five regions, which would satisfy Quebec.' None the less, the status quo was also available as an option – only 11 per cent selected it. ('Le refus global,' *L'actualité*, 15 March 1991, 25)

2 'Quebec can help West get what it wants, Manning says,' *Gazette,* 1 Feb. 1991

3 *Status Report: The Multilateral Meetings on the Constitution* (final version, 16 July 1992), s. 28

4 *Status Report*, s. 29

5 See the discussion of this point by Jacques Frémont in chapter 6 of this volume.

6 Ibid., s. 10

7 Another 'characteristic' of Canada is 'the equality of the provinces' (ibid., s. 1).

8 *Draft Legal Text, October 9, 1992* [a best-efforts text based on the Charlottetown Accord], pp. 3–13.

9 Ibid., pp. 16, 47

10 See Jacques Frémont's analysis in chapter 6 of how the Charlottetown Accord falls short of Quebec's minimal demands regarding the division of powers.

11 *Draft Legal Text*, p. 1

12 Ibid., pp. 11, 13, 25, and 31

13 Reg Whitaker makes many of these points in his piece in this volume (chapter 8). The concept of asymmetry was in fact endorsed at the first of the five public conferences the federal government organized during the winter of 1992. In the words of conference rapporteur Rosalie Abella: 'The government has offered a general devolution of powers to the provinces. You appear to have been reluctant

to accept this and prefer that Canada have a strong central government. Most of you have urged that the federal government address Quebec's needs directly and that such transfers of powers as may be necessary should not for the most part be extended across this country' (Susan Delacourt, 'Forum urges separate deal for Quebec,' *Globe and Mail*, 20 Jan. 1992, 1). For their part, government officials soon dismissed the idea from serious consideration.

14 See, for instance, Gordon Laxer, 'Distinct Status for Québec: A Benefit to English Canada,' *Constitutional Forum constitutionnel* 3, no. 3 (Winter 1992): 60.

15 Jean François-Lisée, 'Dossiers secrets de Bourassa', *L'actualité*, 1 Nov. 1992, 64

16 P. 204

17 Roger Gibbins, 'Something Not So Funny Happened on the Way to Senate Reform,' *Canada Watch* 1, no. 2, September 1992, 22

18 This discussion draws upon my *English Canada and Quebec: Avoiding the Issue*, 6th annual Robarts Lecture (Toronto: Robarts Centre for Canadian Studies, York University 1991).

19 Speech to Quebec Liberal Convention, 28 January 1968, reported in *Ottawa Citizen*, 29 Jan. 1968 (as quoted in George Radawanski, *Trudeau* [Scarborough: Macmillan-NAL Publishing Ltd. 1978], 286).

20 'Des provinces ont prié Ottawa de leur imposer le respect du français,' *Le Devoir*, 23 Oct. 1980, 1

21 Comité pour une politique fonctionnelle (Albert Breton, Claude Bruneau, Yvon Gauthier, Marc Lalonde, Maurice Pinard), 'Bizarre algèbre,' *Cité libre* 20: 82 (décembre 1965): 14. Reputed to be the author of the document, Pierre Trudeau apparently did not sign it because he had entered federal politics.

20

Speculations on a Canada without Quebec

ROGER GIBBINS

The objective of this analysis is to address the possible consequences of Quebec's departure on the residual Canadian state, a state that I assume would encompass the nine remaining provinces and the northern territories. While this objective was first set in the context of the post-Meech constitutional crisis, and at a time when the 26 October referendum was a remote possibility, its relevance has been enhanced by the outcome of that referendum. In the wake of the referendum, it is clear that the threat and possibility of Quebec's departure are not about to leave the Canadian political stage.

To begin this analysis, a number of caveats must be made. The first is that no assumptions are made about the likelihood of Quebec's departure; the 'what if' analysis that follows is predicated on the purely hypothetical case of Quebec achieving full political sovereignty, and not on the assumption that Quebec will leave. Second, no attempt will be made to assess the economic or national-security implications of Quebec's departure, for this is ground that has been extensively covered elsewhere.[1] My focus will be exclusively on the possible impact of Quebec's departure on the Canadian political system, broadly defined. Although the analysis will suggest that Quebec's departure, should it occur, may have some positive benefits, no attempt will be made to add up the totality of costs and benefits. It should also be noted that the analysis will concentrate primarily on the longer-term consequences of Quebec's departure. The immediate consequences, including the dismemberment of the Liberal and Progressive Conservative parties and the implosion of the federal government, are both serious and problematic. However, I will assume that we can make it through this transition period, and will focus, therefore, on the longer-term patterns of change likely to be set into motion by Quebec's departure, whenever that should occur.

TABLE 1
Impact of Quebec's departure on Canada's demographic composition

	1991 Population (%)	Scenario 1 (%)	Scenario 2 (%)
Quebec	25.3	–	–
Ontario	36.9	49.4	50.3
West	29.0	38.7	38.1
Atlantic	8.5	11.4	11.2
North	0.3	0.4	0.4

Scenario 1: Quebec leaves, with no impact on the size or distribution of the residual Canadian population.

Scenario 2: Quebec loses 5% of its population (345,000 persons), who relocate in Ontario.

DEMOGRAPHIC CHANGE

The most immediate political consequences of Quebec's departure would stem from the altered demographic composition of Canada. As scenario 1 in table 1 shows, Ontario would have close to 50 per cent of the remaining Canadian population even if there was no out-migration from Quebec in the wake of separation. If there is modest out-migration, as illustrated by scenario 2, and if that out-migration relocates primarily in Ontario, then Ontario's share of the Canadian population would exceed 50 per cent. Of course, the proportionate size of the other provinces and regions would also increase. In scenario 2, for example, British Columbia and Alberta would end up with 16.1 and 12.5 per cent respectively of the national population and the West's share would increase from 29 to 38.7 per cent. However, the greatest *political* impact would come from the change in Ontario's share of the national population.

    In the short term, Quebec's departure would also alter Canada's demographic structure by constricting the flow of immigration. Potential immigrants would likely pause until Canada had sorted out its political future and until they were convinced there was a country to which it was worth immigrating. The short-term consequences of constricted immigration are not to be taken lightly given the importance of immigration to Canada. However, over the longer run, Canada should be able to restore and perhaps even improve its appeal to potential immigrants.

POLITICAL IMPACT OF DEMOGRAPHIC CHANGE

A stable federal system of government is improbable when one of the constituent states or provinces contains 50 per cent or more of the national population. If, as would be the case in Canada, that state or province is also the economic heartland, the media hub, the home of the largest metropolitan centre, the site of the national capital, and the home of the Blue Jays, then a stable federal system is even more unlikely. The problem, it should be stressed, relates primarily to the configuration of national parliamentary institutions and not to the constitutional division of powers. Under the above conditions, it would be difficult to construct a set of federal arrangements that would give the peripheral provinces, either individually or collectively, sufficient clout within national institutions. Federal states conventionally rely upon second chambers to provide territorial representation, but this strategy would be complicated by Quebec's departure and Ontario's consequent demographic weight. Certainly, anything approximating a Triple-E Senate could not be entertained given the demographic profile depicted in table 1, although regional equality between Ontario and the West might be possible. An approximately equal Senate stripped of any effective power might be possible, but only because it would also be pointless. The issue of regional representation would likely revert to the House of Commons, and a lower house fashioned along contemporary lines – with a rough approximation to representation by population, strict party discipline, and executive dominance – would not meet the challenge of effective regional representation and national integration.

Quebec's departure would, therefore, seriously destabilize the remaining federal system. Put somewhat differently, it would be naïve to assume that Quebec could be plucked out of the existing system and that the federal arrangements now in place would remain more or less intact. But if we assume that some form of federal system must persist if Canada is to survive, that the existing provincial and territorial governments would not quietly fold up their tents and fade away, then what would we have to do to preserve a federal form of government in the face of Ontario's inevitable political, economic, and cultural dominance?

First, Canadians would face much more fundamental institutional reform than was proposed in the Charlottetown Accord. More specifically, we may have to entertain a number of basic and interrelated reforms, including the following:

• The strict application of representation by population in the House of

Commons. This would be essential if Ontario were to accept more federal arrangements in other institutional spheres.

- A congressional form of government that would permit more effective regional or territorial representation within the House of Commons. A congressional form would weaken the linkages between the executive and legislative functions and would, therefore, enable party discipline to be relaxed. This would likely be accompanied by fixed terms for both the House and Senate, a change that would further weaken if not break the hold of party discipline.
- A reformed Senate designed to give expression to territorial and, more important, non-territorial identities, including those based on gender and ethnicity. A Senate along these lines was discussed at the January 1992 constitutional conference in Calgary, but was abandoned in part to meet Quebec's objection to an elected Senate and in part because of a more general wariness about proportional representation.[2]
- An elected president or prime minister to help knit together a geographically disparate community.

If one thing is certain, it is that the institutional and constitutional status quo could not hold. I would also suggest that the institutional configuration that is most likely to emerge would resemble the contemporary American system more than it would the Canadian status quo or the new parliamentary structures envisioned in the Charlottetown Accord. Hopefully, this possibility would not paralyse our political imagination and will.

Second, and in conjunction with the institutional changes noted above, the new federal system would probably be more centralized than the current system and considerably more centralized than that proposed by the Charlottetown Accord. It was Quebec and the attendant linguistic duality that provided the major rationale for a federal system of government in the first place,[3] and it has been Quebec's political élites who have campaigned most incessantly for greater devolution. Admittedly, other provincial governments have ridden on the coat-tails of the nationalist movement in Quebec and have been quick to snap up any powers offered to Quebec. However, they have done so without the same degree of public support and without the same need to protect an arguably distinct society. Other provincial governments have thus been more opportunistic than principled in their pursuit of devolution. When we consider the issues (discussed below) that are likely to dominate the political landscape in a Quebec-less Canada, I would argue that provincial governments will encounter even less support for devolution than they enjoy today. Indeed, administrative decentralization may provide the lifeblood for future provincial governments rather than the devolution of legislative powers and divided sovereignty.⁴

There is, however, an important caveat to note. In the aftermath of any decision by Quebec to leave, and as the federal government implodes, the nine provincial governments may move in on the federal carcass. They, after all, would be the only functioning governments left in the short term. Thus, the prediction of a more centralized federal state is based on the assumption that the federal constitution is not redrawn in the short run and that when it is, players other than provincial governments will also be at the table. The longer we wait, and the more we employ devices like constituent assemblies, the more likely pressure is to build for greater centralization.

Third, and somewhat paradoxically, a viable federal system might only be possible if the primary axes of political debate are no longer regional or territorial in character. If we could shift the terms of political debate on to issues with limited territorial consequences or implications, if we could become less federal as a political community, then the inevitable strains between a massive central province and the regional peripheries might be tolerable. The key is not to pit Ontario against the rest, but rather to frame political debate along axes that cut across the electorates in Ontario and the other provinces. The question, then, is whether we could design political institutions that, over the long run, would channel Canadian political life along non-territorial lines. This question leads in turn to a discussion of new social movements and the changing political agenda.

A NEW POLITICAL AGENDA

Canadian political life has long been dominated by a relatively fixed set of linguistic and territorial concerns. To the despair of many on the left, Canadians approach redistributive politics from the narrow perspective of regional equity; how much is Quebec getting, how much is the West not getting, and so forth. As a consequence and as a reflection, our constitutional politics tend to concentrate on the grievances of the last century rather than on the issues of the next. We are still wrestling with the colonial treatment of Aboriginal peoples and we are still trying to erect walls around the distinct society of Quebec at a time when national boundaries around the world are becoming increasingly permeable and irrelevant. We still give at least the illusion of searching for effective methods of territorial representation at a time when territorial identities are becoming less and less important for Canadians and are being challenged by new identities based on gender, ethnicity, religion, and ideology. In short, we have been trying to come up with the right constitutional package for the nineteenth century rather than for the twenty-first.

There is outside Canada a cauldron of political change in which peoples and states are trying to come to grips with the sweeping reorganization of the international economy, with the globalization of human rights, and with environmental challenges that fail to respect national boundaries. If Quebec were to depart, then Canadians might be better able to embrace this new political agenda, to get beyond the territorial battles, including those masked as linguistic and cultural grievances, which at present limit our political imaginations and sap our energy. I would argue that the politics of the new Canada-without-Quebec would be more ideological and, again, more similar to the contemporary American experience. For example, the first post-Quebec national election would likely pit the NDP against the Reform party or its successor in an ideological contest unlike any we have witnessed before in Canada.

Politics would also be shaped to a much greater extent by such new social movements as feminism and environmentalism and would be more focused on the challenges posed by global economic change to Canadian trade and industrial strategies. Education and the training of human resources would be legitimate matters for national debate. In short, the departure of Quebec might allow us to 'move on,' just as it might allow Quebeckers to move on to the same agenda. Yet, if Quebec stays, neither Quebec nor Canada may be able to move; we will both be locked into an endless debate on helicopter contracts and the constitutional division of powers. 'Lines on maps' will continue to frame our political discourse and cripple our political imaginations.

A NEW NATIONAL GOVERNMENT

Implicit in the above discussion is the assumption that if Canadians are to come to grips with the new political agenda, we will have to fashion more effective instruments of governance than we have now.[5] However, I would argue that recent efforts in this respect have tried to move in the wrong direction. For example, the Charlottetown Accord pointed to a future in which the only effective 'national' strategies towards such things as environmental protection, international trade, and manpower training would have been possible for Quebeckers, but not for Canadians living outside Quebec. In the latter case, the national community and the incumbent instruments of governance would have been divided among nine provincial, two territorial, and countless Aboriginal governments. Coherency, much less efficiency, would have been precluded.

If Quebec remains in Canada, the likely drift of constitutional evolution will be towards the concentration of the instruments of governance within Quebec and the fragmentation of the same outside Quebec. However, if Quebec should leave, there may be strong incentives for Canadians to reconstruct an effective national government for the rest of the country. In this case, the dynamics of reconstruction could result in a more centralized federal state in which Ottawa, and not the provinces, would be empowered to address the concerns of the new political agenda. For example, it does not seem inconceivable that should Quebec leave, Canadians would try to develop a national education strategy, or that the federal government would take a more assertive stance towards environmental protection. Conversely, if Quebec stays, then neither would be possible; education will remain with the provinces and the federal government will limit its environmental initiatives to warnings about excessive sun-tanning.

Should the reconstruction of the federal government come about, it would also entail very substantial changes at the bureaucratic level. The exodus of many federal public servants to Quebec would in itself constitute a major change, particularly within the central agencies of the federal government. Of perhaps equal importance would be the change in recruiting qualifications; the removal of any need for proficiency in both English and French would open up the public service to large numbers of previously excluded people, particularly those raised in Atlantic Canada and the West. While it should not be assumed that the new anglophone recruits would be more competent, they would be a source of new ideas. The infusion of new blood and new ideas that would be part and parcel of the linguistic transformation of the public service could be further enhanced if, in the excitement of building a new national government and a new Canada, the 'best and the brightest' were again attracted to Ottawa and public service.

CHANGE IN THE CANADIAN IDENTITY

Quebec's departure would not only lead to changes in the institutional status quo; it could also set in motion quite significant changes to the Canadian political culture. At the very least we should expect a period of assertive nationalism as Canadians try to redefine their new country and national community; the classic Canadian search for a national identity would come back with a vengeance. This time around, however, Canada would be a very different entity, one in which virtually all citizens shared a single language although obviously not a single ethnic origin. The emotional tone of the new nationalism may be closer to that of John Diefenbaker's 'one Canada' than it would be to contemporary expressions of Canadian nationalism that are muted so as not to offend nationalist sensitivities in Quebec.

The political culture that would likely emerge in the more homogeneous Canadian state would almost certainly offer less support than does the existing political culture for minority language rights. It would be unlikely that francophone minorities would be able to retain any constitutional protection or, indeed, much in the way of programmatic support from the federal or provincial governments. The francophone population, stripped of the political protection afforded by Quebec, would be too small to warrant constitutional protection. In fact, it would be dwarfed by many other linguistic and ethnic groups within the new Canadian community. It is also likely that francophones would bear some of the brunt of the hostility that many English Canadians would inevitably feel at the break-up of their country. This is not to say that francophones would be persecuted, but neither would ongoing constitutional protection be in the cards. In all probability, the official-languages sections of the Charter of Rights and Freedoms would be repealed at the first opportunity.

For somewhat similar reasons, the new political culture would be less supportive of *official* multiculturalism. If there is a tension in the contemporary political culture, and indeed in the Charter of Rights, between the recognition of individual equality on the one hand, and group rights and identities on the other, then I would expect that the new political culture would tip more emphatically towards individual equality. It has been the English-French duality that has provided the umbrella under which official multiculturalism has flourished, and when that duality is removed by the departure of Quebec, there will be less support for the maintenance of official multiculturalism. This is not to say that multiculturalism will diminish as a social reality, but rather that the state will play less of a role in sustaining and promoting multicultural communities. It is official multiculturalism, and not multiculturalism per se, that will be on the block as we move towards something akin to the Reform party position.[6] Of course, any dismantling of official multiculturalism would be fiercely resisted by the political leadership of the multicultural communities. However, the likely reaction of the membership base is not at all clear. It may be that an assimilative nationalism similar in tone to that of the United States may be welcome to Canadian immigrants. In this event, the 'melting pot' may come to a simmer in Canada even as it cools in the United States.

If the new political culture would place greater emphasis on the equality of individuals, and offer less support for linguistic minorities and official multiculturalism, then it is also likely to offer less support for Aboriginal peoples. Relatively large and powerful immigrant groups, if stripped themselves of collective constitutional protection, may be unwilling to extend such protection to Aboriginal peoples.[7] If that protection is already entrenched in the Constitution, they may be unwilling to provide the fiscal transfers necessary to put flesh on the constitutional bones of Aboriginal self-government. This is another one of the ironies of the recent constitutional debate; Quebec may have been seen as the villain of the piece by many Aboriginal leaders, but the departure of Quebec could significantly erode public support for Aboriginal aspirations in the Canada that would remain.

The general point here is a simple one: Canada without Quebec would be a very different political community, not only in its political institutions, but also in its underlying values and beliefs. The presence of Quebec and linguistic duality have shaped the evolution of the Canadian political culture, and in their absence we should expect that the course of evolution will change. While this is not to say that Canada will be better or worse as a consequence, it will be different. Over time, there is also little doubt that the departure of Quebec will accelerate the convergence of political cultures in Canada and the United States, a convergence with both benefits and costs. This convergence would parallel and be reinforced by the institutional convergence predicted above.

CONCLUSIONS

The departure of Quebec would provide the rest of Canada with the chance to get out from under the dead weight of old ideas and old issues, to move to a political agenda that is not dominated by the linguistic and territorial issues that preoccupy the country today. Canadian political life would be less driven by, and less constrained by, the nationalist movement in Quebec. Ideas that cannot be entertained today because of Quebec-based visions of federalism, ideas such as more aggressive national policy on environmental protection or post-secondary education, could at least be put on the table for discussion. This is perhaps one of the major upsides of Quebec's departure; a second is the chance to create a relatively strong national government in Ottawa (as well as in Quebec City), a national government that would be more responsive to regional aspirations beyond those articulated by Quebec.

But what if Quebec does not leave? Can we still move to a new political agenda? Can we revitalize the national government in Ottawa and empower it to tackle the issues that Canadians will confront in the twenty-first century? Can we restructure national parliamentary institutions so as to better reflect regional concerns and aspirations? Unfortunately, the shape of recent constitutional proposals suggests that the answer to all these questions may be 'no.' While this should not lead us to the conclusion that Canadians would be better off if Quebec left, it does suggest that they will continue to pay a significant price to keep the country together, inclusive of Quebec. In asking if that price might be too high, it is useful to consider what Canada might look like if Quebec left.

NOTES

1 For a discussion of the national-security implications of Quebec's departure, see Alex Morrison, ed, *Divided We Fall: The National Security Implications of Canadian Constitutional Issues* (Toronto: Canadian Institute of Strategic Studies 1991).
2 The Australian Senate, and particularly its electoral system, offers some interesting possibilities here.
3 This is not to deny the existence of other considerations, including the pre-existing Maritime colonies, the American precedent, and the sheer size of the Canadian land mass.
4 The German federal experience may, therefore, be of increased relevance for Canada should Quebec leave.
5 This should not be taken as a plea to return to BIG GOVERNMENT; 'big' and 'effective' are not synonymous terms.
6 The Reform position draws from the analogy of a cultural mosaic. The role of the state is to provide the backdrop – a generalized commitment to the equality of individuals – and the binding glue of a shared nationalism by which individual communities are attached to the backdrop. However, the survival and vitality of the individual communities, the pieces of glass that form the mosaic, must depend upon the commitment and private resources of those communities, and not upon state funds.
7 It strikes me that the constitutional protection of Aboriginal rights would have little intrinsic appeal to recent immigrants who, after all, have no parallel claim to advance.

Contributors

MICHAEL ADAMS is president of Environics Research Group Limited, one of Canada's largest and most sophisticated market-research houses, which he co-founded in 1970. Educated at Queen's University and the University of Toronto, his special expertise is the impact of social trends on public policy and corporate strategy.

MAUDE BARLOW is the National Chairperson of the Council of Canadians and is a founder of the Action Canada Network, a coalition of over fifty national groups. Ms Barlow's expertise as a management consultant specialising in pay equity and social change is well known from her tenure as the director of the Office of Equal Opportunity for the City of Ottawa and later as the senior adviser on women's issues to former Prime Minister Pierre Trudeau. She has spoken and written extensively on economic nationalism and the effects of free trade.

Senator GÉRALD-A. BEAUDOIN was most recently a co-chair of two special joint parliamentary committees that examined the process and substance of constitutional renewal. Before being appointed to the Senate in 1988, he was director of the Human Rights Centre at the University of Ottawa, served for a decade as the dean of civil law, and before that was legal counsel at various times to the Department of Justice and the House of Commons. Senator Beaudoin has written several books and many articles on the Canadian constitution.

ANDRÉ BLAIS is a professor in the Department of Political Science, and associate fellow at the Centre de Recherche et Développement en Économique, at the Université de Montréal. His main interests are elections, public opinion, and public policy. He was a research coordinator with the Royal Commission on the Economic Union and Development Prospects for Canada and, until 1991, associate editor of *Canadian Public Policy.*

S H E L A G H   D A Y is vice-president of the National Action Committee on the Status of Women. Educated at Carleton College and Harvard, Ms Day has been the president of LEAF and the director of the Saskatchewan Human Rights Commission. As a human-rights consultant, she has been a leading advocate and supporter of women's rights and those of people with disabilities. Ms Day is the author of several publications on public policy and equality rights.

D A V I D   E L T O N is president of the Canada West Foundation and a professor of political science at the University of Lethbridge, Alberta. Dr Elton was educated at the University of Alberta, and his major areas of reasearch and writing are resource development, transportation policy, economic development, and constitutional reform. He is a frequent commentator on radio and television on public policy and constitutional reform.

J A C Q U E S   F R É M O N T is a professor of law at the Université de Montréal. Educated at Laval University and Osgoode Hall Law School, he has served as a constitutional adviser to the Government of Quebec from 1980 to 1983. Professor Frémont is the author of various articles in the fields of constitutional law and expert systems.

R O G E R   G I B B I N S is a professor and head of the Department of Political Science at the University of Calgary. Dr Gibbins was educated at the University of British Columbia and Stanford; his academic research is in the fields of western alienation, Senate reform, political belief systems, and Aboriginal politics. He has authored numerous articles on these subjects, and is currently a co-editor of the *Canadian Journal of Political Science.*

R A Y M O N D   G I R O U X is an editorial writer and assistant to the editorial page editor with Québec City's *Le Soleil.* He has degrees from the Université de Montréal and Laval, and studied in Paris at the Centre de perfectionnement en journalisme. At *Le Soleil,* M. Giroux has held many assignments, including reporting from the Quebec National Assembly. In 1987, he won the National Newspaper Award for editorial writing.

P E T E R   W.   H O G G is a professor of law at the Osgoode Hall Law School, York University, and has degrees from the University of New Zealand, Harvard, and Monash. Professor Hogg has appeared as counsel in constitutional cases before the Supreme Court of Canada and other courts. He is the author of several works on the Charter of Rights, the Meech Lake Accord, and constitutional and administrative law. The most recent edition of his text *Constitutional Law of Canada* appeared in autumn 1992.

The Honourable PETER LOUGHEED was the premier of Alberta from 1971 to 1985. Mr Lougheed is a lawyer, and earned degrees at the University of Alberta and Harvard. He was first elected to the Alberta legislature in 1967. Mr Lougheed was a central actor in the constitutional debate preceding the patriation of the Constitution in 1982. Upon return to private life, Mr Lougheed has remained active in participating in debates on public policy and constitutional affairs.

KENNETH MCROBERTS is Director of the Robarts Centre for Canadian Studies and professor of political science, York University. A graduate of the University of California, Santa Barbara, and the University of Chicago, Dr McRoberts is the editor-in-chief of the *International Journal of Canadian Studies* and is co-editor of *Canada Watch*. He has written articles and chapters in books on a variety of topics including language policy, Quebec politics, Can-adian federalism, and constitutional questions. He is the author of *Quebec: Social Change and Political Crisis*, he delivered the 1991 Robarts Lecture, *English Canada and Quebec: Avoiding the Issue.*

ERROL P. MENDES is an associate professor of law at the University of Western Ontario. Professor Mendes was educated at Exeter and Illinois, and teaches constitutional law, civil liberties, international business transactions, and public international law. He is the editor of the *National Journal on Constitutional Law.*

PATRICK J. MONAHAN is director of the York University Centre for Public Law and Public Policy and associate professor at Osgoode Hall Law School of York University, having degrees from the University of Ottawa, Carleton, Osgoode Hall Law School, and Harvard. He is the author of *Meech Lake: The Inside Story* (1991) and *Politics and the Constitution* (1987); and is the co-editor of *Canada Watch*, a monthly newsletter on national affairs.

JUDY REBICK is past president of the National Action Committee on the Status of Women, Canada's largest feminist organization. Ms Rebick has spoken frequently on such issues as abortion rights, violence against women, and equality rights, and has been at the forefront of the debate regarding a social charter and gender equality in the central institutions of government. She was formerly Director of Special Projects for the Canadian Hearing Society, and worked for many years with disabled persons as an advocate and supporter, especially in the field of employment equity.

PETER H. RUSSELL is a professor and director of graduate studies in the Department of Political Science at the University of Toronto. He studied at the University of Toronto and Oxford, with constitutional and judicial politics as the focus of his research. His most recent book is *Constitutional Odyssey: Can Canadians Become a Sovereign People?*

JEFFREY SIMPSON is the *Globe and Mail*'s national-affairs columnist and writes a weekly column for *Le Devoir*. Educated at Queen's University and the London School of Economics, Mr Simpson has won all three of Canada's highest literary prizes. He is the author of several books on Canadian politics, and appears frequently on television and CBC Radio's 'Morningside.'

MARY ELLEN TURPEL is an assistant professor of law at Dalhousie University. She was educated at Carleton, Osgoode Hall Law School, the University of Strasbourg, Cambridge, and Harvard. She is a member of the Indigenous Bar Association and acts as legal counsel to several First Nations organizations. Professor Turpel is the author of several articles on the Constitution and aboriginal peoples.

RONALD L. WATTS recently served as assistant secretary to the Cabinet (Constitutional Affairs) in the Federal-Provincial Relations Office. Dr Watts attended the University of Toronto and Oxford, and is a professor of political studies and director of the Institute of Intergovernmental Relations at Queen's University. As a scholar, he has worked for over thirty years on the comparative study of federal systems, a subject on which he has written several books, monographs, and articles.

REG WHITAKER is professor of political science at York University, has degrees from Carleton University and the University of Toronto, and was the director of the graduate program in political science at York. He has written extensively on Canadian politics, political culture and institutions, and issues surrounding Canadian constitutional politics.

Consensus Report on the Constitution
Charlottetown
August 28, 1992
Final Text

TABLE OF CONTENTS

NOTE: Asterisks *in the table of contents* indicate areas where the consensus on some issues under the heading is to proceed with a political accord.

PREFACE

This document is a product of a series of meetings on constitutional reform involving the federal, provincial and territorial governments and representatives of Aboriginal peoples.

These meetings were part of the Canada Round of constitutional renewal. On September 24, 1991, the Government of Canada tabled in the federal Parliament a set of proposals for the renewal of the Canadian federation entitled *Shaping Canada's Future Together.* These proposals were referred to a Special Joint Committee of the House of Commons and the Senate which travelled across Canada seeking views on the proposals. The Committee received 3,000 submissions and listened to testimony from 700 individuals.

During the same period, all provinces and territories created forums for public consultation on constitutional matters. These forums gathered reaction and advice with a view to producing recommendations to their governments. In addition, Aboriginal peoples were consulted by national and regional Aboriginal organizations.

An innovative forum for consultation with experts, advocacy groups and citizens was the series of six televised national conferences that took place between January and March of 1992.

Shortly before the release of the report of the Special Joint Committee on a Renewed Canada, the Prime Minister invited representatives of the provinces and territories and Aboriginal leaders to meet with the federal Minister of Constitutional Affairs to discuss the report.

At this initial meeting, held March 12, 1992 in Ottawa, participants agreed to proceed with a series of meetings with the objective of reaching consensus on a set of constitutional amendments. It was agreed that participants would make best efforts to reach consensus before the end of May, 1992 and that there would be no unilateral actions by any government while this process was under way. It was subsequently agreed to extend this series of meetings into June, and then into July.

To support their work, the heads of delegation agreed to establish a Coordinating Committee, composed of senior government officials and representatives of the four Aboriginal organizations. This committee, in turn, created four working groups to develop options and recommendations for consideration by the heads of delegation.

Recommendations made in the report of the Special Joint Committee on a Renewed Canada served as the basis of discussion, as did the recommendations of the various provincial and territorial consultations and the consultations with Aboriginal peoples. Alternatives and modifications to the proposals in these reports have been the principal subject of discussion at the multilateral meetings.

Including the initial session in Ottawa, there were twenty-seven days of meetings among the heads of delegation, as well as meetings of the Coordinating Committee and the four working groups. The schedule of the meetings during this first phase of meetings was:

March 12	Ottawa
April 8 and 9	Halifax
April 14	Ottawa
April 29 and 30	Edmonton
May 6 and 7	Saint John
May 11, 12 and 13	Vancouver
May 20, 21 and 22	Montreal
May 26, 27, 28, 29 and 30	Toronto
June 9, 10 and 11	Ottawa
June 28 and 29	Ottawa
July 3	Toronto
July 6 and 7	Ottawa

Following this series of meetings, the Prime Minister of Canada chaired a number of meetings of First Ministers, in which the Government of Quebec was a full participant. These include:

August 4	Harrington Lake
August 10	Harrington Lake
August 18, 19, 20, 21 and 22	Ottawa
August 27 and 28	Charlottetown

Organizational support for the full multilateral meetings has been provided by the Canadian Intergovernmental Conferences Secretariat.

In the course of the multilateral discussions, draft constitutional texts have been developed wherever possible in order to reduce uncertainty or ambiguity. In particular, a rolling draft of legal text was the basis of the discussion of issues affecting Aboriginal peoples. These drafts would provide the foundation of the formal legal resolutions to be submitted to Parliament and the legislatures.

In areas where the consensus was not unanimous, some participants chose to have their dissents recorded. Where requested, these dissents have been recorded in the chronological records of the meetings but are not recorded in this summary document.

Asterisks *in the text that follows* indicate the areas where the consensus is to proceed with a political accord.

I: UNITY AND DIVERSITY

A. PEOPLE AND COMMUNITIES

1. *Canada Clause*

A new clause should be included as Section 2 of the *Constitution Act, 1867* that would express fundamental Canadian values. The Canada Clause would guide the courts in their future interpretation of the entire Constitution, including the *Canadian Charter of Rights and Freedoms.*

The *Constitution Act, 1867* is amended by adding thereto, immediately after Section 1 thereof, the following section:

"2. (1) The Constitution of Canada, including the *Canadian Charter of Rights and Freedoms*, shall be interpreted in a manner consistent with the following fundamental characteristics:

  (a) Canada is a democracy committed to a parliamentary and federal system of government and to the rule of law;
  (b) the Aboriginal peoples of Canada, being the first peoples to govern this land, have the right to promote their languages, cultures and traditions and to ensure the integrity of their societies, and their governments constitute one of three orders of government in Canada;
  (c) Quebec constitutes within Canada a distinct society, which includes a French-speaking majority, a unique culture and a civil law tradition;
  (d) Canadians and their governments are committed to the vitality and development of official language minority communities throughout Canada;
  (e) Canadians are committed to racial and ethnic equality in a society that includes citizens from many lands who have contributed, and continue to contribute, to the building of a strong Canada that reflects its cultural and racial diversity;
  (f) Canadians are committed to a respect for individual and collective human rights and freedoms of all people;
  (g) Canadians are committed to the equality of female and male persons; and
  (h) Canadians confirm the principle of the equality of the provinces at the same time as recognizing their diverse characteristics.

(2) The role of the legislature and Government of Quebec to preserve and promote the distinct society of Quebec is affirmed.

(3) Nothing in this section derogates from the powers, rights or privileges of the Parliament or the Government of Canada, or of the legislatures or governments of the provinces, or of the legislative bodies or governments of the Aboriginal peoples of Canada, including any powers, rights or privileges relating to language and, for greater certainty, nothing in this section derogates from the aboriginal and treaty rights of the Aboriginal peoples of Canada."

2. *Aboriginal Peoples and the Canadian Charter of Rights and Freedoms*
   The Charter provision dealing with Aboriginal peoples (Section 25, the non-derogation clause) should be strengthened to ensure that nothing in the Charter abrogates or derogates from Aboriginal, treaty or other rights of Aboriginal peoples, and in particular any rights or freedoms relating to the exercise or protection of their languages, cultures or traditions.

3. *Linguistic Communities in New Brunswick*
   A separate constitutional amendment requiring only the consent of Parliament and the legislature of New Brunswick should be added to the *Canadian Charter of Rights and Freedoms*. The amendment would entrench the equality of status of the English and French linguistic communities in New Brunswick, including the right to distinct educational institutions and such distinct cultural institutions as are necessary for the preservation and promotion of these communities. The amendment would also affirm the role of the legislature and government of New Brunswick to preserve and promote this equality of status.

B. CANADA'S SOCIAL AND ECONOMIC UNION

4. *The Social and Economic Union*
   A new provision should be added to the Constitution describing the commitment of the governments, Parliament and the legislatures within the federation to the principle of the preservation and development of Canada's social and economic union. The new provision, entitled *The Social and Economic Union*, should be drafted to set out a series of policy objectives underlying the social and the economic union, respectively. The provision should not be justiciable.
   The policy objectives set out in the provision on the social union should include, but not be limited to:

   • providing throughout Canada a health care system that is comprehensive, universal, portable, publicly administered and accessible;

- providing adequate social services and benefits to ensure that all individuals resident in Canada have reasonable access to housing, food and other basic necessities;
- providing high quality primary and secondary education to all individuals resident in Canada and ensuring reasonable access to post-secondary education;
- protecting the rights of workers to organize and bargain collectively; and
- protecting, preserving and sustaining the integrity of the environment for present and future generations.

The policy objectives set out in the provision on the economic union should include, but not be limited to:

- working together to strengthen the Canadian economic union;
- the free movement to persons, goods, services and capital;
- the goal of full employment;
- ensuring that all Canadians have a reasonable standard of living; and
- ensuring sustainable and equitable development.

A mechanism for monitoring the Social and Economic Union should be determined by a First Ministers' Conference.

A clause should be added to the Constitution stating that the Social and Economic Union does not abrogate or derogate from the *Canadian Charter of Rights and Freedoms*.

5. *Economic Disparities, Equalization and Regional Development*

Section 36 of the *Constitution Act, 1982* currently commits Parliament and the Government of Canada and the governments and legislatures of the provinces to promote equal opportunities and economic development throughout the country and to provide reasonably comparable levels of public services to all Canadians. Subsection 36(2) currently commits the federal government to the principle of equalization payments. This section should be amended to read as follows:

"Parliament and the Government of Canada are committed to making equalization payments so that provincial governments have sufficient revenues to provide reasonably comparable levels of public services at reasonably comparable levels of taxation."

Subsection 36(1) should be expanded to include the territories.

Subsection 36(1) should be amended to add a commitment to ensure the provision of reasonably comparable economic infrastructures of a national nature in each province and territory.

The Constitution should commit the federal governments to meaningful consultation with the provinces before introducing legislation relating to equalization payments.

A new Subsection 36(3) should be added to entrench the commitment of governments to the promotion of regional economic development to reduce economic disparities.

Regional development is also discussed in item 36 of this document.

6.　*The Common Market*

Section 121 of the *Constitution Act, 1867* would remain unchanged.

Detailed principles and commitments related to the Canadian Common Market are included in the political accord of August 28, 1992. First Ministers will decide on the best approach to implement these principles and commitments at a future First Ministers' Conference on the economy. First Ministers would have the authority to create an independent dispute resolution agency and decide on its role, mandate and composition. (*)

II: INSTITUTIONS

A.　THE SENATE

7.　*An Elected Senate*

The Constitution should be amended to provide that Senators are elected, either by the population of the provinces and territories of Canada or by the members of their provincial or territorial legislative assemblies.

Federal legislation should govern Senate elections, subject to the constitutional provision above and constitutional provisions requiring that elections take place at the same time as elections to the House of Commons and provisions respecting eligibility and mandate of Senators. Federal legislation would be sufficiently flexible to allow provinces and territories to provide for gender equality in the composition of the Senate.

Matters should be expedited in order that Senate elections be held as soon as possible, and, if feasible, at the same time as the next federal general election for the House of Commons.

8. *An Equal Senate*

The Senate should initially total 62 Senators and should be composed of six Senators from each province and one Senator from each territory.

9. *Aboriginal Peoples' Representation in the Senate*

Aboriginal representation in the Senate should be guaranteed in the Constitution. Aboriginal Senate seats should be additional to provincial and territorial seats, rather than drawn from any province or territory's allocation of Senate seats.

Aboriginal Senators should have the same role and powers as other Senators, plus a possible double majority power in relation to certain matters materially affecting Aboriginal people. These issues and other details relating to Aboriginal representation in the Senate (numbers, distribution, method of selection) will be discussed further by governments and the representatives of the Aboriginal peoples in the early autumn of 1992. (*)

10. *Relationship to the House of Commons*

The Senate should not be a confidence chamber. In other words, the defeat of government-sponsored legislation by the Senate would not require the government's resignation.

11. *Categories of Legislation*

There should be four categories of legislation:

1) Revenue and expenditure bills ("supply bills");
2) Legislation materially affecting French language or French culture;
3) Bills involving fundamental tax policy changes directly related to natural resources;
4) Ordinary legislation (any bill not falling into one of the first three categories).

Initial classification of bills should be by the originator of the bill. With the exception of legislation affecting French language or French culture (see item 14), appeals should be determined by the Speaker of the House of Commons, following consultation with the Speaker of the Senate.

12. *Approval of Legislation*

The Constitution should oblige the Senate to dispose of any bills approved by the House of Commons, within thirty sitting days of the House of Commons, with the exception of revenue and expenditure bills.

Revenue and expenditure bills would be subject to a 30 calendar-day suspension veto. If a bill is defeated or amended by the Senate within this period, it could be repassed by a majority vote in the House of Commons on a resolution.

Bills that materially affect French language or French culture would require approval by a majority of Senators voting and by a majority of the Francophone Senators voting. The House of Commons would not be able to override the defeat of a bill in this category by the Senate.

Bills that involve fundamental tax policy changes directly related to natural resources would be defeated if a majority of Senators voting cast their votes against the bill. The House of Commons would not be able to override the Senate's veto. The precise definition of this category of legislation remains to be determined.

Defeat or amendment of ordinary legislation by the Senate would trigger a joint sitting process with the House of Commons. A simple majority vote at the joint sitting would determine the outcome of the bill.

The Senate should have the powers set out in this Consensus Report. There would be no change to the Senate's current role in approving constitutional amendments. Subject to the Consensus Report, Senate powers and procedures should be parallel to those in the House of Commons.

The Senate should continue to have the capacity to initiate bills, except for money bills.

If any bill initiated and passed by the Senate is amended or rejected by the House of Commons, a joint sitting process should be triggered automatically.

The House of Commons should be obliged to dispose of legislation approved by the Senate within a reasonable time limit.

13. *Revenue and Expenditure Bills*

In order to preserve Canada's parliamentary traditions, the Senate should not be able to block the routine flow of legislation relating to taxation, borrowing and appropriation.

Revenue and expenditure bills ("supply bills") should be defined as only those matters involving borrowing, the raising of revenue and appropriation as well as matters subordinate to these issues. This definition should exclude fundamental policy changes to the tax system (such as the Goods and Services Tax and the National Energy Program).

14. *Double Majority*

The originator of a bill should be responsible for designating whether it materially affects French language or French culture. Each designation should be subject to appeal to the Speaker of the Senate under rules to be established by the Senate. These rules should be designed to provide adequate protection to Francophones.

On entering the Senate, Senators should be required to declare whether they are Francophones for the purpose of the double majority voting rule. Any process for challenging these declarations should be left to the rules of the Senate.

15. *Ratification of Appointments*

The Constitution should specify that the Senate ratify the appointment of the Governor of the Bank of Canada.

The Constitution should also be amended to provide the Senate with a new power to ratify other key appointments made by the federal government.

The Senate should be obliged to deal with any proposed appointments within thirty sitting-days of the House of Commons.

The appointments that would be subject to Senate ratification, including the heads of the national cultural institutions and the heads of federal regulatory boards and agencies, should be set out in specific federal legislation rather than the Constitution. The federal government's commitment to table such legislation should be recorded in a political accord. (*)

An appointment submitted for ratification would be rejected if a majority of Senators voting cast their votes against it.

16. *Eligibility for Cabinet*

Senators should not be eligible for Cabinet posts.

B. THE SUPREME COURT

17. *Entrenchment in the Constitution*

The Supreme Court should be entrenched in the Constitution as the general court of appeal for Canada.

18. *Composition*

The Constitution should entrench the current provision of the *Supreme Court Act*, which specifies that the Supreme Court is to be composed of nine members, of whom three must have been admitted to the bar of Quebec (civil law bar).

19. *Nominations and Appointments*

The Constitution should require the federal government to name judges from lists submitted by the government of the provinces and territories. A provision should be made in the Constitution for the appointment of interim judges if a list is not submitted on a timely basis or no candidate is acceptable.

20. *Aboriginal Peoples' Role*

The structure of the Supreme Court should not be modified in this round of constitutional discussions. The role of Aboriginal peoples in relation to the Supreme Court should be recorded in a political accord and should be on the agenda of a future First Ministers' Conference on Aboriginal issues. (*)

Provincial and territorial governments should develop a reasonable process for consulting representatives of the Aboriginal peoples of Canada in the preparation of lists of candidates to fill vacancies on the Supreme Court. (*)

Aboriginal groups should retain the right to make representation to the federal government respecting candidates to fill vacancies on the Supreme Court. (*)

The federal government should examine, in consultation with Aboriginal groups, the proposal that an Aboriginal Council of Elders be entitled to make submissions to the Supreme Court when the court considers Aboriginal issues. (*)

C. HOUSE OF COMMONS

21. *Composition of the House of Commons*

The composition of the House of Commons should be adjusted to better reflect the principle of representation by population. The adjustment should include an initial increase in the size of the House of Commons to 337 seats, to be made at the time Senate reform comes into effect. Ontario and Quebec would each be assigned eighteen additional seats, British Columbia four additional seats, and Alberta two additional seats, with boundaries to be developed using the 1991 census.

An additional special Canada-wide redistribution of seats should be conducted following the 1996 census, aimed at ensuring that, in the first subsequent general election, no province will have fewer than 95 per cent of the House of Commons seats it would receive under strict representation-by-population. Consequently, British Columbia and Ontario would each be assigned three additional seats and Alberta two additional seats. As a result of this special adjustment, no province or territory will lose seats, nor will a province or territory which has achieved full representation-by-population have a smaller share of House of Commons seats than its share of the total population in the 1996 census.

The redistribution based on the 1996 census and all future redistributions should be governed by the following constitutional provisions:

(a) A guarantee that Quebec would be assigned no fewer than 25 per cent of the seats in the House of Commons;

(b) The current Section 41(b) of the *Constitution Act, 1982*, the "fixed floor", would be retained;

(c) Section 51A of the *Constitution Act, 1867*, the "rising floor", would be repealed;

(d) A new provision that would ensure that no province could have fewer Commons seats than another province with a smaller population, subject to the provision in item (a) above;

(e) The current provision that allocates two seats to the Northwest Territories and one seat to Yukon would be retained.

A permanent formula should be developed and Section 51 of the *Constitution Act, 1867* should be adjusted to accommodate demographic change, taking into consideration the principles suggested by the Royal Commission on Electoral Reform and Party Financing.

22. *Aboriginal Peoples' Representation*

The issue of Aboriginal representation in the House of Commons should be pursued by Parliament, in consultation with representatives of the Aboriginal peoples of Canada, after it has received the final report of the House of Commons Committee studying the recommendations of the Royal Commission on Electoral Reform and Party Financing. (*)

D. FIRST MINISTERS' CONFERENCES

23. *Entrenchment*

A provision should be added to the Constitution requiring the Prime Minister to convene a First Ministers' Conference at least once a year. The agendas for these conferences should not be specified in the Constitution.

The leaders of the territorial governments should be invited to participate in any First Ministers' Conference convened pursuant to this constitutional provision. Representatives of the Aboriginal peoples of Canada should be invited to participate in discussions on any item on the agenda of a First Ministers' Conference that directly affects the Aboriginal peoples. This should be embodied in a political accord. (*)

The role and responsibilities of First Ministers with respect to the federal spending power are outlined at item 25 of this document.

E.   THE BANK OF CANADA

24. *Bank of Canada*
    The Bank of Canada was discussed and the consensus was that this issue should not be pursued in this round, except for the consensus that the Senate should have a role in ratifying the appointment of its Governor.

III: ROLES AND RESPONSIBILITIES

25. *Federal Spending Power*
    A provision should be added to the Constitution stipulating that the Government of Canada must provide reasonable compensation to the government of a province that chooses not to participate in a new Canada-wide shared-cost program that is established by the federal government in an area of exclusive provincial jurisdiction, if that province carries on a program or initiative that is compatible with the national objectives.

    A framework should be developed to guide the use of the federal spending power in all areas of exclusive provincial jurisdiction. Once developed, the framework could become a multilateral agreement that would receive constitutional protection using the mechanism described in item 26 of this report. The framework should ensure that when the federal spending power is used in areas of exclusive provincial jurisdiction, it should:

    (a) contribute to the pursuit of national objectives;
    (b) reduce overlap and duplication;
    (c) not distort and should respect provincial priorities; and
    (d) ensure equality of treatment of the provinces, while recognizing their different needs and circumstances.

    The Constitution should commit First Ministers to establishing such a framework at a future conference of First Ministers. Once it is established, First Ministers would assume a role in annually reviewing progress in meeting the objectives set out in the framework.

A provision should be added (as Section 106A(3)) that would ensure that nothing in the section that limits the federal spending power affects the commitments of Parliament and the Government of Canada that are set out in Section 36 of the *Constitution Act, 1982*.

26. *Protection of Intergovernmental Agreements*

The Constitution should be amended to provide a mechanism to ensure that designated agreements between governments are protected from unilateral change. This would occur when Parliament and the legislature(s) enact laws approving the agreement.

Each application of the mechanism should cease to have effect after a maximum of five years but could be renewed by a vote of Parliament and the legislature(s) readopting similar legislation. Governments of Aboriginal peoples should have access to this mechanism. The provision should be available to protect both bilateral and multilateral agreements among federal, provincial and territorial governments, and the governments of Aboriginal peoples. A government negotiating an agreement should be accorded equality of treatment in relation to any government which has already concluded an agreement, taking into account different needs and circumstances.

It is the intention of governments to apply this mechanism to future agreements related to the Canada Assistance Plan. (*)

27. *Immigration*

A new provision should be added to the Constitution committing the Government of Canada to negotiate agreements with the provinces relating to immigration.

The Constitution should oblige the federal government to negotiate and conclude within a reasonable time an immigration agreement at the request of any province. A government negotiating an agreement should be accorded equality of treatment in relation to any government which has already concluded an agreement, taking into account different needs and circumstances.

28. *Labour Market Development and Training*

Exclusive federal jurisdiction for unemployment insurance, as set out in Section 91(2A) of the *Constitution Act, 1867*, should not be altered. The federal government should retain exclusive jurisdiction for income support and its related services delivered through the Unemployment Insurance system. Federal spending on job creation programs should be protected through a constitutional provision or a political accord (*).

Labour market development and training should be identified in Section 92 of the Constitution as a matter of exclusive provincial jurisdiction. Provincial legislatures should have the authority to constrain federal spending that is directly related to labour market development and training. This should be accomplished through justiciable intergovernmental agreements designed to meet the circumstances of each province.

At the request of a province, the federal government would be obligated to withdraw from any or all training activities and from any or all labour market development activities, except Unemployment Insurance. The federal government should be required to negotiate and conclude agreements to provide reasonable compensation to provinces requesting that the federal government withdraw.

The Government of Canada and the government of the province that requested the federal government to withdraw should conclude agreements within a reasonable time.

Provinces negotiating agreements should be accorded equality of treatment with respect to terms and conditions of agreements in relation to any other province that has already concluded an agreement, taking into account the different needs and circumstances of the provinces.

The federal, provincial and territorial governments should commit themselves in a political accord to enter into administrative arrangements to improve efficiency and client service and ensure effective coordination of federal Unemployment Insurance and provincial employment functions. (*)

As a safeguard, the federal government should be required to negotiate and conclude an agreement within a reasonable time, at the request of any province not requesting the federal government to withdraw, to maintain its labour market development and training programs and activities in that province. A similar safeguard should be available to the territories.

There should be a constitutional provision for an ongoing federal role in the establishment of national policy objectives for the national aspects of labour market development. National labour market policy objectives would be established through a process which could be set out in the Constitution including the obligation for presentation to Parliament for debate. Factors to be considered in the establishment of national policy objectives could include items such as national economic conditions, national labour market requirements, international labour market trends and changes in international economic conditions. In establishing national policy objectives, the federal government would take into account the different needs and circumstances of the provinces; and there would be a provision, in the Constitution or in a political accord, committing the federal, provincial and territorial governments to support the development of common occupational standards, in consultation with employer and employee groups. (*)

Provinces that negotiated agreements to constrain the federal spending power should be obliged to ensure that their labour market development programs are compatible with the national policy objectives, in the context of different needs and circumstances.

Considerations of service to the public in both official languages should be included in a political accord and be discussed as part of the negotiations of bilateral agreements. (*)

The concerns of Aboriginal peoples in this field will be dealt with through the mechanisms set out in item 40 below.

29. *Culture*

Provinces should have exclusive jurisdiction over cultural matters within the provinces. This should be recognized through an explicit constitutional amendment that also recognizes the continuing responsibility of the federal government in Canadian cultural matters. The federal government should retain responsibility for national cultural institutions, including grants and contributions delivered by these institutions. The Government of Canada commits to negotiate cultural agreements with provinces in recognition of their lead responsibility for cultural matters within the province and to ensure that the federal governments and the province work in harmony. These changes should not alter the federal fiduciary responsibility for Aboriginal people. The non-derogation provisions for Aboriginal peoples set out in item 40 of this document will apply to culture.

30. *Forestry*

Exclusive provincial jurisdiction over forestry should be recognized and clarified through an explicit constitutional amendment.

Provincial legislatures should have the authority to constrain federal spending that is directly related to forestry.

This should be accomplished through justiciable intergovernmental agreements, designed to meet the specific circumstances of each province. The mechanism used would be the one set out in item 26 of this document, including a provision for equality of treatment with respect to terms and conditions. Considerations of service to the public in both official languages should be considered a possible part of such agreements. (*)

Such an agreement should set the terms for federal withdrawal, including the level and form of financial resources to be transferred. In addition, a political accord could specify the form the compensation would take (i.e. cash transfers, tax points, or others)(*). Alternatively, such an agreement could require the federal government to maintain its spending in that province. A similar safeguard should be available to the territories. The federal government should be obliged to negotiate and conclude such an agreement within a reasonable time.

These changes and the ones set out in items 31, 32, 33, 34 and 35 should not alter the federal fiduciary responsibility for Aboriginal people. The provisions set out in item 40 would apply.

31. *Mining*

Exclusive provincial jurisdiction over mining should be recognized and clarified through an explicit constitutional amendment and the negotiation of federal-provincial agreements. This should be done in the same manner as set out above with respect to forestry. (*)

32. *Tourism*

Exclusive provincial jurisdiction over tourism should be recognized and clarified through an explicit constitutional amendment and the negotiation of federal-provincial agreements. This should be done in the same manner as set out above with respect to forestry. (*)

33. *Housing*

Exclusive provincial jurisdiction over housing should be recognized and clarified through an explicit constitutional amendment and the negotiation of federal-provincial agreements. This should be done in the same manner as set out above with respect to forestry. (*)

34. *Recreation*

Exclusive provincial jurisdiction over recreation should be recognized and clarified through an explicit constitutional amendment and the negotiation of federal-provincial agreements. This should be done in the same manner as set out above with respect to forestry. (*)

35. *Municipal and Urban Affairs*

Exclusive provincial jurisdiction over municipal and urban affairs should be recognized and clarified through an explicit constitutional amendment and the negotiation of federal-provincial agreements. This should be done in the same manner as set out above with respect to forestry. (*)

36. *Regional Development*

In addition to the commitment to regional development to be added to Section 36 of the *Constitution Act, 1982* (described in item 5 of this document), a provision should be added to the Constitution that would oblige the federal government to negotiate an agreement at the request of any province with respect to regional development. Such agreements could be protected under the provision set out in item 26 ("Protection of Intergovernmental Agreements"). Regional development should not become a separate head of power in the Constitution.

37. *Telecommunications*

The federal government should be committed to negotiate agreements with the provincial governments to coordinate and harmonize the procedures of their respective regulatory agencies in this field. Such agreements could be protected under the provision set out in item 26 ("Protection of Intergovernmental Agreements").

38. *Federal Power of Disallowance and Reservation*

This provision of the Constitution should be repealed. Repeal requires unanimity.

39. *Federal Declaratory Power*

Section 92(10)(c) of the *Constitution Act, 1867* permits the federal government to declare a "work" to be for the general advantage of Canada and bring it under the legislative jurisdiction of Parliament. This provision should be amended to ensure that the declaratory power can only be applied to new works or rescinded with respect to past declarations with the explicit consent of the province(s) in which the work is situated. Existing declarations should be left undisturbed unless all of the legislatures affected wish to take action.

40. *Aboriginal Peoples' Protection Mechanism*

There should be a general non-derogation clause to ensure that division of powers amendments will not affect the rights of the Aboriginal peoples and the jurisdictions and powers of governments of Aboriginal peoples.

IV: FIRST PEOPLES

Note: References to the territories will be added to the legal text with respect to this section, except where clearly inappropriate. Nothing in the amendments would extend the powers of the territorial legislature.

A. THE INHERENT RIGHT OF SELF-GOVERNMENT

41. *The Inherent Right of Self-Government*
The Constitution should be amended to recognize that the Aboriginal peoples of Canada have the inherent right of self-government within Canada. This right should be placed in a new section of the *Constitution Act, 1982*, Section 35.1(1).

The recognition of the inherent right of self-government should be interpreted in light of the recognition of Aboriginal governments as one of three orders of government in Canada.

A contextual statement should be inserted in the Constitution, as follows:

"The exercise of the right of self-government includes the authority of the duly constituted legislative bodies of Aboriginal peoples, each within its own jurisdiction:

(a) to safeguard and develop their language, cultures, economies, identities, institutions and traditions; and,

(b) to develop, maintain and strengthen their relationship with their lands, waters and environment

so as to determine and control their development as peoples according to their own values and priorities and ensure the integrity of their societies."

Before making any final determination of an issue arising from the inherent right of self-government, a court or tribunal should take into account the contextual statement referred to above, should enquire into the efforts that have been made to resolve the issue through negotiations and should be empowered to order the parties to take such steps as are appropriate in the circumstances to effect a negotiated resolution.

42. *Delayed Justiciability*
The inherent right of self-government should be entrenched in the Constitution. However, its justiciability should be delayed for a five-year period through constitutional language and a political accord. (*)

Delaying the justiciability of the right should be coupled with a constitutional provision which would shield Aboriginal rights.

Delaying the justiciability of the right will not make the right contingent and will not affect existing Aboriginal and treaty rights.

The issue of special courts or tribunals should be on the agenda of the first First Ministers' Conference on Aboriginal Constitutional matters referred to in item 53. (*)

43. *Charter Issues*

The *Canadian Charter of Rights and Freedoms* should apply immediately to governments of Aboriginal peoples.

A technical change should be made to the English text of sections 3, 4 and 5 of the *Canadian Charter of Rights and Freedoms* to ensure that it corresponds to the French text.

The legislative bodies of Aboriginal peoples should have access to Section 33 of the *Constitution Act, 1982* (the notwithstanding clause) under conditions that are similar to those applying to Parliament and the provincial legislatures but which are appropriate to the circumstances of Aboriginal peoples and their legislative bodies.

44. *Land*

The specific constitutional provision on the inherent right and the specific constitutional provision on the commitment to negotiate land should not create new Aboriginal rights to land or derogate from existing aboriginal or treaty rights to land, except as provided for in self-government agreements.

B.   METHOD OF EXERCISE OF THE RIGHT

45. *Commitment to Negotiate*

There should be a constitutional commitment by the federal and provincial governments and the Indian, Inuit and Métis peoples in the various regions and communities of Canada to negotiate in good faith with the objective of concluding agreements elaborating the relationship between Aboriginal governments and the other orders of government. The negotiations would focus on the implementation of the right of self-government including issues of jurisdiction, lands and resources, and economic and fiscal arrangements.

46. *The Process of Negotiation*
Political Accord on Negotiation and Implementation
— A political accord should be developed to guide the process of self-government negotiations. (*)

Equity of Access
— All Aboriginal peoples of Canada should have equitable access to the process of negotiation.

Trigger for Negotiations
— Self-government negotiations should be initiated by the representatives of Aboriginal peoples when they are prepared to do so.

Provision for Non-Ethnic Governments
— Self-government agreements may provide for self-government institutions which are open to the participation of all residents in a region covered by the agreement.

Provision for Different Circumstances
— Self-government negotiations should take into consideration the different circumstances of the various Aboriginal peoples.

Provision for Agreements
— Self-government agreements should be set out in future treaties, including land claims agreements or amendments to existing treaties, including land claims agreements. In addition, self-government agreements could be set out in other agreements which may contain a declaration that the rights of the Aboriginal peoples are treaty rights, within the meaning of Section 35(1) of the *Constitution Act, 1982*.

Ratification of Agreements
— There should be an approval process for governments and Aboriginal peoples for self-government agreements, involving Parliament, the legislative assemblies of the relevant provinces and/or territories and the legislative bodies of the Aboriginal peoples. This principle should be expressed in the ratification procedures set out in the specific self-government agreements.

Non-Derogation Clause
— There should be an explicit statement in the Constitution that the commitment to negotiate does not make the right of self-government contingent on negotiations or in any way affect the justiciability of the right of self-government.

Dispute Resolution Mechanism
— To assist the negotiation process, a dispute resolution mechanism involving mediation and arbitration should be established. Details of this mechanism should be set out in a political accord. (*)

47. *Legal Transition and Consistency of Laws*
A constitutional provision should ensure that federal and provincial laws will continue to apply until they are displaced by laws passed by governments of Aboriginal peoples pursuant to their authority.

A constitutional provision should ensure that a law passed by a government of Aboriginal peoples, or an assertion of its authority based on the inherent right provision may not be inconsistent with those laws which are essential to the preservation of peace, order and good government in Canada. However, this provision would not extend the legislative authority of Parliament or of the legislatures of the provinces.

48. *Treaties*

With respect to treaties with Aboriginal peoples, the Constitution should be amended as follows:

— treaty rights should be interpreted in a just, broad and liberal manner taking into account the spirit and intent of the treaties and the context in which the specific treaties were negotiated;

— the Government of Canada should be committed to establishing and participating in good faith in a joint process to clarify or implement treaty rights, or to rectify terms of treaties when agreed to by the parties. The governments of the provinces should also be committed, to the extent that they have jurisdiction, to participation in the above treaty process when invited by the government of Canada and the Aboriginal peoples concerned or where specified in a treaty;

— participants in this process should have regard, among other things and where appropriate, to the spirit and intent of the treaties as understood by Aboriginal peoples. It should be confirmed that all Aboriginal peoples that possess treaty rights shall have equitable access to this treaty process;

— it should be provided that these treaty amendments shall not extend the authority of any government or legislature, or affect the rights of Aboriginal peoples not party to the treaty concerned.

C.   ISSUES RELATED TO THE EXERCISE OF THE RIGHT

49. *Equity of Access to Section 35 Rights*

The Constitution should provide that all of the Aboriginal peoples of Canada have access to those Aboriginal and treaty rights recognized and affirmed in Section 35 of the *Constitution Act, 1982* that pertain to them.

50. *Financing*

Matters relating to the financing of governments of Aboriginal peoples should be dealt with in a political accord. The accord would commit the governments of Aboriginal peoples to:

— promoting equal opportunities for the well-being of all Aboriginal peoples;

— furthering economic, social and cultural development and employment opportunities to reduce disparities in opportunities among Aboriginal peoples and between Aboriginal peoples and other Canadians; and

— providing essential public services at levels reasonably comparable to those available to other Canadians in the vicinity.

It would also commit federal and provincial governments to the principle of providing the governments of Aboriginal peoples with fiscal or other resources, such as land, to assist those governments to govern their own affairs and to meet the commitments listed above, taking into account the levels of services provided to other Canadians in the vicinity and the fiscal capacity of governments of Aboriginal peoples to raise revenues from their own sources.

The issues of financing and its possible inclusion in the Constitution should be on the agenda of the first First Ministers' Conference on Aboriginal Constitution matters referred to in item 53. (*)

51. *Affirmative Action Programs*

The Constitution should include a provision which authorizes governments of Aboriginal peoples to undertake affirmative action programs for socially and economically disadvantaged individuals or groups and programs for the advancement of Aboriginal languages and cultures.

52. *Gender Equality*

Section 35(4) of the *Constitution Act, 1982*, which guarantees existing Aboriginal and treaty rights equally to male and female persons, should be retained. The issue of gender equality should be on the agenda of the first First Ministers' Conference on Aboriginal Constitutional matters referred to under item 53. (*)

53. *Future Aboriginal Constitutional Process*

The Constitution should be amended to provide for four future First Ministers' Conferences on Aboriginal constitutional matters beginning no later than 1996, and following every two years thereafter. These conferences would be in addition to any other First Ministers' Conferences required by the Constitution. The agendas of these conferences would include items identified in this report and items requested by Aboriginal peoples.

54. *Section 91(24)*

For greater certainty, a new provision should be added to the *Constitution Act, 1867* to ensure that Section 91(24) applies to all Aboriginal peoples.

The new provision would not result in a reduction of existing expenditures by governments on Indians and Inuit or alter the fiduciary and treaty obligations of the federal government for Aboriginal peoples. This would be reflected in a political accord. (*)

55. *Métis in Alberta/Section 91(24)*

The Constitution should be amended to safeguard the legislative authority of the Government of Alberta for Métis and Métis Settlements lands. There was agreement to a proposed amendment to the *Alberta Act* that would constitutionally protect the status of the land held in fee simple by the Métis Settlements General Council under letters patent from Alberta.

56. *Métis Nation Accord (*)*

The federal government, the provinces of Ontario, Manitoba, Saskatchewan, Alberta, British Columbia and the Métis National Council have agreed to enter into a legally binding, justiciable and enforceable accord on Métis Nation issues. Technical drafting of the Accord is being completed. The Accord sets out the obligations of the federal and provincial governments and the Métis Nation.

The Accord commits governments to negotiate: self-government agreements; lands and resources; the transfer of the portion of Aboriginal programs and services available to Métis; and cost-sharing arrangements relating to Métis institutions, programs and services.

Provinces and the federal government agree not to reduce existing expenditures on Métis and other Aboriginal people as a result of the Accord or as a result of an amendment to Section 91(24). The Accord defines the Métis for the purposes of the Métis Nation Accord and commits governments to enumerate and register the Métis Nation.

V: THE AMENDING FORMULA

Note: All of the following changes to the amending formula require the unanimous agreement of Parliament and the provincial legislatures.

57. *Changes to National Institutions*

Amendments to provisions of the Constitution related to the Senate should require unanimous agreement of Parliament and the provincial legislatures, once the current set of amendments related to Senate reform has come into effect. Future amendments affecting the House of Commons, including Quebec's guarantee of at least 25 per cent of the seats in the House of Commons, and amendments which can now be made under Section 42 should also require unanimity.

Sections 41 and 42 of the *Constitution Act, 1982* should be amended so that the nomination and appointment process of Supreme Court judges would remain subject to the general (7/50) amending procedure. All other matters related to the Supreme Court, including its entrenchment, its role as the general court of appeal and its composition, would be matters requiring unanimity.

58. *Establishment of New Provinces*

The current provisions of the amending formula governing the creation of new provinces should be rescinded. They should be replaced by the pre-1982 provisions allowing the creation of new provinces through an Act of Parliament, following consultation with all of the existing provinces at a First Ministers' Conference. New provinces should not have a role in the amending formula without the unanimous consent of all of the provinces and the federal government, with the exception of purely bilateral or unilateral matters described in sections 38(3), 40, 43, 45 and 46 as it relates to 43, of the *Constitution Act, 1982*. Any increase in the representation for new provinces in the Senate should also require the unanimous consent of all provinces and the federal government. Territories that become provinces could not lose Senators or members of the House of Commons.

The provision now contained in Section 42(1)(e) of the *Constitution Act, 1982* with respect to the extension of provincial boundaries into the Territories should be repealed replaced by the *Constitution Act, 1871*, modified in order to require the consent of the Territories.

59. *Compensation for Amendments that Transfer Jurisdiction*

Where an amendment is made under the general amending formula that transfers legislative powers from provincial legislatures to Parliament, Canada should provide reasonable compensation to any province that opts out of the amendment.

60. *Aboriginal Consent*
There should be Aboriginal consent to future constitutional amendments that directly refer to the Aboriginal peoples. Discussions are continuing on the mechanism by which this consent would be expressed with a view to agreeing on a mechanism prior to the introduction in Parliament of formal resolutions amending the Constitution.

VI: OTHER ISSUES

Other constitutional issues were discussed during the multilateral meetings. The consensus was to not pursue the following issues:

— personal bankruptcy and insolvency;
— intellectual property;
— interjurisdictional immunity;
— inland fisheries;
— marriage and divorce;
— residual power;
— legislative interdelegation;
— changes to the "notwithstanding clause";
— Section 96 (appointment of judges);
— Section 125 (taxation of federal and provincial governments);
— Section 92A (export of natural resources);
— requiring notice for changes to federal legislation respecting equalization payments;
— property rights;
— implementation of international treaties.

Other issues were discussed but were not finally resolved, among which were:

— requiring notice for changes to federal legislation respecting Established Programs Financing;
— establishing in a political accord a formal federal-provincial consultation process with regard to the negotiation of international treaties and agreements;
— Aboriginal participation in intergovernmental agreements respecting the division of powers;
— establishing a framework for compensation issues with respect to labour market development and training;

— consequential amendments related to Senate reform, including by-elections;
— any other consequential amendments required by changes recommended in this report.

Draft Legal Text
October 9, 1992

PREFACE

The attached draft legal text is based on the Charlottetown Accord of August 28, 1992. It is a best efforts text prepared by officials representing all First Ministers and Aboriginal and Territorial Leaders. This draft includes amendments to the following constitutional acts:

- Constitution Act, 1867
- Constitution Act, 1871
- Alberta Act
- Constitution Act, 1982 (including section 16.1, a bilateral amendment by New Brunswick and Canada).

This draft is subject to final review and approval by First Ministers and Leaders to ensure its consistency with the Charlottetown Consensus Report. Officials have made best efforts to ensure that the policy decisions summarized in the Consensus Report on the Constitution of August 28, 1992 have been translated as accurately as possible, in both official languages, into legal text that will serve as the basis for formal constitutional amendments to be presented to Parliament and the provincial legislatures.

The following delegations participated in the drafting of the legal text:

Canada	British Columbia	Yukon
Ontario	Prince Edward Island	Assembly of First Nations
Quebec	Saskatchewan	Inuit Tapirisat of Canada
Nova Scotia	Alberta	Native Council of Canada
New Brunswick	Newfoundland	Métis National Council
Manitoba	Northwest Territories	

TABLE OF CONTENTS

DRAFT

Constitution Act, 1867

1. The *Constitution Act, 1867* is amended by adding thereto, immediately after section 1 thereof, the following section:

Canada Clause

"2. (1) The Constitution of Canada, including the *Canadian Charter of Rights and Freedoms*, shall be interpreted in a manner consistent with the following fundamental characteristics:

(a) Canada is a democracy committed to a parliamentary and federal system of government and to the rule of law;

(b) the Aboriginal peoples of Canada, being the first peoples to govern this land, have the right to promote their languages, cultures and traditions and to ensure the integrity of their societies, and their governments constitute one of three orders of government in Canada;

(c) Quebec constitutes within Canada a distinct society, which includes a French-speaking majority, a unique culture and a civil law tradition;

(d) Canadians and their governments are committed to the vitality and development of official language minority communities throughout Canada;

(e) Canadians are committed to racial and ethnic equality in a society that includes citizens from many lands who have contributed, and continue to contribute, to the building of a strong Canada that reflects its cultural and racial diversity;

(f) Canadians are committed to a respect for individual and collective human rights and freedoms of all people;

(g) Canadians are committed to the equality of female and male persons; and

(h) Canadians confirm the principle of the equality of the provinces at the same time as recognizing their diverse characteristics.

Role of legislature and Government of Quebec

(2) The role of the legislature and Government of Quebec to preserve and promote the distinct society of Quebec is affirmed.

Powers, rights and privileges preserved

(3) Nothing in this section derogates from the powers, rights or privileges of the Parliament or the Government of Canada, or of the legislatures or governments of the provinces, or of the legislative bodies or governments of the Aboriginal peoples of Canada, including any powers, rights or privileges relating to language.

Aboriginal and treaty rights

(4) For greater certainty, nothing in this section abro-gates or derogates from the aboriginal and treaty rights of the Aboriginal peoples of Canada."

2. Section 4 of the said Act is repealed and the following substituted therefor:

Construction

"4. Unless it is otherwise expressed or implied, the name Canada shall be taken to mean as constituted under the Constitution of Canada."

3. Section 17 of the said Act is repealed and the following substituted therefor:

Constitution of Parliament of Canada

"17. There shall be one Parliament for Canada, consisting of the Queen, the Senate and the House of Commons."

4. Sections 21 to 36 of the said Act are repealed and the following substituted therefor:

Constitution of
Senate

"21. (1) The Senate shall consist of sixty-two[1] senators of whom

(a) six shall be elected for each province, namely, Ontario, Quebec, Nova Scotia, New Brunswick, Manitoba, British Columbia, Prince Edward Island, Alberta, Saskatchewan and Newfoundland;

(b) one shall be elected for each territory, namely, the Yukon Territory and the Northwest Territories; and

(c) [Aboriginal representation].*

New provinces

(2) Notwithstanding subsection (1), where a new province is established from the Yukon Territory or the Northwest Territories, the new province shall be entitled to the same representation in the Senate as the territory had.

Summoning of
Senate

22. The Governor General shall from time to time, in the Queen's name, by instrument under the Great Seal of Canada, summon and call together the Senate.

Authority of
Parliament in
relation to
Senate elections

23. (1) Subject to this Act, the Parliament of Canada may provide for all matters relating to the election of senators.

Authority of
legislatures of
provinces or
legislative
authorities of
territories

(2) Subject to this Act, the legislature of any province or the legislative authority of any territory may provide for

1 The number sixty-two is subject to future decisions on the number of guaranteed aboriginal seats. The issue of Aboriginal representation and voting powers of Aboriginal senators is to be discussed in the autumn of 1992, according to the Consensus Report.

(a) the indirect election of senators for the province or territory by the legislative assembly of that province or legislative authority of that territory, and all matters relating thereto;

(b) any special measures to provide for equal representation of male and female persons; and

(c) the determination of electoral districts and the boundaries thereof in relation to the election of senators.

Provincial or territorial law prevails

(3) Where a law of Parliament and a law of a province or territory under paragraph (2)(a) or (b) conflict, the law of the province or territory prevails to the extent of the conflict.

Law of Canada prevails

(4) Where a law of Parliament and a law of a province or territory under paragraph (2)(c) conflict, the law of Parliament prevails to the extent of the conflict.

Limitation

(5) No law made under this section in relation to the direct election of senators shall apply in respect of a general election of senators for which the writs are issued within six months after the law receives the Queen's assent.

Who may not sit as senators

24. No Minister of the Crown and no member of the House of Commons, a legislative assembly of a province or a legislative authority of a territory may be elected, sit or vote as a senator.

Election of Speaker of Senate

25. (1) The Senate on its first assembling after a general election shall, as soon as is practicable, elect one of the senators to be Speaker.

Vacancy in office of Speaker

(2) Where the office of Speaker becomes vacant because of the resignation or death of the Speaker, or for any other reason, the Senate shall, as soon as is practicable, elect a new Speaker from among the senators.

Speaker to preside

(3) The Speaker shall preside at all meetings of the Senate.

Absence of Speaker

(4) In case of the absence for any reason of the Speaker from the chair of the Senate for a period of forty-eight consecutive hours, the Senate may elect another of its members to act as Speaker, and the member so elected shall, during that absence of the Speaker, have and execute all the powers, privileges and duties of the Speaker.

Quorum of Senate

26. (1) The presence of at least ten senators is necessary to constitute a meeting of the Senate for the exercise of its powers, and for that purpose the Speaker shall be counted as a senator.

Voting in the Senate

(2) Subject to this Act, questions arising in the Senate shall be decided by a majority of voices, and the Speaker shall not vote except when the voices are otherwise equal.

Bills materially affecting French language or culture in Canada

(3) For greater certainty, where the Speaker is a French-speaking senator for the purposes of section 36, the Speaker may vote when the votes are otherwise equal among French-speaking senators in relation to a bill that materially affects the French language or culture in Canada.

Duration of Senate

27. On the dissolution of the House of Commons the Senate also stands dissolved, and elections for the Senate shall take place at the same time as those for the House of Commons.

Approval by the Senate of appointments

28. (1) The Parliament of Canada may provide, in respect of any appointment made under its authority, that the appointment is subject to the approval of the Senate.

Head of central bank

(2) No one may be appointed as head of the central bank established by the Parliament of Canada unless the appointment is approved by the Senate.

Deemed
approval

(3) An appointment that is subject to the approval of the Senate under this section shall be deemed to have been approved if the Senate has not voted to withhold its approval of the appointment within thirty days after it has received a request for approval.

Rules relating to Passage of Bills

Application of
general rule

29. (1) This section and sections 30 and 31 apply to all bills except

(a) revenue or expenditure bills, as defined in subsection 32(1);

(b) natural resources tax policy bills, as defined in subsection 34(1); and

(c) bills that materially affect the French language or culture in Canada.

Intergovern-
mental
agreements

(2) Any bill to approve an agreement pursuant to section 126A shall be deemed to be a bill to which this section and sections 30 and 31 apply.

Powers and
procedures

(3) Except as otherwise provided in this Act, the powers and procedures of the Senate and the House of Commons in relation to the consideration and passage of bills under this section and sections 30 and 31 shall be parallel.

General rule for
bills defeated
or amended

(4) Where a bill, having been passed by one House of Parliament, is defeated by the other or is passed by the other with amendments, the House of Parliament where the bill originated may

(a) concur in the amendments made by the other; or

(b) request that a reconciliation committee be established to consider the bill in the form in which it was originally passed in that House.

General rule
for bills not
disposed of
within thirty
sitting days

(5) Where a bill, having been passed by either House of Parliament, is sent to the other House but is not disposed of within thirty sitting days after it is sent or within such longer period as may be agreed to by the Speaker of the House of Parliament where the bill originated, the House of Parliament where the bill originated may request a joint sitting of the Senate and the House of Commons to consider the bill in the form in which it was passed.

Bills amending
the Constitution
of Canada

(6) Notwithstanding subsection (5) and subsection 30(4), no bill to amend the Constitution of Canada in relation to the Senate or the House of Commons may be enacted without the approval of each House of Parliament and no such bill may be sent to a joint sitting of the Senate and the House of Commons.

Rules for
reconciliation
committee and
joint sitting

(7) Subject to sections 30 and 31, the procedures to be followed by a reconciliation committee or a joint sitting of the Senate and the House of Commons shall be established by rules of the Senate and the House of Commons.

Equal number
of members
to serve on
reconciliation
committee

30. (1) The Senate and the House of Commons shall each nominate an equal number of members to serve on any reconciliation committee.

Consideration
of bill by
reconciliation
committee

(2) A reconciliation committee established to consider a bill may, within thirty sitting days after the request that the committee be established, report the bill to the Senate and to the House of Commons with or without amendments.

If Senate and
House of
Commons
approve bill
as reported

(3) If the Senate and the House of Commons each approve a bill as reported by a reconciliation committee, the bill shall be deemed to have been passed by the Senate and the House of Commons in the form in which it was reported by the reconciliation committee.

If bill not
reported or not
approved by
the Senate or
the House of
Commons

(4) If a reconciliation committee fails to report a bill under subsection (2), or if the Senate or the House of Commons does not approve the bill as reported within three sitting days after it is reported, the House of Parliament where the bill originated may request a joint sitting of the Senate and the House of Commons to consider the bill.

Joint sitting of
the Senate and
House of
Commons

31. (1) On a request under subsection 29(5) or subsection 30(4) for a joint sitting of the Senate and the House of Commons to consider a bill, the Speakers of the Senate and the House of Commons shall forthwith convene the joint sitting to consider the bill.

Speaker or
delegate to
preside

(2) The Speaker of the House of Parliament where the bill under consideration originated, or the delegate of the Speaker, shall preside at meetings of any joint sitting convened under subsection (1) to consider the bill.

Consideration
and voting

(3) A joint sitting convened under subsection (1) shall without delay consider and vote on the bill for which it was convened, with such amendments as the joint sitting considers desirable or, in the case of a joint sitting convened pursuant to subsection 29(5), without amendment.

Time limit

(4) The final vote on a bill for which a joint sitting is requested shall take place within ten sitting days after the request is made or within such other period of time as may be agreed to by the Speakers of both Houses of Parliament, and in all cases reasonable time shall be allowed for debate by the joint sitting.

Where bill
approved by
joint sitting

(5) Where a bill is approved by a majority of the senators and members of the House of Commons voting, taken together, in accordance with subsection (3), the bill shall be deemed to have been passed by the Senate and the House of Commons in the form in which it is approved.

Definition of
"sitting days"

(6) In subsection (4), "sitting days" means any days on which the House of Commons sits, either alone or in a joint sitting.

Definition of
"revenue or
expenditure bill"

32. (1) In this section and section 33, "revenue or expenditure bill" means a public bill that is designated on introduction as a revenue or expenditure bill by a Minister of the Crown and that contains only provisions dealing with the following:

(a) the raising of revenues, including the imposition, repeal, remission, alteration and regulation of taxation,

(b) the appropriation of public money,

(c) charges on the Consolidated Revenue Fund,

(d) the public debt, including borrowing authority,

(e) the guarantee of any loan or other debt or obligation, or

(f) subordinate matters relating to any of the matters set out in paragraphs (a) to (e),

but does not include a bill that contains provisions that would result in fundamental policy changes to the tax system.

Revenue or
expenditure bills
defeated in
the Senate or
passed with
amendments not
concurred in by
House of
Commons

(2) Where a revenue or expenditure bill, having been passed by the House of Commons, is defeated by the Senate or is passed by the Senate with amendments, the House of Commons may approve the bill in the form in which it was introduced in the Senate or with such amendments made by the Senate as are concurred in by the House of Commons, whereupon the bill shall, unless the House of Commons directs to the contrary, be deemed to have been passed by the Senate

in the form in which it was finally approved by the House of Commons.

Revenue or expenditure bills not disposed of by the Senate

(3) Where a revenue or expenditure bill, having been passed by the House of Commons, is sent to the Senate but is not disposed of by the Senate within thirty days after it is sent, the bill shall, unless the House of Commons directs to the contrary, be deemed to have been passed by the Senate in the form in which it was sent to the Senate.

Ruling by Speaker of House of Commons

33. (1) Any member of the House of Commons or the Speaker of the Senate may request that the Speaker of the House of Commons consider whether a bill that has been designated as a revenue or expenditure bill is a revenue or expenditure bill, and the Speaker of the House of Commons shall after consulting with the Speaker of the Senate, rule on the matter within five days after the request is made.

Certificate of the Speaker

(2) There shall be endorsed on every revenue or expenditure bill when it is sent to the Senate the certificate of the Speaker of the House of Commons, signed by that speaker, that it is a revenue or expenditure bill.

Idem

(3) A certificate of the Speaker of the House of Commons given under subsection (2) is conclusive for all purposes and shall not be questioned in any court of law.

Definition of "natural resources tax policy bill"

34. (1) In this section and section 35, "natural resources tax policy bill" means a bill that contains provisions that would result in fundamental tax policy changes that are directly related to natural resources or electrical energy.

Disposition of bill

(2) Where a natural resources tax policy bill is passed by the House of Commons and sent to the Senate, the Senate shall dispose of the bill within thirty sitting days after it is sent.

Where bill
defeated in the
Senate

(3) Where a natural resources tax policy bill, having been passed by the House of Commons, is defeated by the Senate, no further action may be taken on the bill.

Identification of
bill

35. (1) A Minister of the Crown may, on introduction of a bill in the House of Commons, indicate that the bill is, in the opinion of the Minister, a natural resources tax policy bill.

Ruling by Speaker
of House of
Commons

(2) Any member of the House of Commons or the Speaker of the Senate may request that the Speaker of the House of Commons consider whether a bill that has been introduced in the House of Commons is a natural resources tax policy bill, and the Speaker of the House of Commons shall, after consulting with the Speaker of the Senate, rule on the matter within five sitting days after the request is made.

Certificate of the
Speaker

(3) There shall be endorsed on every natural resources tax policy bill when it is sent to the Senate the certificate of the Speaker of the House of Commons, signed by that Speaker, that it is a natural resources tax policy bill.

Idem

(4) A certificate of the Speaker of the House of Commons given under subsection (3) is conclusive for all purposes and shall not be questioned in any court of law.

Bills materially
affecting French
language or cul-
ture in Canada

36. (1) A bill that materially affects the French language or culture in Canada must, in order to be passed by the Senate, be approved by a majority of senators voting and a majority of French-speaking senators voting.

Quorum for
vote of French-
speaking senators

(2) A vote of French-speaking senators is not sufficient for the purposes of subsection (1) unless at least one-third of all French-speaking senators are present and voting.

Disposition of bill

(3) Where a bill described in subsection (1) is passed by one House of Parliament and sent to the other House, the House to which the bill is sent shall dispose of the bill within thirty sitting days after it is sent.

Where bill defeat-
ed in either House
of Parliament

(4) Where a bill described in subsection (1) is defeated in either House of Parliament, no further action may be taken on the bill.

Exception

(5) This section and section 36A do not apply to revenue or expenditure bills, as defined in subsection 32(1).

Identification of
bill

36A. (1) Any senator, on introducing a bill into the Senate, or any member of the House of Commons, on introducing a bill that originates in the House of Commons, may indicate that the bill is, in the opinion of the senator or member, a bill that materially affects the French language or culture in Canada.

Ruling by Speaker
of Senate

(2) Any senator or the Speaker of the House of Commons may request that the Speaker of the Senate consider whether a bill materially affects the French language or culture in Canada and the Speaker of the Senate shall, after consulting with the Speaker of the House of Commons, rule on the matter within five sitting days after the request is made.

Certificate of
Speaker

(3) There shall be endorsed on every bill that materially affects the French language or culture in Canada, when it is presented to the Governor General for the Queen's assent, a certificate of the Speaker of the Senate, signed by that Speaker, that it is a bill that materially affects the French language or culture in Canada and that it has received the requisite approval.

Idem

(4) A certificate of the Speaker of the Senate given under subsection (3) is conclusive for all purposes and shall not be questioned in any court of law.

French-speaking
senators

36B. (1) For the purposes of section 36, senators are, subject to subsection (2), French-speaking if they identify themselves to the Speaker as French-speaking on first taking their seats in the Senate.

Idem

(2) The Speaker of the Senate may resolve any dispute about whether a senator is French-speaking, and the decision of the Speaker is conclusive for all purposes and shall not be questioned in any court of law.

Definition of
"sitting days"

36C. In sections 28 to 30 and 34 to 36A, "sitting days" means any days on which the House of Commons sits."

5. Sections 51A and 52 of the said Act are repealed and the following substituted therefor:

Principle of
proportionate
representation in
the House of
Commons

"51A. (1) In readjusting the number of members in the House of Commons, the Parliament of Canada shall be guided by the principle that the proportion of members of the House of Commons representing a province shall be based on the proportion of the population of Canada from that province.

Special rules
relating to the
constitution of
the House of
Commons

(2) Notwithstanding anything in this Act,

(a) a province shall always be entitled to a number of members in the House of Commons not fewer than the number of senators by which the province was entitled to be represented on April 17, 1982;

(b) Quebec shall always be entitled to a number of members in the House of Commons that is no fewer than twenty-five per cent of the total number of members in the House of Commons;

(c) except as a result of the application of paragraph (b), no province shall have fewer members in the House of Commons than any other province that had, at the then latest general census, a smaller population;

(d) in any readjustment of the number of members in the House of Commons, no province shall have its representation reduced by more than one member; and

(e) the Yukon Territory and the Northwest Territories shall always be entitled to a number of members in the House of Commons not fewer than the number of members to which they were entitled on the coming into force of this section, and this entitlement applies to any new province established from either of them.

Increase of number in House of Commons

52. Subject to section 51A, the number of members of the House of Commons may from time to time be increased by the Parliament of Canada."

6. Sections 55 to 57 of the said Act are repealed and the following substituted therefor:

Royal Assent to bills

"55. Where a bill passed by the Houses of the Parliament is presented to the Governor General for the Queen's Assent, the Governor General shall declare, according to the discretion of the Governor General, but subject to Her Majesty's instructions, either that the bill is assented to in the Queen's name, or that the Queen's Assent is withheld."

7. Section 90 of the said Act is repealed and the following substituted therefor:

Application to legislatures of provisions respecting money votes and assent

"90. The provision of this Act relating to the recommendation of money votes and the assent to bills in the Parliament of Canada apply to the legislatures of the provinces with the substitution of the Lieutenant Governor of the province for the Governor General and of the Governor General for the Queen."

8. The said Act is further amended by adding thereto, immediately after section 91 thereof, the following section:

Application of

"91A. For greater certainty, class 24 of section 91

applies, except as provided in section 95E, in relation to all the Aboriginal peoples of Canada."

9. (1) Paragraph (c) of class 10 of section 92 of the said Act is repealed and the following substituted therefor:

"(c) such works as, although wholly situate within the Province, are before or after their execution declared by the Parliament of Canada, where authorized by resolution of the Legislative Assembly of the Province, to be for the general advantage of Canada or for the advantage of two or more of the Provinces."

(2) Section 92 of the said Act is further amended by adding thereto, immediately after class 12 thereof, the following:

"12A. Labour market development and training in the Province."

(3) Section 92 of the said Act is further amended by adding thereto, immediately after class 16 thereof, the following:

"And,

(a) for greater certainty, any declaration made under paragraph (c) of class 10 and in force immediately before this paragraph comes into force remains in force until it is repealed in accordance with paragraph (b); and

(b) no declaration made under paragraph (c) of class 10 may be repealed by the Parliament of Canada except where authorized by resolution of the legislative assembly of the province within which the works in respect of which declaration is made are situate."

10. The said Act is further amended by adding thereto, immediately after section 92A thereof, the following heading and sections:

"Culture

Laws in relation
to culture

92B. (1) The legislature of each province may exclusively make laws in relation to culture in the province.

National cultural
matters

(2) The Government of Canada retains its role in relation to national cultural matters, including national cultural institutions and grants and contributions delivered by such institutions.

Authority not
extended

(3) Nothing in subsection (2) extends the authority of the Parliament of Canada.

Agreements on
culture with
provinces

92C. (1) The Government of Canada shall negotiate with the government of any province that so requests an agreement on culture for the purpose of ensuring that both governments work in harmony, recognizing the lead responsibility of the province for culture in the province.

Agreements on
culture with
territories

(2) The Government of Canada shall negotiate with the government of any territory that so requests an agreement on culture for the purpose of ensuring that both governments work in harmony.

Telecommunications

Agreement on
telecommu-
nications

92D. The Government of Canada shall negotiate with the government of any province or territory that so requests an agreement on telecommunications for the purpose of coordinating and harmonizing the procedures of their respective regulatory agencies."

11. The said Act is further amended by adding thereto, immediately after section 93 thereof, the following heading and sections:

"Urban and Municipal Affairs, Tourism, Recreation,
Housing, Mining and Forestry

Exclusive

93A. (1) It is hereby affirmed that the following

provincial
authority

matters in each province come within the exclusive legislative authority of the legislature of the province:

(a) urban and municipal affairs;
(b) tourism;
(c) recreation;
(d) housing;
(e) mining; and
(f) forestry.

Agreements to
withdraw from
grants and
contributions

(2) The Government of Canada shall, at the request of the government of any province or territory, negotiate with that government for the purpose of concluding an agreement under which the Government of Canada is required to withdraw partially or completely as soon as is practicable from any program of grants or contributions in respect of the province or territory that relates to any of the matters listed in subsection (1) and is required to provide reasonable compensation to the province or territory.

Agreements to
constrain
expenditures

(3) The Government of Canada and the govern-ment of any province or territory may enter into an agreement under which any expenditure of money in respect of the province or territory by the Government of Canada in relation to any of the matters listed in subsection (1) is constrained, whether or not the agreement relates to a withdrawal from a program of grants or contributions.

Maintenance of
spending

(4) Where an agreement is concluded with the government of any province or territory pursuant to subsection (2) or (3), the Government of Canada shall, at the request of the government of any other province or territory, negotiate with that government for the purpose of concluding an agreement under which the Government of Canada is required to maintain its expenditure of money in respect of that province or territory in relation to the matter that is the subject of the agreement.

Reasonable
time

(5) Where a request is made under subsection (2) or (4), the Government of Canada and the government of the province or territory that made the request shall conclude an agreement within a reasonable time.

Equality of
treatment of
provinces

(6) Where an agreement is being negotiated pursuant to this section, the province negotiating the agreement shall, with respect to the terms and conditions of the agreement, including compensation, be accorded equality of treatment in relation to any other province with which an agreement has been concluded pursuant to this section in relation to the same matter in the context of the different needs and circumstances of the provinces.

Equality of
treatment of
territories

(7) Subsection (6) applies in respect of territories so as to accord a territory equality of treatment in relation to another territory in the context of the different needs and circumstances of the territories.

Labour Market Development and Training

Negotiated
withdrawal

93B. (1) The Government of Canada shall, at the request of the government of any province or territory, negotiate with that government for the purpose of concluding an agreement under which the Government of Canada is required to withdraw partially or completely, as soon as is practicable, from any program or activity in respect of the province or territory that relates to labour market development or training, including labour market training in the province or territory under any unemployment insurance program or activity, and is required to provide reasonable compensation to the province or territory.

Withdrawal

(2) Where the government of a province or territory requests the Government of Canada to withdraw partially or completely from any program or activity in respect of the province or territory described in subsection (1), the Government of Canada shall, in

accordance with the request, do so as soon as is practicable.

Unemployment insurance

(3) For greater certainty, nothing in this section abrogates or derogates from the legislative authority of the Parliament of Canada in relation to unemployment insurance.

Job creation programs

(4) Nothing in subsections (1) and (2) precludes the Government of Canada from making expenditures on job creation programs.

Maintenance of spending

(5) Where an agreement is concluded with the government of any province or territory pursuant to subsection (1), or the Government of Canada withdraws from a program or activity in any province or territory pursuant to subsection (2), the Government of Canada shall, at the request of the government of any other province or territory, negotiate with that government for the purpose of concluding an agreement under which the Government of Canada is required to maintain its expenditure of money in respect of that province or territory in relation to labour market development or training.

Reasonable time

(6) Where a request is made under subsection (1) or (5), the Government of Canada and the government of the province or territory that made the request shall conclude an agreement within a reasonable time.

Equality of treatment of provinces

(7) Where an agreement is being negotiated pursuant to this section, the province negotiating the agreement shall, with respect to the terms and conditions of the agreement, including compensation, be accorded equality of treatment in relation to any other province with which an agreement has been concluded pursuant to this section in the context of the different needs and circumstances of the provinces.

Equality of

(8) Subsection (7) applies in respect of territories so

treatment of
territories

as to accord a territory equality of treatment in relation
to another territory in the context of the different needs
and circumstances of the territories.

National
objectives for
labour market
development
programs and
activities

93C. (1) Where the Government of Canada withdraws
from a program or activity pursuant to subsection 93B
(1) or (2), the government of the province or territory
that requested the withdrawal shall ensure that all
labour market development programs and activities in
the province or territory, considered together, are
compatible with national objectives established under
subsection (2) in the context of the different needs and
circumstances of the provinces or territories.

Establishment
of national
objectives

(2) For the purposes of subsection (1), the Government of Canada shall, from time to time, with the
governments of the provinces and territories, establish
national objectives in relation to national aspects of
labour market development programs and activities,
taking into account the different needs and circumstances of the provinces and territories.

Regional Development

Negotiated
agreement

93D. (1) The Government of Canada shall, at the
request of the government of any province or territory,
negotiate with that government for the purpose of
concluding an agreement relating to regional
development in that province or territory.

Reasonable time

(2) Where a request is made under subsection (1),
the Government of Canada and the government of the
province or territory that made the request shall
conclude an agreement within a reasonable time.

Equality of
treatment of
provinces

(3) Where an agreement is being negotiated pursuant to this section, the province negotiating the
agreement shall, with respect to the terms and conditions of the agreement, be accorded equality of
treatment in relation to any other province with which
an agreement has been concluded pursuant to this sec-

tion in the context of the different needs and circumstances of the provinces and, in particular, with regard to the need for a special focus on provinces, or regions within provinces, suffering the greatest disparities.

Equality of treatment of territories

(4) Subsection (3) applies in respect of territories so as to accord a territory equality of treatment in relation to another territory in the context of the different needs and circumstances of the territories.

Legislative Powers not Extended

Legislative powers not extended

93E. Nothing in sections 93A to 93D extends the legislative powers of the Parliament of Canada."

12. The said Act is further amended by adding thereto, immediately after section 95 thereof, the following heading and sections:

"Agreements on Immigration and Aliens

Negotiated agreements

95A. (1) The Government of Canada shall, at the request of the government of any province, negotiate with the government of that province for the purpose of concluding an agreement relating to immigration or the temporary admission of aliens into that province that is appropriate to the needs and circumstances of that province.

Reasonable time

(2) Where a request is made under subsection (1), the Government of Canada and the government of the province that made the request shall conclude an agreement within a reasonable time.

Equality of treatment

(3) Where an agreement is being negotiated pursuant to this section, the province negotiating the agreement shall, with respect to the terms and conditions of the agreement, be accorded equality of treatment in relation to any other province with which an agreement has been concluded pursuant to this section in the context of the different needs and circumstances of the provinces.

Agreements

95B. (1) Any agreement concluded between Canada and a province in relation to immigration or the temporary admission of aliens into that province has the force of law from the time it is declared to do so in accordance with subsection 95C(1) and shall from that time have effect notwithstanding class 25 of section 91 or section 95.

Limitation

(2) An agreement that has the force of law under subsection (1) shall have effect only so long and so far as it is not repugnant to any provision of an Act of the Parliament of Canada that sets national standards and objectives relating to immigration or aliens, including any provision that establishes general classes of immigrants or relates to levels of immigration for Canada or that prescribes classes of individuals who are inadmissible into Canada.

Application of Charter

(3) The *Canadian Charter of Rights and Freedoms* applies in respect of any agreement that has the force of law under subsection (1) and in respect of anything done by the Parliament or Government of Canada, or the legislature or government of a province, pursuant to any such agreement.

Proclamation relating to agreements

95C. (1) A declaration that an agreement referred to in subsection 95B(1) has the force of law may be made by proclamation issued by the Governor General under the Great Seal of Canada only where so authorized by resolutions of the Senate and House of Commons and of the legislative assembly of the province that is a party to the agreement.

Amendment of agreements

(2) An amendment to an agreement referred to in subsection 95B(1) may be made by proclamation issued by the Governor General under the Great Seal of Canada only where so authorized

(a) by resolutions of the Senate and House of Commons and of the legislative assembly of the province that is a party to the agreement; or

(b) in such other manner as is set out in the agreement.

Application of sections 46 to 48 of *Constitution Act, 1982*

95D. Sections 46 to 48 of the *Constitution Act, 1982* apply, with such modifications as the circumstances require, in respect of any declaration made pursuant to subsection 95C(1) or any amendment to an agreement made pursuant to subsection 95C(2).

Métis and Métis Settlement Lands in Alberta

Métis and Métis settlement lands in Alberta

95E. In the context of section 91A, the legislature of Alberta may make laws, and the Parliament of Canada may make laws, in relation to the Métis in Alberta and to Métis settlement lands in Alberta and, where such a law of Alberta and a law of Parliament conflict, the law of Parliament prevails to the extent of the conflict."

13. The said Act is further amended by adding thereto, immediately before section 96 thereof, the following heading:

"General"

14. The said Act is further amended by adding thereto, immediately before section 101 thereof, the following heading:

"Courts Established by the Parliament of Canada"

15. The said Act is further amended by adding thereto, immediately after section 101 thereof, the following heading and sections:

"Supreme Court of Canada

Supreme Court continued

101A. (1) The court existing under the name of the Supreme Court of Canada is hereby continued as the general court of appeal for Canada, and as an additional court for the better administration of the laws of Canada, and shall continue to be a superior court of record.

Composition

(2) The Supreme Court of Canada shall consist of a chief justice, to be called the Chief Justice of Canada, and eight other judges who shall be appointed by the Governor General in Council.

Who may be appointed judges

101B. (1) Any person may be appointed a judge of the Supreme Court of Canada who, after having been admitted to the bar of a province or territory, has, for a total of at least ten years, been a judge of any court in Canada or a member of the bar of any province or territory.

Three judges from Quebec

(2) At least three of the judges shall be appointed from among persons who, after having been admitted to the bar of Quebec, have, for a total of at least ten years, been judges of any court of Quebec or of any court established by the Parliament of Canada, or members of the bar of Quebec.

Names of candidates

101C. (1) Where a vacancy occurs in the Supreme Court of Canada, the government of each province or territory any submit to the Minister of Justice of Canada the names of at least five candidates to fill the vacancy, each of whom is qualified under section 101B for appointment to the Court.

Appointment from names submitted

(2) Where an appointment is made to the Supreme Court of Canada, the Governor General in Council shall, except where the Chief Justice is appointed from among members of the Court, appoint a person whose name has been submitted under subsection (1) and who is acceptable to the Queen's Privy Council for Canada.

Appointment from Quebec

(3) Where an appointment is made under subsection 101B(2), the Governor General in Council shall appoint a person whose name is submitted by the Government of Quebec.

Appointment from other province or territory

(4) Where an appointment is made otherwise than under subsection 101B(2), the Governor General in Council shall appoint a person whose name is submitted by the government of a province, other than Quebec, or of a territory.

Interim judges

101D. (1) Where a vacancy in the Supreme Court of Canada is not filled and at least ninety days have elapsed since the vacancy occurred, the Chief of Justice of Canada may in writing request a judge of a superior court of a province or territory or of any superior court established by the Parliament of Canada to attend at the sittings of the Supreme Court of Canada as an interim judge for the duration of the vacancy.

Interim judge
from Quebec

(2) Where a vacancy in the Supreme Court of Canada results in there being fewer than three judges on the Court who meet the qualifications set out in subsection 101B(2), no judge may be requested to attend as an interim judge under subsection (1) unless the judge meets those qualifications.

Tenures, salaries,
etc., of judges

101E. Sections 99 and 100 apply in respect of the judges of the Supreme Court of Canada.

Relationship to
section 101

101F. (1) Sections 101A to 101E shall not be construed as abrogating or derogating from the powers of the Parliament of Canada to make laws under section 101 except to the extent that such laws are inconsistent with those sections.

References to the
Supreme Court
of Canada

(2) For greater certainty, section 101A shall not be construed as abrogating or derogating from the powers of the Parliament of Canada to make laws relating to the reference of questions of law or fact, or any other matters, to the Supreme Court of Canada."

16. The said Act is further amended by adding thereto, immediately after section 106 thereof, the following section:

Shared-cost
program

"106A. (1) The Government of Canada shall provide reasonable compensation to the government of a province that chooses not to participate in a national shared-cost program that is established by the Government of Canada after the coming into force of this section in an area of exclusive provincial jurisdiction, if the province carries on a program or initiative that is compatible with the national objectives.

Legislative powers not extended

(2) Nothing in this section extends the legislative powers of the Parliament of Canada or of the legislatures of the provinces.

Section 36 of *Constitution Act, 1982* not affected

(3) For greater certainty, nothing in this section affects the commitments of the Parliament and government of Canada set out in section 36 of the *Constitution Act, 1982.*"

17. The said Act is further amended by adding thereto, immediately after Part VIII thereof, the following Part:

"VIII.I INTERGOVERNMENTAL AGREEMENTS

No inconsistent laws

126A. (1) Where the Government of Canada and the government of one or more provinces or territories enter into an agreement that is approved under this section, no law made by or under the authority of the Parliament of Canada or of any legislature of a province or legislative authority of a territory that is a party to the agreement and has caused it to be approved under this section may amend, revoke or otherwise supersede the agreement while the approval of the agreement remains in force.

Approval

(2) An agreement is approved when the Parliament of Canada and the legislature of a province, or the legislative authority of a territory, that is a party thereto have each passed a law that approves the agreement and that includes an express declaration that this section applies in respect of the agreement.

Amendment revocation, etc.

(3) An agreement approved under this section may be amended, revoked or otherwise superseded only in accordance with its terms or by a further agreement approved under this section.

Duration of

(4) An approval under this section expires no later

approval

than five years after it is given, but may be renewed under this section for additional periods not exceeding five years each.

Equality of
treatment of
provinces

(5) Where an agreement between the Government of Canada and the government of any province is approved under this section, the Government of Canada, at the request of the government of any other province, shall negotiate and conclude an agreement within a reasonable time with that other government and shall, with respect to the terms and conditions of that agreement, accord that other government equality of treatment in the context of the different needs and circumstances of the provinces, and the Government of Canada shall cause the agreement to be placed before the Parliament of Canada for approval under this section.

Equality of
treatment of
territories

(6) Subsection (5) applies in respect of territories so as to accord a territory equality of treatment in relation to another territory in the context of the different needs and circumstances of the territories.

Application
of section to
Aboriginal
governments

(7) This section applies, with such modifications as the circumstances require, in respect of any agreement entered into between a government of the Aboriginal peoples of Canada and the Government of Canada or the government of a province or territory.

Definition of
"agreement"

(8) In this section, "agreement" includes any agreement, contract or other arrangement."

18. The said Act is further amended by adding thereto, immediately before section 128 thereof, the following section:

Non-derogation

"127. (1) For greater certainty, except to the extent that is otherwise agreed by the Aboriginal peoples concerned, none of the provisions referred to in subsection (2), and no agreement made under any provision referred to in subsection (2), abrogates or derogates from

(a) the legislative authority of the Parliament of

Canada under class 24 of section 91 consistent with section 91A, as modified by section 95E;

(b) the federal fiduciary responsibility for Aboriginal peoples; or

(c) the aboriginal, treaty or other rights or freedoms that pertain to the Aboriginal peoples of Canada, including

(i) any rights or freedoms that have been recognized by the Royal Proclamation of October 7, 1763,

(ii) any rights of freedoms that now exist by way of land claims agreements or may be so acquired,

(iii) the inherent right of self-government referred to in section 35.1 of the *Constitution Act, 1982* and the powers and jurisdictions set out in self-government agreements, and

(iv) any rights or freedoms relating to the exercise or protection of their languages, cultures or traditions.

Application

(2) This section applies in relation to the following provisions:

(a) paragraph (c) of class 10 of section 92 and all that portion of section 92 following class 16 thereof;

(b) class 12A of section 92;

(c) sections 92B to 92D;

(d) sections 93A to 93D;

(e) sections 95A to 95D;

(f) section 95E;

(g) section 106A; and

(h) section 126A."

19. (1) Notwithstanding sections 41 and 44 of the *Constitution Act, 1982*, the amendments in this section are made in accordance with section 41 of that Act.

(2) Rules 1 and 2 in subsection 51(1) of the *Constitution Act, 1867* are repealed and the following substituted therefor:

Rule

"1. After the completion of the 1991 decennial census, the House of Commons shall consist of three hundred and thirty-seven members and there shall be assigned to each of the provinces and territories the following numbers of members: one hundred and seventeen for Ontario; ninety-three for Quebec; eleven for Nova Scotia; ten for New Brunswick; fourteen for Manitoba; thirty-six for British Columbia; four for Prince Edward Island; twenty-eight for Alberta; fourteen for Saskatchewan; seven for Newfoundland; one for the Yukon Territory; and two for the Northwest Territories."

Adjusted representation

(3) After the completion of the 1996 census, the representation of the provinces in the House of Commons shall be readjusted by adding eight members, of which three shall be for Ontario, three for British Columbia and two for Alberta.

TRANSITIONAL

First election of senators

20. (1) Notwithstanding section 27 of the *Constitution Act, 1867*, as enacted by section 4 of this amendment, Parliament may provide for the first general election of senators to take place within one year after this section comes into force, whether or not it occurs at the same time as a general election of the House of Commons.

344   Appendix 2

Delay of application

    (2) Subsection 23(5) of the *Constitution Act, 1867*, as enacted by section 4 of this amendment, does not apply for one year after this section comes into force.

Continuation

    (3) Until the first general election of senators is completed, the provision enacted by sections 3 and 4 of this amendment do not apply and the Senate shall continue as if those provisions had not come into force.

CONSTITUTION ACT, 1871

Establishment of new provinces in territories in Canada

21. Section 2 of the *Constitution Act, 1871* is repealed and the following substituted therefor:

"2. (1.) The Parliament of Canada may from time to time establish a new province in any territory forming for the time being part of the Dominion of Canada, but not included in any province thereof, at the request of the legislative authority of the territory, and may, at the time of such establishment, make provision for the constitution and administration of any such province, and for the passing of laws for the peace, order and good government of the province, and for its representation in the House of Commons.

First Ministers' Conference

    (2) Before a new province is established under subsection (1), a conference of the Prime Minister of Canada and the first ministers of the provinces shall be convened to take into account the views of the provinces."

22. Section 3 of the said Act is renumbered as subsection 3(1) and is further amended by adding thereto the following subsection:

Consent of territories

"(2) The Parliament of Canada may not, pursuant to subsection (1), alter the limits of any territory forming for the time being part of the Dominion of Canada, except with the consent of the legislative authority of the territory."

23. The *Alberta Act* is amended by adding thereto, immediately after section 24 thereof, the following section:

Definitions

"24.1 (1) In this section,

"Métis Settlements General Council"
« *Conseil* ... »

"Métis Settlements General Council" means the Métis Settlements General Council incorporated by the *Métis Settlements Act* (Alberta);

"Métis settlement land"
« *terres* ... »

"Métis settlement land" means land held in fee simple by the Métis Settlements General Council under letters patent from Her Majesty in right of Alberta.

Expropriation

(2) The fee simple estate in Métis settlement land, or any interest in it less than fee simple, may not be acquired through expropriation by

(a) any person,

(b) Her Majesty in right of Alberta, or

(c) Her Majesty in right of Canada, except with the consent of the Governor in Council after consultation between the Government of Canada and the Métis Settlements General Council,

but an interest less than fee simple may be acquired in that land in a manner permitted by the *Métis Settlements Land Protection Act* (Alberta).

Exemption from seizure

(3) The fee simple estate in Métis settlement land is exempt from seizure and sale under court order, writ of execution or any other process whether judicial or extra-judicial.

Restriction on Legislature

(4) No Act of the Legislature may

(a) amend or repeal the *Métis Settlements Land Protection Act* (Alberta),

(b) alter or revoke letters patent granting Métis settlement land to the Métis Settlements General Council, or

(c) dissolve the Métis Settlements General Council or result in its being composed of persons who are not settlement members,

without the agreement of the Métis Settlements General Council.

Restriction on Parliament of Canada

(5) No Act of the Parliament of Canada may dissolve the Métis Settlements General Council or result in its being composed of members who are not settlement members without the agreement of the Métis Settlements General Council.

Application of laws

(6) Nothing in this section shall be construed as limiting

(a) the application of the laws of Alberta or Canada to, or

(b) the jurisdiction of the Legislature of Alberta or the Parliament of Canada to enact laws in and for Alberta applicable to,

Métis settlement land and any activities on or in respect of that land, except to the extent necessary to give effect to this section.

Non-derogation

(7) Nothing in this section shall be construed so as to abrogate or derogate from any rights referred to in Part II of the *Constitution Act, 1982*."

Constitution Act, 1982

24. Section 3 of the *Constitution Act, 1982* is repealed and the following substituted therefor:

Democratic
rights of citizens

"3. Every citizen of Canada has the right to vote in an election of members of the House of Commons or of a legislative assembly of a province and to be qualified for membership therein."

25. Section 25 of the said Act is amended by striking out the word "and" at the end of paragraph (a) thereof, by adding the word "and" at the end of paragraph (b) thereof and by adding thereto the following paragraph:

"(c) any rights or freedoms relating to the exercise or protection of their languages, cultures or traditions."

26. Subsection 32(1) of the said Act is amended by striking out the word "and" at the end of paragraph (a) thereof, by adding the word "and" at the end of paragraph (b) thereof and by adding thereto the following paragraph:

"(c) to all legislative bodies and governments of the Aboriginal peoples of Canada in respect of all matters within the authority of their respective legislative bodies."

27. The said Act is further amended by adding thereto, immediately after section 33 thereof, the following section:

Application of
section 33 to
aboriginal
legislative bodies

"33.1 Section 33 applies to legislative bodies of the Aboriginal peoples of Canada with such modifications, consistent with the purposes of the requirements of that section, as are appropriate to the circumstances of the Aboriginal peoples concerned."

28. (1) Subsection 35(1) of the English version of the said Act is amended by substituting the expression "Aboriginal peoples of Canada" for the expression "aboriginal peoples of Canada".

(2) Subsection 35(2) of the said Act is repealed and the following substituted therefor:

Definition of
"Aboriginal
peoples of
Canada"

"(2) In *the Constitution of Canada,* "Aboriginal peoples of Canada" includes the Indian, Inuit and Métis peoples of Canada."

(3) Subsection 35(4) of the said Act is repealed and the following substituted therefor:

Access by all
Aboriginal
peoples

"(4) For greater certainty, all the Aboriginal peoples of Canada have access to the aboriginal and treaty rights recognized and affirmed in this Part that pertain to them."

29. Section 35.1 of the said Act is repealed and the following substituted therefor:

Inherent right
of self-
government

"35.1 (1) The Aboriginal peoples of Canada have the inherent right of self-government within Canada.

Three orders of
government

(2) The right referred to in subsection (1) shall be interpreted in a manner consistent with the recognition of the governments of the Aboriginal peoples of Canada as constituting one of three orders of government in Canada.

Contextual
statement

(3) The exercise of the right referred to in subsection (1) includes the authority of duly constituted legislative bodies of the Aboriginal peoples, each within its own jurisdiction,

(a) to safeguard and develop their languages, cultures, economies, identities, institutions and traditions, and

(b) to develop, maintain and strengthen their relationship with their lands, waters and environment,

so as to determine and control their development as peoples according to their own values and priorities and to ensure the integrity of their societies.

Issues before
court or tribunal

(4) Where an issue arises in any proceedings in relation to the scope of the inherent right of self-

government, or in relation to an assertion of that right, a court or tribunal

(a) before making any final determination of the issue, shall inquire into efforts that have been made to resolve the issue through negotiations under section 35.2 and may order the parties to take such steps as may be appropriate in the circumstances to effect a negotiated resolution; and

(b) in making any final determination of the issue, shall take into account subsection (3).

Land

(5) Neither the right referred to in subsection (1) nor anything in subsection 35.2(1) creates new aboriginal rights to land or abrogates or derogates from existing aboriginal or treaty rights to land, except as otherwise provided in self-government agreements negotiated under section 35.2.

Commitment to negotiate

35.2 (1) The government of Canada, the provincial and territorial governments and the Aboriginal peoples of Canada, including the Indian, Inuit and Métis peoples of Canada, in the various regions and communities of Canada shall negotiate in good faith the implementation of the right of self-government, including issues of

(a) jurisdiction,

(b) lands and resources, and

(c) economic and fiscal arrangements,

with the objective of concluding agreements elaborating relationships between governments of Aboriginal peoples and the government of Canada and provincial or territorial governments.

Process of negotiation

(2) Negotiations referred to in subsection (1) may be initiated only by the representatives or governments of the Aboriginal peoples concerned, and shall, unless

otherwise agreed by the parties to the negotiations, be conducted in accordance with the process for negotiations outlined in an accord entered into by the government of Canada, the provincial and territorial governments and representatives of the Aboriginal peoples.

Equitable
access

(3) All the Aboriginal peoples of Canada shall have equitable access to negotiations referred to in subsection (1).

Agreement
may allow
participation of
all residents

(4) An agreement negotiated under this section may provide for bodies or institutions of self-government that are open to the participation of all residents of the region to which the agreement relates as determined by the agreement.

Different
circumstances

(5) The parties to negotiations referred to in subsection (1) shall have regard to the different circumstances of the various Aboriginal peoples of Canada.

Where rights
are treaty rights

(6) Where an agreement negotiated under this section

(a) is set out in a treaty or land claims agreement, or in an amendment to a treaty including a land claims agreement, or

(b) contains a declaration that the rights of the Aboriginal peoples set out in the agreement are treaty rights,

the rights of the Aboriginal peoples set out in the agreement are treaty rights under subsection 35(1).

Non-derogation
Delay of
justifiability

(7) Nothing in this section abrogates or derogates from the rights referred to in section 35 or 35.1, or from the enforceability thereof, and nothing in subsection 35.1(3) or in this section makes those rights contingent on the commitment to negotiate under this section.

35.3 (1) Except in relation to self-government agreements concluded after the coming into force of this section, section 35.1 shall not be made the subject of judicial notice, interpretation or enforcement for five years after that section comes into force.

For greater certainty

(2) For greater certainty, nothing in subsection (1) prevents the justiciability of disputes in relation to

(a) any existing rights that are recognized and affirmed in subsection 35(1), including any rights relating to self-government, when raised in any court; or

(b) the process of negotiation under section 35.2.

Idem

(3) Nothing in subsection (1) abrogates or derogates from section 35.1 or renders section 35.1 contingent on the happening of any future event, and subsection (1) merely delays for five years judicial notice, interpretation or enforcement of that section.

Application of laws

35.4 (1) Except as otherwise provided by the Constitution of Canada, the laws of Canada and the laws of the provinces and territories continue to apply to the Aboriginal peoples of Canada, subject nevertheless to being displaced by laws enacted by legislative bodies of the Aboriginal peoples according to their authority.

Peace, order and good government in Canada

(2) No aboriginal law or any other exercise of the inherent right of self-government under section 35.1 may be inconsistent with federal or provincial laws that are essential to the preservation of peace, order and good government in Canada.

Legislative authority not extended

(3) For greater certainty, nothing in this section extends the legislative authority of the Parliament of Canada or the legislatures of the provinces or territories.

Affirmative action

35.5 (1) Subsections 6(2) and (3) of the *Canadian Charter of Rights and Freedoms* do not preclude a legislative body or government of the Aboriginal peoples of Canada from exercising authority pursuant to this Part through affirmative action measures that have as their object the amelioration of conditions of individuals or groups who are socially or economically disadvantaged or the protection and advancement of aboriginal languages and cultures.

For greater
certainty

(2) For greater certainty, nothing in this section abrogates or derogates from section 15, 25 or 28 of the *Canadian Charter of Rights and Freedoms* or from section 35.7 of this Part.

Interpretation
of treaty rights

35.6 (1) The treaty rights referred to in this section 35(1) shall be interpreted in a just, broad and liberal manner taking into account their spirit and intent and the context of the specific treaty negotiations relating thereto.

Commitment to
processes to
clarify,
implement or
rectify treaties

(2) The government of Canada is committed to establishing treaty processes to clarify or implement treaty rights and, where the parties agree, to rectify terms of the treaties, and is committed, where requested by the Aboriginal peoples of Canada concerned, to participating in good faith in the process that relates to them.

Participation of
provinces and
territories

(3) The governments of the provinces and territories are committed, to the extent that they have jurisdiction, to participating in good faith in the processes referred to in subsection (2), where jointly invited by the government of Canada and the Aboriginal peoples of Canada concerned or where it is specified that they will do so under the terms of the treaty concerned.

Spirit and
intent

(4) The participants in the processes referred to in subsection (2) shall have regard to, among other things and where appropriate, the spirit and intent of the treaties, as understood by the Aboriginal peoples concerned.

Equitable
access

(5) For greater certainty, all those Aboriginal peoples of Canada who have treaty rights shall have equitable access to the processes referred to in this section.

Non-derogation

(6) Nothing in this section abrogates or derogates from any rights of the Aboriginal peoples of Canada who are not parties to a particular treaty.

Rights of the Aboriginal peoples of Canada guaranteed equally to both sexes

35.7 Notwithstanding any other provision of this Act, the rights of the Aboriginal peoples of Canada referred to in this Part are guaranteed equally to male and female persons.

Commitment to participate in constitutional conference

[35.8* The government of Canada and the provincial governments are committed to the principle that, before any amendment described in section 45.1 is made,

(a) a constitutional conference that includes in its agenda an item relating to the proposed amendment, composed of the Prime Minister of Canada and the first ministers of the provinces, will be convened by the Prime Minister of Canada; and

(b) the Prime Minister of Canada will invite representatives of the Aboriginal peoples of Canada to participate in the discussions on that item.]

Constitutional conferences

35.9 (1) At least four constitutional conferences on aboriginal issues composed of the Prime Minister of Canada, the first ministers of the provinces, representatives of the Aboriginal peoples of Canada and elected representatives of the governments of the territories shall be convened by the Prime Minister of Canada, the first to be held no later than 1996 and the three subsequent conferences to be held one every two years thereafter.

---

* The final wording of this provision (based on existing section 35.1 added in 1984) is to be revisited when the consent mechanism is finalized for section 45.1, at which time concerns will be addressed in respect of amendments directly referring to Aboriginal peoples in some but not all regions of Canada.

Agenda

(2) Each conference convened under subsection (1) shall have included in its agenda such items as are proposed by the representatives of the Aboriginal peoples of Canada.

Power of
territories not
extended

35.91 For greater certainty, nothing in this Part extends the powers of the legislative authorities or governments of the territories."

30. (1) All that portion of subsection 36(1) of the said Act preceding paragraph (a) thereof is repealed and the following substituted therefor:

Commitment to
promote equal
opportunities

"36. (1) Without altering the legislative authority of Parliament, the provincial legislatures or the territorial legislative authorities, or the rights of any of them with respect to the exercise of their legislative authority, Parliament, the provincial legislatures and the territorial legislative authorities, together with the government of Canada and the provincial and territorial governments, are committed to"

(2) Subsection 36(1) of the said Act is further amended by striking out the word "and" at the end of paragraph (b) thereof, by adding the word "and" at the end of paragraph (c) thereof and by adding thereto the following paragraph:

"(d) ensuring the provision and maintenance of reasonably comparable economic infrastructure of a national nature in each province and territory of Canada."

(3) Subsection 36(2) of the said Act is repealed and the following substituted therefor:

Commitment
respecting
equalization
payments

"(2) Parliament and the government of Canada are committed to making equalization payments so that provincial governments have sufficient revenues to provide reasonably comparable levels of public services at reasonably comparable levels of taxation.

Consultation

(3) The government of Canada is committed to meaningful consultation with provincial governments before introducing legislation relating to making equalization payments.

Commitment to regional economic development

(4) Parliament, the provincial legislatures and the territorial legislative authorities, together with the government of Canada and the provincial and territorial governments, are committed to the promotion of regional economic development to reduce economic disparities."

31. The said Act is further amended by adding thereto, immediately after Part III thereof, the following Parts:

"PART III. I

THE SOCIAL AND ECONOMIC UNION

Commitment respecting social and economic union

36.1 (1) Without altering the authority of Parliament, the provincial legislatures or the territorial legislative authorities, or of the government of Canada or the governments of the provinces or territories, or the rights of any of them with respect to the exercise of their authority, Parliament, the provincial legislatures and the territorial legislative authorities, together with the government of Canada and the provincial and territorial governments, are committed to the principle of the preservation and development of the Canadian social and economic union.

Social union

(2) The preservation and development of the social union includes, but is not limited to, the following policy objectives:

(a) providing throughout Canada a health care system that is comprehensive, universal, portable, publicly administered, and accessible;

(b) providing adequate social services and benefits to ensure that all individuals resident in Canada have reasonable access to housing, food and other basic necessities;

(c) providing high quality primary and secondary education to all individuals residents in Canada and ensuring reasonable access to post-secondary education;

(d) protecting the rights of workers to organize and bargain collectively; and

(e) protecting, preserving and sustaining the integrity of the environment for present and future generations.

Economic union   (3) The preservation and development of the economic union includes, but is not limited to, the following policy objectives:

(a) working together to strengthen the Canadian economic union;

(b) the free movement of persons, goods, services and capital;

(c) the goal of full employment;

(d) ensuring that all Canadians have a reasonable standard of living; and

(e) ensuring sustainable and equitable development.

Interpretation of Charter rights and freedoms not modified   (4) This Part does not have the effect of modifying the interpretation of the rights and freedoms referred to in the *Canadian Charter of Rights and Freedoms*.

Monitoring   36.2 The Prime Minister of Canada and the first ministers of the provinces shall, at a conference convened pursuant to section 37.1, establish a mechanism to monitor the progress made in relation to the objectives stated in subsections 36.1(2) and (3).

PART IV

FRAMEWORK FOR CERTAIN EXPENDITURES BY THE GOVERNMENT OF CANADA

Framework for
certain expend-
itures of money

37. (1) The government of Canada and the governments of the provinces are committed to establishing a framework to govern expenditures of money in the provinces by the government of Canada in areas of exclusive provincial jurisdiction that would ensure, in particular, that such expenditures

    (a) contribute to the pursuit of national objectives;

    (b) reduce overlap and duplication;

    (c) respect and not distort provincial priorities; and

    (d) ensure equality of treatment of provinces while recognizing their different needs and circumstances.

Review at First
Ministers'
Conferences

(2) After establishing a framework pursuant to subsection (1), the Prime Minister of Canada and the first ministers of the provinces shall review the progress made in achieving the objectives set out in the framework once each year at conferences convened pursuant to section 37.1.

PART IV.I

FIRST MINISTERS' CONFERENCES

First Ministers'
Conferences

37.1 A conference of the Prime Minister of Canada and the first ministers of the provinces shall be convened by the Prime Minister of Canada at least once each year, the first within twelve months after this Part comes into force."

32. Sections 40 to 42 of the said Act are repealed and the following substituted therefor:

Compensation

"40. Where an amendment is made under subsection 38(1) that transfers legislative powers from provincial legislatures to Parliament, Canada shall provide reasonable compensation to any province to which the amendment does not apply.

Amendment by
unanimous
consent

41. An amendment to the Constitution of Canada in relation to the following matters may be made by proclamation issued by the Governor General under the Great Seal of Canada only where authorized by resolutions of the Senate and House of Commons and of the legislative assembly of each province:

(a) the office of the Queen, the Governor General and the Lieutenant Governor of a province;

(b) the powers of the Senate and the selection of senators;

(c) the number of senators by which a province or territory is entitled to be represented in the Senate and the qualifications of senators set out in the *Constitution Act, 1867*;

[(c.1)* the number of senators by which the Aboriginal peoples of Canada are entitled to be represented in the Senate and the qualifications of such senators;]

(d) an amendment to section 51A of the *Constitution Act, 1867*;

(e) subject to section 43, the use of the English or the French language;

(f) subject to subsection 42(1), the Supreme Court of Canada;

* The issue of Aboriginal representation is to be discussed in the autumn of 1992, according to the Consensus Report.

(g) an amendment to section 2 or 3 of the *Constitution Act, 1871*; and

(h) an amendment to this Part.

Amendment by general procedure

42. (1) An amendment to the Constitution of Canada in relation to the method of selecting judges of the Supreme Court of Canada may be made only in accordance with subsection 38(1).

Exception

(2) Subsection 38(2) to (4) do not apply in respect of amendments in relation to the matter referred to in subsection (1).

New provinces

42.1 Subsection 38(1) and sections 41 and 42 do not apply to allow a province that is established pursuant to section 2 of the *Constitution Act, 1871* after the coming into force of this section to authorize amendments to the Constitution of Canada and, for greater certainty, all other provisions of this Part apply in respect of such a province."

[33. The said Act is further amended by adding thereto, immediately after section 45 thereof, the following section:

Amendments where Aboriginal peoples of Canada directly referred to

"45.1* (1) An amendment to the Constitution of Canada that directly refers to, or that amends a provision that directly refers to, one or more of the Aboriginal peoples of Canada or their governments, including

(a) section 2, as it relates to the Aboriginal peoples of Canada,** class 24 of section 91, and sections

---

* A mechanism for obtaining aboriginal consent would be worked out prior to the tabling of a Constitution resolution in Parliament.

** A reference to any provision relating to aboriginal representation in the Senate would be added here.

91A, 95E and 127 of the *Constitution Act, 1867*, and

(b) section 25 and Part II of this Act and this section, may be made by proclamation issued by the Governor General under the Great Seal of Canada only where the amendment has been authorized in accordance with this Part and has received the substantial consent of the Aboriginal peoples so referred to.

Initiation of amendment procedures

(2) Notwithstanding section 46, the procedures for amending the Constitution of Canada in relation to any matter referred to in subsection (1) may be initiated by any of the Aboriginal peoples of Canada directly referred to as provided in subsection (1)."]

34. Subsection 52(2) of the said Act is amended by striking out the word "and" at the end of paragraph (b) thereof, by adding the word "and" at the end of paragraph (c) thereof and by adding thereto the following paragraph:

"(d) any other amendment to the Constitution of Canada."

35. Section 61 of the said Act is repealed and the following substituted therefor:

References

"61. A reference to the *Constitution Act, 1982* or a reference to the *Constitution Acts, 1867 to 1982* shall be deemed to include a reference to any amendments thereto."

Constitution Act, 1982

(Bilateral amendment – New Brunswick and Canada)

1. The *Constitution Act, 1982* is amended by adding thereto, immediately after section 16 thereof, the following section:

English and
French linguistic
communities in
New Brunswick

"16.1 (1) The English linguistic community and the French linguistic community in New Brunswick have equality of status and equal rights and privileges, including the right to distinct educational institutions and such distinct cultural institutions as are necessary for the preservation and promotion of those communities.

Role of the
legislature and
government of
New Brunswick

(2) The role of the legislature and government of New Brunswick to preserve and promote the status, rights and privileges referred to in subsection (1) is affirmed."

Official Voting Results, by Province
26 October 1992

APPENDIX 3

Official voting results, by province, 26 October 1992

Province	Population (1991 census)	Electors on the list	Total ballots cast for		Total valid votes	Rejected ballots	Total votes cast	% of electors who voted
			Yes/ percentage*	No/ percentage*				
Newfoundland	568,474	398,269	133,583/63.2	77,742/36.8	211,325	1,068	212,393	53.3
Prince Edward Island	129,765	93,534	48,541/73.9	17,128/26.1	65,669	305	65,974	70.5
Nova Scotia	899,942	664,594	218,967/48.8	229,690/51.2	448,657	2,065	450,722	67.8
New Brunswick	723,900	529,071	234,469/61.8	144,885/38.2	379,354	2,642	381,996	72.2
Ontario	10,084,885	6,719,895	2,409,713/50.1	2,395,465/49.9	4,805,178	29,564	4,834,742	71.9
Manitoba	1,091,942	740,627	199,905/38.4	320,918/61.6	520,823	2,370	523,193	70.6
Saskatchewan	988,928	664,917	203,525/44.7	251,441/55.3	454,966	1,644	456,610	68.7
Alberta	2,545,553	1,679,700	484,472/39.8	732,457/60.2	1,216,929	2,958	1,219,887	72.6
British Columbia	3,282,061	2,183,398	528,773/31.7	1,139,127/68.3	1,667,900	6,047	1,673,947	76.7
Northwest Territory	57,649	34,333	14,723/61.3	9,280/38.7	24,003	169	24,172	70.4
Yukon	27,797	17,628	5,360/43.7	6,916/56.3	12,276	66	12,342	70.0
National totals (not including Quebec)	20,400,896	13,725,966	4,482,031/45.7	5,325,049/54.3	9,807,080	48,898	9,855,978	72.0
Quebec	6,895,963	4,872,965	1,709,075/43.3	2,236,144/56.7	3,945,189	87,832	4,033,021	82.7
National totals (including Quebec)	27,296,859	18,598,931	6,191,106/45	7,561,163/55.07	13,752,269	136,730	13,888,999	74.7

* Percentage of total valid votes

SOURCES
– Provinces and Territories outside Quebec: Chief Electoral Officer of Canada, Elections Canada
– Quebec totals: Directeur Général des élections du Québec